CANADIAN COMMERCIAL LAW

Richard A. Piner LL.B.

Fanshawe College
London, Ontario

Copp Clark Pitman Ltd.
Toronto

ISBN 0-7730-4281-4

Edited by Robert Billings and Charles Casement

Canadian Cataloguing in Publication Data

Piner, Richard.
    Canadian commercial law

ISBN 0-7730-4281-4

1. Commercial law — Canada.   2. Commercial law —
Canada — Cases.   I. Title.

KE919.P56   346.7107   C80-094304-X

Copp Clark Pitman Ltd.

Table of Contents

Introduction /iv

Chapter 1   Sources of Law   /1

Unit I: How to use this book   /2
Unit II: How to solve legal problems   /3
Unit III: Sources of law   /5
Checklist   /17
Review   /18

Chapter 2
The Law of Torts and Business Crimes   /19

Checklist   /31
Review   /34

Chapter 3   Contracts   /35

Unit I: Mutual agreement   /36
Unit II: Consideration   /43
Unit III: Legal capacity   /48
Unit IV: Lawful object   /51
Unit V: Genuine intention   /54
Checklist   /59
Review   /60
Unit VI: Remedies on breach of contract   /61
Checklist   /68
Review   /69

Chapter 4   Sale of Goods   /70

Unit I: The sale of goods contracts   /71
Unit II: Effects of the sale contract   /81
Unit III: Right of unpaid sellers   /85
Unit IV: Special business transactions   /90
Review   /98
Checklist   /99
Review   /100

Chapter 5   Consumer Law   /101

Checklist   /108
Review   /108

Chapter 6   Employment Law   /110

Unit I: The relationship between employers
and Employees   /111
Unit II: Federal and provincial law relating
to employment   /119
Checklist   /123
Review   /124

Chapter 7
Insurance and Business Risks   /125

Unit I: Structure of Canadian insurance law   /126
Unit II: Types of insurance   /133
Checklist   /138
Review   /139

Chapter 8
Legal Forms of Business Organization   /141

Unit I: Sole proprietorship   /142
Checklist   /145
Unit II: Agency   /147
Checklist   /152
Review   /153
Unit III: Partnership   /154
Checklist   /163
Review   /166
Unit IV: Corporations   /167
Checklist   /173
Review   /174

Chapter 9
Industrial and Intellectual Property   /175

Unit I: Patents, trade secrets, industrial design   /176
Unit II: Copyright   /182
Unit III: Trade Marks   /187
Checklist   /191
Review   /192

Chapter 10   Creditors' Rights   /194

Unit I: Collection of debts   /195
Unit II: Bankruptcy   /200
Checklist   /206
Review   /208

Solutions to cases   /209

Index   /214

Introduction

Canadian Commercial Law is a manual for Canadians who are preparing for careers that demand a knowledge of business law. It is for those who recognize the importance of having a practical guide through what may be called the "legal jungles" of life.

Everyone should know certain basic facts about law. In the every-day traffic of business life, we are constantly running legal red lights and paying dearly for our inability to recognize them before it is too late.

The approach taken in this book is based on three main objectives:

1. To identify legally acceptable rules.
2. To examine law as a "live" subject, not as a matter of history or theory.
3. To sharpen the ability to think and reason.

The individual who first said, "What you don't know can't hurt you" was not thinking about the law. In a civilized society, the law touches us all. It is as ever present and essential as air and water. Whether we are aware of it or not, whatever our goals, wherever we go and whatever we do, we cannot escape the "long reach" of the law. If we recognize this, an understanding of legal principles will serve us well.

One does not have to be a lawyer to recognize a legal red light. It is possible for everyone to learn when to stop, look and listen and when to consult a lawyer before it is too late. However, legal problems sometimes lurk behind the most innocent circumstances. We should know at least enough law to suspect the possible existence of these problems *as they arise.* Our guided tour over the broad field of Canadian business law should provide an "enlightened suspicion."

In practice, business people consult lawyers when they are confronted with legal pitfalls. However, all too frequently they do not actually "see" the problem before it is too late. This book contains numerous cases from the author's 20 years of legal practice which outline the bitter experiences of clients (identified by fictitious names) who have shrugged their shoulders in complaint, saying, "But. . .I never dreamed!"

The paragraphs that follow will serve as an overview of the types of problems this book is designed to solve. A reading of the cases and comments set out below will also provide you with a check-up on your present knowledge of business law.

Shapiro was the manager of an apartment complex. He found Fisher, who had been previously warned in person and by registered mail to stay away from the premises, in the lobby. Shapiro ordered Fisher to leave and Fisher, after a brief protest, reluctantly and slowly complied. As Fisher was leaving he swore repeatedly. In order to hurry him on his way Shapiro shoved the trespasser who unexpectedly fell and struck his head. Shapiro was prosecuted and convicted for assault. In addition, Fisher obtained damages for assault in the civil courts against Shapiro and his employer. Shapiro learned in the school of hard knocks the dangers of running a business without an adequate knowledge of the law of civil wrong. This is explained in Chapter 2 which deals with Torts and criminal wrongs.

Nichols worked long and hard to find a buyer for his business. During the period of negotiations which formed the basis of a mutual agreement between herself and a buyer named Knockwood, Nichols made certain representations honestly believing them to be true. When Knockwood discovered that some of the representations were untrue, he wanted out of the deal. Nichols agreed to adjust the price because of her error, but maintained that because she was honest Knockwood should not be able to rescind the entire contract. She was shocked to learn that her representations were "innocent misrepresentations" which did in fact give the other party to the contract the right to get out of it completely. We discuss this type of problem in Chapter 3: Contracts.

Bardos agreed to purchase a diamond from Roman Jewellers Ltd., which agreed as part of the purchase price to set the diamond in a ring. Bardos paid the purchase price in full and was told that the diamond would be "set in a day or two." After the work was completed but before Bardos returned to pick up "her ring," armed robbers stole it and other merchandise. When Bardos demanded her ring or her money back the manager replied, "Your ring was stolen. It just wasn't our fault. We can't give you a refund." Under certain circumstances the manager is right. Under others he is wrong. An understanding of the Sale of Goods Contract is necessary to provide an answer. This information may be obtained in Chapter 4: Sale of Goods.

German, an accountant, refused to comply with orders from his immediate supervisor because he considered them unreasonable. The company fired him for insubordination saying, "It wasn't his place to make that sort of judgment. He should have registered his complaint and then done the job." German was unable to obtain suitable employment in a related field partly because his supervisor grossly exaggerated the reasons for German's dismissal. German sucessfully sued his former employer on the grounds of unlawful dismissal and libel and slander. In this case, the supervisor totally misunderstood the law relating to employment and civil wrong. These matters are examined in both Chapter 2: Torts and Chapter 6: Employment Law.

Disney's business was retail sales. A customer wanted to purchase a $1 000 television set with $100 down and the balance to be paid in 30 days. Disney was prepared to deal on that basis and was given the name of an established business person, Yull, as a guarantor. Disney telephoned Yull who confirmed that if the customer did not pay he would personally guarantee payment of the balance. The customer walked off with the set and was never seen again. Disney demanded payment from Yull who refused to pay. Could Disney hold Yull responsible? Not on this type of oral guaranty: this is one of those types of contracts that must be in writing to be enforceable. This type of problem is discussed in Chapter 3: Contracts and Chapter 7: Insurance.

Webb and Gowan are partners in a used car business. Their partnership name is publicly registered and they have a Partnership Agreement that restricts Webb's authority to running the office, keeping records and making purchases of supplies. The Agreement specifically prohibits him from "dealing directly with customers, handling cash or negotiating or signing contracts with customers." In Gowan's absence, a customer dealt directly with Webb and gave him cash. Webb gave a receipt, delivered the Bill of Sale and disappeared. When Gowan returned, he refused to deliver the vehicle which was still on the lot in spite of the customer's demands, claiming the Bill of Sale was void because it was signed by an unauthorized person. Was Gowan right? The answer lies in Chapter 8 which deals with Partnerships and other legal forms of business organization.

Regier, a child-genius, developed a new and useful device which she had perfected by the time she was fourteen. She made dozens of them over the year and sold them to friends and neighbours for amounts sufficient to cover her costs. Several years later, her studies as a college Marketing student revealed to her the commercial value of the device. When she attempted to obtain Patent pro-

tection, she found that an important time limitation had slipped by which prevented her from obtaining exclusive rights to her own invention. The law relating to protection of inventions, processes and business secrets is set out in Chapter 9: Industrial and Intellectual Property.

Jacobus struggled to collect an overdue account of $7 000 from Green. Jacobus was aware that Green was selling off parts of his inventory in bulk out of the ordinary course of business, but was confident in his own ability to collect and did not want to incur the legal expenses of working through a lawyer. In a lightning-flash of activity Green disposed of his assets and absconded, leaving Jacobus and other creditors "high and dry." Jacobus failed to understand that creditors (like consumers) have rights that must be exercised at the right times. Perhaps if Jacobus had read Chapter 10 on Creditors' Rights he would have found a quick and effective procedure for appointing a Receiver in Bankruptcy to take over the Green business legally and thereby avoid such losses as occurred in this case. However, it still may not be too late for Jacobus if he will only examine the rules of Bulk Sales in Chapter 4: Sale of Goods. A last ditch remedy may well be found there.

The point of presenting these cases here is to point out that most of the unfortunate experiences could have been avoided by an "enlightened suspicion." We do not suggest that people should become their own lawyers, thereby fulfilling the old adage that people who act as their own lawyers have fools for clients. But we do hope to accomplish two things. First, to set up an early warning system in which a bell will sound in your computer when you approach a legal pitfall, no matter how cleverly it is disguised. Second, to alert you to situations in which it is essential for you to consult a lawyer so that unfortunate consequences may be averted.

You will learn from this book that our lives are intimately controlled by the law. We get up in the morning having slept on a bed purchased by a contract of sale; we breakfast on food likewise obtained. We then go to work, either as an employer or an employee, a relationship governed by a contract of employment. All day long we proceed to make one contract after another, by letter, telephone, or face to face, and only in special situations with the help and guidance of a lawyer. It is a fact that from the cradle to the grave, life is one contract after another. Therefore, it is clear from the nature of our existence, whether or not we know it, and whether or not we like it, that we must all learn something about the law, either by sad experience, or by intelligent understanding.

Space will not permit acknowledgment of the assistance I have received from numerous associates in the practice. However, I wish to acknowledge special indebtedness to Arthur Wishart, Q.C. an outstanding lawyer (to whom I was an Article-Student-At-Law) for so patiently and persistently planting the seeds of love for the practical aspects of the law; and to Gerald Nori, Q.C. for assistance for which no repayment is possible.

Richard A. Piner

CHAPTER 1

Sources of Law

Unit I How to use this book

1. You are the Jury

Most of us relate to problems involving clear-cut, factual situations. We feel comfortable discussing them. Each unit begins with You Are The Jury, which provides an opportunity to discuss legal issues in the context of a given set of facts that require a solution. You can make best use of this section by reading and discussing these problems before examining the material that follows. In this way, you will have already given some thought to the aspects of law you are about to encounter. This should also give you a clearer idea of your present level of experience and knowledge. After you have read and mastered the unit, it would be a good idea for you to come back to this section. You may be pleasantly surprised to find that your competence and knowledge have increased to a satisfying degree. A Key to You Are The Jury cases will be found at the end of each unit.

2. Objectives

Following the You Are The Jury section you will find a brief list of the major objectives of each unit. This list will alert you to the goals which that particular unit has been designed to accomplish.

3. Lexicon

Understanding legal terminology is half the battle. Each unit includes a list of legal words and phrases. Examine the list carefully. Study the unfamiliar terms until you feel at ease with them. In this way, when you study the text you will be able to get to grips with the issues straightaway without being baffled by the language of the law.

4. Case Studies

The central part of each unit contains a detailed examination of the law concerning the subject under discussion. Since it is generally easier to remember factual situations than bald statements of rules, the more vital and complex legal rules are illustrated by Case Studies and/or brief simulated situations. These are designed in part as instant review material and in part as a test of your ability to identify the rules properly and to understand their practical application.

5. Checklist

This is a point-by-point list designed as a quick reference to all the essential ingredients of the law covered in the unit or chapter. The Checklist offers suggested steps and precautions which, if followed, will enable you to avoid costly and time-consuming mistakes in handling your personal and business affairs.

6. Review

The Review is composed of fact situations drawn from selected cases to which you can apply your newly-acquired legal knowledge. Have you in fact mastered the material? Are you able to recall the rules discussed quickly and effectively? Do you have enough knowledge and the right approach to solve problems? Use the Review as a diagnostic tool to evaluate progress. If there are gaps in your memory, re-examine the material *now* and strengthen recollection.

The best use of your time at the end of each unit is disciplined use of the Review. In this way, you can master the essentials of the unit before moving on to the problems that will be presented in the next unit.

Unit II How to solve legal problems

YOU ARE THE JURY

Walter, a weekend golfer, purchased a backyard driving range to improve his game. Advertisements described the apparatus as "totally safe." Following instructions, Walter drove two pegs into the ground and attached an elastic cord to both pegs and the ball. Walter picked up his club and swung mightily. The ball sailed into the yard, then rebounded and hit him on the head causing a concussion.

"I'm suing the company," moaned Walter. The company's lawyer replied, "Walter should have ducked. He was the author of his own misfortune - he should have ducked."

This unit will explain the five steps that must be taken in order to solve a legal problem. Using this method and common sense, you should be able to resolve the majority of legal problems that life has to offer. Of course, this is not a magic formula which will do away with the necessity of consulting a lawyer on substantive issues. Remember that old adage - "One who acts as his own counsel has a fool for a client." This text is a useful tool that should be used with discretion.

How do we solve the above case? Let's try! Begin by asking, "What is the *key* to the situation? What are the relevant facts? What is this all about?" List the important points that come to mind.

We will, in fact, immediately identify two significant obstacles. First we find we have no "game plan." We lack a practical formula to apply against such a complex legal problem. Second, we have no rule book. We lack knowledge or relevant legal rules. This unit is designed to hurdle the first barrier; the remaining units, the second.

The approach to solving any legal problem may be broken down into five steps:
1. Identify the problem - classify the general area of law involved.
2. Establish an issue - "whether or not . . . "
3. Identify the legal rule - common law rule or statute.
4. Argument - apply the law to the facts.
5. Conclusion - the result of disciplined, logical thinking.

Imagine these five elements as stepping stones in a treacherous stream. One false step and you'll end up battered and bruised, fighting for your life in the muddy waters. If you do not proceed carefully in sequence from one step to the next, you will not arrive at a correct, effective solution.

1. Identify the Problem   Lawyers have known for centuries that all law can be classified into recognizable topics. The first step, then, is to identify the broad area of law into which the facts will comfortably fit. Of course, it is not possible for anyone to have all the legal rules instantly at his fingertips. It is possible, however, for anyone presented with a legal problem to be able to identify broad, general categories of laws. Once this ability is mastered, a person can then go to a law resource book and examine the rules. In Walter's case, the first thing you should do, then, is "pigeonhole" his problem.

2. Establish the Issue   Once the problem has been classified, it is usually fairly easy to determine the issue. Examine the hard facts. Distil from them the real substantial issue to be decided. Write down the issue in the form of a question.

The idea is to ask one or two (never any more) material questions, whose answers will provide an effective solution to your problem. It is here that you attempt to discover the key to the situation. If you were presented with a problem and were permitted to ask an expert one question, you would make that question count. That is the type of inquiry you must develop at this stage.

3. Identify the Legal Rule   Once you are able to pigeonhole your case into an identifiable area of law and have written down the essential issue, you must then search for and identify the legal rules applicable to the case. You will have to read the appropriate resource book or statute to do this. In time, many of the rules will become second nature and they will readily come to mind as required.

4. Argument. Apply Law to the Facts   Now you know where you are going. You have identified the problem, established the issue to be resolved and researched the rules that apply to the case. You are now ready to argue your case by applying the law to the facts.

The first three steps are developed through critical thinking. This fourth step gives you an opportunity to visualize and verbalize through creative thinking. Be a free thinker here. Explore all the angles. Write them down as fast as they occur to you. Remember there are two sides to most

stories so you must look at the problem as objectively as possible. There should be only one constraint on your creativity. You must always keep in mind the issue you have chosen and keep searching for the answer to the question you have established for yourself in step two.

5. Conclusion   The final step is to mentally assemble all that you have done and write down the most probable result. Who is right? Who is wrong? What remedies are available? When asked to suggest a solution to a legal problem most people immediately state their conclusion without first working through the discipline of all the steps in our method. This is a natural tendency but it is guess-work, gambling which has no place in the correct approach to solving legal problems. You want your conclusions to pinpoint an effective solution. If they do, you manage to aim at your target with an accurate, high-powered rifle rather than with a shotgun into which you have poured a handful of buckshot.

KEY TO YOU ARE THE JURY

Walter's Case   If you were to use the approach outlined above in solving Walter's problem, the five steps might look like this:
Identify Problem: Sale of goods . . . Product liability . . . Advertising products . . . Guarantees . . .
Issue: Whether or not the advertised endorsement "totally safe" renders the company liable for Walter's injuries.
Law: Sale of Goods Act (province); Contract of Guarantee.
Argument: The "driving range" may be categorized in law as "goods." The seller of goods to a consumer is liable for express or stated warranties and guarantees and representations. The statement "totally safe" was a representation in the form of an express warranty. Walter was entitled to rely on the company's statement. His injuries clearly show that the representation was false.
Conclusion: The company pays. It is liable on the ground of false representation and breach of express warranty.

This five-step formula can be a satisfying and rewarding adventure in logical problem solving. Practise the method as often as you need until you feel comfortable with it. Use it to solve problems that arise in the following units.

Unit III Sources of Law

YOU ARE THE JURY

REGINA v. DAVIS

A city in Eastern Canada passed a local by-law prohibiting the sale of canned beverages within the municipality as part of its ecology program. The municipality had been given the authority by the Province to pass by-laws to regulate business and commerce within the city limits. Davis, a vendor of canned soft drinks challenged the law. Davis claimed the city did not have the authority to prohibit trade entirely, as it had only the power to regulate trade. The city prosecuted, arguing that the law was enforceable through the courts. What are the issues? How would you decide?

OBJECTIVES

- to define the concept of law.
- to identify the three essential elements of every law.
- to identify the main sources of our laws.
- to understand how laws are enforced through the civil courts.

LEXICON

Affidavit   Written statements made under oath before a lawyer or officer for taking oaths.

Execution   A method by which a person who has obtained a judgment through the courts may seize lands or goods from a debtor in satisfaction of a claim.

Judgment   A written decision in favour of a party to a court action who has been successful, setting out the relief awarded by the court.

Litigation   The process of bringing a civil case to trial.

Pleadings   The written statements of parties to a court case, setting out what they hope to prove at trial and stating the relief they request from the court.

Statute   Written law as set out in acts or legislation of a provincial legislature or the federal government.

Statement of Claim:

~~**Writ of Summons**~~   The document by which a party to a court case commences the action. It omit contains a brief statement of the claim and informs the other party as to what must be done to defend the action.

Why we need laws

If we were able to live completely separate and alone, laws would not be necessary, since we would have only ourselves to think of in regulating our behaviour. But this is not the case in our society. While we remain individuals who wish to enjoy things, own property, and act in a way which will result in personal success and pleasure, the fact is that we have elected to live in communities with other people. Under these circumstances, some things cannot be done without creating conflict of interest between two or more individuals. Furthermore, society itself considers some conduct unacceptable and raises prohibitions.

Conflicts that arise in a society can be resolved in a variety of ways. If we followed the example of the animal kingdom, brute force would bring about a quick, effective, and conclusive solution. But, as civilized people, we felt that the rules of the jungle were incompatible with the dignity of human society and we came to the conclusion that we needed rules, or *laws*, to encourage socially acceptable behaviour and to punish or restrain unacceptable behaviour.

Our laws have been developed over many centuries and in the course of time a certain mystique has grown up around them. We believe that laws are difficult to understand. The terminology alone is sufficient to make most of us cringe. The underlying reality, however, is that laws are nothing more than a group of rules or principles that we ourselves have created from our own group conduct to regulate our lives. Anyone can develop an understanding of our laws by considering a simple definition of law together with the three essential elements of every law and then applying them through an understanding of the structure of our legal system.

The definition of law

Law is a civilized people's attempt to regulate life in society by dictates of reason and fairness as opposed to brute force.

Analyze this definition. Spend some time with it. Laws are meant to regulate life in society. Some laws prohibit certain conduct. Can you think of instances where our lawmakers have made bad laws by attempting to prohibit rather than regulate? Take note of the word "attempt." Nowhere does anyone suggest that we have been entirely successful in our lawmaking or that any of our laws are necessarily perfect. One hundred years

from now we shall still be making new laws and changing old ones because law, like society itself, is constantly changing.

Finally, you should note that the rule of law is based on two major concepts - *reason* (law) and *fairness* (equity). These are principles which must be understood in order to appreciate how our legal system works.

Essential elements of every law

A law professor once illustrated the three essential elements that every law must have in order to be enforceable by telling a story about a person who lived one million years ago. "This person's laws must have been simple, personal, and highly practicable, probably somewhat along this style: If anyone touches my tiger skin, I will strike them with my cave-bear thighbone club."

We have here all the essential elements of every law, whether made a million years ago or today. These elements are: *authority, promulgation*, and *enforcement*. All three elements must be present or the law will be unenforceable. Frequently, laws are challenged in the courts on the grounds that one or more of the elements is missing. If you are confronted with a law which will effect your rights, never assume that the law is enforceable just because it is "on the books." Always begin with the position that the law may be inoperative.

Authority
A law will only be valid if it is passed by a branch of government that we as a people have authorized to make such laws. In Canada, we have divided the power to make laws among our federal and provincial governments through a statute called the *British North America Act*. The provinces further delegate authority to municipal councils which have the power to pass by-laws.

Promulgation
Before a law may take effect, it must be published in a form accessible to the public. Laws are passed in the form of statutes and are published in the *Canada Gazette* or one of the provincial gazettes (depending on whether they are federal or provincial laws). They are also made available to the public in printed form. (Copies of statutes can be obtained from government bookstores or by writing to the government department concerned.)

Enforcement
A law passed by an appropriate authority and published must be enforceable through a court or

tribunal system. It follows then that in order to enforce one's rights, one must be able to identify the proper forum in which to seek relief. In Canada we have devised a system of courts and tribunals to provide enforcement of most of our rights. The existence of this system means that if you have a matter to be tried, you must first identify a court or tribunal within the system which has been given the statutory power to deal with and decide the issues involved in such a matter.

Before you move on, review the definition of law and the three essentials. Reconsider *Regina v. Davis* in the light of the definition and essentials. This should help reinforce these basic concepts.

Putting our laws in perspective

Criticizing laws because they are imperfect is unproductive. We have already conceded that we *need* laws, while at the same time we agree that they will never be perfect.

Many of us think of law in terms of fairness and justice, and we are disappointed (perhaps even angry) when we find that some laws don't measure up. The application of legal principles does not always result in "justice being done." Some laws are designed to be discriminatory. Some laws have been created to fill a particular need of society for its preservation. Some laws which made sense years ago have been made obsolete by changing morality and business practice. Some laws are based on logic, while others were passed for the sole purpose of creating a set of rules to guide people in their business dealings. It is a mistake to continue to view the law unrealistically or to expect the law to provide a perfect or near-perfect solution to our problems every time.

In the past twenty years, more than ever before in our history, our laws have been constantly reviewed and updated by government and the courts to make them reflect more consistently the realities of modern society. For example, the Canadian government has:
- made comprehensive revisions to the federal *Bankruptcy Act* which are designed to deal with an increasing tendency among business people to engage in rash and tricky practices.
- revised the procedures for incorporating a federal Limited Company to meet business' need for more streamlined organizations.

The sources of law

Where do our laws come from? How were they created in the past? How are they created today and how will they be created tomorrow? There are three major sources of law: *common law, equity* and *statute law*.

Common law
In the past, disputes were brought by citizens to the courts. In attempting to resolve civil disputes and arrive at a judgment based on realistic standards, the judges placed great emphasis on the customs of the people. They heard evidence from witnesses on how people in the community governed their own businesses and affairs; and they looked to the usual accepted practices in business and the customs of the various trades.

Judgments resulting from court hearings were (and still are) written down, and the more important decisions were collected in special volumes for future study and reference. Lawyers would research past decisions and refer to them in their arguments before other judges in later cases. Legal writers began analyzing these decisions and found that there were distinct, recognizable customs and practices which had been recognized by the courts and which could be expressed in the form of identifiable rules. This created a branch of law known today as the common law. Lawyers refer to this source of law as "case law," that is, law learned and identified from cases tried in court.

Today we still apply the decisions of the past to help resolve present problems. In Canada we have a large body of case law which provides a guide as to how legal principles will probably be applied to a particular set of facts.

The courts in Canada are heavily committed to follow the doctrine of *stare decisis* (Let It Stand Decided), the practice of following the precedents of earlier decisions. The practice is that decisions of the Supreme Court of Canada, the highest court in the country, are binding on all lower courts; in the provinces the decisions of higher courts of the province are binding on the lower courts of that province; and decisions of courts of other provinces are not binding but may be referred to as a precedent likely to influence. To be "binding" means that the lower court must obey and follow the decision of the higher court. For example, the Supreme Court of a province must follow the decision of the Supreme Court of Canada. The role played by precedent may best be clarified by examining *Diamond v. Ho*, a hypothetical business law case.

CASE 1 DIAMOND v. HO

Ho entered into a contract to supply furnaces to buildings constructed by Diamond for the "1982–83 building season." In March 1983 Ho declared his obligation ended as he interpreted this to mean buildings commenced before the end of 1982. "Time for a new price," said Ho. Diamond disagreed, "Wrong! The '82–83 season includes all buildings I started up to December 31, 1983. If you don't supply at the same price, I'll sue." Diamond sued for breach of contract in a provincial Supreme Court.

Lawyers for both sides prepared for trial by examining law reports of past court judgments which dealt with and decided construction contract disputes. In these cases judges had analyzed the custom of the building trade, reviewed and considered existing legal principles (as they interpreted them) and gave reasons for judgment. None of the facts or issues raised in these cases were precisely the same as those in the Ho case, but in the view of the lawyers they were similar enough to be of value in supporting their respective cases. Diamond's lawyer found support for the contractor's side in a previous decision of the provincial Supreme Court and several decisions of the Supreme Courts of other provinces. Ho's lawyer relied on a decision of the Supreme Court of Canada. Although the lawyers attempted to settle the case without going to trial, they were unable to agree that one or more of the previous decisions was sufficiently "on point" to win the case for either side.

At the trial each lawyer challenged the application of the previous decisions used by his opponent to the facts and issues of this particular case. If the trial judge concluded that the issue decided by the Supreme Court of Canada in the precedent case cited applied to the Ho case, then the trial court (being a lower court) would be bound by it and Ho would win. If the judge found that the Supreme Court of Canada decision was distinguishable from the facts of the Ho case, that decision would not apply and the trial court would be bound by its own previous decision - in which case Diamond would win. The decisions of the Supreme Courts of other provinces would not bind the trial judge because he is free to follow or disregard them; but they are useful as "precedents of influence" which may sway the trial judge's decision by the pure logic and analysis employed by another judge in similar circumstances. British, American, Australian and other commonwealth decisions may also be used as "precedents of influence."

Equity

Another peculiarity of our law which must be identified to understand how our laws work is its division into two separate and distinct parts. One is known as law; the other as equity. We have been conditioned for so long to think only in terms of law that we have developed a distorted view of our system. In order to overcome this we will take a bit of trouble to examine both branches.

Our definition stated that law is based on two principles: reason and fairness. The first principle is well illustrated by the approach taken in the development of common law. Not only did common law reflect accepted customs and practices, but also the doctrine of *stare decisis* or the rule of precedent ensured that the law was consistently applied.

However, in the course of time a serious weakness in this system became apparent. What happened was that the courts became extremely rigid and inflexible in their interpretation of the law. Possibly this was due to the fact that precedents went unchallenged even though the circumstances in which they had arisen had long since become outdated. For whatever reason, the law became harsh and unbending, a fact that caused considerable resentment among people whose cases came before the courts.

The authorities in power began thinking there was a better way and as a result they developed an alternate court called the Court of Equity (Chancery). This court was designed to provide justice and a relief against the harsh, unbending rules created by the law courts. Our courts today retain the dual concepts of law and equity and every judge is a judge of both law and equity. Many of our written laws contain principles of equitable relief as well.

CASE 2 SQUIRE v. WARKINGTON

Squire leased premises on a long term lease to Warkington who ran a children's wear business. Squire felt the rent was insufficient and, although he had never complained to Warkington, he was unhappy because she was always 15 to 20 days late with her monthly payments. Squire was offered a more attractive rent by a corporation but with the provision that he could give possession in 30 days. As Warkington's rent was still in arrears, Squire immediately and without notice changed the locks and posted an eviction notice on the front door. He later told Warkington he had seized her inventory and fixtures as security for rent. Warkington brought an application to permit her to pay the rent which was overdue and for an order declaring the lease valid and in force. The provincial *Landlord and Tenant Act* provided that in spite of a legal term in a lease giving the landlord the right to evict for non-payment of rent, the court had a power to give relief which was called "relief against forfeiture." The court was influenced by the following facts:

- rent was in arrears only 18 days and was in the sum of only $200.
- the lease had another 15 years to run.
- Squire's actions put Warkington out of business.
- in the past Squire had never complained about late payments.

The court judgment reads in part, "In effect Squire lulled Warkington into a false sense of security leading her to believe that late payment would not lead to serious consequences. It would be shocking if I were to deprive her of the substantial benefit of the lease. It would be equitable for me to restore Warkington's privileges as a tenant and I so order on condition that Warkington pay all arrears forthwith and make all future payments under the lease promptly." Although the term in the lease supported Squire, equity supported Warkington. Whenever Law and Equity are in conflict, Equity always prevails.

Statute law

Statutes are the most important legal source of law. Under the major written component of the Canadian constitution, namely, the *British North America Act*, there are eleven sovereign legislative bodies in Canada. One is the Parliament of Canada, and the others are the ten provincial legislatures. By the provisions of the *B.N.A. Act*, each is granted legislative authority to enact statutes. The legislative power of each is, however, specifically limited to certain classes of matters. It is important to realize that a sovereign legislative body can enact statutes only in accordance with its legislative competence. Such legislation is referred to as "primary legislation" in that it is passed by the sovereign legislative body itself. There is another category of legislation in Canada, and this is referred to as "subordinate legislation."

Subordinate legislation is legislation enacted by a person, body or tribunal, subordinate to a sovereign legislative body. Subordinate legislation takes many forms: by-laws, ordinances, statutory instruments, orders in council, rules and regulations. The body enacting subordinate legislation must do so only in accordance with the authority granted it by the sovereign legislative body. In other words, the sovereign legislative body enacts legislation that spells out just what the subordinate body can or cannot do. In many instances, what happens is that the sovereign body delegates authority in certain matters to a subordinate body. A good example of a delegated authority is a municipal council. Under enabling provincial legislation, municipalities are created and municipal councils are granted authority to enact by-laws. But they may only enact by-laws in those areas designated by the provincial legislation.

The function of the legal profession

The first significant step in the enforcement or the defence of a civil claim is the interview between a lawyer and his client. The essential function of the interview is to inform the solicitor of the facts of the case. It is imperative that a client give his solicitor a full and frank account of all the facts, both favourable and unfavourable. It is on the basis of the client's account that a solicitor must advise the client as to his legal rights and duties, and it is on the basis of this advice that a client may determine what steps he should take to enforce or defend a claim. It is foolhardy, therefore, for a client to withhold relevant information from his solicitor. It is a bit late for a lawyer to learn the truth at the trial, and a misinformed solicitor should not be blamed for a lost cause.

When a client has informed his solicitor of the facts, the solicitor will inform himself on the law. The length of time and the amount of effort which is required to advise a client soundly as to his legal position varies with the complexity of the problem. So does the fee.

The trial of a civil action: From writ to judgment

When a solicitor advises his client that he has a case, the client must decide whether or not to pursue his claim in the courts. The decision is not one to be made lightly, for the pursuit of a claim requires professional assistance and may take considerable time. Although a person who is not legally trained is permitted to take his own case, it is wise to remember that a person is rarely capable of seeing his own case objectively and in perspective. In many instances the best advice a solicitor can give his client is to settle the case out of court. For instance, a plaintiff may have an excellent case, but the amount involved or the uncertainty of collection may make litigation unwise.

Again, the plaintiff's case may be uncertain, or, even though it is clear on the facts as then known, the case may be hard to prove. These considerations apply equally to determining whether a claim should be defended. Particularly where business relationships are involved, it may be better to forego pursuing or resisting a claim for business reasons, quite apart from the legal right of the parties.

It is open to the parties to settle their differences out of court at any time. Each step in the pre-trial procedure that is outlined below could be followed by settlement instead of pursuing the case to trial.

Pre-trial procedure

The procedure for getting a case to trail is designed to provide adequate information to the three persons who must be informed of all relevant matters if surprise and delay are to be avoided: the plaintiff, the defendant, and the court.

The first step is the issuance of a *Writ of Summons*. This document is issued out of the Court Registry on the instigation of the plaintiff, and is addressed to the defendant. It sets out the names of the parties and outlines the nature of the plaintiff's claim. The writ is served on the defendant, and an affidavit proving delivery is filed in the registry. The defendant in turn "enters an appearance" to the action at the Court Registry by filing a document which, in effect, says the defendant will appear in court to defend. If he does not do so within a prescribed time limit, the plaintiff may obtain judgment by default. When the defendant has entered an appearance, he serves notice of appearance on the plaintiff's solicitor.

The next step is the preparation of the most important document in the pleadings: the plaintiff's *Statement of Claim*. It is a detailed document which sets out paragraph by paragraph the facts of the plaintiff's claim against the defendant and the relief claimed. It is served on the defendant and a copy is filed at the registry. This step is followed by the defendant's response, the *Statement of Defence*, in which the defendant disputes the plaintiff's claim in detail. This document is delivered to the plaintiff and a copy is filed at the registry.

The plaintiff may, if he chooses, file a reply to the defence. If there is no reply, the pleadings are closed and the parties are said to have "joined issue" on the pleadings.

Before the actual trial, two further steps may be taken to ascertain relevant facts. One step is *Discovery of Documents* and the other is *Examination for Discovery*. Either party may issue a demand for discovery of documents. The other party replies by affidavit, listing the documents that may be introduced in evidence at the trial. Inspection of documents may follow.

Examination for discovery is a process whereby each party may be cross-examined by the opposing party's lawyer. Persons who are witnesses only (i.e., who are not parties to the action) may not be examined for discovery. Evidence of the examination may be introduced at the trial. It sometimes happens that evidence received through these processes of discovery may induce a solicitor to advise his client not to proceed further with the case. But if the case is to go on, the plaintiff sets it down for trial and serves notice of trial on the defendant. Subpoenas may be issued at this point, ordering persons to appear at the trial to give evidence or to produce documents. The action is now ready for trial.

Procedure in court

When the judge enters the courtroom from his chambers behind the bench, those present rise until the judge is seated. The clerk reads out the name of the case. It is customary for counsel at this point to introduce themselves to the court and to identify themselves with their clients. The judge then invites counsel for the plaintiff to put in his case. Counsel for the plaintiff usually outlines his case in summary form to indicate to the judge what he proposes to establish. He then calls his witnesses, who are put under oath by the clerk of the court and are examined by counsel for the plaintiff. They may also be cross-examined by counsel for the defendant. In examination, counsel may not ask his own witness leading questions, that is, questions which indicate to the witness what answer is sought. In cross-examination leading questions are permitted; but the art of advocacy often lies in restraint. It is proper for counsel to interview and review evidence with his witness prior to the trial, but it is completely improper for counsel to instruct a witness as to the testimony that he is to give.

When the plaintiff's case has been presented, counsel for the defence has two courses before him. He may be sufficiently confident that the plaintiff has not established a case to move for a dismissal. The danger is that if he so moves and is unsuccessful, he debars himself from introducing evidence on his own behalf. Therefore, he usually follows the second course and proceeds with his defence. He summarizes his case, calls his witnesses (who are examined and cross-examined in the usual way), and closes his case.

Amended Sept. 1975

United Stationery Co. Limited, Legal Department
30 Production Dr., Scarborough, Ontario

Form L426 Writ of Summons S.C.O.—General   No.   A.D. 19

In the Supreme Court of Ontario

Between

                                                                    PLAINTIFF

                                    AND

                                                                    DEFENDANT

(SEAL)

In describing the Court, insert County, United Counties, District, Regional Municipality or Judicial District where appropriate. For place of residence, insert appropriate County, District, Regional Municipality, etc.

Elizabeth the Second, by the Grace of God, of the United Kingdom, Canada and Her other Realms and Territories Queen, Head of the Commonwealth, Defender of the Faith.

TO

Insert Defendant's Name and Address

We Command that, if you wish to defend this action, either you or your lawyer shall file an Appearance in the office of this Court at
within ten days after the day this Writ was served upon you; AND TAKE NOTICE that, where a Statement of Claim is also served with this Writ, or is served upon you at some later date, and you fail to serve upon the plaintiff   or   lawyer AND file your Statement of Defence in the same Court office within twenty days after the Statement of Claim has been filed and served upon you, pleadings may be noted closed against you and you may not be permitted to deliver your Statement of Defence;

And Further Take Notice that where pleadings have been noted closed against you, you may be deemed to have admitted the plaintiff's claim and you may not be entitled to notice of any motion for judgment or notice of trial, AND JUDGMENT MAY BE GIVEN AGAINST YOU IN YOUR ABSENCE.

In Witness Whereof this Writ is signed for the Supreme Court of Ontario by
                    Registrar of the said Court at

this   day of   19

                                        (signature of officer)

N.B.—This Writ is to be served within twelve calendar months from the date thereof, or if renewed, within twelve calendar months from the date of such renewal, including the day of such date and not afterwards.

Page 1 of Writ of Summons in the Supreme Court of Ontario.

11

At this point the plaintiff may introduce rebuttal evidence, but only if the defendant has opened new ground.

Counsel for the defendant now sums up his case in terms of evidence and argument, followed by the plaintiff. Occasionally the defendant may reply to the plaintiff's summing up, but on matters of law only. This is not a debate. The judge is interested in argument, and judgment is to be determined by the merits of the case, not by the histrionics of counsel.

The judge may give oral judgment immediately after the summing up by counsel, but usually he reserves judgment, giving reasons for judgment at a later date. The victor prepares the formal judgment and submits it to the loser for approval. If there is a dispute, it is settled by the judge or the registrar. The victor then draws his bill of costs, which is frequently assessed by the registrar under a procedure called "taxation of costs." As a general rule, costs follow the decision (i.e., the loser has to pay the costs of the victor).

The loser has the right to appeal. If the case is appealed, the judgment and order for costs are suspended pending the decision of the appeal court. There is no inherent right to appeal, although most cases can in practice be appealed. The Court of Appeal may confirm the judgment of the trial court or may reverse the judgment on a point of law or, very occasionally, on a finding of fact. Alternatively, the Court of Appeal may order a new trial. The jurisdiction of the Supreme Court of Canada on appeal from the Court of Appeal is much the same.

The judgment

Once a judge has heard a case, he must determine its outcome. Usually he writes a judgment, giving reasons for the decision. Much has been written on the judicial process of making law. In theory, it is basically a matter of taking the relevant law and applying it to the relevant facts of a case to arrive at a conclusion. But in reality the process is really much more subtle and complex.

It is the responsibility of counsel to see that the facts and the relevant law are before the court. Because of the nature of their function and responsibilities, counsel are said to be officers of the court. Counsel who has prepared, presented and argued his case well will have assisted the court immeasurably in the performance of its function. The key to the problem is the word "relevant." Often a conclusion cannot be reached as to what law is relevant until the facts have been adduced. This is one reason why the pleadings which are

exchanged before trial are so important. The writ states the general nature of the plaintiff's claim, and the subsequent steps in the pre-trial procedure should help both counsel and the court to determine with a high degree of accuracy what are the significant facts and what is the relevant law.

Although no two judgments take exactly the same form, most judgments follow a pattern which should become familiar as one examines them. First, a judgment should set out the nature of the proceedings and the remedy sought. For instance, it may read: "This is an action for damages for breach of contract." The reader thus already knows two important aspects of the case: why the plaintiff is suing, and what he is seeking. The reader's thoughts have already been given direction.

Second, a judgment should set out the facts. For instance, it may read: "On 30 June, 1959, the defendant ordered from the plaintiff and the plaintiff agreed to sell the defendant ten crates of strawberries for immediate delivery. The plaintiff put the goods in the hands of a common carrier, a trucking firm, for delivery to the defendant. The truck carrying the strawberries was in an accident and some of the strawberries were destroyed. The defendant refused to accept any of the strawberries, and the plaintiff claims damages for breach of the contract of sale." The reader now knows what happened, and is ready to consider the rights of the parties.

At this point, the judgment should set out the legal issues. Who owned the goods at the time of the accident? Whose agent was the carrier? Does it matter whether the carrier was at fault? Must the purchaser accept part delivery or may he reject delivery unless the entire contract is performed? These issues should be determinable from argument of counsel, who will have spoken to those points in the presentation of the case.

And now, the final question that must be answered is: What is the law? The judgment should review the relevant case law and statutes, in this case particularly the *Sale of Goods Act.* The judge then reaches a decision based on stated reasons.

As we have seen, the common law is built on a system of precedent. It is sensible that similar cases should be treated in a similar way, and it is useful to a court to know how other courts have dealt with cases of a like nature. Not only is it useful, but if a principle of law has been stated by a higher court the lower court is bound by law to follow it. This is the principle of *stare decisis:* "let it stand decided." Of course, cases are frequently "distinguishable" on their facts. Sometimes

judges state views on the law which are not necessary for deciding the case before the court (these statements are known as *obiter dicta*). And frequently cases arise which have never been tried before. Consequently, a judge may be called upon to rework a legal principle, or to extend a principle, or to consider the applicability of an old principle to a modern situation. The judge is thus in a position to *create* law. This is what a famous judge once described as "the process by which law is continually working itself pure." Judicial creativeness was more succinctly recognized by a New Hampshire judge: "Do judges make law? 'Course they do. Made some myself.''

The enforcement of judgments

When a litigant has obtained a judgment in his favour directing the loser to pay money or deliver up real or personal property, it is not necessary for him to demand fulfillment of the judgment; service of the order compels its fulfillment without demand. If the person (including a corporation) against whom the judgment is directed (known as the "judgment debtor") fails to meet the judgment, there are several legal ways in which the judgment can be enforced. These are, with certain outstanding exceptions, directed against the property of the judgment debtor. Enforcement is effective, therefore, only if the defaulter has the means with which to satisfy the terms of the judgment. The proposition that you cannot get blood out of stone holds true in law. All persons with valid claims are entitled to share the available assets of the debtor.

Since property may be held in a variety of ways which make the amount of property difficult to ascertain, the law provides a method of ascertaining the nature and extent of the defaulter's property and means called *Discovery in aid of Execution.* The Rules of the trial courts allow a person entitled to enforce a judgment to apply to the court for an order that the judgment debtor (including an officer of a debtor company) be examined orally as to his "means." The court appoints an officer of the court before whom the examination is held, and may compel the production of the judgment debtor's documents or books. The examination may be conducted by counsel.

If the person ordered to attend for oral examination fails to appear, he is in contempt of court, and an order may be made for his committal to prison for the contempt. In certain circumstances, property transferred by the debtor to escape payment of his debts may be traced and applied in satisfaction of the judgment.

Execution

The trial court Rules provide for "issuing execution against a judgment debtor." This means the issuing of such process against his person or property as is applicable to the case. The form of execution adopted depends mainly upon two factors:

(a) the terms of the order, for instance, whether it orders the payment of money or delivery of property; and

(b) the nature of the debtor's assets as disclosed by previous examination or otherwise, for instance, movable goods or real property, bank deposits or shares.

The following paragraphs deal with some of the most common forms of execution for obtaining satisfaction of a judgment.

Execution against goods The goods and chattels of a judgment debtor are liable to seizure and sale under a *writ of execution.* This writ takes the form of an order of the court directed to a sheriff ordering him to seize the goods and chattels of the debtor to the approximate extent of the judgment, and to sell them to satisfy the judgment and costs of the process. (The debtor's personal property is,

to a certain extent, exempt from seizure.) This writ is known as *Fieri Facias,* from the Latin whose English equivalent now found in the writ instructs the sheriff "that you cause to be made" a sum of money from the assets of the judgment debtor. Where the judgment debtor has no assets which the sheriff may seize under the writ, the sheriff returns the writ marked "nulla bona," meaning literally "no goods."

The law makes provision to ensure that one creditor is not able to seize all the goods and chattels of a judgment debtor to the exclusion of other creditors. Seizures are a matter of public record, and other creditors may take summary proceedings to establish their claims and share in the results of execution.

Execution against land A judgment or order may be registered in any or all of the Land Registry or Land Titles Offices in the province. From the time of registration, the judgment forms a charge on all the lands of the judgment debtor in the particular registration district. This registration must be renewed periodically to be kept alive.

The holder of the judgment may apply to the court for an order for the sale of a particular

WRIT OF FIERI FÁCIAS

(Rule 556)

(Court and Cause)

(Seal)

Name and title of Sovereign

To the Sheriff of . . . . greeting:

We command you that of the goods and chattels and lands and tenements in your bailiwick of C.D. you cause to be made the sum of $ . . . . and also interest at the rate of. . . . . per cent per annum thereon from . . . . 19 . . . ., (*day of the judgment or order, or day on which the money is directed to be paid, or day from which interest is directed by the order to run, as the case may be*), which sum of money and interest were by a judgment in this action bearing the date of . . . . 19 . . . . , adjudged to be paid by the said C.D. to A.B., and also the further sum of $ . . . . for the taxed costs of the said A.B., mentioned in the said judgment, together with interest at the rate of . . . . per cent per annum thereon from . . . . 19 . . . ., (*the date of the judgment awarding the costs*) and we further command you that so much thereof as you shall have made from the said goods and chattels and lands and tenements be paid out according to law, and if required to do so, make appear to our Justices of the Supreme Court of Ontario in what manner you shall have executed this our writ.

In witness whereof this writ is signed for the Supreme Court of Ontario by . . . . (Local) Registrar of the said Court at . . . . this . . . . day of . . . . 19 . . . .

. . . .
(signature of officer)

Endorsements

The . . . . is entitled to receive for this and other writs and renewals of the same, the following sums:

For this writ, $ . . . .
                                         (signature of officer)

For 1st renewal, $ . . . .
                                         (signature of officer)

For 2nd renewal, $ . . . .
                                         (signature of officer)

Etc., etc. (*as may be necessary*).

MR. SHERIFF: Levy the sum of $ . . . . with interest at . . . . per cent per annum from . . . . 19 . . . ., and the sum of $ . . . . for costs, with interest at . . . . per cent per annum from . . . . 19 . . . ., and for this writ $ . . . . together with your own fees and incidental expenses.

. . . .
(signature of person filing writ)

. . . .
(address)

Writ of Fieri Facias.

parcel of land in order to satisfy the judgment. This application is followed by a court inquiry into the debtor's interest in the land, priorities between judgments, and the method of fair distribution of the proceeds of sale. This is followed by an order of the court for the sale of the interest in question, for notices, advertisements, sale, payment of proceeds into court, and finally for distribution among all creditors entitled to share in the proceeds. Where more than one judgment is involved, the court will determine which judgment(s) should have priority and how the proceeds of the sale should be distributed among the creditors entitled to a share.

Execution against the person　A judgment debtor may not be taken into custody for non-payment of the judgment unless it can be shown that he has defrauded or intends to defraud his creditors. Under the *Fraudulent Debtor's Arrest Act*, a judgment debtor may be arrested as follows:

(i) *Process commencing before judgment*　If the plaintiff can show that the defendant is about to leave the province unless apprehended, the plaintiff may obtain a court order that the defendant be held to bail. The amount of the bail is determined by the judge and may not exceed the amount of the claim against the defendant. Having obtained this order, the plaintiff may obtain a *Writ of Capias* directed to the sheriff to arrest and imprison the defendant. The defendant remains in custody until he furnishes bail bond to the sheriff or deposits the necessary amount (including costs) in court. The defendant may apply to the court for an order calling upon the plaintiff to show cause why he should not be released from custody.

After judgment has been passed (and assuming the plaintiff wins his case), the judge may order the defendant's discharge if he is satisfied the defendant has no means of payment. (It is up to the defendant, however, to request discharge.) If it appears to the judge on the evidence that the judgment debtor has incurred the debt by fraud, or has concealed or made away with his property to defraud his creditors, the judge may order the defendant to be committeed to jail with or without hard larbour for a term not exceeding twelve months, or until satisfaction of the judgment. A further term may be imposed if it is disclosed that the judgment debtor has the means to pay.

(ii) *Process commencing after judgment*　A plaintiff who has won his case and who establishes that the judgment debtor is about to leave the province with intent to defraud his creditors, may obtain an order for the arrest of the judgment debtor for

examination. If examination discloses a fraud, the judge may order imprisonment on the same terms as those stated above.

There are numerous other processes which are available to a judgment creditor. *Garnishment* is perhaps the most familiar of these. By this order, a judgment creditor or a plaintiff in an action may obtain the seizure of such assets as bank accounts, wages, and other sums of money owed to the debtor. A *Writ of Possession* is issued to obtain the delivery of possession of land directed to be delivered by a judgment. Thus, the debtor gives up possession irrespective of ownership. A *Writ of Delivery* may be issued on the order of a judge to enforce a judgment for the recovery of property other than land or money.

KEY TO YOU ARE THE JURY

REGINA v. DAVIS

Davis won. The province had given the municipality authority to regulate trade and business within its boundaries but not the right to prohibit trade. The municipality could only act within the powers actually transferred to it by statute. The effect of the by-law was to prohibit Davis from carrying on a specific trade or business. The by-law lacked two essential elements - authority and a court prepared to enforce the penalty. Review the case and try and determine what alternative solution might have been available to achieve the municipality's objectives and yet remain within the law.

Checklist: Sources of law; legal proceedings

Here is a list of things to do after you have taken reasonable steps to avoid legal problems, but you are nevertheless going to be involved in a legal action.

1. Document   Courts rely heavily on documented evidence. Trust written records more than oral recollection of what happened. Collect letters, information, invoices, contracts, agreements, receipts, quotations, figures. Arrange in chronological order, and place in one central file. Leave nothing out, even if you believe a document will hurt your case.

2. Record Events   Take time to record events and activities in note form. Be accurate regarding dates, times.

3. Confirm   Confirm conversations and oral agreements. Make comprehensive notes at the time. Place in file. Follow up letter to other person setting out facts agreed to as you understand them.

4. Consult Lawyer   As soon as possible. Select lawyer carefully. Choose best. Check out reputation with business people and others using legal services. Choose specialist in your immediate problem.

5. Be Prepared   First contact with lawyer sets tone for future relationship and lawyer's opinion of value of case. Tell whole story, be honest, open. Lawyer will ask pointed questions, test truthfulness, pry for weaknesses as well as strengths.

6. Discuss   Discuss mechanics of court procedure and processing claim through courts. Don't assume you are familiar with procedure. Don't be afraid to ask or show ignorance of process. Will have bearing on your ultimate decision to proceed, settle or drop claim.

7. Deliver Documents and Records   Lawyer needs documents to study. Arrange in package, in chronological order. Remember to keep copies for your records as backup in case originals are lost and so they will be available to study yourself as case proceeds.

8. Fees; Costs   Request estimates of legal fees and costs. Lawyer will give estimate and advise how much must be paid immediately as a retainer (be prepared to pay a minimum deposit of $500 for higher court claims) and will discuss orderly

payment of balance according to law firm's practice.

9. Appraisal   Ask for a frank, realistic appraisal of chances of success or failure; factors which might limit success; general value of claim in terms of dollars; dangers of launching an unsuccessful law suit. Lawyer may give general opinion. If he needs time for assessment, he will arrange second interview for this purpose.

10. Explore Dangers   Ask lawyer to give estimate on liability for court costs should your claim prove unsuccessful (if you are thrown out of court you usually are responsible for part of other person's costs).

11. Retainer   Lawyer will require retainer fee be paid immediately. Pay retainer. Lawyer may also ask you to sign written general retainer authorizing firm to act and proceed.

12. Second Meeting   Request advice whether claim worth pursuing. Lawyer will give realistic appraisal of chances of success (expressed as percentage); value of claim (expressed in dollar figures); anticipated time to obtain judgment; what you may expect from law firm; and what lawyer will require of you as matter progresses. Lawyer will specify details. Request lawyer send you details in writing. (Studies show clients understand only one-half of what lawyer tells them in interview; so get it in writing.)

13. Follow Instructions   Follow lawyer's instructions and advice.

14. Lawyer Prepares   Lawyer will prepare summons, pleadings and court notices. Ask to be kept informed. Lawyer will set down for trial; examine law and precedents; interview witnesses; prepare trial brief; arrange Examination for Discovery.

15. Examination For Discovery   Pre-trial hearing of parties under oath arranged by lawyers. Both sides to be questioned at examiner's offices. Take great care in preparation. You will be interrogated by opposing lawyer. Answers will be recorded in transcript which may be used against you at trial. Lawyer also observing you, assessing you as reliable, unreliable, strong, weak. Be assertive, truthful, know what you are talking about. Lawyers will use strengths which appear from examination to attempt settlement.

16. Production of Documents   Each side is entitled to preview records of others. You are required to produce for other's inspection business records you intend to introduce at trial. If not produced at this stage, they cannot be used at trial without special permission of the court.

17. Prepare for Trial   Don't wait until last minute. Don't wait for lawyer to instruct or review with you (lawyers have been known to leave this to last minute, may catch you short). Review records from your own files. Ask lawyer to give you copies of the trial papers and pleadings so you can study them. Visit courtroom in advance. Watch a trial. Observe procedure.

18. Day Of Trial   Set everything else aside. Clear mind of other problems. Dress conservatively, properly. Maintain good appearance, posture. When giving evidence be frank, open, honest, serious. Give evidence directly to judge (or jury). Be prepared for vigorous cross-examination and testing of evidence by other lawyer. Court wants facts not generalities, opinions or hearsay. Don't argue. Don't exaggerate. Be responsive but don't volunteer unnecessary information to other lawyer.

19. Psychological Winner   The poise and confidence of a winner will help your case. But be prepared for the possibility of loss in whole or in part. No lawyer can give guarantee of success. Remember, every trial is a horse race.

20. Settlement   Lawyer will spend time during process of case attempting to settle claim. Be open at every stage to reasonable settlement. Trust lawyer's independent advice and outlook more than your personal view of what is absolutely right. Be prepared to compromise as long as settlement gets you reasonable results and compensation. Don't be too stubborn on matters of principle or showing the other guy how tough you are. In the end, the right compromise might be best for you.

Review

1. GORNIAK v. ARCHER.   Archer owns a commercial building worth $250 000. Gorniak holds a mortgage against the property which has a present principal balance of $20 000 and requires monthly payments of $800. The mortgage has two more years to run before maturity. Archer has been faithfully paying it off but she has failed to make the last two payments. The mortgage gives Gorniak the legal right to foreclose if a single payment is overdue by 45 days. Gorniak now attempts to foreclose and take over the property. Consider the rules of law and equity and the definition of law and decide whether or not Gorniak will be successful. Consider as well what general remedies Archer may reasonably expect to be available to her.

2. Review the definition of law. Identify one key point that truly interests you or at least provokes feelings in you. Turn it over in your mind critically and write a one-page report using your own experience, views, prejudices and thoughts. Read the report. You'll find it reveals much about you as a person and about your view of the law.

3. Becker, a contractor, is in the middle of an important trial in your province's major city. Oosterhoff, also a contractor, is engaged in court in a small county town several hundred miles away. The facts of both cases are substantially the same. What assurances may be given that the trial judges will both come to the same conclusions by delivering basically similar judgments? What aspects of the law make this a real probability?

4. List the steps necessary to process a typical civil trial from commencement to judgment. Comment on each step. Then review Unit Three to identify those steps which you did not recall or understand. This is an important exercise for any serious student because of the basic importance of legal procedures.

CHAPTER 2

The Law of Torts and Business Crimes

YOU ARE THE JURY

1. CHAMPION v. TURNBULL

Turnbull, the owner of a self-serve 24-hour laundromat, had warned Champion, a heavy drinker, to stay away from the premises. Later, Turnbull found Champion "doing his laundry." He advanced to within a few feet of the startled Champion, raised his arm and shouted, "If you're not out of here with those rags in one minute I'll break both your legs." Champion began to comply but suffered a heart attack in the process. After recovering, Champion sued Turnbull for assault. Should the action succeed?

2. SILVESTER v. DUNGWORTH

Dungworth, a department store manager, called an employee, Silvester, into her office. "I've been examining some records and your shifts coincide exactly with these drug thefts we've been having in the drug department. I think you're the thief." Silvester responded that if the accusation was made again he would sue. Several days later the manager approached Silvester at work and whis-pered, "I still think you're a crook." The manager and the owners of the store received letters from Silvester's lawyer advising that he intended to sue for slander. Does Silvester have a case?

3. STOUT v. HARDCASTLE

Stout picked up a package in a department store honestly believing it was her own. The particular parcel was actually the property of the store. Two employees ran after Stout and had her arrested. After Stout proved her innocence in court, she sued the department store and the two employees involved for malicious prosecution. Is Stout entitled to succeed?

OBJECTIVES

- to identify legal rights to personal security and property security.
- to identify the duties owed to others in the conduct of business and personal affairs.
- to list and define wrong conduct most commonly encountered in business (business torts).
- to define negligence and identify the elements of the standard of care

LEXICON

Assault Unlawfully harming another person, including the least touching of another person wilfully or in anger. Sometimes referred to as "assault and battery." Practically, "harm" has a wide definition, including attempts to restrain or touch another person without consent. Assault also includes the attempt or threat to harm another without actual touching of the person and whether or not any actual suffering occurs. The victim may sue for damages, institute a criminal prosecution, or both.

Damages An injury or loss to a person or property for which a court will award a sum of money as compensation.

Disparagement The general term for words, either written or spoken, which tend to injure another's property rights.

Induce To persuade someone to act to the detriment or injury of one person, and the advantage of another.

Libel Written statements, published or made available to one or more third parties, which are false and cause injury to another.

Negligence Failure to exercise the due care towards others that reasonable people in similar circumstances would have exercised, and which results in injury. Negligence is a question of fact for the judge (or jury) to decide on the merit of each case. It is necessary to prove a higher degree of negligence in criminal cases than in civil cases.

Tort A civil wrong which results in injury to person or property and for which the victim may sue for damages in civil court.

Wrong An act which unlawfully deprives or interferes with another person's personal or property rights. Used in the same sense as a tort.

The preceding three You Are The Jury cases illustrate that business activities may lead to conflicts in which one of the participants suffers harm or injury. The purpose of the branch of law known as Torts is to provide a court-based system with powers to provide a suitable remedy – usually monetary compensation.

Rights and duties

We Canadians are a bundle of rights and duties. Your rights represent my duty to you and my rights represent your duty to me. The objective of the law of torts is to preserve our rights while at the same time compelling us to do our duty. Do I have the right to enter your store? If so, you have the duty to maintain safe premises. Do you have a right to expect that I will complete my part of our contract? If so, I have a duty to perform it.

It would be impossible to discuss business law without a clear grasp of our mutual rights and duties. Rights are either *absolute* or *contractual*. Absolute rights arise naturally out of our status as human beings and include personal security, personal liberty, integrity of reputation and property ownership. Contractual rights arise when two or more persons reach a mutual agreement which creates a legally binding contract.

Personal security

Personal security consists of the peaceable enjoyment of life, body, health and reputation. It may be violated in terms of either civil law (negligence, assault, libel, slander and malicious prosecution) or criminal law (criminal assault, arson, robbery and criminal libel). Under our system of government, Canadians cannot (except by operation of law) be prevented from going where they please nor compelled to go where they do not want to nor in any way imprisoned or confined.

Property

Our property laws give Canadians the right to exclusive use and possession of real and personal property. Owners have the right to assert their ownership, prevent use of property by others and prevent trespass.

Contractual rights and duties

These are the rights and duties which arise out of a contract which has been mutually agreed to including contracts for sales, employment, insurance, agency and business organization.

Civil and criminal wrongs

A legal wrong is the violation of some right or duty. "Wrongs" are either civil or criminal (although the same act may constitute both a civil and criminal wrong: i.e., an act which injures a person by assault; reckless driving). Civil wrongs (Torts) violate private rights or duties and therefore concern people individually rather than the public as a whole. Civil wrongs are remedied by private court actions. Walter, the weekend golfer of Chapter One, would bring his action in the civil courts as would all of the injured parties in the You Are The Jury cases in this chapter. A criminal wrong, or crime, violates a public right or duty and will therefore result in prosecution through the courts which have the power to fine or imprison the offender. We will consider both civil and criminal wrongs in this chapter.

Meaning of Tort

The English word Tort has its roots in the Latin verb *torquere*, to twist. To commit a tort means to do something twisted or crooked, or in effect, to commit a legal wrong. Specifically, the term tort refers to a wrongful act, committed by one person against another, for which the injured person is entitled by law to a civil court remedy – usually in the form of a monetary award. The injured party must prove that the act complained of amounted to a tort, and must produce evidence to show that injury resulted. The judge (or jury), if satisfied that a tort resulted in injury meriting an award of damages, sets the compensation to be awarded.

For example, in the *Stout v. Hardcastle* case, Stout as plaintiff must sue the store in a civil court and must prove that the actions of the store's employees amounted to the tort of malicious prosecution. She must also provide facts to show the extent of her discomfort, inconvenience, loss of liberty, and loss of reputation. As defendant, the store has the right to submit in its defence that the employees acted in good faith and on reasonable and probable grounds that a crime had been committed which warranted prosecution. At the conclusion of the trial, the court would give judgment for one party or the other, and if it found that a tort had been committed it would further be required to assess the damages in dollars and cents. The store would then be required to pay Stout the amount of the damages as compensation.

There are four major classifications of torts:
- *Intentional Injury to the Person* in which a person deliberately causes harm or loss to another.
- *Intentional Injury to Property* in which a person deliberately causes damage or loss to the property of another.
- *Unintentional Injury (Negligence)* in which a person acts carelessly or negligently thereby causing unintentional loss, harm or damage to another or the property of another.
- *Business Torts* which consist of a group of wrongs commonly encountered in the course of business including interfering in the contracts of others, maliciously harming the business of another, sending threatening letters and infringing on another's Patent or Trade Mark rights.

Intentional torts to the person

Wrongs to the person

Wrongs to the person may involve assault on one's body, freedom, security or reputation. These are commonly referred to, respectively, as assault, false imprisonment, malicious prosecution and defamation.

Assault

Under our present laws, a person may commit an assault in two ways: first, by intentionally applying force by physically touching, pushing, hitting or restraining another without that person's consent; and second, by attempting or threatening by action of gestures to apply such force at a time when the victim might reasonably believe that force will in fact be applied.

CASE 1 MATTHEWS v. MARKLE

Matthews looked out his kitchen window and saw Markle pointing a gun at him. Matthews' complaint to the police resulted in a criminal prosecution, and Matthews also sued Markle in the civil courts in tort (assault). Although Markle was able to establish that the gun was not loaded, both courts found that he had committed an assault because Matthews had reasonable grounds to believe that he was in danger. Markle was found guilty in the criminal prosecution and assessed a fine of $200. The civil court awarded Matthews damages in the sum $1 000.

CASE 2 EVAN v. ODEON THEATERS

A disruptive person was asked to leave a theater by an usher. The customer began to leave but the usher, believing the customer was moving too slowly, reached out to hurry him along. The customer fell and sued the theater company for assault. The court awarded damages to the customer finding that the employee had no right to touch the customer as he was leaving the theater of his own free will.

Except in genuine cases of self-defence, no-one is justified in assaulting another person. When aggravated, insulted or verbally abused by another, the victim is expected to prudently withdraw as far as possible to avoid conflict. If the victim retreats as far as possible and it then becomes necessary for him to protect his person or property, he is entitled to use whatever force is reasonable under the circumstances, but no more.

CASE 3 MANN v. KING

King operated several variety stores in a major Canadian city. He instructed his staff to confront any customer suspected of shoplifting and gave them authority to advise such customers not to return to the store in the future. Young customers who claimed to have been falsely accused of thefts

demonstrated in front of King's stores, and one employee told King she had been threatened by a demonstrator. King began driving his staff home after work. On one such occasion, King found several persons outside an employee's home shouting, "Get King! Get King!" King went into his employee's home briefly and then emerged to confront the hecklers. Mann pushed King, whereupon King stabbed the youth in the leg severing an artery. Mann was hospitalized for a long time. He sued for damages. King said, "If Mann had stayed home, he would not have been hurt. If he hadn't pushed me, I wouldn't have had to defend myself."

The court held that King was right to withdraw to the safety of the house but that he was wrong in emerging to confront the demonstrators. He had other options – such as calling the police – and in any event the force he used was excessive. In spite of the finding that Mann's conduct was reprehensible, the court awarded him damages for assault.

False imprisonment (false arrest)

Any unlawful interference with the right of people to go or stay where they please constitutes false imprisonment. One Canadian judge described it as "the intentional and unjustified total restraint of a person's movement by actively confining or preventing that person from exercising the privilege of leaving a place." A false imprisonment occurs in each of the following situations:
- physical restraint is applied to the person to compel compliance.
- the person is threatened with physical restraint in the event of non-compliance and submits to detention without actually being touched.
- no physical restraint and no threat of physical restraint, but the person restrained is given the impression that non-compliance with the order to remain will cause public spectacle and embarrassment.

The term false arrest is used interchangeably with the term false imprisonment but is more specifically a detention with the intention of turning the person over to the authorities for criminal prosecution.

CASE 4 KRANE v. NU-SHOPPER INC.

The employees in a store suspected a customer, Krane, of shoplifting. Krane complied without question when asked to return to the store. The customer again complied when a second employee told him, "it would be best for you to come in the back room." No force or threats were used. The employees discovered that they had been mistaken in their belief that the customer had stolen merchandise, apologized and told him he was free to go. The customer had been detained for 20 minutes. The customer sued and was awarded judgment in the sum of $2 500.

CASE 5 STARR v. XYZ RAILWAY COMPANY

Two employees detained Starr after recognizing her from a missing person poster in their office. After being coaxed and gently pushed into a private office, Starr complained that she had been home for several months and was no longer a missing person. One half hour later, police confirmed this. Starr sued. The court held that the good intentions of the railway employees were not a defence to a civil action for false imprisonment and awarded Starr $3 000 for her ordeal.

Our discussion of assault and false imprisonment should bring home a clear message to Canadian business people. Great risks await those who take the law into their own hands. A "citizen's arrest" should only be made when one is absolutely certain of the facts; and only in the most extreme circumstances should a person resort to self-defence.

Malicious Prosecution
A malicious prosecution is one brought in bad faith for improper motives. An innocent person accused of a crime by a vindictive person may sue and recover damages against the latter in tort. In order to succeed the following four elements must be present: the accuser must be shown to have acted in bad faith; there must not be reasonable or probable grounds to the charges; charges must be laid; the charges must be dismissed or withdrawn.

CASE 6 MAY v. STEENHUIS

An employee made up a story of wrongdoing against her employer and produced documents to the police who accepted the information. They used it to lay criminal charges. Before the trial, the Crown discovered the evidence was false and withdrew the charges. The employer sued the employee, Crown attorney and investigating officers for malicious prosecution. Judgment was entered against the employee in the sum of $8 000, but the case against the Crown Attorney and police was dismissed as they proceeded in good faith and had reasonable and probable grounds to believe that a crime had been committed.

Defamation (Libel and Slander)
Defamation means unjustifiably injuring a person's name, character or reputation by false statements. In Canadian law protection of a person's reputation and good name is based on the torts of libel and slander in civil courts and by criminal prosecution based on the offence of libel. Libel consists of written, printed or other graphic defamation such as signs, marks, pictures, motion pictures or television. Slander consists of verbal defamation. Civil libel as a tort differs from criminal libel chiefly in the remedy sought: i.e., damages rather than prosecution, conviction and punishment.

In order to succeed in an action based on the torts of libel and slander, the victim must prove that the defamatory statement was (1) false (2) published by being shown to or spoken in the presence of a third party (3) injury, loss or harm has resulted. Defamation actions have been lost under the following circumstances:

- defendant called the plaintiff a liar and the "accusation" was proven to be true and justified.
- defendant accused the plaintiff of being a thief. The plaintiff was not in fact a thief but no-one else was present so the statement could not be considered to have been "published."
- defendant published a false statement against the plaintiff but no-one believed it so that the plaintiff suffered no actual, provable harm.

CASE 7 STORTINI v. BOARD OF EDUCATION

Stortini had been laid off from his position with the Board. He persistently attended a Board office seeking a job. On one of these visits he happened to see the word "crazy" written in large handwriting on the front cover of his file. Later, one of the office's employees admitted that she had written the comment on the file after a particularly frustrating session with Stortini. Stortini sued for damages based on the tort of libel. The court held that the written word "crazy" constituted a libel which may have affected Stortini in his "calling, vocation or work." The court awarded damages in the sum of $500 and ordered the Board to pay Stortini's court costs.

The law recognizes that there are situations in which people should be encouraged to write and speak freely without the risks of being sued in tort. Therefore certain statements are permitted on the grounds of absolute privilege, qualified privilege and fair comment.

Absolute privilege from a suit in torts for defamation is given to Members of Parliament engaged in parliamentary proceedings; judges engaged in court proceedings; lawyers, witnesses and jury members during the course of a trial; all inquests and the proceedings of Royal Commissions. This absolute privilege is designed to encourage fearless, unhindered arguments in court and forceful debate in Parliament and other forums.

A *qualified privilege* is available to persons who are required to give certain information. This privilege protects the individual from a defamation suit provided that the information is given in good faith, without malice and with an honest belief in its truth. Employers, teachers and business associates who are requested to provide letters of reference cannot be sued for defamation even if a statement turns out to be false. Qualified privilege also extends to accurate reports of meetings, court proceedings, and parliamentary and provincial legislative proceedings. A further protection is given by rules of fair comment on matters of public interest. Therefore a person is allowed to critically express an opinion provided he can demonstrate an honest belief in the opinion given, good faith, lack of malice and no intention to cause harm.

Intentional torts affecting property

The torts affecting property are conversion, nuisance, waste, and occupier's rights and duties.

Conversion (Replevin)

The tort of conversion consists of unlawfully assuming and exercising the right of ownership over personal property which belongs to another. In one case merchandise belonging to one merchant was mistakenly delivered to another who sold the merchandise to customers. The first merchant successfully sued the second for damages based on the tort of conversion. Where personal property is wrongfully withheld from the true owner, the latter, instead of suing for conversion and damages, may bring a replevin action requesting the court to order the return of the article itself. For further particulars on replevin see Chapter 10: Creditors' Rights.

Nuisance

The tort of nuisance means any unlawful, improper or indecent conduct which produces substantial annoyance, inconvenience, discomfort or injury to some person, persons or to the public. A person complaining of a legal nuisance may bring an action in tort and recover damages.

CASE 8 YOUNG v. DAVIS AUTO REPAIR INC.

Young had lived for twelve years in an apartment over a garage operated by Davis. Davis converted his business to a new process which gave off odourless fumes which seeped up into the apartment nearly killing Young. After a long period of hospitalization, Young sued. Young succeeded in tort and recovered $20 000 in damages.

Waste

If a person, such as a tenant, has possession but not ownership of real property, then the property must be used in such a way that when the possession ceases the premises will not have suffered any substantial damage or depreciation other than ordinary wear and tear. If damage has been done, the landscape disfigured, useful trees chopped down or if the premises have been allowed to fall into decay, the tenant has committed the tort of waste and may be sued for damages by the owner.

CASE 9 FELKER v. HUMANN

Felker leased a farmhouse and adjoining land to Humann. Felker discovered that Humann had excavated part of the land and removed gravel which he had sold at a profit. Felker sued his tenant successfully in tort for waste and was awarded monetary damages equivalent to the value of the gravel removed.

Occupier's liability

The person in possession of land, whether he is the actual owner or only a tenant, is liable for injuries sustained by visitors, invitees, licensees and trespassers, on the basis of a type of sliding scale applied by the courts.

An invitee is a person who has been directly or indirectly invited to come to the premises to transact or engage in business. Clients of professional people and customers of tradespeople fall into this category. The occupier must take care to prevent injuries of which he, as a reasonable and responsible person, ought to anticipate under the circumstances. A licensee is a visitor who enters the premises of the occupier as a guest as opposed to someone who has come to transact business. For example, a dinner guest who has come to your home for the evening; a member of an association who has come to your office for the purpose of a meeting unconnected with your business; or a guest of an apartment tenant, while in the vestibule or common areas owned by the landlord.

The occupier's liability may be somewhat less to a licensee than to an invitee. Liability to a licensee has been accurately described as limited to ensuring that there are no "hidden traps" on the premises which are likely to result in injury. In one case, a licensee seriously twisted an ankle while stepping through a loose floorboard which showed no visible signs of defect. This was considered to be a hidden trap. A second licensee failed to recover for similar injuries caused by loose floor tiles which were visibly in a loose and dangerous condition.

A trespasser is a person who is not lawfully on the premises. This classification includes people who have come for some criminal purpose; those who have come for no improper purpose but who have been previously warned to stay away; those who trespass in ignorance; and those who realize the property belongs to someone else but who simply want to get from point A to B by the quickest possible route. The occupier owes this class of person the lowest duty and accordingly is only required not to deliberately set traps to cause harm. Needless to say the duty owed the criminal is absolutely minimal.

CASE 10 TINKERS, EVERS AND CHANCE v. CUMMINS

Suppose Cummins is the owner of three apartment buildings set some distance back from the street. Suppose weather conditions have created a treacherous sheet of ice and this is hidden beneath a soft blanket of newly-fallen snow. Suppose as well that Cummins is not aware of the ice under the snow and therefore has been tardy in clearing off the walkways to make them safe to walk on. Suppose further than Tinkers has come to talk to Cummins about buying the buildings; Evers has come to visit the tenants in apartment 312-A and Chance is a student who has learned that the quickest way to get to his classes is a straight line that takes him across Cummins' property. Suppose now all three fall simultaneously on the ice while on Cummins' lands. Each fractures a pelvis and is hospitalized for eight weeks. What do you think Cummins' liability will be to each?

Occupier's rights and duties regarding trespassers

When occupiers (persons in possession of property whether owners or tenants) of lands or buildings find a trespasser on the premises, they have the right to order the trespasser from the premises. If the trespasser refuses to leave, the occupier has the right to use reasonable force to

"evict" the trespasser. The trespasser must be permitted to leave willingly and reasonable force may only be applied if the trespasser refuses to leave.

Both the civil and criminal law provides occupiers with remedies against trespass. Each province has passed legislation against "petty trespass" which gives powers of arrest, trial by provincial courts and punishment by fine. In the alternative or in addition, the occupier may sue the trespasser in the civil courts in tort for damages.

CASE 11 WINDER v. CARROTHERS

Construction workers and machinery under the control of a contractor, Carrothers, crossed over Winder's residential property daily to get to the construction site. Winder complained to Carrothers, but when nothing was done Winder sued. The court held that the tort of trespass is a continuing offence so that the trespasses of each day must be considered as separate, intentional wrongs. Winder was therefore allowed a greater amount of damages than if the offence had occured only once. The court awarded Winder $5 000 in damages.

When it appears that the trespass is likely to be a continuing wrong, the civil courts also provide the remedy of injunction by which the court orders the trespasser to refrain from further trespass activity or suffer the consequences of further court penalty.

Negligence

Standard of care
In the conduct of their affairs all Canadians have a duty to take reasonable care not to injure another person or another person's property. In determining in any given case whether or not a particular person has exercised reasonable care, the courts use the test of "foreseeability of harm." In reviewing the facts the court must ask itself whether a reasonable, prudent person, possessing average skill and knowledge, would have foreseen the probability of injury. If the courts decide that there has been a failure to take due care, the defendants are guilty of negligence and are legally liable for the injury they have caused. Negligence has been specifically defined as the doing or failing to do something which a reasonable person would or would not do under the circumstances;

and failing to exercise a duty of care towards others where a reasonable person could foresee injury to another.

In the diagram below those persons who act in ways listed above the line will not be liable in tort even though some person may have been injured as a direct or indirect result of their conduct. Those persons who fall below the line will be liable.

- Acts with superior skill, knowledge, due care.
- Acts with above average skill, knowledge, due care.
- Acts with average skill, knowledge, due care.
- Acts but could not reasonably have foreseen injury.
- Acts cause injury but owed no duty to injured party.
- Acts imperfectly but can't be judged careless.

Conduct of Reasonable Person

- Acts below average standard of care.
- Acts carelessly without sufficient thought.
- Acts without good judgment: not in control.
- Acts without considering probable consequences.
- Acts without steps to avoid injury to others.

In order to be successful in a tort action based on negligence the injured party must prove three essential elements:
- the defendant owed this particular injured party a duty of care under these particular circumstances.
- the defendant fell below the minimal standard of care set for the reasonable, prudent person.
- the defendant's act caused injury or loss which can be translated into an award of damages by a court.

Defences to a negligence action
Once a plaintiff in a negligence action has established the three elements listed above, it becomes the responsibility of the defendant to establish that the plaintiff is not entitled to a court judgment awarding damages. The defendant may challenge the plaintiff's evidence by establishing that the damages were "too remote to justify recovery," or that the plaintiff's conduct contributed to the damage thereby making the plaintiff at least partly responsible for the injury.

The court must be able to establish a reasonable relationship between the defendant's conduct and the injuries sustained by the plaintiff. Otherwise the plaintiff's action must be dismissed on the grounds the injuries complained of were too remote.

CASE 12 MONCKTON AND OTHERS v. PORTER

Suppose Monckton carelessly discarded a cigaret near a service station thereby causing an explosion that created this sequence of events:

- demolition of Albert's car.
- incineration of Albert's hairpiece and his hospitalization.
- frightening of Albert's wife who was half a block away causing her to faint. Several weeks later she had a miscarriage.
- damaging of the service station which put it out of business for several weeks.
- Frank, come unexpectedly upon the prostrate form of Albert's wife, suffering a heart attack while trying to assist her.
- June, who had her car in for repairs, having to make alternative arrangements with another service station and missing out on her vacation.

Monckton would be responsible for all of the injuries that were a direct result of his negligence, or which could reasonably be shown to be part of an unbroken series of events which he started. Most assuredly, he will be responsible for all of the injuries to Albert and a substantial part of the loss caused to the service station, including loss of business and profits over a reasonable period of shutdown. The fainting injury of Albert's wife is also actionable. However, the remaining events are too remote to warrant recovery.

A second type of defence open to a defendant in a negligence action is to establish that the plaintiff was also negligent, and was therefore guilty of contributory negligence under circumstances which would render it reasonable to divide the loss between the plaintiff and defendant.

CASE 13 MacGREGOR v. SCHNYDER

MacGregor inched his car into an intersection to determine whether the way was clear. He proceeded thinking that it was and was struck by Schnyder who had the right of way. MacGregor was seriously injured and sued Schnyder, relying on a provision of a provincial highway traffic act which potentially deprived Schnyder of her defence of right of way. The jury found on the facts that MacGregor was 75% to blame for the accident and Schnyder was 25% to blame. It assessed the damages at $30 000, and the judge accordingly limited Schnyder's liability to $7 500.

Business torts and crimes

Business torts

The term "business torts" may be applied to a group of wrongs commonly encountered in the course of business. These include fraud and deceit; false disparagement of a competitor's business or products; wrongful interference with other people's contracts; the sending of threatening or intimidating letters; and patent, copyright and trade mark infringements. Many of these civil wrongs also contravene Canadian criminal law.

Fraud and deceit

Fraud constitutes a tort for which damages may be recovered through the civil courts. The effect of fraud on contracts will be discussed in Chapter Three.

Disparagement

Disparagement of things is very like defamation of person, and many of the rules relating to defamation may be applied to this branch of law. There are two types of disparagement:

- Slander of Title.
- Slander of Quality.

The courts have defined slander of title as a "false and malicious statement disparaging a person's title to property causing special damage." The courts have also expanded the definition of the term slander to include written statements when the wrong relates to property rather than persons or reputation. However, there can be no slander of title unless the statement is both false and malicious, and unless it results in special damage to the owner. For further discussion of these points, see Chapter Three.

CASE 14 ALCROFT v. CUTSEY

Cutsey honestly but mistakenly believed that he was the legal owner of a section of development land which actually belonged to Alcroft. This "challenge" to Alcroft's title or ownership resulted in the loss of a sale for the property and Alcroft suffered financial injury. Alcroft had his accountant calculate the amount of the loss and had his lawyer sue Cutsey in tort. Alcroft was compelled to withdraw the suit at a preliminary stage (before trial) because it became clear that Cutsey's conduct did not amount to a slander of title: he acted in good faith and, although mistaken, lacked the necessary malicious intent to support an action in tort.

The second type of disparagement, slander of quality, makes anyone who circulates or publishes an untrue statement of fact (not opinion) which disparages the quality of another person's merchandise or other property, causing loss through impairment ''in the salability of such merchandise or property,'' liable for such loss if it could have been reasonably foreseen that such loss might result. Malice or honest mistake are not factors in this type of disparagement and therefore are immaterial when considering whether or not a person has committed the tort of slander of quality.

Disparagement and special defences

As in defamation, in cases of disparagement one may plead privilege. For example, suppose you owe a special duty to a third party. Perhaps you are a relative, a close friend, a business person responding to an inquiry, a civil servant in the course of duty, or a professional whose business requires giving advice to consumers. Must you remain silent to avoid a disparagement suit? No! If you merely try to protect a third party against loss, you may express a reasonable belief that a product is inferior.

Wrongful interference with contract

Any wrongful interference with an existing contract, by obstructing, delaying or preventing its performance in whole or in part, gives an injured party an action in tort. The most common tort under this heading is inducing one person to break an existing contractual commitment to another person. As one judge put it, ''A person who induces a party to a contract to break it, intending thereby to injure another person or to get some personal advantage, commits an actionable wrong unless the evidence discloses legal justification for interference.''

CASE 15 ZANDRI v. BAINES

Zandri, a travel agent, obtained a contract with a foreign corporation appointing him the exclusive agent for offering the corporation's services in Ontario. Baines, another travel agent, knew about that contract but induced the corporation to extend the same rights to him. Baines argued, ''I acted in good faith without malice. Besides I've got the right to compete. I was only going after my rights. That's legal. Isn't it?''

Zandri won. The court pointed out that the absence of malice does not justify persuading another person to break a contract. The act is

wrong if done intentionally and with knowledge of the existing contract. The judge said, "It is one thing to compete for a contract not yet awarded, but a wholly different thing . . . amounting to tort, to procure a contract for one's self by inducing the breach of another contract."

There are situations where a person may legally advise another person to refrain from the performance of a contract. A solicitor may advise a client not to complete a contractual undertaking. A physician may counsel a young hockey player to abandon a career in sports (resulting in the breach of a contract of employment by the patient). A concerned mother may induce her son to cancel a contract for the purchase of shares. These are all good examples of the type of justification which will be recognized by the courts as a defence to an action in tort against the person inducing a breach of contract.

Malicious injury to business
The Canadian free enterprise system permits all Canadians to engage freely in business, even if in so doing other similar businesses sustain loss. However, where people embark on a competitive venture not for business reasons, but for the malicious and wilful purpose of injuring another person already engaged in such business, they are merely using their own venture as an instrument for achieving a wrongful purpose.

CASE 16 BUCK v. REDRUPP

Redrupp ran the only sheet metal business in a small Northern Canadian city. Each time a competitor set up business, Redrupp reduced his prices to a low level, thereby diverting business away from the competitor. As soon as the competitor had been driven out of business, the bargains stopped and prices were raised. Buck, one such unfortunate competitor, sued for damages. The court held that Redrupp's conduct amounted to "a wanton wrong actionable in tort."

Business correspondence
In attempting to make collections by mail businesses (collection agencies in particular) must walk the fine line between collection demands and collection threats. Any creditor has the right to make vigorous and insistent demands for payment and to state that non-payment may result in a lawsuit. However, threats that amount to mental harassment and annoyance are recognized by the courts as inflicting a type of injury for which damages are recoverable. The attitude of the courts may be observed in the following two cases.

CASE 17 WILLIAMSON v. COWDREY COLLECTION SERVICE

Cowdrey sent Williamson, an employed widow, a series of letters threatening to sue and to "bother your employer until he is so disgusted with you he will throw you out the back door. We can tie you up tighter than a drum, you know, unless we are paid in full." Williamson became nervous and unable to work. She suffered mental pain, and eventually had to rest in bed. She sued and recovered a judgment based on tort because the court decided that Cowdrey's acts had been done for the "purpose of harassing and annoying Williamson mentally."

CASE 18 CARRIER v. INTEGRITY BUSINESS SCHOOLS

Carrier signed a contract for a correspondence course. When he did not pay tuition, he received, over a period of twelve months, thirty letters which varied from polite reminders to threats to garnishee his wages, to accusations of "moral unworthiness" which were obviously calculated to force payment. Carrier sued. Judgment was given in tort for worry, humiliation and loss of sleep based on the court's finding that the school's intent was to harass Carrier until he paid.

Infringement of industrial or intellectual property
Industrial or intellectual property includes patents, copyright, industrial designs, trade marks and trade names. As you will discover in Chapter Nine, this type of industrial property is protected by law in the same way other property is protected. If any person violates any property right, the owner is entitled to sue in tort. This type of offence is known as infringement and is fully discussed in Chapter Nine.

Other considerations
Further material on tort is available in this book. Liability arising out of contract is dealt with in Chapter Three: Contracts. Employer's liability is covered in Chapter Six: Employment Law. As people naturally attempt to anticipate tort liability and avoid the consequences through insurance coverage, refer also to Chapter Seven: Insurance and Business Risks.

KEY TO YOU ARE THE JURY

1. CHAMPION v. TURNBULL   Turnbull wins. Champion was entitled to order Turnbull from the premises, but was not entitled to use force as long as Turnbull was complying. Champion's gesture and words constituted an assault even though he did not touch the intended victim. The assault was unjustified, and reasonably foreseeable injuries resulted.

2. SILVESTER v. DUNGWORTH   Silvester has no case. In addition to proving the statements were false, Silvester must establish that they were "published" by being spoken in the presence of a third party who actually heard the accusation. Dungworth avoided liability for slander by being discrete.

3. STOUT v. HARDCASTLE   Charges were laid and dismissed but Stout must prove that, through its agents, the store acted in bad faith. Under the circumstances of this case, it should have been obvious to a prudent person that Stout probably made a mistake in picking up the parcel and therefore there was no reasonable and probable ground for insisting on prosecution. Stout succeeded in an action based on malicious prosecution.

Checklist: Torts

A. The Injured Party

1. As soon as you realize you are the probable victim of a tort, open a file and begin to document facts, dates, events, names of witnesses. System should be suitable for daily records, updates, correspondence receipts, reports. Remember best documented cases are most successful in court or result in better, quicker settlement.

2. Solicitor-client relationship. First meeting sets tone for future activity. Be prepared with documentation to discuss elements and facts of your case including liability of other party and probable damages. Lawyer needs sufficient facts to make preliminary assessment.

a) Be prepared to tell full story, endure some pointed questioning and have lawyer test your truthfulness and reliability.

b) Encourage a general discussion of the mechanics of pursuing a claim in tort. Lawyer may assume you are aware of steps. Insist on knowing. Will help you to deal with and decide matters as they arise if you can see whole picture.

c) Discuss fees. Lawyer will charge fees for services rendered but cannot legally base fee as percentage of recovery or agree to charge fee only if successful. Expect to pay retainer at this interview – usually $500 for claim involving several thousand dollars and up, less for smaller claims.

d) Request frank appraisal of probable award by court, factors which could prevent your recovering damages completely or in part in court, time limitation periods and the general value of the claim for settlement purposes. Lawyer will probably want to delay assessments until a future meeting to become better acquainted with facts, consider additional factors to provide more meaningful estimates. This is usual procedure and you should agree to such delayed opinion.

3. Solicitor-client second meeting. Solicitor will advise whether claim worth pursuing and will confirm willingness or competence to pursue claim further. If lawyer agrees to pursue case, make certain that this person will carry matter through to trial. If other lawyers in office may be asked to take over at trial stage, insist the lawyer you retained carry through to end unless you are not concerned who takes case to trial. In any event, if possiblity another may take over file in future ask for explanation of the procedure.

4. After a realistic appraisal of the merits of case by lawyer, decide whether you will pursue claim on terms established by lawyer's practice.

a) Lawyer will give chances of success in rough terms as percentage.

b) Lawyer will give damage figure as estimated range.

c) Lawyer will estimate total fees based on other cases of similar complexity and discuss policy of interim billings and times when fees generally due. Usually all fees required to be paid before actual trial.

d) Lawyer will discuss costs advising what part of legal costs you might expect to recover through court or from other parties, insurance company (if covered).

e) Lawyer will request authority to retain experts, technical witnesses, medical witnesses, etc. and advise how expenses for same will be handled.

f) Lawyer will discuss probable out-of-pocket expenses and disbursements and ask for agreement on extent of authority to incur such expenses.

g) Lawyer will advise how much time you must devote to case, attendances at law firm, pre-trial hearings, attempt to settle meetings and to generally assist in fact-finding activities. Proper handling of the case will require time and effort on your part. Don't expect lawyer to handle every detail.

5. As matters progress maintain personal record keeping. Be careful to record thoughts on paper as they come and keep in file for next meeting with lawyer. Records should be as specific as possible. Generalities do little in court and little to promote good settlement. Be realistic. Don't exaggerate. In particular record:

a) Names, addresses and phone number of prospective witnesses; brief statement of what they can prove.

b) Names of participants in conversations relating to case and substance of what was said.

c) If tort results in personal injury, also record whether anyone photographed or drew diagrams of scene (i.e., police); whether any criminal charges were laid against other party; details about other parties' condition and behavior (i.e., drinking, disorientated, under influence of drugs).

d) Personal history of self if tort results in personal injury. Medical background, including prior illnesses, surgeries, other personal injury claims; identify doctors, hospitals, therapists who examined or treated you. Include any insurance applications which required you to report on your physical condition in past seven years.

e) Personal injury claim including personal details, marital status, details of family. Job information, position, responsibility; how much time off work related to injury.

f) For torts resulting in personal injury, obtain medical report identifying medical care received; out-of-pocket expenses for medication; treatment; details of hospitalization; effect of injury on job related activities; missed opportunities; ability to sleep; emotional and other changes; extent of pain and suffering; extent of permanent physical disability.

6. Sign release permitting lawyer to obtain information from physician, x-ray, hospitals, employer, police and other officials.

7. If claim includes loss of income or diminished ability to earn, gather any receipts, bills, income tax returns for past eight years.

8. A diary of events must include unusually painful episodes, unsuccessful attempts to participate in activities and the rigours of enduring medical treatment, as well as each stage in returning to good health.

9. At this stage, lawyer attempts settlement with other party or insurance company. Instruct lawyer to consult with you before committing you to any settlement of your case. Ask lawyer to keep you advised as matters proceed and communicate to you forthwith any offer of settlement. Don't assume lawyer will do this automatically without such request.

10. Pre-trial hearing (examination for discovery). If case cannot be settled without trial, you will be required to attend pre-trial hearing to be questioned by other lawyer under oath at examiner's office. Written records made of questions and answers result in transcript which can be used against you at trial. Prepare as carefully as you would to testify before the judge. Other lawyer intends to discover weaknesses and strengths of your case and will also test your honesty/reliability, and will size you up as good, poor, or bad witness. Lawyer will use this as basis for further settlement negotiations.

11. Settlement. Negotiations for settlement most fruitful after discovery. Assist lawyer in reaching right compromise acceptable to you. Be prepared to consider weak points in case. Don't let emotions sway judgment. If you have trust in lawyer so far, assessment by lawyer is probably good. Give full weight to solicitor's judgment and experience. Deal with and decide on proposed settlement. Be prepared to sign releases to other party if case settled.

12. Preparing for trial. If case can't be settled, ask lawyer for interview well in advance of trial. Review the written court records and examination for discovery with lawyer. Ask for copies so you can study on own. Carefully read and consider contents.

13. Visit scene where tort committed. Refresh memory on pertinent physical facts. Visit courtroom in advance. Spend time watching court procedure.

14. For trial dress neatly and conservatively. When called as witness speak directly to judge or jurors. Speak firmly, loudly enough to be heard, slowly enough for court reporter to record evidence. Listen carefully to each question. Think before answering. You have right to ask that question be repeated. Don't be argumentative. Answer honestly, frankly. Don't volunteer information not specifically asked for.

B.   The Party Committing The Tort

1. Time to consider consequence of tort is before it happens. Frankly assess your failure/success record dealing with people; proneness to negligence; tendency to make serious errors. Keep temper and nerves under control. Don't be too bold or too meek. When taking action, carefully consider the probable results. Avoid activities likely to harm others or their property. Correct careless habits.

2. If you are an employer, assess reliability of employees. When hiring, interview should be designed to reveal facts or traits that may indicate employee likely to involve you in tort situation.

3. Review nature of your business or activities that put you in contact with others. Assess probable injuries or damage which may result. Attempt to obtain adequate insurance coverage for foreseeable risks (see Checklist for Chapter Seven: Insurance).

4. Establish test of reasonable, prudent person as guide for activities. Identify those classes of person to whom legal duty of care required.

5. Up-date skills through refresher courses, reading and study to maintain competence of an average person in your trade or calling. Provide opportunity to employees to maintain skills and study to maintain level of competence.

6. Avoid self-help, taking law into one's own hands. Take only prudent steps to protect self or property. Avoid false imprisonment, assault situations when harassed, aggravated.

7. Be able to identify probable liability to consumers or customers for injuries which may result from use of product sold by your firm.

8. Review safety of premises. Occupier owes duty to public to take care to prevent injuries from hazards which were known or of which you ought to have been aware had you properly inspected premises.

9. Be able to write memoranda, letters and other records with care to avoid false statements which may be libelous. Restrict spoken communication to avoid slander which may result in civil or criminal action.

10. Review checklist A. Most points there are also applicable to person who causes tort injury or damage. Will also alert you to activities of other side and will assist in preparation of defence to tort claim. Prepare as recommended in Checklist A for lawyer interview, examination for discovery, trial and settlement.

Review

1. List reasons why we need a comprehensive system of tort law.

2. Canadians are a "bundle of rights and duties." Discuss in view of what has been written in this chapter.

3. List and discuss the elements which must be proven by a plaintiff in a negligence action.

4. Why is it important for us to accept the rule of the reasonable and prudent person in establishing a legal standard of care? What difficulties would arise if we adopted a test based on requiring evidence that a defendant did in fact foresee any danger?

5. What precautions should an employee take before deciding to stop a customer suspected of theft?

6. **COLEMAN v. LANGFORD.** Coleman was a dinner guest of the Langfords for the first time. Chico, Langfords' pet, was an "angelic looking but snappy dog," with two known bites to his credit. Mrs. Langford told Coleman that Chico was neurotic and was not to be petted. The following events occurred:

- Chico had the run of the house and was in no way restrained.
- Coleman passed some time throwing a ball which Chico would fetch. The dog appeared friendly during this interval.
- while at the table Coleman offered Chico a bit of meat and was bitten on the nose.
- Coleman was in great discomfort while leaving for the hospital, tripped on a loose step and broke her ankle.
- Coleman was hospitalized for two weeks, underwent plastic surgery, anti-rabies shots and a setting of the ankle.

Coleman sues. If you were the judge in this case how would you decide it, and on what grounds?

7. How would you decide the following cases and on what grounds?

KUHN v. ERIE TRANSPORT

Kuhn sued the transport company for damages. He claimed that several barrels of oil had been insufficiently secured and as a result they rolled downhill and collided with a moving locomotive which sparked the oil and caused it to catch fire, run into a stream and ignite Kuhn's barn.

LOMBARDO v. GABLE

Lombardo paid a fee in order to use the facilities in a public lavatory operated as part of Gable's business. She was unable to get out of the cubicle because the handle on the inside was defective. Quite some time passed in which no-one responded to her calls for help, so she attempted to climb out. In spite of a valiant effort, she was unable to do so. When she attempted to climb back down, she fell and sustained injuries.

CHAPTER 3

Contracts

Unit I Mutual agreement

YOU ARE THE JURY

JARVIS v. STOKES

Jarvis asked several contractors to send him sealed tenders quoting their price for the construction of a building. Nine tenders were received in sealed envelopes which were opened and reviewed by Jarvis and his architect on January 11th. Stokes' bid was the lowest, but no final decision was made to accept any of the tenders at that meeting. The following day Jarvis received a registered letter and a telephone call from an apologetic Stokes advising that he was no longer in a position to actually undertake the work and he was accordingly withdrawing his bid. Jarvis advised Stokes his bid was the lowest but said nothing further. One week later Jarvis wrote to Stokes confirming that his bid had been the lowest and saying, "I accordingly accept your bid and expect you to commence construction within 30 days." Stokes refused and was sued by Jarvis for breach of contract. What is Stokes' legal position?

OBJECTIVES

* to be able to identify the five essential elements of a legally binding contract.
* to be able to identify the essential elements of a mutual agreement in which one party makes a definite offer to another party who unconditionally accepts.
* to be able to recognize when no legal contract is created by failure to reach the mutual agreement stage.

LEXICON

Consensus ad idem A legal phrase meaning that the parties have reached a "meeting of the minds" through one party making a definite offer to contract which the other unconditionally accepts.

Counter-offer A situation in which a party to whom a definite offer has been made changes the offer in a material way by adding new terms, or deleting or changing terms, thus creating what is in effect a new offer which the other party is free to accept or reject.

Lapse A legal rule which provides that if no time limits are stated by the parties in which to arrive at a consensus, then the transaction will automatically become void and unenforceable after a "reasonable time" has passed.

Revocation An act or statement by a person making a definite offer which clearly indicates to the other party that the offer is being withdrawn or cancelled. To be effective, the act of revocation must be made within a strict time limitation.

When confronted with the question, "What is a contract?" most of us picture a formal document prepared by a lawyer and displaying a generous sprinkling of legal phrases beginning with "whereas" or "heretofore." We do not, unfortunately, think in terms of contractual business we do every day.

We make a legal contract whenever we buy goods at a store, have a television set serviced, go to work for an employer, or accept the offer of admission from a college. To put this interpretation of contracts into clearer focus, ask yourself one question. Is there anything of value that you own which was not acquired through a contract processed by yourself (or in the case of a gift, by the donor)?

A study of contract law will, therefore, not only prepare you for that rare "big deal" but also help you cope with all the simple, basic contracts that occur almost every day of your life.

How, then, can we define a contract? A contract is "an agreement between two or more legally competent persons to do a lawful act with genuine intention to be legally bound." A close examination of this definition reveals *five essential elements* which must be present to create a valid contract. They are:

1. Mutual agreement (offer/acceptance).
2. Legal consideration.
3. Legal capacity.
4. Lawful object.
5. Genuine intention.

Since all five essentials must be present to create a legally binding contract, each element will be examined separately in the above sequence.

The bargaining process

All contracts are preceded by a bargaining or negotiation stage in which the parties concerned seek to obtain an advantage. The parties should be feeling each other out at this point and do not intend their preliminary conduct to result in legally binding obligations. The negotiations may be carried on indefinitely until one of the parties takes the first serious step toward forming a contract by making a *definite offer*. The law recognizes this "ritual" and will permit the parties to bargain freely without interference until the definite offer is made.

CASE 1   BASSFORD v. WILLIS

Willis wrote to Bassford, "I will buy the business at the agreed price provided my accountants are favourably impressed after their audit." Are the parties still in the negotiation stage? Has Willis made a legally binding offer?

The chain concept

A legal contract may be likened to a chain composed of six separate interlocking and interdependent links. To create this chain, we must weld each link to the next in proper sequence. The chain will be as strong as its weakest link. Should a single link prove defective, it will break away from the rest, leaving us with useless chunks of metal. So it is with a legal contract. If one element is materially defective, the contract is unenforceable and invalid.

Use the chain concept as a means of visualizing the essentials of a contract. For example, in analyzing a problem concerning the validity of a contract, take six paperclips, each one representing one of the essential elements of a contract. As you go through the problem, make certain that all the elements are present. If you end up with an unbroken chain, you have a legally binding contract; if not, the contract is void.

The offer   (The first link)

The bargaining process is successfully concluded when one party makes a *definite offer* and the other party *unconditionally accepts*. This is the element of mutual agreement, which is the first essential element of a contract. Note that it is composed of two basic links – offer and acceptance.

The offer must be definite. It must be communicated to the other party in a clear, unambiguous manner. If the offer is incomplete or too vague, it will not constitute a legal offer. It must be more than a mere statement of intention or a mere quotation of price.

CASE 2   PIERCE v. CRAWFORD

Leonard Pierce says to Crawford, "I'm thinking of selling my car. Will you give me $500.00?" Has Pierce made a legal offer to sell? Consider carefully what was said. Be analytical and critical.

Contrary to popular belief, the offer should always be in written form. The disadvantage of oral contracts it that they are open to misunderstanding of what has been agreed. To avoid this possibility, the offer should always be in written form. Some contracts *must* be in writing in order to be enforceable.

The statute of frauds
Each province has a civil Statute of Frauds which requires the following contracts to be in writing: leases for a term of three years or more; guarantees to answer for the debt of a third party; sale of lands; and contracts which will take more than one year to perform. Almost all other legal contracts can be made without any writing signed by the parties.

CASE 3   VANCE v. LEIGH

Leigh offered to buy a parcel of land from Vance through a written document that read in part, "Leigh agrees to buy Blackacres from Vance for the price of $58 000.00 with $15 000.00 paid down as a deposit and balance to be secured by a mortgage to be given back by Leigh on closing. . . ." The terms of the mortgage were not otherwise identified. Both Leigh and Vance signed and the deposit was advanced, but Leigh later demanded his money back and refused to complete the transaction. Vance sued Leigh for breach of contract. In his defence, Leigh claimed the contract was not binding because it was incomplete.

In this case, no mutual agreement was reached between Vance and Leigh, because Leigh did not make a legally definite offer. The offer that was made was incomplete and too vague to create a legal obligation. For example, the terms of the mortgage did not specify how and over what period it was to be paid or what interest rate was to be charged.

The court made an important statement that we must always bear in mind. The judge said, "What is the function of the courts in these matters? It is our responsibility to interpret and enforce whole contracts in which all the essential elements are definite and clear. It is not our function to make contracts for the parties or to create and impose missing terms."

There is a lesson to be learned from this case: Always make certain that all essential elements are spelled out in the agreement in clear, unambiguous language.

The statement of intention

We must also be careful of persons who, by their words or conduct, appear to made a definite offer but who, in reality, are merely stating an intention to do something in the future without necessarily meaning to become legally obligated.

CASE 4   IN RE FICKUS

Fickus, anxious to marry off a particularly ugly daughter, wrote to a young man, ". . . if you marry my daughter, she will have the bulk of my estate after I am dead." The young man married the lady and was shocked when she received only a small inheritance after Fickus died. The court held that under the circumstances Fickus was merely stating an intention to act in the future and he was in fact legally free to change his mind without penalty.

CASE 5   FOXX v. MILLS

Patricia Foxx decided to drop out of college. Her uncle Wilbur wrote to her promising $5 000 if she would continue her studies and graduate. Patricia decided to complete her education and did in fact graduate. However Wilbur refused to give her the money. The court refused to find that Wilbur's letter constituted a legally binding, definite offer, and having regard to all of the circumstances found that Wilbur merely expressed an intention to do something in the future for which he could not be legally bound.

How do we deal with the problem posed by the Mills and Fickus cases? Simply take the time to redraft the promise in concrete, clear terms so that it constitutes a definite offer and have the offeror sign the new agreement. There are no magic words or phrases to be learned, just keep the principles in this unit in mind and write down the specifics in plain language; or, if this is not possible or the stakes are too high, take it to a lawyer for advice and redrafting.

The invitation to buy

Does a merchant who displays merchandise in a store or catalogue make a definite offer to sell to customers? Or is the display an invitation to the public to make offers to buy? The basic rule is that it is the customer who must make a definite offer to purchase, which the merchant is then free to accept or reject. This rule is designed to bring order to the business community and in effect protects the merchant in a variety of circumstances.

CASE 6   LINCOLN v. LAVINE

Lincoln, a customer, took a book to the store's cashier but the proprietor, Lavine, stepped in and refused to accept Lincoln's money saying, "This is terrible. It's a mistake. This book is not for sale." Lincoln points out a price tag on the inside cover. Assume the mistake was genuine and there is no question of prejudice against Lincoln. May Lavine legally refuse to sell the book?

CASE 7   SKEFFINGTON v. SALLY SHOPPES

A young nurse, Skeffington, entered a Sally Shoppe to purchase a fur coat. The coat she wanted was on sale but was being "tried on" by an elderly and valued client of the establishment. As soon as the client put the coat down, Skeffington picked it up and brought it to the front desk. On seeing this, the client made up her mind to purchase the coat and demanded that Skeffington give it up so that she might purchase it. The owner took the coat away from Skeffington and gave it to the other customer. Advise Skeffington.

Time limitations

If the offer is specific enough, it will bind the *offeror*. The person to whom the offer is made (called the *acceptor*) thus has an advantage. The acceptor may now accept or reject the offer and he will be under no legal liability until the offer is actually accepted. Suppose the acceptor decides to hold off – to get a better offer or "see which way the wind blows" – will the offeror be indefinitely bound while the acceptor remains free to deal?

The offeror can protect himself when making a definite offer by including a term limiting the time in which the offer may be accepted. This limitation clause will specify that if the offer is not accepted by a certain date, then the offer will be automatically revoked. This is an important legal device to force the acceptor to decide within the time limit set. In the event of non-acceptance, this has the added benefit of releasing the offeror from a committed obligation within a foreseeable period of time.

Termination of offer

We must now consider the circumstances in which an offer may be terminated. It may lapse; it may be answered by a counter-offer; it may be revoked; it may be subject to a condition that cannot be satisfied; or it may be terminated by the death of either of the parties.

1. *The Doctrine of Lapse*

In the event the offeror has not set a time limit for acceptance, the legal doctrine of lapse will even matters out. This doctrine states that a legal offer must be accepted within a "reasonable time," otherwise the offer will lapse and be rendered null and void. One should not, however, depend too greatly on this rule since the courts have not given any exact definition of the phrase "reasonable time." Each case depends on its own particular facts.

CASE 8   GARDI v. CELLARMASTER

The Cellarmasters, commercial winemakers, offered to purchase a quantity of berries from Gardi. The offer was made by mail and Gardi responded by a letter of acceptance mailed one week later. In the meantime, Cellarmasters purchased their berries from a third party. They advised Gardi that due to the delay in his reply they were "forced to go elsewhere." Gardi's lawyer argued that a mutual agreement had been created by the exchange of letters. Opposing counsel argued a defence based on lapse.

The court considered the custom of the commercial winemaking trade and the time of the year. It held that under the circumstances a delay of only a few days was critical. The offer, not having been accepted within a reasonable time, had lapsed and no mutual agreement had been reached.

What is a "reasonable time"? Remember each case must stand on its own facts. The courts will consider such matters as custom of a trade, perishability (of produce), changes in the market (stock market), or durability of subject matter (land).

2. *The Counter-offer*

The proposed acceptor is often generally agreeable to the offer but may not be satisfied with all of its terms. Consequently, he will add to, delete from or alter the offer, initial the changes, sign it, and return it. This is known as a *counter-offer* and, as its name indicates, it is by nature an offer. In fact, it is intended to replace the original offer by bringing everything back to square one. It is *not*

intended to operate as an acceptance. Its legal effect is to revoke the original offer and require the original offeror to accept what is in reality a fresh offer.

CASE 9   HYDE v. WRENCH

Wrench wrote to Hyde offering land for sale at a specified price. Hyde countered by "accepting" the offer at a reduced price. Wrench refused to sell at the lower price and then Hyde agreed to pay the original price. By this point, however, Wrench had decided not to sell, and Hyde went to court.

The court held that the original offer had not been accepted, and that Hyde had made a counter-offer which had legally destroyed the original offer. Hyde had substituted a new offer which Wrench was free to accept or reject. When Wrench rejected the counter-offer he terminated it. The end result was that all offers made in the transactions had been terminated, and thus it was not possible for the parties to reach a mutual agreement. It was also not possible for Hyde to revive and act on the original offer. Hyde had broken a link in the chain and, once broken, the link could not be repaired.

---

3. *Revocation*

In the event that an offeror has a change of heart after an offer has been made, it is legally possible to revoke (withdraw) the offer at any time before acceptance by the other party. Up to the time of acceptance, the legal obligation arising out of an offer can be wiped out by a *clear* act of revocation. The offeror must communicate the decision to withdraw to the proposed acceptor.

Suppose the offeror realizes that a mistake has been made: new facts recently learned disclose that the transaction will "ruin" the offeror; a better opportunity has suddenly appeared out of nowhere; circumstances have changed; or the offeror just gets cold feet. What opportunity, if any, does the offeror have to withdraw a definite, legal offer?

The time between the making of an offer and its acceptance by the other party is crucial because after acceptance the offer cannot be revoked. Let us assume, however, that the offer has not yet been accepted. It is not sufficient for the offeror simply to have a change of mind. The decision to revoke must be communicated to the intended acceptor by clear, effective action. The offeror will be required to prove that steps were taken amounting to revocation, that the other party was aware of the action being taken, and that this occurred before acceptance.

The sequence for revocation would look like this:

- make a definite offer.
- communicate the offer to the other party.
- decide not to go through with the contract.
- make it clear that the offer is being revoked.
- get the message to the other party before the offer has been accepted.

In the event that it becomes necessary to revoke, it is best to state clearly what is happening in writing and immediately deliver this to the other side. The need for speed may dictate that a telephone call be made at once or a telegram sent off. The law recognizes any reasonable attempt to revoke but does insist that the steps be taken before acceptance of the offer.

Suppose the offer states that the offeror will keep the offer open for a given period. Must the offeror wait for this time to expire before acting? The courts have held that even under these circumstances the offeror is free to withdraw, provided that steps to revoke are communicated to the other party before acceptance.

CASE 10   ROUTLEDGE v. GRANT

The purchaser offered to buy a house, giving the owner "a period of six weeks to accept." Within the six weeks, the purchaser withdrew the offer and the owner sued in contract. The court held that the purchaser "could withdraw at any moment before acceptance even though the time limit had not expired."

It is obvious that this rule for revocation may save the day for many an offeror, but it does create uncertainty in business, and to avoid the rule many professionally prepared contracts contain a term that the offer will be *"irrevocable"* by the offeror for a specified time. This is a perfectly legitimate device and very commonly used.

Revocation may take many forms, including the written and spoken word and the conduct of the parties. It does not seem to matter how the decision to revoke comes to the attention of the other party, only that it be communicated by some clear means prior to acceptance. Case 11 may prove instructive.

CASE 11   JORDAN v. BROWN

Dave Brown offered to sell his sports car to Connie Jordan and agreed to hold the car for her until the following day to give her an opportunity to get the purchase price from her bank. On her way to the bank the next day, Connie spoke to Frances Tikk who told her that she had purchased the car from Dave that very morning. Connie obtained her money and went to Dave demanding ''my sports car or else.'' What is Connie's legal position?

Brown's offer was left open to permit Jordan an opportunity to accept it by going to the bank, obtaining the funds and returning. In the meantime Brown, according to the general rules of contract was free to withdraw his offer at any time provided that the withdrawal was effectively communicated to Jordan before actual acceptance. Jordan's meeting with Tikk provided the necessary notice. The source of the notice makes no difference; therefore it does not matter that Brown in this case took no active steps to notify Jordan of his ''change of heart.''

4. Death

In the event that either party dies after an offer has been made but before acceptance, the offer becomes null and void and is of course unenforceable. If death occurs after acceptance, the contract can be kept alive and carried through the deceased party's representative or executor.

5. Failure to satisfy a condition

Another device used effectively in today's business practice is the *conditional offer.* The offer itself is definite and complete, but its operation is suspended until specific conditions explained in the offer have been met.

Suppose I wish to buy a house, and the owner and I have reached agreement on all the terms, but I do not yet have all the money I will need to close the deal. Let's say we have agreed to close in 60 days. Let's further suppose that I must borrow at least part of the purchase price from the bank and it's possible that the bank may turn down my application. What shall I do in such circumstances? If my offer is accepted and I am in fact unable to find the money required, I could find myself in an embarrassing position if the other party insisted on the contract being honoured. The solution is simple: I will make a written offer containing all the terms of purchase, but I will include a clause that the contract is conditional upon my bank advancing me the loan; otherwise the sale is to be null and void. If I am unable to obtain the funds, a condition attached to the offer has failed and I do not have to complete the transaction.

CASE 12   PINTIER v. MCGUGAN

McGugan planned to purchase two buildings adjacent to each other. She signed an unconditional agreement of purchase and sale for one building with Pintier. She honestly believed that an agent in another part of the country had obtained a firm offer for the other property, but she was mistaken. As the success of her business scheme depended on ownership of both buildings, the Pintier building proved to be of no use to her. Nothing in the written offer with Pintier made it conditional on the purchase of the other building and Pintier forced McGugan to complete the purchase of his building. This resulted in a substantial financial loss to her.

In contrast, under similar circumstances a purchaser, Markestein, had the following conditional clause inserted into his agreement:

> The purchasers may cancel the agreement of sale arising out of this offer if, prior to the date of completion, the purchasers have not obtained contracts for the purchase of the property known as Lot 14 Plan 800; and upon cancellation the deposit shall be returned to the purchasers and this transaction shall be null and void.

Acceptance (The second link)

We have discussed how an offer is made and how it can be terminated before acceptance. We will now discuss what happens after an offer has been communicated to a party who is prepared to accept.

The act of acceptance must be clear, unambiguous, and unconditional. The acceptor must communicate his decision to accept by clear action or words (or both) to the offeror within the time specified (or if no time is stipulated, then within a reasonable time).

The steps, action or words by which acceptance is communicated to the offeror are critical. We must observe some visible form of activity of the sort that would clearly show a reasonable, prudent person that a mutual agreement had been reached. One cannot accept an offer by silence. For example, suppose you were to say to me, ''I'll buy your boat for $3 000.00. If I don't hear from you by midnight tonight, it's a deal.'' If I, in fact, say and do nothing, then there is no visible act and therefore no legal acceptance and, of course, no contract.

The acceptance must be complete and unconditional. It should always be in written form and should be communicated by the most reliable means available.

CASE 13   SPOTISWOOD v. DORIAN

Dorian and a partner made an offer to lease office space from Spotiswood. The landlord's acceptance contained a clause that it was subject to a satisfactory credit check and would also be subject to terms to be set out in a formal written lease. Dorian found other, more suitable quarters and Spotiswood sued on ''his contract.'' Would Spotiswood succeed? Discuss.

A valid, binding contract can only be created if the parties take pains to communicate well with each other in clear, simple language. The parties must set out all the essential terms in sufficient detail. Otherwise the agreement will be unenforceable for uncertainty. Remember the courts are not designed to make contracts for people, only to interpret those that the parties have made for themselves.

KEY TO YOU ARE THE JURY

JARVIS v. STOKES

The written tender submitted by Stokes did not contain any provision that the bid contained therein would be irrevocable and open for any period of time. Like any other offer silent as to the time of acceptance, the tender could be revoked at any time before acceptance provided notice of revocation was given. The registered letter and telephone call represented an effective withdrawal of the offer contained in the tender and this withdrawal notice was received by the other party before the actual legal acceptance. Consequently, Jarvis failed.

Unit II Consideration (the third link)

YOU ARE THE JURY

AMBEAULT v. SILVER

Sterling Silver, a lawyer, in a written memorandum (not under seal) agrees to assist Robert Ambeault's non-profit association to incorporate. His memo states that he will charge no fee for his services. Robert eagerly accepts the offer. When nothing further is done and Robert presses Silver, the lawyer tells Robert that he is just too busy, "go find yourself another boy." Robert now seeks to enforce the "contract." Discuss.

OBJECTIVES

- to identify the five rules that must be followed to create a legally binding contract by providing legal value.
- to identify eight types of legal consideration that amount to legal value.
- to be able to apply the rules in a variety of factual situations involving different types of consideration.

LEXICON

Consideration An act or promise made by the party who will benefit by the contract which is in itself of a sufficient recognizable value according to the rules of the law. For example, consideration may be in the form of money, goods or land.

Forbearance A deliberate action by which a person refrains from or postpones doing something which he has a legal right to do. For example, if Nixon had the right to sue Walton for a bad debt and agreed to postpone taking any action for six months to give Walton a chance to pay voluntarily, Nixon would be exercising forbearance.

Gratuitous Promise A promise given freely by one party to do something for another party which is not required to be done by law and for which nothing is to be given in return.

Promissee A party to a contract who will benefit from it and who has agreed to give legal value in order to secure the act or promise from the other party.

Promissor A party to a contract who in return for value must provide a benefit to the other party.

Not every mutual agreement is legally enforceable. The courts will not enforce every and any promise regardless of what it involves and the way in which it was made. In particular, the courts are not to be used to enforce a gratuitous promise nor are they to be used to support an agreement that lacks *consideration* – our third link in the chain.

Contracts under seal

A document under seal is a writing upon which a gummed wafer or seal has been affixed opposite the signatures of the parties. The seal is still used in all of the provinces, but there is evidence that its use is becoming less and less common. Some provinces, such as British Columbia and Ontario, are investigating the validity or need for such a formality and in the years ahead the practice of sealing may well be abolished.

For our purposes, we must recognize that when people place seals on their contracts it means they really mean business, and the presence of a seal will thus satisfy the requirement for consideration. If there are seals on the contract, they take the place of consideration and we need not insist upon proving the existence of consideration to enforce or support the contract.

Necessity for consideration

Most contracts made today are not under seal and therefore require consideration. This is true for both written and oral contracts.

What then is legal consideration (or, as it is sometimes called, "valuable consideration")? This is not a difficult question to answer if we can analyze it in concrete terms. In order to do this we apply two tests.

First, let's consider what is necessary to prove a contract in court. Plaintiff must prove that the promise on which he is suing is part of a contract to which he has made a contribution. It is necessary for him to prove that he "*bought*" the other party's promise either by doing some act in return or by offering a counter-promise to do something.

Second, note well the necessity of "buying one's way into a contract." This clearly shows the commercial aspect of contracts that will help elevate them to the class of legally enforceable agreements. Let's take this a step further. Let's say Robert Adams goes to Sasha's fur store and receives from Sasha a fur hat. In return Adams gives Sasha $300.00. Has either party given valuable consideration to the other? If so, what? Go back for a moment and review *Ambeault v. Silver.*

Are you able to detect any material differences in the facts?

Consideration is easy to understand and corresponds to the normal exchange of promises made by people in this country every day. It also emphasizes the commercial nature of the Canadian contract. This way of looking at consideration has the further benefit of exposing the simplicity of the concept which has unfortunately been clouded under legal jargon and complicated explanations for too long. The concept of consideration is real and rational and, when analyzed as an essential third link in the chain, is the true symbol of a legally enforceable negotiated contract.

First, however, let us examine the items of acceptable value that will amount to legal consideration and thus support a contract.

1. *Money in its various forms.*
   Cash; the promise to pay money through cheques, drafts, promissory notes, bills of exchange.
2. *Work and services.*
3. *Tangible goods or chattels.*
   Motor vehicles, equipment, furnishings, personal effects, livestock, any type of consumer goods.
4. *Stocks, bonds, securities.*
5. *Mortgages against real estate or personal property.*
6. *Real property.*
   Real estate, lands, houses.
7. *Forbearance of a legal right.*
   This will be discussed in some detail later in this unit.
8. *An exchange of bare promises to provide any of the above.*

Rules of consideration

The most important rules of consideration are as follows:

1. Consideration must move from the person benefiting from the promise (who is called the *promisee*). In the *Ambeault v. Silver* case, Robert Ambeault is the promisee and Sterling Silver is the promisor. Review the case once again. Are you able to identify any consideration moving from Ambeault to Silver? If no consideration moves from the promisee, then the contract is unenforceable.
2. Consideration must be of some ascertainable value in the cold eyes of the law. Natural love and affection between members of a family do not have such value. Neither does the gift of property or services under a gratuitous promise.

3. The consideration must be legal. Promises to do something unlawful obviously will not be enforceable. (This is discussed in detail in Unit 4: Lawful Object.)
4. Consideration need not be "adequate." Remember it is the function of the courts to interpret and enforce contracts, not to make them. The parties must make their own contracts and the courts will not step in later to evaluate how well each did in the process.

Suppose Guest purchases land from Stenning and discovers that he paid too much. May he go to court to have the contract reviewed? Will a court order that the overpayment be returned to Guest? No. If a court were to do that, it would be making or re-making a contract for the parties. Transactions are, however, reviewable when the consideration given is so grossly out of line as to amount to civil fraud. (This exception to the rule is discussed below.)
5. The consideration must not be *past consideration*. To be effective, consideration must flow from the agreement now reached. The courts will not recognize consideration which has already been completed and which may have arisen out of some past transaction.

Now that the principles and rules of consideration have been stated, we can examine them in more detail.

The gratuitous promise

A gratuitous promise will not be enforced in the courts of any province (except Quebec which recognizes the *Code Civile* and consequently may enforce a contract de bienfaisance).

CASE 14   DOWNS v. SMYTHE

Smythe, who was about to secure a long-term lease for lands, discovered that Downs, a neighbour, would substantially benefit from a right-of-way over the leased property. Smythe gratuitously agreed to "grant a right-of-way over the southerly 20' of Greenacres as soon as I have the lease." When, subsequently, Smythe refused to grant the right-of-way, Downs sued. "I have his promise right here in this letter he signed," he said. Who is right?

CASE 15   FLEMING ET AL. v. SHORT

Fleming, a minister, asks one of his congregation, Short, an accountant, to prepare the financial statement for the church. In a burst of generosity, Short agrees to perform the service at no charge.

He instructs a young student, Robert Bruce, to do the work but not to spend too much time at it. "This is a freebie, so get back fast." Bruce works with dispatch. He does not follow ordinary accounting procedures (which would reveal that a church employee is stealing regularly). Short and Bruce carry on in this fashion for two years. The stolen $8 000. Is Short liable?

First, let's examine these facts in light of the law of contracts. The church was the promissee. The church gave no valuable consideration; Short's undertaking was gratuitous; there was no contractual relationship between the parties and therefore no remedy available under this branch of law.

Now follows a very important observation. Is the promissee without remedy simply because the promissor was working under an unenforceable contract? Not at all. The law states that while a gratuitous promise to perform services cannot be enforced, if, in fact, the services are undertaken, they must be properly carried out. If loss results to the promissee through improper conduct or negligence, then the promissor will be liable for the loss.

There is an essential lesson to be learned from the Short case. While it is perfectly in order for you (in fact, imperative) to study the rules one at a time in isolation, you must not forget that the law functions as a whole and applies the principles of its many branches to each case. The plaintiff in the Short case will fail under contract law but will succeed under the law of negligence. Therefore, it is important to never take a narrow view of any legal position. Cases are seldom solved by applying only one principle of law.

Consideration must move from the promissee

Only those persons who have paid the "price" for a promise may apply to the court to enforce it. They must prove their share in the bargained contract. The essential rule of Canadian law is that a legal contract is the result of a bargain. If parties provide no consideration, they take no part in the bargain. If they take no part in the bargain, they take no part in the contract.

CASE 16   TALLON v. COSTA

Costa turns down a request from his niece for a loan to be made to her friend, Tallon. However, Costa agrees that if his niece does some work for

him, he will give the money to Tallon. The niece does the work but she also breaks off her relationship with Tallon. Costa therefore does not pay the money, his reason being, "They're not going together now, so why should I pay the money." Tallon counters, "That has nothing to do with the agreement. Pay me or I will sue."

In order to succeed Tallon must show legal consideration moving from him to Costa. In a similar case (*Tweddle v. Atkinson*) the judge said, "It is now established that no *stranger* to the consideration can take advantage of a contract although made for his benefit." Thus, Tallon cannot show consideration passing from him to Costa because he did not do the work. Indeed, he was not a party to the contract.

The adequacy rule

It is well established that the courts will not inquire into the adequacy of the consideration, nor will they attempt to weigh the comparative value of what each party gives. They will not overturn an agreement merely because it "seems unfair." The courts do not lightly interfere in a contract once it is made: it is not their function to protect the improvident or foolish party who makes a bad deal.

CASE 17   LEHAY v. RUSS

LeHay agrees to purchase an apartment block from Russ for $200 000.00. He then discovers that a fair market value for the property is between $150 000.00 and $180 000.00. Can you distinguish these facts from those in Wolfe v. Fawcette below?

There is one exception to the adequacy rule. In the event that the consideration is so grossly inadequate that it "shocks the conscience" or creates a suspicion of fraud, then evidence of the inadequacy of the consideration may be introduced to establish fraud or lack or genuine intention, and if either be proven, then the agreement may be declared void and set aside.

CASE 18   WOLFE v. FAWCETTE

Fawcette, concerned over the militancy of her creditors, transfers the title to her office equipment and luxury car to her husband for $3 000.00. The property actually has a total value of $25 000.00.

Wolfe, representing the creditors, wants the "contract" reviewed and set aside. Assume he has the legal right to made such application and that Mr. Fawcette has actually advanced the $3 000.00. Wolfe wants control of the property so that he can sell it to help satisfy the debts owing to the creditors.

Fawcette would undoubtedly argue that he made an exceptionally good deal and that the courts should not be concerned about inadequacy of consideration. He would argue that a mutual agreement was formed and would prove his consideration in that he had paid his wife for the goods. Wolfe would argue that the relationship of husband and wife created sufficiently suspicious circumstances to warrant a review of the contract. He would point out Mrs. Fawcette's financial position and argue that the $3 000.00 represented grossly inadequate consideration under the circumstances.

Wolfe would succeed. If this were not so, people could defraud others through the use of the adequacy rule. In fact, all the provinces have confirmed this exception to the adequacy rule by passing fraudulent preference legislation which makes the giving of preference, such as the Fawcette contract, unlawful.

Past consideration

When a mutual agreement is formed, the supporting consideration must arise out of and be part of the agreement. If promises are made subsequent to and independent of the original agreement, they must be regarded as mere intentions to act or as a gift or as a preference and no contract will arise out of these new promises. These promises are said to arise out of past consideration and past consideration is considered *no consideration*.

CASE 19   FOX v. WELLINGTON

Wellington, a contractor, has received loans and advances from his mother over the past six years. She does not ask for and does not receive any security, and the advances total $40 000.00. It is understood, however, that these are loans and some day will be repaid. Wellington, realizing that he is unable to meet his debts generally as they arise, signs a bill of sale for all his equipment transferring title to his mother. The consideration in the deed is said to be $40 000.00. Creditors who attempt to seize the equipment discover that Wellington is no longer the owner. Assume that

Wellington has not declared bankruptcy and the creditors are restricted to the laws of contract in your province. Discuss, then examine the solution below.

Since all of the money had been advanced completely and independently before the document was signed, this was a case of past consideration and the deed could not be supported as a binding contract. The original transactions represented a series of unsecured loans. The giving of the transfer was subsequent to and independent of those original transactions. The Wellingtons may well also be caught by the fraudulent preference statutes in your province.

CASE 20   JANEWAY v. GIGILO

Gigilo accompanies Aunt Mary on a world tour. She agrees to pay all expenses. After the trip and as an afterthought she signs and hands Gigilo a promissory note payable to him in 60 days. Mary dies shortly afterwards and her personal representatives refuse to honour the note. Gigilo sues. Will he succeed? Drawing on the rules for consideration only, identify and resolve the main issue.

Businessmen and financial institutions have discovered an effective device for securing their relationships with falter clients. It will be appropriate, at this stage, to see how it works. Realizing that past consideration is no consideration, they meet with their client, review the security they presently hold, identify what other assets might be tied up, transferred or mortgaged, and then agree to continue a line of credit or to make a further (usually modest) advance of funds in return for the additional security. The documents are signed and the advance is made. A new agreement has been created and fresh consideration has been provided. Consideration must move from the promissee (in this case the bank) and the consideration is the promise to continue doing business or the advance of further funds. A modest advance may thus secure all of the past indebtedness as well by getting around the past consideration rule. If the contents of this paragraph are clear then move on; if not, then review the past consideration rule until you fully comprehend the difference between the situation outlined in this paragraph and the Wellington and Gigilo cases.

Forbearance of a legal right

Forbearance means the giving up, either temporarily or permanently, of a legal right that one

party can assert over another. For example, suppose Smith owes me $5 000.00 and I have the right to sue him for the debt. Smith makes an agreement with me that if I don't issue a writ against him, he will give me a mortgage against his cottage and discharge the debt within one year. I agree and instruct my lawyer to discontinue action. The exchange of promises constitutes a mutual agreement. As I am the promisee I must demonstrate that I have given legal consideration. It is recognized in law that the surrender of a legal right is valuable consideration which will support a contract. Try to decide what will happen if Smith refuses to give me the promised security, and I want it?

CASE 21   THE BANK v. BROOM

A customer, Broom, owed the bank $20 000 on an unsecured loan and under pressure agreed to give security to cover the debt. The bank instructed its lawyer not to take any action as "the case has been settled." Broom, however, refused to complete the necessary documents and the bank sued him on the promise. The court gave judgment for the bank and ordered that the promised security be delivered to it. The judgment read in part:

> When the bank threatened suit and in consequence Broom agreed to give certain security, the effect was that the bank did in fact give (and Broom received) the benefit of forbearance which Broom would not have received if he had not made the agreement. The surrender of a legal right such as the right to sue is legal consideration sufficient to support an enforceable contract.

KEY TO YOU ARE THE JURY

AMBEAULT v. SILVER   Robert will discover that the contract is unenforceable. True, there was a definite offer and an unconditional acceptance – a mutual agreement (links one and two). However, the law will not enforce a gratuitous promise unless it was made under seal. A promise to make a gift without receiving valuable consideration is unenforceable, as is a promise to act without receiving consideration in return. If Robert had insisted on making even a nominal payment for the services (and had Silver agreed), the contract would have been enforceable.

Unit III Legal capacity (the fourth link)

YOU ARE THE JURY

YOUNG v. S J & A INC.

Roberta Young, age 17, purchased a "brass bed" from S J & A Inc., giving $100.00 in cash and a series of four post-dated cheques for the balance. When the bed was delivered, her father objected to the purchase because, "Bobby already had a fine bed and this one is not brass." Roberta stopped payment on her cheques and advised the merchant to "return her money and come pick up his iron bed." The merchant threatened suit for the balance owing. Identify the main issue and consider the merits of both sides of the case.

OBJECTIVES

- to identify the classes of "persons" who lack the capability of entering into contracts by legal rules.
- to be able to recognize the consequences of entering into transactions with those persons who have legal disabilities.
- to distinguish between the creation of void and voidable contracts.

LEXICON

Void Contract   A contract having no force or effect; an unenforceable legal nullity.

Voidable Contract   A contract unenforceable by a wrong-doer, but enforceable at the option of the victimized party.

The parties to an agreement must have the legal *capacity* to contract in order for their agreement to be completely binding or enforceable. If this capacity is lacking, then the fourth link in the chain will not fit into place.

Most people have the capacity to contract, and so this link is usually secure. We shall, therefore, make the best use of our time by examining the rules that relate to those persons who lack capacity, including corporations, agents, infants, mental incompetents, and drunken persons.

Corporations and their officers

Corporations (more fully described in Chapter Eight, Unit 4) are limited companies incorporated under either federal or provincial law and are identified by the inclusion of the words Limited or Incorporated (often abbreviated to Ltd. or Inc.) after the firm name. Under our present laws, corporations have broad powers, but nevertheless they do not have the full capacity of a natural adult. Furthermore, they carry on business through officers, agents, and employees whose terms of authority are often limited by internal corporate rules. When dealing with corporations, we should make reasonable inquiries to be certain that the officers or agents we actually deal with have the authority to act and bind the corporation.

Agency and partnerships

An agent acting for a third party often has limited authority to act, as does a partner representing his firm and other partners. Again, we must make reasonable inquiries to be certain that the persons with whom we deal have the power to bind the principal or the firm. The specific rules concerning agents and partners are set out in the Agency and Partnership Units of Chapter Eight.

Infants and minors

A person who has not yet reached majority or come of age is referred to in law as an "infant" or a "minor." For our purpose, all persons who are not yet adults will be described by the general term "infant." In some provinces the legal age of majority is 21; in others 19; and in others 18. You should know what is the legal age in your own province.

An infant enjoys a special status under the law. He is protected against advantage that might be secured by an older, wiser adult. Infants do have the capacity and right to contract. The general rule, however, is that once made, the contract is voidable at the option of the infant.

All provinces have passed statute laws called *Infants' Act* (or *Infants' Relief Acts*) which apply special rules to infants' contracts. When an actual problem involving questions of infancy arises, the statute in force at the time (available in the public libraries) should be consulted. The rules that follow are applicable to all provinces.

The infant's contract for luxuries

The *Infant's Acts* of each province render an infant's contract for luxuries absolutely void and unenforceable. Luxuries are defined as goods which are not considered necessary to enable the infant to live or work having regard to the circumstances or the lifestyle of the infant, and goods of which the infant already has a sufficient supply. For example, a car used to drive to and from school when there are other adequate means of travel; a pair of shoes when there are several serviceable pairs in the closet; the latest records; non-essentials of all descriptions: these would be considered as luxuries.

A merchant selling luxuries to an infant cannot compel completion of the contract or sue for payment. If the infant has paid for the goods in whole or in part, he is entitled to a refund of his money.

The infant's contract for necessities of life

Infants are in a different position when they purchase necessities. These are goods considered necessary for the sustaining of life, having regard to surrounding circumstances and the infant's "station in life." Courts have identified the following items as necessities: physicians' accounts, dental bills, flashlights, clothing when there is not a sufficient supply, food and fuel, and where the infant is a parent, baby clothing.

The legal rule is that contracts made by infants for necessities are valid *but reviewable*. The law recognizes that infants must be able to buy the necessities of life. Infants, therefore, have the capacity to enter into contracts for necessities and such contracts are enforceable against them.

The problem of an adult taking advantage of an infant still remains, however, so the courts have the power to review the terms of the contract and adjust them (which might include a reduction in price) if necessary.

CASE 22 SUGERMAN v. HARTEN

A high school dropout, Harten, took a job as a door-to-door salesman. He needed a car for business purposes. On the strength of a good sales record Harten, who was still an infant, persuaded Sugerman to sell him a used car for $2 500.00 with $600.00 down and the balance to be paid monthly on settled terms. A short time afterward, Harten lost his job and brought the car back for a refund. Sugerman demanded that the balance of the car payments be made and when this was not done, he sued for the outstanding balance ($1 700.00).

The court held that the contract was valid and enforceable by Sugerman in spite of Harten's infancy. The car fell into the category of necessities since it was essential to Harten's livelihood. The terms were reviewable, however. In particular, the court considered that the price paid ($2 500) was too high and reduced it by $500.00. Since Harten had already paid $800.00, judgment was entered against him for $1 200.00 and not $1 700.00.

Loans to infants

Loans to infants are void and cannot be recovered even though the money has been advanced, since the *Infant's Acts* of each province have declared that infants do not have the capacity to enter into such contracts.

Beneficial contracts of service

Infants have the capacity to enter into contracts of apprenticeship or service since such contracts provide a means whereby infants can learn a trade and earn a livelihood. Such contracts therefore are valid and binding on infants.

Mental incompetents and drunken persons

Agreements made by persons impaired by drugs or alcohol and those made by mental incompetents are voidable. What is meant by the term "voidable"? We have seen that some contracts made by infants are "void and unenforceable." What distinction must be made between void and voidable?

A *voidable* contract occurs when one party is disabled, is under a legal disability, or has been taken advantage of in some serious manner. The "disabled" party is presumed in law to be the victim of the other party and is given the advantage of a choice: he can either treat the contract as valid and thus enforceable or he can declare it invalid and thus avoid any liability he might otherwise have incurred.

The other party, however, does not share this advantage and must go along with the decision of the disabled party. This legal rule should be committed to memory since it has widespread applications to many situations.

The advantage conferred by the "victim concept" is extraordinary in that it allows the victim to gain substantially. But he must act within the rules as set out below before declaring the contract voidable:

1. That impaired persons or their legal representatives must establish that the impairment, whether it be from alcohol, drugs or mental incompetence, was sufficiently serious that they were unable to understand the nature and consequences of their actions.

2. That the other party knew or ought to have known (say, from the surrounding circumstances) of the degree of impairment described in (1) above.

3. That the agreement was repudiated within a reasonable time. Since the option is an extraordinary relief, the party seeking to make a contract voidable on any of these grounds will be expected to act quickly. Steps must be taken to cancel out the transaction immediately, including notifying the other party, returning goods, and doing everything necessary to put the parties back to the position they were in before the agreement was made.

CASE 23   DISNEY v. COHOL

Alexander Cohol, an alcoholic, who has been drinking heavily, purchases a colour TV set from Disney. He receives a copy of the Bill of Sale and the set is delivered to his home. He is to have a week's ''free viewing'' to make certain he gets a good picture. Disney misplaces the bill and fails to follow up. His bookkeeper finds the bill several weeks later and notes that it has not been paid. When Cohol receives the account in the mail, he calls Disney, ''Take your set back. It's fuzzy and it's got some cigar burns on it.'' Advise Disney of his legal position.

Note: The above case also deals with problems arising out of the Sale of Goods. Make a point of coming back to this case after you have examined Chapter Four: Sale of Goods.

KEY TO YOU ARE THE JURY

YOUNG v. S J & A INC. At 17, Roberta is an infant and as such, although she has the capacity to contract generally, she is afforded special protection under the law. In law, the bed is a chattel or goods. These items fall into two categories: luxuries or necessities.

If Roberta already has a serviceable bed at home and lives there with father, the bed falls into the luxury category. It is nice to have; but there is no absolute need for it. Infant contracts for luxuries are void. The company must therefore refund the $100.00. It is, however, entitled to take steps to get the bed back.

Suppose Roberta does not now live at home and is setting up housekeeping away from her parent's home. Suppose she must furnish her place on her own and needs the bed. The bed

then is a necessity and the contract is valid. The store keeps the $100.00 and may insist that the balance be paid. However, the contract is reviewable and the court may adjust the price if Roberta paid too much.

This case suggests another problem as well. Did she contract for a brass bed and get an iron one? Did the store misrepresent what it sold? We'll come back to this case in Unit 5: Genuine Intention.

Unit IV Lawful object (the fifth link)

YOU ARE THE JURY

MOFFAT v. PORTER

Moffat, a contractor, requires each labourer to sign a work contract in which it is agreed that the employee will not exercise the legal right to file a mechanics' lien against any property upon which the Moffat Company does work. Porter, a carpenter, files such a lien for unpaid wages and this lien is challenged because of the "contract" signed earlier. A provincial statute *(Mechanics' Liens Act)* makes it unlawful for such employees to enter into such restrictive contracts.

OBJECTIVES

- to be able to identify seven examples of contracts which contain terms considered in law to be illegal to the point that the contract will be unenforceable.
- to be able to identify terms in a contract which are considered against public policy to the point that the contract will be unenforceable.

LEXICON

Illegal The word "illegal" as used in this unit includes any act which would amount to a crime under Canadian law and any act which is unlawful under federal or provincial civil laws.

Public Policy A general rule of law that prevents two otherwise legally capable persons from entering into a private contract which will be contrary to the interests of society as a community. In these cases the general good of all is considered more important than the private good of the parties, and their contract will therefore be unenforceable (void).

Restraint of Trade Any agreement by which one party is required to give up usual employment in a trade or profession as a term of a contract. Such transactions are against public policy if the terms are considered unreasonable by objective legal test.

Tort A legal term for conduct that amounts to a civil (as opposed to a criminal) wrong by which one person is harmed or injured by either the deliberate act or negligence of another.

If we have a mutual agreement supported by valuable consideration, then the next step is to ex-amine the purpose or object behind the contract. If the object is unlawful, then the contract will be absolutely void and unenforceable by any party to the agreement.

Agreements for an unlawful object fall into two broad categories: illegal object, and objects which offend "public policy."

Illegal object

Both common law and statute law prohibit or regulate conduct. These laws are binding on everyone. It is not possible for some citizens to contract out of the law of the land by making a private contract among themselves. If this were permitted, it would effectively allow people to make their own laws and otherwise flout existing laws. A short list of illegal contracts follows:
1. agreements to do an act that is prohibited by federal or provincial statutes.
2. agreements to commit an act designated by law as a crime.
3. agreements to commit a tort or fraud against a third party.
4. agreements that promote corruption in public life.
5. agreements involving sexual immorality.
6. agreements that prejudice public safety.
7. agreements to defraud the provincial or federal government of revenue.

CASE 24 ANDERSON v. DANIEL

A manufacturer, Anderson, delivers ten tonnes of manure to Daniels together with an invoice which states the tonnage and price but which does not specify the percentages of the various component chemicals. A statute requires that the supplier provide an invoice identifying the chemicals by percentages. When Daniel fails to pay, Anderson sues. Daniels sets up the defective invoice in defence. How was this case decided?

Daniel argued that the object of the contract was for an unlawful purpose. The court agreed. "It is not unlawful to sell these chemical products but it is unlawful to sell them without the required 'percentage breakdown' invoice. The contract is void and unenforceable. The way in which this contract was performed was illegal and Anderson cannot recover the purchase price."

CASE 25 PIONEER v. ADARO

James Adaro misappropriated $2 300.00 from his employer's account. Pioneer commenced prosecution in the criminal courts. Before the trial, James's father agreed in writing to repay the amount personally in consideration that Pioneer would not proceed against James. Pioneer gave no evidence and consented with leave of the court to dismissal of the charge. Shortly afterwards James left town and his father refused to pay. If Pioneer sues for the debt, consider the probable results.

Objects which offend public policy

As we saw in Unit 2, Consideration, the courts will not lightly interfere in private agreements – a rule to which we should add a very important "but". Freedom to make contracts must be upheld, *but* any contract that tends to prejudice the interests of the community as a whole must be forbidden. The decided cases clearly indicate that the courts will not tolerate any contract that is injurious to the economic and social health of society.

The two major categories of contracts that offend against public policy are:
1. agreements to restrict access to the courts.
2. agreements in restraint of trade.

Agreements to restrict access to the courts

It has been established that agreements that destroy the right of any party to submit questions of law to the courts are contrary to public policy and therefore void.

CASE 26   BAKER v. JONES

An association is formed, and control over regulations is placed in the hands of a board of directors. The constitution reads in part, " . . . the Board is to be the interpreter of the rules . . . and its decisions will in all cases and in all circumstances be *final*." Baker does not agree with a Board decision and brings an action against the association. What are possible results and arguments in light of the above comments?

It was held in the Baker case that the powers given to the Board were void. The courts reserve the right to review decisions to determine whether any error in law has been made and to assist any person who has been denied natural justice. Under our system of justice, an injured party must be able to obtain a final decision from an independent tribunal.

It should be noted that the common business practice of requiring arbitration of business disputes by a private arbitrator or board before the issue can be taken to court is valid and enforceable. Such agreements must, however, recognize the rights of the parties to submit questions of law to the courts after the final internal decision has been made.

Agreements in restraint of trade

Agreements which *unreasonably* restrict the right of parties to carry on their trade or profession are of three types:
a. Agreements by which employees promise that after leaving their present employment they will not compete against their employer, either by setting up a rival business or by going to work for a competitor.
b. Agreements by which an owner selling his business contracts that he will not carry on a similar operation in competition with the new owner.
c. Agreements by which businesses or suppliers agree to fix selling prices and otherwise combine to regulate trade.

If the restrictions contained in any of these agreements are *unreasonable,* they will offend against public policy and be unenforceable. It must be realized, of course, that in certain circumstances restrictions on trading activities are justified. Suppose you were to purchase a thriving business only to find the former customers of your establishment flocking across the street to a new business opened by the previous owner. Or, suppose you teach several employees the "tricks of your trade" and encourage customers to deal directly with them only to find one day that they have all resigned and opened their own business taking 40% of your clientele with them.

One large Canadian firm makes a practice of having all new key employees sign an employment contract containing a term that, in the event their employment is terminated for any reason, they will not take up employment with several named competitors for a period of 18 months. Lawyers acting for purchasers of business make a practice of including a term that the old owners will not go into competition for a specific period of time within an identified geographic area.

CASE 27   CURLEY COSMETICS LTD. v. HARRY

Al Harry took a job in sales with the Toronto branch of Curley Cosmetics. He signed an employment agreement in which he agreed " . . . not to solicit or sell cosmetic products to any Curley customer with whom the salesperson [i.e., in this case, Al] dealt during the course of employment for a period of 20 months after employment is terminated for any reasons.'' Al actually contacted 492 such customers all in the Toronto area in which there are 1552 potential customers. Al quit and now runs a rival business out of his basement. He is actively and persistently soliciting many of his old customers.

Agreements such as the one in the Curley case are common. They are in restraint of trade and do not have the full support of the courts. Judges recognize that employers must protect themselves against certain skilled employees who leave, but if the agreement in any way appears unjust or unreasonable as to terms, the courts are likely to declare such provisions void and unenforceable.

Let's analyze the Curley contract. If the matter is taken to court, obviously the onus will be on the employer (Curley) to prove that the restrictive terms are reasonable under the circumstances.

First, the agreement does not restrict Harry from carrying on *any* trade, only that of cosmetic sales. In fact, Harry is still free to carry on sales in the field anywhere in the world; he is simply forbidden to contact Curley customers with whom he has dealt in a sales capacity. If he wishes to sell cosmetics in Toronto he still has over 60% of the market to work. Secondly, the 20-month period seems short and Harry will be free to contact even ''his old customers'' after that period in direct competition with Curley. The restrictions being reasonable, they do not offend public policy and will be enforceable. Curley will be able to obtain a court order restraining Harry from the prohibited competition.

A contract restricting competition for a five-year period was judged unreasonable by a British Columbia court, and a Manitoba court declared that an agreement restricting competition ''in any part of Southern Manitoba'' offended against public policy. In the first case, the time restriction was judged too long, and in the second, the territorial restriction was too great.

The second type of agreement in restraint of trade is that designed to restrain the sellers of businesses from competition. When a business is sold, the owners are required (by careful purchasers) to sign an agreement not to carry on a similar business in competition with the new owners. Such agreements are valid only if they are no wider than is necessary to protect adequately the interests of the purchasers of the business. Again, the court will pay particular attention to the two issues of geographic restriction and time restriction. If the restrictions on area and time are unreasonable, the agreement will be void.

The following rules summarize the law concerning agreements in restraint of trade:

1. The general rule is that all restraint terms are *presumed* to be against public policy and therefore void.
2. The presumption can be set aside (rebutted) by proving the restraint to be reasonable.
3. To be considered reasonable, the restraint must be no greater than is necessary to protect the interest of the person benefiting from the agreement. The court must be satisfied that the restraints in regard to time, area, and subject matter are not excessive.
4. The person to be restrained must possess some special skill, or must have knowledge of trade secrets or special techniques, or must represent some serious competitive potential which will amount to a danger to the business sold or left behind.

The third type of agreement in restraint of trade deals with arrangements made to fix prices or business marketing practices by manufacturers and suppliers. These practices are covered by a federal statute – *The Combines Investigation Act* – which applies with equal force to all Canadians. This topic is covered in Chapter Five.

KEY TO YOU ARE THE JURY

MOFFAT v. PORTER The issue in this case is whether or not a labourer (Porter) will be bound by an agreement to give up a right conferred by a provincial statute. The provincial *Mechanics' Lien Acts* provide labourers with the important right to file a lien against any property which they have improved through their labour to secure unpaid wages. The object of the statutes is to provide workers with a remedy should they not be paid for their labour, and they provide the additional safeguard of outlawing any agreement which an overbearing employer may be able to extract from a worker as the price of employment or remaining employed. Moffat's agreement is unlawful and cannot be used to interfere with Porter's right to file a lien and secure his wages against the property.

Unit V Genuine intention (the sixth link)

YOU ARE THE JURY

LESLIE TRUCKS INC. v. MERKOSKI

Merkoski purchased a tractor from Leslie Trucks for $40 000, believing it to be new. In fact an X had been placed by Leslie in the box opposite the word ''new'' and the box labelled ''used'' was blank. Later, when he learned that the unit had previously been leased to one Sanderson, Merkoski returned the tractor and demanded a refund. Leslie refused as no-one could recall telling Merkoski that the unit was new. Merkoski sued. How would the case be decided?

OBJECTIVES

- to be able to distinguish situations in which the mistake of one or more of the parties renders the contract void from those in which mistake does not affect the validity of the contract.
- to identify the legal rules arising out of misrepresentations and to be able to distinguish the remedies available for innocent and fraudulent misrepresentation.
- to be able to identify the following rules and the remedies that flow from them: non est factum; duress; undue influence.

LEXICON

Duress   The use or the threat of force by one party capable of causing harm against another party, which is intended to make that other party act in a certain way.

Misrepresentation   Any ''statement'' about a material term of the contract which is untrue; is made with the intention that the other party rely on it; and does in fact influence the judgment of that other party. All three of these elements are necessary.

Non Est Factum   A phrase meaning ''this is not my deed.'' This is a defence which can be raised when there is a forgery; when a party signing a contract has been misled as to the nature of the document; or where a document with the signature of the party has been obtained by deceit or fraud. The general rule is that if one signs a document, legal responsibility follows. Therefore the defence of non est factum depends on the party being defrauded.

Recision   The act by which one party, who has been wronged by another party, cancels all legal obligations arising out of the agreement and requires the other party to treat the agreement as void. The usual remedy is to put the parties as close as possible back to their original positions before the contract was made.

Genuine intention to create legally binding obligations is the final and decisive link that keeps the agreement. It is the last to be added and joins all the others together to form an unbreakable chain. The conduct of the parties must be such as to lead a reasonable, prudent person to conclude that their intention must have been to agree that legal obligations would flow from their bargain.

A person would not, of course, make a contract without knowing what it was about unless he was mistaken as to its nature and consequences, or was tricked or pressured into it. But when this does occur, the contract may be declared void because of a lack of genuine intention. It would be a mistake, however, to believe (as many of us do) that no effect should be given an agreement based on an obvious misunderstanding. The law does not take the position that a contract is void simply because one or more of the parties would not have made it had they known the true facts. For example, suppose Hogan agrees to buy a service station situated near a busy highway from Preston, and unknown to the purchaser, but known to the seller, the highway will shortly be bypassed, leaving the station in the ''middle of nowhere.'' The purchaser, Hogan, cannot avoid the contract by pleading *mistake*. If, during the negotiations, the purchaser is actually misled by the seller's conduct or statements, he may be able to avoid the contract, not because of mistake but because of the additional ground of *misrepresentation*.

In order to identify those instances in which the lack of genuine intention will destroy a contract, we must examine the legal implications of:
1. Mistake (Somebody goofed!).
2. Misrepresentation (I've been a liar all my life!).
3. Non Est Factum (It's not my deed).
4. Duress (Sign or I'll break your arm).
5. Undue Influence (It will be good for your soul).

Mistake

The possibility of avoiding contractual liability because of a mistake is extremely remote. The general rule is that contracts once made should be upheld wherever possible. Thus the doctrine of legal mistake is very narrowly and technically defined by the courts. A person may not argue, for example, that he was mistaken about the applicability of a law, for every person is presumed to know the law. Each of us must be as alert and knowledgeable in this regard as possible, for "ignorance of the law is no excuse."

Having stated the general rule, we must note certain exceptions. There are three types of mistake that by their nature will definitely render an otherwise sound contract void.

Mutual mistake

When the parties fail to communicate properly and talk at "cross-purposes," they misunderstand each other and a fundamental mistake occurs, which destroys the validity of the contract.

CASE 28   PSYCHOGAS v. JORDAN

Georgia, the owner of several parcels of land, agreed with Constance to "sell 80 acres of land in Aweres Township for $80 000.00 cash." Georgia actually owned two parcels of land in the township. She believed Constance wanted "Greenacres" when in reality Constance was bargaining for "Blackacres."

The parties obviously contracted at "cross-purposes." This is an example of mutual mistake. In such a case the courts would rule that the agreement was void and unenforceable by either party.

Common mistake

When both parties are mistaken about the same fundamental fact, they have fallen inadvertently into the trap of common mistake and their contract will be void and unenforceable.

CASE 29   MITCHELL v. LEGROS

Elly Mitchell (as vendor) and Roland Legros (as purchaser) signed a contract for the purchase of a cottage. Unknown to either of them, the cottage had been completely destroyed the previous night. Is this an example of common mistake? How does the destruction of the subject matter of the contract affect the contract itself?

Unilateral mistake

In the case of unilateral mistake, only one of the parties is mistaken and the other party knows or ought to know from the surrounding circumstances of the mistake. The mistake must go to

the root of the bargain and it must be material to the contract. In other words, it must be a mistake of some consequence. Unilateral mistake renders a contract void and unenforceable.

CASE 30   YOUNG v. S. J. & A. INC

Roberta Young asks to see a brass bed. She is shown such a bed, but feels it is too expensive. The clerk smiles, says nothing, and takes Roberta to another bed. The bed is painted white, but small brass knobs shine, one at each corner. She purchases the bed and later discovers that the painted parts are "only iron." Is this a case of unilateral mistake?

The solution to this case is difficult. The clerk did not say that the second bed was a brass bed and we must attempt to interpret the conduct of the store in the overall context of what actually happened – and in the light of our definition of unilateral mistake. Was Roberta mistaken? Did she believe she was buying a brass bed? Couldn't she have examined it more closely? Remember, we looked at this case earlier and were told Roberta was 17 years old. Should her youth be a factor? How should this case be argued?

First, if she asked to see brass beds and believed she was being shown such items, it is logical to assume that she was actually mistaken. This is confirmed when she attempted to rescind the contract on learning the "real facts." We can be certain that the store was not mistaken and a reasonably prudent clerk ought to have realized that Roberta was mistaken. The customer, by specifying the type and quality of the item, made "brassness" a material, substantial element of the contract. Roberta will succeed in rescinding the contract and will be entitled to receive her money back.

Roberta may also be able to argue *misrepresentation* by conduct. For its part, the store would argue the doctrine of *caveat emptor*. Both are discussed in the following section.

Misrepresentation

A general rule of contract law is *caveat emptor* – let the buyer beware. The buyer must be cautious since the risk is his.

The seller, as a rule, does not have any legal duty to disclose facts that might affect the purchaser's decision or judgment. This rule applies to most contracts, the exceptions being where there exists a special position of trust between the parties or where the contract is said to be one of utmost good faith.

While a party may often be allowed to remain silent, the law does not permit active misrepresentation of material facts. There are two types of misrepresentation – *innocent* and *fraudulent* – which are discussed below.

But first, we must consider the definition of a contractual "representation." This is a statement made by one party to the other regarding an existing fact or circumstance which induces or influences the other party to act – for example, a statement that the profit for the business in the past has been $100 000.00 a year; or that a tractor is new and has never been used; or that a basement is dry. A representation may also be interpreted from conduct such as where a clerk (*Young v. S. J. & A.*) shows goods of one kind and then, without more than a smile, switches the customer to goods of another quality.

Note that a representation means a statement of *fact* and does not include expressions of opinion or law. All persons selling are entitled to "puff up" their wares ("This is a great little car" or "This is a home any discriminating family would be proud to own"), and since we are all presumed to know the law, we are expected to make our own investigation on this count.

A misrepresentation is a false statement of fact or of circumstances intended to induce the other party to act.

Innocent misrepresentation

Innocent misrepresentation consists of any false statement of a material fact, made with intent that another act on it, which falls short of being fraudulent. In other words, the misrepresenting party may believe in what he is saying so that the conduct does not amount to a deliberate lie.

All that is important here is that the statement be "untrue." The misstatement must be one of material fact that goes to the root of the contract. It must be such that if the true state of affairs were known, the person to whom the statement is made would have said, "No! I would not even for a moment consider this contract." There must also be some evidence that the misled party was influenced to act on the basis of the misrepresentation. If all these factors are present, we have what amounts to innocent misrepresentation and *the contract is voidable at the option of the "victim" who was induced to act.*

The lesson to be learned is that we must all take great care in making statements designed to inform or influence the other party, for if we are wrong in a statement of fact, even though we act *honestly*, we must pay the price for our error.

Fraudulent misrepresentation

Fraudulent misrepresentation is a misstatement made by one party who knows it to be false and makes the statement recklessly. The statement must be equivalent to a deliberate lie. It must be a misstatement of a material fact and must go to the root of the contract. The statement must be made with the intent that the other party should rely on it and that party must, in fact, be shown to have relied on the misrepresentation. Evidence of inducement through misrepresentation must be present. If all of the above factors are present, *the party who is the victim of a fraudulent misrepresentation may treat the contract as voidable.*

Obviously the element of fraud adds a sinister note. The injured party has the additional right to claim money damages. To this extent, the remedy for fraudulent misrepresentation is different from that for innocent misrepresentation.

Recision

In the event a contract is found to be voidable for misrepresentation, the main remedy available is that of *recision*. The injured party is entitled to cancel the transaction and to have his money or his property returned, so that he returns to the position he was in before the contract was made.

This is an extraordinary remedy and in order to pursue such a powerful option, the injured party has a duty to give notice of recision as soon as he becomes aware of the truth.

Both the remedy of recision and damages are explored in detail in Unit Six: Remedies on Breach of Contract.

CASE 31   GROSSET v. DUNLOP

Grosset has agreed in writing to sell a large old home to Dunlop. Grosset tells Dunlop that the property has been re-zoned for commercial use and that he is completing the apartment units in the structure under the authority of a building permit issued by the city. Grosset honestly believes that the area has been re-zoned for business (though in fact it has not) but he knows that he does not have the permit. Nothing is mentioned about the representations in the offer to purchase. Before a deed is given and the transaction is completed, Dunlop discovers the true state of affairs. He refuses to close and demands the return of his deposit. Grosset demands he take the property "as is."

Grosset has been guilty of both innocent and fraudulent misrepresentations. Dunlop will have difficulty proving innocent misstatement, but he should be able to avoid the contract on the grounds of fraud. The court will order his deposit returned and may also award damages in the form of an additional award to cover his costs and time thrown away in this fruitless endeavour.

Non est factum

When one party to a contract says *"non est factum"* (this is not my deed) he is attempting to suggest he is not responsible for a contract he appears to have made. The general rule is that you are presumed in law to have read the contents of every document you have signed and therefore you are bound by your signature whether you read the document or not. Non est factum is an exception to the rule. It means literally "the act is not mine" or "my mind did not go with my pen." In such cases agreements are utterly void.

CASE 32   DUNN v. KLAUS

Christopher Klaus, age 87, signed a document which he was told was a personal guarantee for his son's loan. Later he discovered that the document was actually a mortgage on his house. When the son failed to repay the loan, Dunn, the lender, took foreclosure proceedings against the home. Dunn said, "I don't know anything about any trick. I just want my money or the house."

The old gentleman may well be able to apply the defence non est factum because his "mind never went with his pen." Klaus would avoid liability from foreclosure and would be able to force Dunn to remove the mortgage from the title to the house.

Duress and undue influence

The rules with respect to duress are very similar to those for undue influence. Duress means, quite simply, force. We shall therefore confine our comments to undue influence which is rather more complex. Undue influence consists of the improper use by one person of power or influence over another. The parties may be related or circumstances may have thrown them together in such a way that one is "superior" to the other. Examples are: Doctor-Patient; Lawyer-Client; Priest-Confessor; or a sick person dependent on a healthy person for care. In the event that the contracting parties are not strangers dealing at "arm's length" but are subject to some special relationship, a legal presumption will arise that the contract lacks the necessary genuine intention to create a valid contract.

Legal presumptions, however, are rebuttable or may be reversed. The "superior" parties must prove that they did not exercise any undue influence. To avoid the defence of undue influence, such parties must be able to prove that:

(i) they made full disclosure of all of the material facts;
(ii) the consideration was fair;
(iii) the weaker party was in receipt of independent legal advice.

CASE 33   YAKE v. LOWW

A lawyer, Belle Yake, signed an Offer to Purchase for a business block from Mel Loww, a client, on terms rather beneficial to her. Loww later attempted to back out of the transaction.

Yake's position as lawyer for Loww places her in a legally "superior" position. In order to avoid Loww's defence of undue influence she will have to prove all three elements listed above. She would have to prove that she made full disclosure of any material facts surrounding the transaction, including disclosure that she was purchasing the property on her own account. There must also be evidence that Loww received an adequate and fair price, and that he received independent legal advice. This is usually done by sending parties in the inferior position to a lawyer of their choice to provide them with an opportunity to reconsider the contract in an atmosphere removed from any pressure and with the added assistance of an independent professional.

If all of these things were done, the presumption of undue influence will be set aside – and Yake will have bought herself a piece of real estate.

CASE 34   IN RE FLANNAGAN'S WILL

At Flannagan's request Father Murphy assisted Flannagan to prepare his will. When Flannagan died, his will disclosed that a significant amount of money had been left to the church. Apply the rules of undue influence to these facts and determine the validity of the gift.

KEY TO YOU ARE THE JURY

LESLIE TRUCKS INC. v. MERKOSKI   This case presents a problem of misrepresentation. The issue is whether or not the bill of sale representing the tractor to be new is sufficient to create a lack of genuine intention.

The seller may not have a duty to disclose that the unit was used but he does have a legal duty not to misrepresent. In the absence of any explanation, the marking of the machine as "new" amounts to a misstatement of a material fact and if Merkoski is able to prove that he was influenced to buy the tractor because he believed it was new, he will succeed. If he can prove that Leslie was fraudulent or reckless and careless of the truth, he may be able to establish fraudulent misrepresentation and in addition to recision may be awarded money damages.

The contract will be cancelled and Merkoski will have his money returned.

Checklist: Contracts

1. **(a) Begin to negotiate; bargain;** opinion, sales pitch (puffing) permitted. Separate fact from opinion, specifics from generalities, truth from fiction (as farmer would wheat from chaff).

   (b) Analyze progress. Is one party ready to make an offer? Can you persuade other party to make the offer? Will you have to make the offer? Are you prepared to do so?

2. **Draft offer in written form.** Does it contain all terms you want? Is it clear, unambiguous, more than a statement of intention? Does it have value of a legally binding offer? Prepare offer in final form.

3. **Presentation.** Consider best means of delivering offer to other party. Personal delivery? Through agent? Registered mail? Courier? Include specific instructions, method by which other party may communicate *acceptance* and set time limit for response.

4. **Acceptance.** Examine acceptance from other party.

5. **Change of Heart.** If circumstances indicate it wise to withdraw offer, may this be done legally? Consider appropriate steps to withdraw before acceptance. Take steps so identified. Communicate withdrawal to other party by quickest, surest means. Document steps taken in writing. Note for file and correspondence letters confirming action taken to other party and any other who must know of decision.

6. **Acceptance.** If other party accepts and offer not withdrawn, examine acceptance carefully. Does it appear to be legally binding? Is it unconditional? Are conditions attached? Has acceptance been communicated on time by proper method?

7. **Counter-offer.** Is the acceptance in form of counter-offer? If so, are terms agreeable? What steps must you take to accept the counter-offer to create a binding legal agreement? If unacceptable counter-offer received, what steps must you take to reject and call deal off?

8. **No acceptance.** If other party has not accepted, has there been a rejection of the offer? Should you re-negotiate? If no response by deadline or reasonable time, has offer lapsed? Are you free to deal with another? What steps should be taken to clearly inform other party the offer has

lapsed and is now null and void? Take such steps required.

9. **Consideration.** Has the person benefiting from the contract given legal value? Usually safe if both parties have given legal value (i.e., money, cheque, draft, money in any form, work, services, property including lands, buildings, personal property, goods or firm promise to exchange or give legal value as a result of contract).

10. **If no consideration given.** Will contract be void as a gratuitous promise? What steps to be taken to make binding? Consider giving nominal value (i.e., $2 to bind transaction) or use legal seal or waiver to take place of consideration. These precautions not necessary in Quebec which recognizes validity of gratuitous promise.

11. **Lawful Object.** Consider whether contract is for legal purpose? Will its object contravene any criminal or civil law? Any federal, provincial or municipal law? If in doubt, consult lawyer.

12. **Genuine Intention.** Do we both intend to be legally bound? Review contract. Is it possible you are mistaken about a term? Is it possible both parties are mistaken? Consider unilateral, common and mutual mistakes. As you go along, look for signs of misrepresentation. Has other party been untruthful about material term, intending you to act? Consider both intentional and unintentional (innocent) conduct on other party's part.

13. **Mistake. Misrepresentation.** If legal mistake or misrepresentation is identified, you must notify other party at earliest opportunity or lose right to rescind or call deal off. Consider whether your best interests require you to get out of deal. Decide whether you want to complete transaction or exercise right as victim to rescind.

14. **Time to double check.** If no difficulties are apparent on the surface, it's time to review anyway. Set aside a few moments for thought. Consider danger of fraudulent conduct or deliberately withheld information. Act if you detect any danger signals at this stage.

15. **Independent legal advice.** If there is some special relationship between the parties (parent/child, lawyer/client, employer/employee, wife/husband, etc.) it may be necessary for a party to have independent legal advice from a lawyer of that person's choice. In such cases consider

whether you or the other party should be required to seek independent legal advice.

16. Complete contract.
If all goes well, contract concluded without incident.

17. Breach.
If one party breaks a term of the contract, consider consequences. If important term breached, victim entitled on learning of breach to repudiate it and in effect get out of it (that is, to be put back in same position as before contract made). In case of fraud or bad faith of other party, you may also be entitled to money damages. See Breach of Contracts Checklist for more details and Chapter Four: Sale of Goods for remedy of damages.

18. After contract concluded.
If you discover misrepresentation after contract has been concluded, consider whether you as victim should take steps to repudiate contract. Consult lawyer. Take steps immediately on discovery or rights to reverse contract lost.

19. General check.
Remember contract should always be in writing, signed by both parties. All representations given should be included. Read fine print. Ask questions until contract thoroughly understood. Remember no-one can protect you against foolishness. If you pay too much, accept opinion as fact, fail to get specifics in writing, or make a mistake not on the list above, the law will not take extraordinary measures to protect you.

Review

If you were the jury, how would you decide the following cases and on what grounds?

1. GOLDTHORPE v. LOGAN Greta, a pretty woman plagued with persistent facial hairs which formed an unmistakable mustache read an advertisement, "HAIRS . . . removed safely. Permanently. Results Guaranteed." Greta answered the ad and was told, "We guarantee our work. You'll shortly be a ravishing beauty." Greta paid for and received five treatments but the results were unsatisfactory. The hairs were not permanently removed and in fact grew in more luxuriantly than before.

2. CARTON ENTERPRISES v. SWANSON
A farmer signed a contract for sale of lands with Chinook, in spite of the fact that he had previously offered them to Carton. When Carton discovered the Chinook sale, its president called a meeting at which were examined documents including a letter from the farmer which read, "I hereby offer you my property Block A Concession 13 at a price of $200 000. My offer is open for acceptance for six months from the date hereof." Carton's president noted that the time limit was not yet up and persuaded the Carton directors to "accept" the offer. Carton then delivered a formal written acceptance by hand to the farmer. When the farmer refused to deal further with Carton, the company sued him for specific performance.

3. COHOL v. LYON Cohol refused to carry out the terms of a "contract" by which he had agreed to sell his business to Lyon, claiming that
• he had been drinking heavily at the time and

did not fully understand the contract on the day it was signed.
• the contract was drawn by Lyon's lawyer, who attended at Cohol's home with Lyon and an accountant.
• the lawyer commented at the time, "this guy's a nervous wreck. It's two in the afternoon, and he is still in his bathrobe." Lyon said in reply, "He's lucky to be getting out of this business. Maybe he can take it easy and get off the stuff."
• Cohol did not read the contract before he signed it.

4. KANTER v. SINAH Sinah undertook gratuitously to invest money for Kanter, who gave Sinah the funds and instructions. Sinah invested the money in spite of the fact that she found she could not follow Kanter's instructions. The money was lost. Sinah's lawyer argued that she could not be sued in contract, could only be liable for negligence, and that she had not been negligent. Assume that Sinah's conduct had not amounted to legal negligence. Was her lawyer correct in law?

5. BREMER v. KIEL A creditor, Bremer, threatened to sue a company of which Kiel was an officer. Although Kiel was not personally liable on the debt, he gave the creditor a promissory note agreeing to pay the debt to avoid the law suit against the company. The creditor thereupon halted all further legal steps against the company. After several months without payment the creditor sued Kiel, having come to the conclusion that it would be easier to collect from Kiel than from the company.

Unit VI Remedies on breach of contract

YOU ARE THE JURY

OTTENBRITE v. SIPPI

Laura Ottenbrite sold her thriving beauty salon business to Sippi. In the written contract Laura undertook "not to engage in the beauty salon trade nor the sale of cosmetics or related products for a period of 18 months within a radius of two miles of the said business." Laura left the city for a brief period but returned six months later to open a rival salon across the street from Sippi. Discuss the implications of Laura's actions and consider the remedies available to Sippi, if any.

OBJECTIVES

- to be able to identify actions leading to breach of contract which give rise to legal remedies.
- to be able to identify the legal rules under which an award of money damages may be made.
- to be able to choose the appropriate legal remedy, given choices of specific performance, replevin, injunction, and/or recision.

LEXICON

Breach Failure of a party to a contract to carry out any part of an essential term of the agreement.

Condition A term of a contract which is so essential that failure to perform it will amount to a breach of contract.

Damages An amount of money expressed in terms of dollars and cents which a court will award an injured party in compensation for loss arising *directly* from a breach of contract committed by another party.

Injunction A court order prohibiting a party to a contract from breaching its terms or continuing conduct which amounts to a breach.

Mitigation Action taken by the injured party to avoid or reduce a loss caused by the misconduct of the other party.

Replevin A court proceeding in which an officer of the court is empowered to seize and hold goods or property until a formal hearing has determined the rightful owner.

Quantum Meruit A method of legally calculating the value of work or services which have been only partly performed but for which some compensation must be awarded.

Specific Performance An equitable relief of an extraordinary nature available (at the discretion of the court) to compel a defaulting party to a contract to deliver to another the subject matter of the contract, usually when a money award would be grossly inadequate compensation.

In Unit Two we concentrated on how a contract is made and on the qualities necessary to make it valid and binding. In this part we focus on what happens after a contract has been made, and in particular what happens when one of the parties to a contract does not live up to his bargain. A discussion of breach of contract does, in fact, go straight to the heart of why we use contracts at all, and provides an excellent opportunity to analyze the practical value of creating legally binding agreements. You will see just why it is that prudent people never plan business activities requiring the expenditure of funds, time and effort without the assurance of a contract which defines the obligations of the other parties.

CASE 35   SHAVER v. WEBB

Webb ordered some specially-designed plastic clamps from Shaver, who was to manufacture and deliver them within six months. Shaver completed his part of the contract on time, but Webb then refused to take delivery claiming that circumstances had changed and he no longer needed the clamps.

Consider the implications of the Shaver case. Any supplier receiving an order from a customer will want to make sure that the goods will be accepted on delivery and that they will eventually be paid for. He will want an assurance that the customer is bound by the contract and unable to opt out of it merely because he changes his mind. The supplier will likewise seek protection in the event that the customer is unable to take delivery because of a change in circumstances or for any other reason beyond the control of the seller.

The main purpose of a contract is to make people live up to their promises. Many will do so only if the penalty for failure is clearly defined and substantial. What can Shaver do now that Webb has refused to take delivery? The law says that if a party fails to perform as promised, this constitutes a *breach* of contract and the injured party is entitled to *damages* as compensation for loss. Generally the amount of the damage award is designed to put the injured party in as good a position as he would have been in had the contract actually been performed.

Money damages is the usual remedy available for breach of contract, but there are circumstances in which the harm done cannot be assessed in terms of dollars and cents. In such cases, a court may order a party to perform the contract under a remedy called *specific performance.*

A fourth remedy available on a breach of contract is an *injunction* by which a court may restrain one party from doing an act prejudicial to the other. We shall now examine these remedies in greater detail and the availability of a fifth remedy *recision,* which has already been discussed in connection with misrepresentation.

Discharge

Contracts may be discharged or ended in the following ways:
- by performance of the terms.
- by subsequent agreement.
- by impossibility of performance.
- by acts of one party failing to complete terms thus relieving other party of obligation.
- by operation of law.

Discharge by performance
The obligation of a contracting party is clearly discharged or ended when all the terms undertaken to be done have in fact been done. The party having done all that is necessary is naturally relieved of further responsibility under the contract.

Discharge by subsequent agreement
After parties have entered into a contract, there is nothing to stop them from mutually agreeing in the form of a second contract to release each other from the terms of the first contract, thus discharging it. The exchange of promises to release is a sufficient legal consideration to support a subsequent agreement. Often, business people terminate their original contracts by substituting a new agreement which expressly or by implication rescinds former contracts.

Suppose Lalonde agreed to buy a certain lot from Young, upon which Young was to construct a certain model home. Later the same parties

agreed that a different model be built on a different lot and a new contract was signed. Theoretically, Lalonde has signed to buy two lots and have two homes constructed because no steps were taken to "cancel" the first agreement. But practically, Lalonde and Young are bound only to complete the second contract which by implication automatically cancels out the first.

Impossibility of performance
The general rule of law is that any person who enters into a legal contract must complete the terms thereof even though subsequent events make it impossible to perform the contract. The promissor remains liable and will be liable in damages for failure to complete the terms of a contract. It is for this reason that prudent business people attempt to anticipate events which might render it impossible for them to complete their part of a bargain. They do so by including an express term in the contract specifying that their liability is conditional on possibility of performance. For example, transport companies limit their liability by stipulating that they are not responsible for failure to deliver goods in the event of certain "Excepted Risks" such as union strikes and "acts of God."

Right to discharge by other's breach
In most contractual arrangements, the failure by one party to carry out the terms of the contract releases the other from further obligation. In order to amount to a discharge, the conduct of the other party must strike at the root of the contract and must demonstrate that the defaulting party no longer intends to be bound. When one party fails to complete an essential part of the contract, the other may treat the contract as at an end and sue for damages.

CASE 36   SMITHERS v. TRAVERS

Smithers and Travers entered into a contract by which Smithers was to manufacture and supply goods on a regular basis by instalments. After several deliveries had been made, and without just cause, Travers advised Smithers that he would not accept any more deliveries. Smithers could sue Travers for damages provided he himself remained ready, willing and able to make future deliveries.

Discharge by operation of law
At times, although the parties remain willing to complete the terms of their agreement, one or

both is prevented from carrying out the terms because a rule of law makes it unlawful for them to pursue their intended goal. Examples are:

- Richard convinces Connie to invest in a mail order business, but halfway through the scheme Richard discovers that the scheme contravenes a provincial anti-Pyramid Act.
- Gregory has retained a non-lawyer firm to assist him to obtain a divorce but before the divorce can be processed a law is passed making such businesses unlawful.
- Walter, who has been unable to pay a contractual debt, declares bankruptcy and obtains an order of the bankruptcy court discharging all his debts.

Damages

In the event that one contracting party substantially breaches a contract by refusing or neglecting to complete it, the other has the right to treat the contract as discharged and may sue for damages for breach of contract. The injured party must prove:

1. Substantial breach of one or more material conditions of the contract by the other party.
2. The injured party's readiness to complete the contract at all times.
3. That steps were taken by the injured party to reduce or avoid loss.
4. The amount of the loss (converted into dollar values) *directly* caused by the breach of the other party.

Assuming the dispute is taken to court, the onus or responsibility is on the plaintiff (the injured party) to prove the four elements of the breach listed above. The plaintiff must prove that the conduct of the defendant (the party in breach) amounted to a failure to perform a condition or material term of the contract. A condition of a contract may be described as a part of it which is so vital that no reasonable, prudent person would go through with the contract if the other party failed to complete such an important part. Webb's refusal to take delivery of the clamps was clearly a breach of a fundamental term or condition. On such breach the plaintiff is entitled to treat the contract as discharged which paves the way for a suit for damages.

The plaintiff must prove a readiness, willingness, and capability to complete his own part of the contract at all times and that there was no breach on his side which would have prevented the contract from being completed.

The injured party has an obligation to take all reasonable and necessary steps to avoid or reduce

loss caused directly by the other side. Such action is referred to as *mitigation* – that is, steps are taken by the plaintiff to "mitigate" loss caused by the default of the other party. This is a way of demonstrating good faith. The courts will not look kindly on people who, faced with a loss resulting from breach of contract, take no steps to avoid or reduce such loss. For example, if a vendor of a large quantity of highly perishable goods finds that a purchaser will not take delivery, immediate steps must be taken to find another buyer to purchase the goods (even if it means selling at a lower price) rather than simply allow the goods to rot on the assumption that the original buyer may be sued for the entire value.

The plaintiff must next establish the amount of the loss by producing the necessary documents or records of the transaction. Note that it is not for the court to calculate this figure for the plaintiff but it will consider sums "proved" by the plaintiff in accord with the rules of the court. Ideally, damages should be sufficient to make the plaintiff "whole again" – that is, the plaintiff should not have to suffer any loss. But in fact this does not always happen as Canadian judges base decisions on established legal guides in making damage awards. The fundamental rule is that money damages are to compensate for loss caused *directly* by the breach but shall not necessarily include all loss actually sustained. Judges refer to the "remoteness test" in identifying damages for which they will not allow compensation. Whether damages are direct or remote are questions of fact to be decided on the merits of each individual case.

CASE 37   HADLEY v. BAXENDALE

Hadley was a miller. A broken crank shaft had shut down his business and in order to have a new shaft manufactured it was necessary to send the old one to a factory some distance away. Hadley hired Baxendale Transport to make the delivery. Baxendale handled the contract negligently and caused a lengthy delay. Consequently, Hadley's business was completely shut down for a longer period than necessary. Hadley sued for damages which included loss of profits. If Hadley is to succeed, what must be proven? Consider as a fact that Baxendale had no knowledge of the shutdown.

The court did award damages. However, it found that Baxendale was liable only for those damages which could be considered the "natural result of the delay which were reasonably in the contemplation of the parties at the time they made the contract." Since Baxendale had no actual knowledge that the delay would shut down the mill, he was not responsible for the loss of profit to the mill.

The test adopted by Canadian courts may be stated as follows:

Any damage actually caused by a breach of contract is recoverable providing that when the contract was made it was reasonably foreseeable that such loss was liable to result from the breach.

CASE 38   SULLIVAN v. KIDD

Sullivan ordered a tractor from Kidd and made it known at the time that delivery was required immediately and that it was essential that the machine be in "perfect working order" since it was urgently needed to complete important work he had undertaken for a third party. Kidd delivered on time but the machine was defective and Sullivan lost the contract as a result. Sullivan sued for damages, including $3 500 for loss of profit. Will Sullivan succeed?

In a similar case decided by a Manitoba Court of Appeal it was held that a loss of profit was in fact a reasonably foreseeable result of the defendant's breach of contract. Great weight was attached to the fact that the party in breach had been made aware of the consequences of breach in clear terms at the time the contract was made. Review the Hadley and Sullivan cases to make sure you understand the material differences between the two situations.

CASE 39   TALIANA v. ARROW TRANSPORT

Taliana sold a quantity of imported shoes at an exceptionally high price to a firm in Vancouver and contracted with Arrow to transport them to British Columbia. It was a condition of the original sale contract that the shoes be delivered by a certain date and Arrow agreed to the deadline for delivery. Arrow delivered the shoes late and the Vancouver firm rejected them and repudiated its contract with Taliana (which it had the legal right to do). Taliana was able to sell the shipment to another firm but for a price somewhat less than the average going rate for such goods. Taliana then sued Arrow for the difference in price. Consider the main issues before reading on and attempt to come to a solution.

If you had difficulty identifying the issues you should go back and review the material in this section. If you had difficulty arriving at a satisfactory conclusion, that's not surprising, since one fact was deliberately omitted. Arrow was not aware of the exceptionally high price the original purchaser had contracted to pay. Take a moment to reconsider the problem.

Applying the Foreseeability Rule, Arrow would not be liable for the loss arising out of the difference between the exceptionally high contract price and the "market price" for the shoes. There was, however, a slight loss which resulted from the emergency sale and Arrow would be liable for this, since such a loss was reasonably foreseeable.

If Taliana had been able to mitigate damages by a fortunate sale at the market value for such goods, he would have suffered no damages and consequently would be unable to establish a loss recoverable in court. (Though in such cases the courts have awarded nominal damages against defendants.)

Other rules to consider under damages include:
- no damages will be awarded for interest unless the contract specifies that interest shall be paid by a writing (*Interest Act*, Canada).
- no damages will be awarded for mere inconvenience or injured feelings that might arise incidentally out of breach.
- while it is the duty of the plaintiff to mitigate damages, there is also a heavy burden on the defendant to prove that the plaintiff did not take all reasonable steps to mitigate.

Quantum meruit (Part performance)

The principle of *quantum meruit* arises where a contract that has been partly performed by one party is discharged by the breach of the other party. When this occurs, the injured party is entitled to be paid a reasonable amount for what has been done.

CASE 40   SILVER v. KELLY

Sterling Silver was retained by Kelly to institute a libel action against Kelly's employer, Slade. Kelly agreed to pay a fee of $3 000. Several days before the trial but after Silver had done most of the work on the file, Slade published a complete retraction. Kelly instructed Silver to discontinue all further action. Is Silver entitled to the fee agreed upon in advance? Part of the fee? Nothing?

On the strength of "part performance," Silver is entitled to be paid a sum equivalent to the value of the work actually performed and Kelly would be liable to pay this sum, but not the full $3 000.

Specific performance

An order to pay damages does not mean that the defendant actually has to perform the contract. The court does not order defendants to live up to their promises but only to compensate their "victims" for loss arising out of breach. The courts do, however, have the power to order defendants to perform certain contractual promises through the remedy of "specific performance." This is an extraordinary, equitable remedy which is available (at the discretion of the court) only where the subject matter of the contract is unique so that a mere damage award could not satisfy the expectations of a reasonable, prudent person.

CASE 41   RAJNOVICH v. BOURDEAU DEVELOPMENTS INC.

The development company contracted in writing to sell an apartment/office complex to Rajnovich. The company later refused to complete the sale transaction.

The courts have held that no two parcels of land are identical. Each is unique and therefore no damage award could possibly put purchasers of lands in as good a position as they would have been in if their land sale contracts had been carried out. Rajnovich may sue the company for specific performance of the contract and the court has power to order Bourdeau to complete its sale contract by delivering title to the property to Rajnovich on the terms and conditions set out in the contract. If Bourdeau Developments still persists in its refusal to sell, it would then be guilty of contempt of court and for such an offence its officers could be imprisoned or fined or both.

Specific performance may also be available as a remedy where contracts involve antiques, original paintings, rare coins, and objects which have "one-of-a-kind" characteristics. Breach of contract for the sale of commercial goods will not give rise to a specific performance remedy because the goods are not "unique" and a plaintiff who receives money damages can easily purchase similar goods elsewhere.

Replevin

It often happens during the course of a commercial transaction that one party has possession of goods which are owned by the other party. When the contract goes sour, the party with possession may refuse or neglect to give up the goods to the rightful owner. At other times, both parties may honestly believe that they are the legal owner of goods which one of them has in his possession. It is an unfortunate fact in these situations that a party who seeks legal remedy through the courts must normally await the outcome of the proceedings before an effective demand may be made for possession of the goods. If the proceedings drag on too long, the wrong person may have possession for such a long time that the goods may become "lost" or damaged or otherwise put out of the reach of the true owner.

In order to avoid such a scandalous situation the law has developed a remedy called *replevin*. Persons who claim to be owners of goods which they allege are wrongfully in the possession of a third party who will not willingly give them up, may bring an immediate application before a judge who has the power to direct the sheriff of the County or District to seize the goods and hold them until a formal hearing can take place to determine the true owner. In this way the property in question is kept safe and intact under the watchful eye of the sheriff until the dispute between the contracting parties can be settled in court.

Injunction

An injunction is an order of a court commanding one person not to do or to cease doing an act which contravenes a term or condition of a contract which has been breached by that person.

CASE 42   A & A INC. v. PIONEER

A recording company entered into a contract with a little-known singer whereby she would record exclusively for them for a period of two years. Soon afterwards, Pioneer's career "took off" and in spite of the contract with A & A she entered into a new contract with a larger company to record exclusively for them. In this case an injunction would be granted by the court to forbid Pioneer from making recordings for other studios during the time remaining on the original recording contract.

An injunction would also be an appropriate remedy for those situations listed in the section on Lawful Object in Unit Four.

Recision

The final remedy on breach of contract is recision. The injured party is entitled to treat the contract as discharged and to be put back into the

same position as before the contract was made. In other words, he may be entitled to receive his money back or have his property returned.

This is an important option available for consideration, particularly in cases where money damages would provide wholly inadequate relief. It is an extraordinary remedy and in order to pursue it, the plaintiff has a duty to give notice of recision as soon as he becomes aware of the breach.

CASE 43   FAIRBAIRNE v. PAYEUR

Payeur agreed to sell Fairbairne a large building which she had converted into several "apartments." Those on the first and second floors were finished and occupied. Two units in the basement were still under construction. Fairbairne received assurances from Payeur that all work completed and in progress had been authorized by municipal permits. In fact, no such authority existed. After the transaction was completed, Fairbairne, as owner, was advised by the municipality that all work on the building must cease and that Payeur had never applied for permits. Fairbairne was further advised that the area was not zoned for "multiple dwelling use," therefore occupation of the building by more than one family was prohibited.

Review the remedies previously discussed. Do any appear to be appropriate? Consider this question only from the point of view of Fairbairne against Payeur. Don't get sidetracked into considering whether Fairbairne has a claim against any others, such as her lawyer or other agent.

In this case Payeur made a false statement, certainly with full knowledge of her misrepresentation, which Fairbairne relied on and which most likely was made to induce Fairbairne to contract. This type of conduct amounts to a breach of the element of genuine intention required to make an agreement valid. Fairbairne, as the victim of the fraud, has the option to demand recision of the contract. In other words, Fairbairne has the legal right to insist that Payeur return the purchase price and take back the title to the building with all its headaches.

In addition to being able to reverse the transaction completely, Fairbairne is also entitled to an award of damages for breach of contract, which should result in a judgment of the court against Payeur to pay money damages equivalent to the expenses incurred by Fairbairne in taking over the property.

Remember, however, that in order to preserve rights of recision, people in Fairbairne's position have a duty to advise the other side immediately on discovery of the breach that they intend to seek this remedy; otherwise, a delay in advising the other party may prevent the raising of a claim for recision on technical legal grounds.

You should by now be aware that there is a certain element of risk in making any contract. Some people find it easy to be fraudulent when it suits their purposes and others can be incredibly stupid or incompetent in the handling of their business affairs. At times people may be forced by circumstances beyond their control to breach a contract; the apparent honesty of such persons is therefore no guarantee that they will be able to live up to their promises. It is the responsibility of the contracting parties to try to minimize this element of risk by anticipating what action the other party is likely to take. If they can predict what pressures may force the other party to breach the contract, they can include appropriate safeguards in the contract. They can then reasonably expect adequate compensation in court should a breach occur. Bear in mind that if the consequences of breach are nominal, others will find it easier to commit a breach against your contract.

So far our discussion of breach of contract has been based on the assumption that the matter is taken to court to collect damages or obtain some other remedy. There are, however, practical considerations, particularly in terms of business practice, that may make it advisable not to go to court. In some cases it is a custom to permit customers to cancel even though technically they are bound by a contract to accept the goods ordered and may be liable to pay damages for breach. In fact, in certain cases it will be poor business to insist on all of your legal rights. It is important to bear this in mind when instructing your lawyers on your contract business. Your lawyers may not always know how you feel about enforcing contract rights and they may not be fully aware of the custom of your trade in these matters. They must know, however, what action you would be willing to take in the event of a breach of contract before they can effectively advise you what ought to be put into a formal commercial contract or provide you with an opinion as to how well a contract will protect you.

It may be, then, that you have no intention of going to court when your contract is breached. But you will still find that a contract has its uses. Even if other parties know that you are not likely to go to court, they will be reluctant to show bad faith and injure their reputations by breaching a formal contract. The contract will also serve to identify the terms of the agreement clearly enough to prevent misunderstandings. The important thing is to understand just what you can expect the contract to do for you. Don't fall into a trap by over-estimating its true usefulness.

KEY TO YOU ARE THE JURY

OTTENBRITE v. SIPPI   The main issue in this case is whether or not Laura Ottenbrite breached a condition of the contract. One condition of the contract was that Laura undertook not to compete with Sippi for a specified time and within a specified area. By opening a rival salon across the street only six months later, she clearly acted in breach of that condition.

Most likely mere money damages would not give Sippi adequate compensation because the continued presence of Laura's salon would affect her business. In fact it would be shocking if Laura were able to ignore her own negative covenant by paying what would amount to a "fine." Sippi has a good claim for an action in injunction whereby a court will forbid Ottenbrite to compete with Sippi for the term and in the area specified in the contract.

Checklist: Remedies on breach of contract

The step-by-step activities to ensure proper remedy available in event other party defaults or breaches contract are:

1. Review steps required to create a legally binding contract (see Unit Two).

2. Express all essential terms of the contract in a written statement signed by the parties.

3. Include details and exact amount of interest expected to be recovered, particularly in event of delay.

4. Clearly define the purpose of contract to other party from your point of view and identify all consequences that can reasonably be anticipated by a breach, including significance of transaction, special circumstances, loss of profit and necessary background to be certain other party appreciates gravity of consequences in event of failure.

5. Document information regarding consequences in form of letter or memorandum. Sign. Send copy to other party. Retain copy for your files.

6. On becoming aware of breach, consider necessity of contacting lawyer for advice immediately.

7. Contact other party. Make it clear you are ready, willing and able to complete your part of bargain. Advise you expect compliance. Re-affirm consequences. Document conversation in writing and send to other party. Retain copy for your records.

8. Review and analyze nature of breach; essential term (condition); warranty; minor term.

9. Consider remedies available; damages; specific performance.

10. Notify other party of remedy you intend to seek. Document. Send to other party; retain copy for your files. Be particularly prompt if specific performance or injunction an appropriate choice.

11. If replevin appropriate, instruct lawyer to take steps to obtain immediate possession of property through sheriff or court officer.

12. Begin to document loss damages. Document as you go along.

13. Take steps to avoid or lessen loss by selfhelp. Follow reasonable course of action to mitigate damages.

14. If necessary to advise other party of intention to rescind, this must be done as soon as possible after you are aware of facts amounting to breach by other party in order to avoid defence of other party on legal grounds of delay. Document. Send writing to other party. Retain copy for your files.

15. Continue to establish loss. Document fully.

16. Keep lawyer advised on an ongoing basis if possibility of law suit. Retain lawyer as soon as possible, but do not abdicate your responsibility to make decisions and take appropriate steps required.

Review

What progress have we now made? We have had the unique opportunity to examine many cases that have come before the courts. We should have developed by now a feel for an effective approach to legal problems. If this has in fact happened, it is an important accomplishment because they are different from any other problem in business. Have we been able to take the first step by identifying the legal problem? If so, in some cases we have found it an easy matter; in others we may have found it difficult to separate important, urgent facts and problems from those of trivial value. Have we been able to take the next step by establishing a main issue to identify the questions that must be answered to find a solution to the problem? We should have discovered that this step has helped to sort out alternatives available for evaluation. Through the use of the resource material provided by this book, have we been able to list legal rules available as guides? Have we found, once having done this, that we have been able to apply the law to the facts to assist us in making appropriate choices of action leading to proper legal remedies? If we have been able to develop this systematic approach stand up and cheer, for we have found that situations that have appeared at first to be hopelessly complicated are not really so hard to deal with when put under the disciplined microscope of "the system."

1. List the four elements that must be proven in an action for damages arising out of a breach of a material term.

2. TURNER v. STINSON Turner developed a highly secret process which will enable him to produce a device which will be superior but less expensive than similar devices now known. He secured contracts with several large companies to market his device and went to a great expense to retool his operation for production. At the same time, Turner ordered from Stinson, a manufacturer, a plastic component part. Stinson received instructions to produce the ordinary-looking part by a specific date. Later, Stinson realized he had overextended himself and decided to cut back on his operation. Stinson advised Turner he could not provide him with the part. Turner was unable to find an alternate source of supply and lost several of the lucrative contracts he had arranged. Could Turner sue Stinson for damages? Could he claim the loss of cancelled sales as damages?

3. BARBER v. FIELDS Barber decided to forsake city life for a life in the country. Fields offered to transfer title to 300 acres of land in return for 5 years' work. Barber was to receive a small allowance, food and living quarters. Barber accepted and after working three years was advised by Fields that he intended to convey title to only 200 acres because of the rapid rise in land prices. Barber quit, returned to the city and sued Fields for three years' wages. Would Barber succeed?

4. BLAKEY v. WATTS Blakey discovered an original Picasso drawing in the attic of an old theatre he had purchased. Blakey accepted an offer to purchase from a collector, Watts. Both knew the drawing was a Picasso, but it was only after the contract was made that Blakey realized the drawing was worth much more than he had thought. Blakey now refuses to deliver the drawing. What is the most appropriate remedy, if any, available to Watts? Give reasons.

CHAPTER 4

Sale of Goods

Unit I The sale of goods contract

YOU ARE THE JURY

KOHAL v. McDONALD

Kohal sold a car to McDonald, who paid a deposit of $100 and agreed to pay the balance when the bank opened on Monday morning. Kohal signed the ownership permit over and delivered the car to McDonald, who broke her promise to pay as agreed. McDonald refused to return the car saying, "Sue me." What are Kohal's rights?

OBJECTIVES

* to define a sale of goods.
* to define the requirements for making binding enforceable sale of goods contracts.
* to be able to identify conditions of sale contracts and consequences of breach of a condition therein.
* to be able to identify warranties as terms of sales contracts and consequences of breach of warranty.

LEXICON

Caveat Emptor   Let the buyer beware. Legal rule placing a duty on buyers to take reasonable care to inspect goods before purchasing and make certain that they are reasonably fit for the intended use.

Conditions   Essential terms in sales identifying the main purpose of the contract; they are so essential that a breach thereof will lead to the remedy of recision entitling the injured party to be put back to the same position as before the contract.

Delivery   The voluntary transfer of the possession of goods from the seller to the buyer.

Warranty   A term in a sale contract collateral to the main purpose, the breach of which gives rise to a claim for damages but not the right to rescind the contract or reject the goods.

A sale of goods contract is one in which a seller transfers or agrees to transfer the property in goods to a buyer for a price, which always consists of money consideration. This branch of the law represents the most important and often most misunderstood area of Canadian business. We live in an age of consumption in which we all buy goods in greater quantities than ever before in our history. Sellers are faced with problems arising from dealings with dishonest purchasers who refuse to take delivery or pay as agreed or who fail to keep other undertakings without apparent shame or concern for the consequences.

The consumer purchases goods from large corporate outlets which may have head offices in distant cities and rarely comes into contact with an owner/seller. Our purchases have become increasingly impersonal. At the same time we appear to have more legitimate complaints over the servicability and quality of purchased goods.

The combination of experiences listed above, coupled with recent Canadian legislation designed to protect the consumer, have resulted in a rash of cases before the courts in the last few years. Actions arising out of disputed sales issues are now the most common civil matter handled by Canadian judges. It is therefore most important for you to be able to identify and use the rules relating to sale of goods.

Note that for the sake of consistency all references in this chapter are made to the Ontario *Sale of Goods Act*. However, all the provincial *Sale of Goods Acts* are similarly worded, and by using the conversion table on page 000, you will be able to find the corresponding section number of your own province's Act.

How to approach sale of goods issues

The subject of sale of goods must be approached carefully. Sale of goods is a specialized branch of contract law. Therefore, you will need to master the principles set out in Chapter Three. These should be reviewed again and again until they become second nature to you. They will be useful only if you are able to use them by immediate recall in a variety of circumstances.

Secondly, you must remember that the law relating to the sale of goods is regulated in each province by a statute entitled the *Sale of Goods Act* (except in Quebec which embodies its written rules in the Civil Code of Quebec). You will find it necessary to think in the context of a narrow group of rules that may apply only to sale of goods activities. The rules as set out here are so specialized that I must caution you not to attempt to apply the principles in this part to other branches of the law such as real property (real estate), contracts for services or insurance. We have been dealing so far with common law problems; now we examine laws as they are formally enacted in written form by provincial governments. Once the law is set out in the form of a statute, the courts interpret wording strictly. The statutes themselves are designed to be inflexible, giving those who need to relate the law to any particular set of facts a solid guide to follow.

Thirdly, the key to the sale of goods lies in the transfer of title to or ownership of goods from one person to another. In this regard we must also consider aspects of the law of property.

Fourthly, it will be essential to determine the legal duties of sellers on the one hand and of buyers on the other in order to appreciate what effect certain conduct would have on the sale of goods transaction. In doing so, it is important to recognize the two essential types of terms which make up every sales contract. These are identified as *conditions* and *warranties*.

Fifthly, we must be able to identify the types of remedies that are available to a party to a sales contract: to correct for defective goods, compel the other party to comply with the terms of the contract, and in serious cases to allow a party to repudiate the contract altogether.

The sale of goods is a complicated subject and it is essential to approach it in a disciplined, logical way; otherwise you may look forward to becoming enmeshed in a hopeless morass of conflicting facts, red-herrings, false assumptions, and misleading arguments. As a first step, it may be useful to review the five points listed above. They form the basis of the following list of questions which you should always ask yourself when faced with an issue involving the sale of goods.

1. Which of the five essential elements of a general contract are most pertinent to this issue?
2. Is this a sale within the meaning of the *Sale of Goods Act* in my province (or the Quebec Civil Code)?
3. Are goods the subject matter of this transaction?
4. If the answers to 2 and 3 are Yes, then the *Sale of Goods Act* applies. Which section(s) of the Act relate to this transaction?
5. What legal duties of the buyer and/or the seller are relevant?
6. Can the relevant term of the sale contract be identified as either a condition or a warranty?
7. What remedies are available to each of the parties?

The object in asking these questions is to identify the rules and anticipate the problems that are likely to arise in a sales transaction. In this way you will train yourself to be aware of the disputes that may occur, and to identify those risks that you may be prepared to run and those that you will want to avoid at all costs.

The Sale of Goods Acts

Each province has codified the law of sale of goods into a statute that applies only to sales transactions in which the property in goods or chattels is intended to be passed to a buyer for a money consideration called the "price." The code for your province will be found in a statute known as the *Sale of Goods Act* (if you live or do business in Quebec the law is codified there as part of the Civil Code of Quebec).

The Acts and the units of this chapter, then, deal only where the transaction is a sale as defined in the first paragraph of this unit. Therefore, in order for the law of sales to apply the intent of the transaction must be to pass title from a seller to a buyer.

The consideration moving from the purchaser must be expressed in money or be capable of being expressed in terms of money without changing the intentions of the parties. Otherwise there is no sale and the sale of goods rules cannot apply. For example, it is possible to enter into a barter transaction in which goods are exchanged for other goods. Since the consideration moving from the buyer is not in the form of cash, the sale of goods rules do not apply to the barter system. Nor may we apply sale of goods rules to such common commercial transactions as consignment, in which only possession is transferred to the consignee (the person who ultimately disposes of the goods or sells them to third parties). In consignment the owner retains ownership and title to the goods until they are finally sold. See Unit Four for a detailed analysis of consignment.

The *Sale of Goods Acts* apply only where the subject matter of the contract is to be "goods" within the meaning of the Acts. Goods are defined as "all chattels personal," which include items such as clothing, furniture, equipment, trucks, appliances, and similar tangible, movable property. The Acts also include as "goods" industrial growing crops. The Acts specifically exclude property in the form of personal rights attached to items such as shares, bonds, bills of exchange, promissory notes, and money.

Avoid the trap of attempting to apply any of the special rules relating to sale of goods to anything that does not fall under the legal definition of goods. To give some further examples, you cannot apply them to problems arising out of real estate transactions, or to contracts involving personal services, i.e., carpentry services in which a workman installs cupboards, or the services of a photographer or painter commissioned for a portrait.

There are two fundamental concepts we must remember. They are the need to recognize the right of contracting individuals to establish their own rules and working relationships; and the need to define the serious consequences that flow from "ownership of goods."

The provincial Acts do not attempt to formulate any new law. They are simply intended to restate the law as it is known through court decisions and custom in one convenient written document passed by the authority of government. While the *Sale of Goods Acts* list rights, duties and liabilities, they acknowledge the right of contracting parties to negate or vary them by express agreement, or through understandings developed between the parties in the course of business over a period of years or as a result of the custom established in their trade. We might well ask, "What, then, do these Acts actually do? How are they applied to disputes?" What happens is that if the parties have made their own rules (and they are not unlawful in themselves) then they will permit settlement of differences according to ordinary contract law; but if the parties are silent on a point, having failed to express any definite intention, then the rule set out in the Acts will be used as a guide and settlement of differences will have to be made by applying the rules stated in the Acts themselves.

For example, section 53 of the Ontario Act allows parties to sales contracts to incorporate exclusionary clauses which will establish the rules for sale. These clauses are generally referred to as the "fine print." A vendor may insert a clause specifying that, "There are no representations, conditions or warranties which affect this contract except those in writing herein." By such a clause the vendor intends to avoid the conditions and warranties implied by the *Sale of Goods Act* and those limiting liability. Section 18 of the Act gives the parties to a sales contract the freedom to dictate the exact moment when title will pass. The Acts democratically give business people the first opportunity to settle on the precise terms of their sale of goods contracts. If they fail to do so, the implied terms contained in the Acts will be used by the courts to assist in the settlement of disputes.

Now we come to the concept of transfer of ownership. The general rule is that "Risk Follows Title." The main purpose of a sale of goods contract is to transfer legal title from one person to another. As we shall see, at stages of the contract the title is vested first in one and then in the other. It is sometimes difficult during the course of many transactions to be able to quickly and with certainty identify the real owner at any given moment. Such is the complexity of commercial sales.

How to make a sale of goods contract

A contract of sale may be made in writing or by word of mouth or partly in writing and partly by word or mouth, or it may be implied by the conduct of the parties.

It is advisable for parties always to set out the terms of their contracts in writing and in doing so take advantage of the right to contract out of the *Sale of Goods Acts* with all their technicalities by clearly expressing their intentions on each important step. It is clear, however, that even if only part of the contract has been put in writing, we are free to treat oral statements as part of the transaction. What was said, then, in the process of making the contract may well be as important as what has been written. There is misconception that oral contracts are invalid and unenforceable. In some areas of law oral contracts are not permitted, it is true, but this is the exception rather than the rule and we must think in terms of the validity of the spoken parts of the contract for sale of goods. You should also remember that the conduct and actions of the parties may be considered in attempting to reconstruct a contract or interpret what the parties intended to happen.

Section 4 of the Ontario Act makes it clear that a contract for sale of goods may be made entirely of spoken words (though this is subject to the other rules of the Act which we will consider in this unit).

Enforceability of sales contracts

Most sales contracts that meet the specifications set out in the above paragraphs will be enforceable in Canadian courts, but not all. Which contracts are enforceable? Which are not? The position is that the *Sale of Goods Acts* will not enforce sales contracts where there is little evidence of the actual terms of the contract. Thus, the Acts of each province prohibit enforcement of sales contracts unless:

1. the buyer has accepted part of the goods and actually received at least part of them; or
2. the buyer has made a part payment or has given a deposit to bind the transaction; or

3. there is some note or memorandum of the contract in writing which has been signed by the party to be "charged."

Note that only *one* of these conditions need be present in order for the contract to be enforceable by court action. In other words, the contract will not be enforceable only if *all three* conditions are absent. The key section to examine is section 5 of the Ontario Act. (See the Conversion Table for the equivalent section in the Acts of other provinces.)

CASE 1   CREMA v. GOLD

Crema manufactured and sold fine furniture. He had in stock an expensive dining-room suite, consisting of table, chairs and hutch. Gold agreed to purchase the suite if Crema would make some minor modifications to a design in the middle of the table and on the back of the chairs. At first Crema refused, saying, "It will absolutely ruin them," but after Gold had drawn some sketches of what she wanted, he agreed. They renegotiated the price to cover the additional work. When the design work was completed, Crema called Gold.

When she saw the furniture Gold said, "You were right all along, Crema, the furniture is ruined," whereupon she told the cabinetmaker that she did not want any of the furnishings. Nevertheless, on the advice of his lawyer, Crema deposited all of the furniture in Gold's garage later that day without her knowledge or consent. Crema's lawyer recommends court action if Gold refuses to pay. Gold's advises her not to pay.

Gold's defence to any claim by Crema is that since furniture is goods within the meaning of the *Sale of Goods Act* and since she intended to pay cash, the transaction was a sale; hence the Act would apply and not the general law of contract. Her defence under Section 5 of the Ontario Act (and under equivalent sections in the other provinces) is that the contract cannot be enforced in court since she signed nothing, paid no deposit, and did not accept the goods. If Crema is to succeed at all, it will be on the grounds that Gold's actions throughout were consistent only with the fact that she recognized she had made a binding contract, and that she had in fact by her conduct prior to the last meeting "accepted" the goods in a legal sense.

This case illustrates the difficulties that can arise when common words such as "acceptance" are given special meaning by definitions set out in the Acts. When this is done, the words or phrases are said to be "terms of art" and must be understood as having the special meaning given by the Act. In this case, Section 5 of the Ontario Act defines the word "acceptance" as follows:

S 5 (3). There is an acceptance of goods within the meaning of this section when the buyer *does any act in relation to the goods that recognizes a pre-existing contract of sale. . .*

Gold's actions directing the carving of a special design can only be interpreted as recognition of a sales contract enforceable through court action. The designs, while not technically a writing, would be admissible to show how closely she or-

chestrated the work and that she consented to it being done. Crema would succeed.

It must be noted here that Gold's defence is not that there was no contract; she simply asserts that the requirements of the Act were not met and that therefore the courts cannot enforce the contract. If they can't, then Crema has no effective remedy and Gold wins. Another way of expressing her argument would be to say that what was otherwise a valid sales contract is not legally binding because it failed to meet the requirements established by Section 5 of the Act.

You should note that contracts for small amounts of money (less than $40 in Ontario; similar sums in other provinces) are exempt from these technical demands and they are accordingly enforceable if otherwise legally binding.

Sale of goods: Conversion table

References in the text are to the section numbers in the Ontario *Sale of Goods Act*.
This conversion table gives the corresponding section number of the other Acts in force in Canada.

ALTA	B.C.	MAN	N.B.	NFLD	N.S.	ONT	P.E.I	SASK	YUK	NWT
2	2	2	1	60	1	1	1	2	2	2
6	10	5	4	4	5	4	5	5	5	5
7		6	5	5	6	5	6	6	6	6
15	18	14	13	13	14	13	14	14	14	14
17	20	16	15	15	16	15	16	16	16	16
20	23	19	18	18	19	18	19	19	19	19
21	24	20	19	19	20	19	20	20	20	20
28	32	29	25	26	28	26	27	27	26	27
30	34	31	27	30	30	28	29	29	28	28
31	35	32	28	31	31	29	30	30	29	29
32	36	33	29	32	32	30	31	31	30	30
33	37	34	30	33	33	31	32	32	31	31
37	41	38	34	37	37	35	36	36	35	35
38	42	39	35	38	38	36	37	37	36	36
39	43	40	36	39	39	37	38	38	37	37
40	44	41	37	40	40	38	39	39	38	38
41	45	42	38	41	41	39	41	40	39	39
43	47	44	40	43	43	41	43	42	41	41
44	48	45	41	44	44	42	44	43	42	42
45	49	46	42	45	45	43	45	44	43	43
46	50	47	43	46	46	44	46	45	44	44
49	53	50	46	49	47	47	49	48	47	47
50	54	51	47	50	50	48	50	49	48	48
55	69	56	52	55	55	53	55	54	53	53
56	70	57	53	56	56	54	56	55	54	54

Note: The Quebec Law of Sale is similar, but is incorporated into the Civil Code of Quebec.

Essential terms of sales contracts

All sales contracts can be divided into two types of terms. One consists of those statements which are intended as contractual promises; these are called *conditions*. The other type consists of statements (or representations) which are designed only to influence the purchaser to buy; these are called *warranties*. One could say, in fact, that contracts are really just bundles of conditions and warranties. If we are ever to understand the true nature of sales contracts, we must take them apart and isolate the various conditions and warranties they contain.

In attempting to determine which terms are conditions and which are warranties, you must bear in mind that each contract stands on its own facts. Even when dealing with preprinted "standard" commercial contracts, you must train yourself to think of "this contract" as though it were individually drafted by the parties. Your best approach is to put yourself in the shoes of the parties concerned so as to identify their actual intentions. Did they intend this part to be a condition? Does this term amount to a contractual promise to be treated as though it were a condition? Should a certain term be listed as a warranty because it is obvious it could only have been intended as an inducement to the buyer to deal? This should prove to be a simple procedure to adopt and follow. You need only analyze the words used in the contract and observe the conduct of the parties. The only difficulty you will encounter will be when the parties have failed to express their intentions clearly or when the situation is otherwise too murky to permit you to come to logical conclusions. In these cases, the provincial *Sale of Goods Acts* come to the rescue by listing and identifying *implied conditions and warranties*. These are presumed to exist in every contract in which the parties have failed to express their intentions either through words or actions.

Your task, then, in distinguishing between conditions and warranties is first to look for the expressed intentions of the parties and then, if this is not helpful, to look at the Act for the implied rule to apply. Why follow this procedure at all? The answer will be found in the paragraphs below in which conditions and warranties are discussed in detail.

Conditions

In the law of the sale of goods, a *condition* is a technical expression used to identify a vital term, the breach of which will give the injured party the right to treat the contract as repudiated. Conditions are contractual promises which are so essential and fundamental that if they are not honoured, any reasonable, prudent person would immediately treat the contract as broken and seek recision as the appropriate remedy. (As you will recall, the effect of recision is to put the injured party back into the same position as before the contract was made.)

Lawyers think of conditions as "going to the root of the contract." This will be a useful analogy for us to consider. Any gardener knows that if you pull a weed entirely from the ground, it has been effectively destroyed. If you simply snap it off above the ground it will grow again. Examples of implied conditions in sales of goods are in the following paragraphs.

The right to sell

In every contract for sale, the seller gives the purchaser the legal right to transfer the title to goods to the purchaser. This undertaking amounts to a condition and if a seller does not have the title to the goods, a condition of the contract has been breached. The buyer may then treat the contract as broken, reject the goods, and either collect back the purchase price or refuse to pay for them.

CASE 2 MOONEY v. DOWKER

Dowker purchased a used car from Mooney, a Canadian retail car dealer. Several months later, an RCMP officer seized the car from Dowker, advising that the car had been identified as one illegally imported into Canada by one Charrelle. Under the *Customs Act of Canada* the car was absolutely forfeited to the Federal Government. Dowker demanded the return of his purchase price, but Mooney declined, arguing, "Look I dealt with the Charrelle for years. Never had trouble. I had no idea! I gave no guarantees. Here's the contract. Show me why I should lose."

In this case Mooney gave no written or oral representations or promises upon which Dowker could rely and Mooney was telling the truth when he described himself as innocent and having no knowledge of Charrelle's smuggling activities. What should Dowker do? He must first look to the contract. He will find no express condition or warranty which would lead him to an appropriate remedy. He now must take one further step: examine the *Sale of Goods Act* for his province. In doing so, he will find the rule that will assist him. All of the *Sale of Goods Acts* provide that:

In a contract of sale, unless the circumstances of the contract are such as to show a different intention, there is an implied condition on the part of the seller that in case of a sale he has a right to sell the goods.

Therefore the Act incorporates into the Dowker contract an implied condition that Mooney had the legal right to pass title to the car on to the purchaser. He was not able to perform this contractual promise; therefore he was in breach of a condition. The remedy available to the purchaser is to treat the contract as broken, claim recision, and demand to be put back into the same position as before the contract was formed. So Mooney must return the purchase price to Dowker. Of course Mooney will have a claim against Charrelle on the basis of a similar argument applied to the contract he made with Charrelle.

This case also serves to illustrate a point made in Chapter One, that we do not always have the villain of the piece before us. At times, we have two "innocent" parties and the legal process must be used to determine which of the two is "less innocent" in order to provide a remedy.

The duty to deliver

The seller has a duty to deliver the goods and this duty amounts to a condition.

Delivery means the voluntary transfer of possession from one person to another. It is the seller's duty to deliver the correct quantity of goods, of the right quality, to or at a place specified in the contract or determined by operation of law or custom, and to make delivery within a certain time limit.

CASE 3   FELKER v. DISNEY DRUGSTORES LTD.

Ronald Disney, an associate in a retail drug store chain signed a contract to purchase "100 Felker Model B units at $200 each unit to be delivered on or about December 1st, this year." After discussion with his associate, Ronald realized that he had made an incredible blunder which would lead to substantial loss for his business. The shipment from Felker arrived on the 2nd day of December and was made up of 102 Model A items packed in bundles of three. Ronald noticed that he had been billed for only 100 units at the price of the B units even though the A units were of better quality than those ordered. In an attempt to get out of a bad deal at the last moment, Ronald called the company lawyer before signing for and accepting

the shipment. On the advice of the lawyer, Ronald refused delivery. Felker immediately advised that he intended to sue.

A seller who has contracted to send goods to a buyer must send the right quantity ordered if he is to fulfill his part of the contract. If he sends the wrong quantity, he breaches a condition of the contract and the purchaser is entitled to treat the contract as broken, reject the goods, and refuse to pay (or, if any payment has been made, to recover the money paid). Thus, since the Felker company delivered the wrong quantity, it was in breach of its condition to deliver. Felker can't instruct Disney to return two units and pay for the rest; nor can it take the position that it didn't charge for the two extra units. Felker can't insist that Disney keep the excess as a gift; nor would Felker have been in any better position if it had sent 99 units and amended its billing to charge for one less unit than the quantity ordered. Felker's shipper has made a fundamental error which has resulted in breach of a condition.

The seller is also required to deliver the right quality of goods where the goods are ordered by description or as a certain type or model. If a seller fails to deliver the right quality, a condition of contract is broken and the purchaser is entitled to treat the contract as broken, reject the goods, and refuse to pay the purchase price. Therefore, it is clear that Felker was also in breach of contract since the goods shipped were of higher quality than those ordered. The rule is clear that the goods must be of the right quality, and the seller who substitutes because of his own inventory limitations at the time does so at his own risk.

If the seller delivers the wrong quantity or quality of goods, it is not open to him to argue "mistake" and promise to remedy the situation by a fresh delivery, since the breach has already occurred. Once a contract condition has been broken, the contract itself is no longer in existence.

Of course a purchaser has the option of taking the goods even if they are not in the proper quantity or of the right quality, but in doing so he is making an entirely new contract: the seller's delivery represents an offer which the purchaser accepts by taking the goods.

Note that the right quality rule applies only to contracts in which the goods are identified by description, model or sample. Many sale contracts do not specifically identify the goods in these ways. The ordinary rule as to quality is dealt with under the heading "Caveat emptor." When dealing with quality matters we should also review *caveat emptor* (buyer beware) principles to develop a complete picture. On the other hand, the rule relating to quantity will apply to all sales contracts.

The time of delivery

The seller has a duty to deliver on the date specified in the contract, if the parties have agreed to such a date. Time is then said to be "of the essence." If no time is specified, the seller must still deliver within a reasonable time. What is a reasonable time will depend on the commodity to be shipped and the surrounding circumstances.

The duty to deliver on time is a *condition* of the contract. If the time is fixed, then failure to deliver at that time will be a breach of condition which will permit the purchaser to refuse delivery.

In cases where the seller foresees difficulties in making delivery, he will protect himself by inserting in the contract a clause that he will use "best efforts" to deliver by a certain date. If in spite of such efforts the seller is unable to deliver on time, he must still deliver the goods within a "reasonable time" of the contemplated date; otherwise he will be in breach of his term of delivery condition, which will enable the buyer to repudiate the contract. The buyer may reject the goods even though no damage will be caused by the delay.

If the sales contract requires delivery by installments to be paid for by the buyer on the delivery of each shipment, and the seller fails to deliver an installment on time or within a reasonable time, then the buyer may be able to repudiate the entire contract and refuse to take delivery of all future shipments. The same remedy is open to the seller, so that in the event that it is the buyer who defaults by a refusal or neglect to pay for a shipment as agreed, the seller may treat the contract as broken and may advise the buyer that no further installments will be sent. The *Sale of Goods Acts* of each province, however, specify that in order for either the seller or the buyer to elect to take such drastic remedial action, the injured party must be reasonably satisfied that the default of the other is evidence of a fundamental breach of contract and that it is one which on the balance of probabilities is likely to be repeated.

Fitness of goods for buyer's purpose

A buyer who wishes to use goods for a particular purpose not ordinarily within the knowledge of the seller must set out such use clearly along with the purchase order if he wishes to hold the seller liable in the event the goods prove unfit for the intended use. Buyers who require unusually high standards (above trade norms) must bring their needs to the attention of the seller if they expect to have a remedy should the goods delivered fail to meet their requirements. These words of caution are necessary because the general rule is that there are no implied conditions or warranties that any goods supplied under a sales contract will be fit for any particular purpose.

The general rule is *caveat emptor* (let the buyer beware). In effect this means that all a seller has to do is supply goods of a type normally used without regard for the particular needs or standards of the individual buyer. *Caveat emptor* means that the buyer must take reasonable precautions in purchasing goods to make certain that they will suit his needs and meet the standards required. In doing so he must rely on his own judgment, and if the goods are not fit for his purpose, he has no-one to blame but himself. The seller will have a good defence under *caveat emptor*.

The *caveat emptor* rule is a sensible one when specific items are being purchased and the buyer has an opportunity to examine them. It is less satisfactory when the purchase consists of items in bulk or when the buyer does not have an opportunity to examine the goods properly. An investigation of Canadian cases also shows that the rule is not at all rigid and court decisions tend to vary from case to case. Therefore, it is best to avoid situations to which the rule could apply. Buyers may do this in two ways.

First, include in the contract a statement clearly setting out the exact specifications as to quality and describing any use for the goods which may differ from the normal uses of such goods. In this way the contract will provide evidence of an express intention by the buyer and the statement will be part of the contract. If the goods do not meet the specifications or suit the intended use, the seller has breached a condition and the goods can be rejected. *Caveat emptor* cannot be applied in these circumstances.

Secondly, take advantage of a provision of the *Sale of Goods Act* which identifies the following rule:

Where the buyer, expressly or by implication, makes known to the seller the particular purpose for which the goods are required so as to show that the buyer relies on the seller's skill or judgment, and the goods are of a description that it is in the course of the seller's business to supply (whether he is the manufacturer or not), there is an implied condition that the goods will be reasonably fit for the purpose, but in the case of a contract for the sale of a specified article under its patent or other trade name there is no implied condition as to its fitness for any particular purpose. (Ontario, Section 15 (1). See the Conversion Table for the applicable section in your province.)

CASE 4 VENUS ELECTRIC LTD. v. BREVEL PRODUCTS LTD.

Venus assembled hairdryers for sale to Simpsons-Sears Limited. Brevel manufactured and supplied the motors for the hairdryers. The motors supplied were not defective and would have worked satisfactorily had not Venus made some modifications to its dryers that rendered the motors incompatible with the plastic housing and fan its machines used. Simpsons returned unsold dryers as a result of customer complaints that the dryers did not work. It was found that the motors caused the units to crack and the type of oil used in them badly damaged the fans. Venus sued Brevel, relying on the implied condition in the Act. What do you think was the result?

CASE 5 SUTHERLAND v. MURRAY

Sutherland told Murray, a car dealer, that he wished to purchase a taxi suitable for trips over rough country roads. Murray assured him that a Bugatti car would meet his needs and showed him a Bugatti he had on the lot. Sutherland signed an order for an "eight-cylinder Bugatti." The Bugatti which was delivered to Sutherland was totally unsuitable for his taxi business. Sutherland brought the car back and demanded the return of his purchase price.

In this case Sutherland carefully outlined the special use to which the goods would be put in such a way that he showed that he relied on Murray's skill in making an appropriate choice. The Bugatti was a type of car usually carried by Murray in his business, therefore the implied condition as to fitness for purpose contained in the *Sale of Goods Act* applied. Murray had not supplied goods which were reasonably fit and was accordingly in breach of a condition. Sutherland was entitled to return the vehicle for a full refund of the purchase price.

In a similar case the court further held that the implied condition of fitness in the Act applied even though the goods were sold under their trade name. A buyer who relies on the skill and judgment of the seller to make a decision to supply goods which are reasonably fit for a named purpose has not bought goods under a trade name within the meaning of the exception contained in the last part of Section 15(1).

Warranties

Warranties are terms of a sales contract which are considered to be subordinate to the main purpose of the contract. The breach of a warranty gives the injured party the right to claim damages but not to reject the goods or to treat the contract as repudiated.

Time of payment

Payment of the purchase price and terms giving time for payment are warranties, not conditions. If the purchaser refuses to pay for delivered goods, the seller has only the right to sue for the price (damages) and not the right to claim recision and consequently the return of the goods.

CASE 6 TALBUT v. SQUIRE

A manufacturer, Talbut, contracted with Squire to manufacture and deliver a quantity of end tables. Under the terms of the contract, Squire was to pay for the goods within 30 days of delivery to her place of business. Talbut delivered the goods which Squire accepted and immediately placed in her store for resale. Squire failed to pay Talbut for the goods within the required time. Talbut made inquiries and discovered that Squire was in deep financial trouble and was believed to be liquidating her stock at an alarming rate at sales below cost. Talbut wishes to take steps to repossess the unsold end tables still in Squire's possession. Can Talbut get the goods back?

Quiet possession and freedom from encumbrances

It is an implied term of the contract of sale that the buyer will have quiet possession and enjoyment of the goods. In other words, once there has been a transfer of title, the buyer's right to possession will not be interfered with by the seller or anyone else. This term has the value of a warranty; therefore, if it is breached the buyer will have a remedy in damages but no right to repudiate the contract.

CASE 7 NIBLETT LTD. v. CMC LTD.

Niblett purchased canned goods from CMC. The labels bore a symbol that infringed the trade mark of a third company which successfully restrained Niblett from marketing the goods. Niblett's attempt to repudiate the contract with CMC failed. The labels were removed from the cans which were then sold at a substantial loss.

In this case the injury to Niblett arose out of an

interference with quiet possession and accordingly CMC was liable on a breach of warranty. Niblett could claim damages to compensate for the loss sustained by forced sale, but could not return the goods to CMC and demand repayment of the purchase price.

A further implied warranty is that the goods are free of any charge, lien or mortgage in favour of a third party, which was not revealed to the buyer at the time of making the sale contract.

CASE 8   WALKER v. HUNT

Walker purchased a used car from Hunt. Several days after delivery, the vehicle was seized by a bailiff acting on behalf of a bank claiming under a type of chattel mortgage which secured a loan. The bank advised Walker that he could have the car back on payment of $550 which was the balance owing to them. What is Walker's position?

A security such as a chattel mortgage is an encumbrance against the title to goods. Presumably Hunt did not disclose the existence of the encumbrance to Walker and was therefore in breach of an implied warranty that the goods were free of any charge or encumbrance in favour of a third party. Although Walker must pay the bank to obtain possession of the vehicle, he has the right to sue Hunt for damages equivalent to the loss.

Statements and representations

Statements that are intended to induce the buyer to purchase are express warranties for which the seller will be liable in damages if the statements prove incorrect or are materially misleading.

CASE 9   DUNSTER v. PICCOLO

Dunster purchased a quantity of cosmetics from Piccolo who assured her that there was a ready market for this type of goods. In fact none of the goods were marketable and Dunster learned later that Piccolo had been unable to sell the cosmetics until she came along.

Piccolo's statement amounted to a representation of fact made to induce the purchaser to buy, amounting to an express warranty which was breached providing Dunster with a remedy in damages but not the right to rescind.

This case is useful and deserves another look. The statement we examined was one of fact. Under other circumstances it is not hard to imagine Piccolo saying, "Well I thought there was a market. I guess it was just my opinion and I was

wrong." Statements of opinion, sales talk and puffing by the seller are not strong enough to be warranties. We must therefore be careful in identifying statements as such in order to be certain we include only statements of fact.

Dunster may well feel cheated by the law: there would be certain advantages to her if she were permitted to repudiate the contract entirely. But the law of sale of goods will not permit this. We said before that sales are one branch of contract and, if we just for a moment look over the fence into the contract patch, we might be able to identify another source of help for Dunster which will yield a more satisfactory remedy. If Piccolo's statement amounted to a false misrepresentation then that would affect the *genuine intention* of the agreement which in turn will provide Dunster with the right of recision. Under the general law of contract, this will permit her to repudiate the contract, give back the goods and receive back her purchase price. The advantages of this are that she can divest herself of the responsibility of storing the stock and taking steps to mitigate her damages. The lesson to be learned here is that you should never become so insular in your thinking that you box yourself into looking at only one branch of law for a solution. Look at as many topics of law as the number of subdivisions which arise from your problem.

KEY TO YOU ARE THE JURY

KOHAL v. McDONALD   The agreement was a sale of goods within the meaning of the law in the province in which the parties lived. Therefore the *Sale of Goods Act* applies. The purpose of a sales contract is to transfer title to the goods to the buyer. The delivery of the goods effectively transferred the ownership and McDonald became the owner of the car. Her undertaking to pay the balance at a specified time was a term of the contract. In failing to pay as agreed, McDonald breached a warranty. Kohal is entitled to sue for damages equivalent to the unpaid amount, but he is not entitled to repossess the car as he gave up his right to ownership by the delivery of the car under these circumstances.

Unit II Effects of the sale contract

YOU ARE THE JURY

SHAWE v. SHARPPE MOTORS INC.

Shawe agreed to buy a new car if Sharppe would install a heavy duty battery and upgrade the tires. The parties signed a contract in which Sharppe consented to the terms. Shawe paid the full purchase price and advised that she would return the following day for the vehicle. Sharppe performed the required work and returned the vehicle (which was particularly attractive) to the showroom. Early next morning an arsonist set fire to the building and the vehicle was damaged. Shawe demanded the return of her purchase price. Sharppe argued that he had done all he promised; they had a contract and he was entitled to keep her money. "Sue the guy who set the fire. I'm in no position to help you. In fact we took real good care of your car, putting it in the showroom and all." What is Shawe's position? Suppose that no valid insurance coverage exists.

OBJECTIVES

- to identify the rules which determine the point in time when property in goods is transferred from the seller to the buyer.
- to define terminology relating to the concept of title and delivery.
- to list rules which will determine whether or not a seller has legally delivered the goods to the buyer.

LEXICON

Deliverable State Goods are in a deliverable state when they are in such a condition that a buyer under the contract would be required to accept the goods. When the buyer requests something be done to the goods to put them in such condition, they are not in deliverable state until the thing is done.

Delivery A legal term used to describe the process by which the seller voluntarily transfers possession of goods to a buyer. The word must be strictly defined as outlined in this unit.

Sale on Approval A sale of goods in which the buyer receives physical possession of goods with authority to retain them or return them. Buyer has right to reject goods within certain time limitations.

Specific Goods Goods which have been actually selected as the subject matter of the contract as opposed to goods not yet manufactured or available.

Trustee in Bankruptcy An official representing interests of creditors generally with certain powers to seize or take into possession assets of debtors for the benefit of creditors.

We completed a study of the nature of sales contracts in Unit One of this chapter. In this unit we consider the two elements that contribute most to the need to give contracts of sale special treatment. The first is the need for title to pass from one person to another; and the second results from the restricted meaning given to the term *delivery*.

Title to goods

A sale of goods requires the transfer of property in, or title to, goods from the seller to the buyer. This is an important aspect of the transaction to keep in mind particularly in light of the rule that *Risk Follows Title*, which may be more clearly expressed as "he who is the legal owner at the moment of loss or damage must bear the loss."

The Act distinguishes between *specific* and *unascertained goods*. Specific goods are those goods which have been identified and agreed upon at the time of the making of the contract. They are the very goods that the seller must deliver. For example, in *Shawe v. Sharppe* the car chosen by Shawe is the one that must be delivered. No other will do. Not even a reasonable equivalent which is similar in every respect.

The Act provides that the title to specific goods is transferred to the buyer at such time as the parties to the contract intend it to be transferred (S18 Ontario). Therefore, during the course of a transaction we must pay particular attention to the statements and conduct of the parties which will reveal their intention with respect to ownership. If some event occurs which results in damage to or loss of the goods during the course of the contract, we must be able to ascertain whether the seller still has title or whether it has passed to the buyer in order to determine which will bear the loss and what remedies, if any, are open to the loser.

If the parties have expressed themselves well, this procedure will not be difficult. But what if they have not clearly stated their intentions, and no definite intention can be discovered from their conduct? In this case the Act provides rules for ascertaining the intention of the parties as to the passing of title.

Section 19 (Ontario). Unless a different intention appears, the following are rules for ascertaining the intention of the parties as to the time at which the property in the goods is to pass to the buyer.

Rule 1. Where there is an unconditional contract for the sale of specific goods in a deliverable state, the property in the goods passes to the buyer when the contract is made and it is immaterial whether the time of payment or the time of delivery or both is postponed.

CASE 10   ROWE v. BEDARD

Rowe examined a china cabinet on a showroom floor of Bedard's furniture store. Bedard told her that he would sell this one item at a reduced price if she would take it "as is." She agreed, paid for the cabinet and received a receipt marked "Paid in full. To take as is. Cabinet to be sent by Speedy tomorrow latest. Signed D. Bedard." The following day a trustee in bankruptcy took possession of all the store's assets on behalf of the creditors. The trustee refused to give up the cabinet. He would also not return the purchase price to Rowe.

Neither Rowe nor Bedard considered passing of title of great importance at the time of making the contract and no clear mention was made of when ownership would pass. We must look then to the Act for the rule. The goods were specific within the meaning of the Act. The contract was unconditional. Therefore Rule 1 applied, making Rowe the owner of the goods at the time the contract was made. As she, not Bedard, was the real owner the trustee had to give the cabinet to Rowe.

Both *Kohal v. McDonald* and *Shawe v. Sharppe* turn on similar facts. These cases appear in the You Are The Jury sections of Units One and Two of this chapter. Review both cases to see if we are now in a better position to resolve them. Does Rule 1 apply to either of them?

Rule 2. Where there is a contract for the sale of specific goods and the seller is bound to do something to the goods for the purpose of putting them into a deliverable state, the property does not pass until such thing is done and the buyer has notice thereof.

CASE 11   LAFRENTZ v. HOGAN

Hogan purchased twelve used typewriters from Lafrentz who was to clean them by a specified commercial process. Hogan arranged to have them transported to his store after the work was completed. The typewriters were stolen before Hogan had a chance to pick them up. Consider the issues.

Would it make any difference whether the equipment was stolen before or after the cleaning? If the cleaning job had been completed before the theft, was there something further Lafrentz should have done? Try to list the circumstances in which Hogan would not bear the loss.

Review *Shawe v. Sharppe* once more to see if Rule 2 is of assistance in resolving the dispute in that case.

Rule 3. Where there is a contract for the sale of specific goods in a deliverable state but the seller is bound to weigh, test or do some other act or thing with reference to the goods for the purpose of ascertaining the price, the property does not pass until such act or thing is done and the buyer has notice thereof.

CASE 12   WOLFE v. EIDELBERG

The parties were a furrier and a trapper. They agreed that pelts of a certain description on the trapper's premises at the time were to be purchased by the furrier, who agreed to pay a price based on a $15 a pelt. The trapper counted the pelts and prepared his bill; but before he notified the purchaser of the total price, the goods were stolen. Before title could pass the trapper was bound to establish the price by counting the pelts and to notify the purchaser. As the goods were stolen before this could be completed and as *risk follows title*, the trapper must bear the loss.

Rule 4. When goods are delivered to the buyer on approval or on "sale and return" or other similar terms the property therein passes to the buyer
(i) when he signifies his approval or acceptance to the seller or does any other act adopting the transaction;
(ii) if he does not signify his approval or acceptance to the seller but retains the goods without giving notice of rejection, then if a time has been fixed for the return of the goods, on the expiration of such time, and, if no time has been fixed, on the expiration of a reasonable time, and what is a reasonable time is a question of fact.

CASE 13   MENDLOWITZ v. FINLAYSON

Mendlowitz persuaded Finlayson to purchase a colour television set by saying, "Take it home. Try it. Listen, if you don't like it just let me know; we'll tear this contract up. Keep it a while." Finlayson signed the order and the set was delivered. The invoice was inadvertently misplaced and six months later Mendlowitz realized Finlayson had not paid for the set. He sent a bill whereupon Finlayson called saying, "I'm not

This is a sale of goods, therefore the Act applies. In particular it is a sale on approval within the meaning of Rule 4. The parties did not express themselves very well, so it will do no good to examine their conduct in order to discern their intention. However, we can identify relevant guidelines from the Act. Finlayson never did signify his approval in any unequivocal way: however he retained the goods without giving Mendlowitz any notice of rejection. Moreover, he kept them for over six months and the Act specifies that he must give some notice of rejection within a reasonable time; otherwise title will pass to him by default. The court held in this case that the customary time for approval in the appliance trade was one to two weeks and that Finlayson had retained the goods beyond a reasonable time and property in the set had passed to him. Finlayson paid.

Unascertained goods are dealt with in Rule 5 which reads as follows:

Rule 5.   Where there is a contract for the sale of unascertained or future goods by description and goods of that description in a deliverable state are unconditionally appropriated to the contract, either by the seller with the assent of the buyer or the buyer with the assent of the seller, the property in the goods thereupon passes to the buyer, and such assent may be either express or implied and may be given either before or after the appropriation.

Where there is a contract for the sale of unascertained goods the title cannot be transferred until sufficient steps are taken to assure that they are in a deliverable state and some act has been done that makes the goods specific. Unascertained goods may be goods identified only by description, or they may be goods to be manufactured or acquired by the seller. They may be a portion of the inventory in the seller's warehouse.

CASE 14   IN RE TOWERS

Perrin bought and paid for a quantity of barley and delivered to Towers sacks bearing the Perrin trade mark with instructions to fill them with the barley. Towers' workmen had filled half of the bags when work was halted by the sheriff of the county who seized the assets of Towers' business on behalf of certain judgment creditors. Perrin brought an action asking for a declaration identifying him as owner of the barley he had paid for. The court held that the barley which had in fact been placed in Perrin's sacks had been appropriated to the contract and those goods were now ascertained and specific, but that the remainder which had not yet been appropriated maintained the character of unascertained goods the title of which could not be passed. Perrin was declared owner of the barley in the sacks.

Delivery

Delivery as used in sales contracts is a term of art and does not have the same meaning as it does in ordinary usage. The Act defines delivery as the "voluntary transfer of possession" from one person to another. It is the duty of the seller to deliver the goods. The Act does not define what is meant by possession so it will be our task to determine what actions taken by the seller will amount to a transfer of possession to the buyer. This will not be an easy matter because the legal definition of the word "possession" is notoriously complex. The following rules should serve to adequately explain that delivery in law does not always require a seller to move goods, pick them up, ship or send them on to the buyer.

Unconditional contract

In an unconditional contract for the sale of specific goods, the title passes to the buyer at the time the contract is made. The duty of the seller to deliver is to make the goods available at the seller's place of business for the buyer to collect. In the *Rowe v. Bedard* case the seller completed the responsibility to deliver on making the contract by having them available at his premises. While the seller retained physical possession of the goods, he held them as a trustee or bailee for the new owner, Rowe. This is the general rule for delivery.

Goods in warehouse of a third party

In a sale of goods which are at the time housed in the warehouse of a third party, title passes and delivery is complete as soon as the seller advises the warehouseman of the sale and the warehouseman in return advises the buyer that the goods are held at the warehouse on the buyer's behalf. The seller bears the risk of loss up to the point these things are done. Thereafter the buyer bears the risk. Notice that in both situations delivery in law is effected without any physical movement of

the goods and without them being actually deposited with the buyer.

Delivery by custom

By their conduct over the years, certain businesses have established rules for delivery. Companies such as Eaton's, Simpson's and The Bay, which operate partly as order houses, agree as part of the contract of sale to transport the goods directly to a customer's home. In such cases delivery must mean the physical transportation of the goods to the place designated by the buyer. This is a rule established by usage or custom.

Express term in contract

The parties may themselves place their own interpretation on the meaning of delivery by spelling out clearly the precise steps the seller will be expected to take in order to contractually deliver the goods to the buyer. It is always open to the parties to make their own rules if they wish to do so.

Special contracts

Delivery is subjected to still other meanings in special contracts used by Canadian businesses. These contracts are known as C.I.F., F.O.B., and C.O.D. contracts, all of which are described in detail in Unit Four of this chapter.

KEY TO YOU ARE THE JURY

SHAWE v. SHARPPE A car has the nature of goods and the price paid by Shawe was money. Therefore the *Sale of Goods Act* of the province applies to this contract. The main issue is whether title had passed to the buyer at the time the goods were destroyed in the fire. The general law which will apply is that risk of loss follows title. More specifically, Sections 18 and 19 of the Act may apply. As the parties did not themselves clearly state when title was to pass, we cannot rely directly on their contract, statements or conduct to decide who should be identified as owner of the car at the relevant time. Section 19 provides that where the seller must do some act to put the goods into a deliverable state, the action must be complete and the buyer must be advised (notified) that that which was required to be done has been done. Only after these things are accomplished does title pass from seller to buyer. In this case, although the work had been done Sharppe had done nothing to notify Shawe and therefore no title had passed. Sharppe is still legal owner of the car and as owner must bear the loss. Shawe will be entitled to the return of her purchase price. Section 19 restricts this result to those cases in which the goods are in the specific category and as this was *the* car, it falls into that category.

Unit III   Rights of unpaid sellers

YOU ARE THE JURY

IN RE FLYNN

Flynn sold a quantity of truck tires to an old customer, Sussex, under a sales agreement by which Flynn was to arrange for transportation of the goods to the Sussex warehouse and Sussex was to pay 60 days after the tires were actually delivered. The tires were appropriated to the contract and placed on a transport for delivery. The following day, before the goods arrived at their destination, Flynn learned that creditors of Sussex had put him into bankruptcy (receivership). Flynn telephoned the transport company to advise it not to make the delivery and to re-route the goods to another destination. The company followed these instructions. The trustee in bankruptcy took the position that, as credit had been extended, Flynn had no right to the goods. Flynn's lawyer advised the trustee that if he wanted the goods it would be necessary to sue. Weigh the merits of both arguments. Consider this case as it relates to the property in goods and the right to possession.

OBJECTIVES

- to identify rules that give the seller the right to sue for the price, retain the goods, claim a lien against the goods and/or claim damages.
- to define the term *damages* as it applies to the right of an unpaid seller.
- to list the rights against an insolvent buyer.
- to list rights sellers may acquire by express agreement.

LEXICON

Bankrupt A person who has ceased to meet obligations generally as they arise, who has declared bankruptcy through a licensed trustee or been forced into bankruptcy by creditors.
Carrier A transport company, railway or shipper engaged to transport goods to the buyer.
Insolvent A person (buyer in this case) who has ceased to meet financial obligations generally as they arise so as to become a serious credit risk.
Lien A legal right which gives a person in the position of a creditor the right to possession of goods as security for payment and if he is unpaid the further right to sell the goods.
Mitigate The legal duty of a person to lessen the amount of a loss through prudent steps of self-

help before claiming damages for loss from another party.
Receivership Action taken by creditors, through a licensed trustee in bankruptcy, to seize assets of a debtor. A form of involuntary bankruptcy.

No doubt, we have by now come to appreciate the distinction between the property in goods and mere possession of them. This difference will prove vitally important in our consideration of the rights of sellers, who are given a wide range of rights and protection under the Act.

Suit for price and damages

The most obvious right of the seller is the power to sue for the price of the goods when the buyer wrongfully neglects or refuses to pay for them according to the requirements of the contract.

If the buyer wrongfully refuses or neglects to accept the goods and pay for them, the seller has a right of action for damages for *non-acceptance*. What amount of damages might the seller reasonably expect to collect? Would the seller be better off relying only on a general right to the price or will there be some advantage to a claim for damages? The measure of damages will be an amount equivalent to the estimated loss directly and naturally resulting in the ordinary course of events from the buyer's breach.

First of all, the seller is now "stuck with the goods" but will have the right to dispose of the goods to another. If this is done and the price obtained on the re-sale is less than on the original, obviously the difference should be calculated as part of the loss.

At times it may not be practicable to resell the goods to establish loss before action is taken against a defaulting buyer. In that case, we have to apply a rule in the Act which states that where there is an available market or current price, the measure of damages may be calculated on the basis of the difference between the original contract price and the usual current price for similar goods.

In either event, a calculation can be made. The seller will either lose money on resale, make a larger profit, or the formula established by the Act will produce a similar loss or profit figure.

If we recall the nature of the claim in damages, we know we must go further. In one case, the court held, "in giving damages for breach of contract, the party complaining should, so far as it can be done by money, be placed in the same position as if the contract had been performed."*

Damages will include all loss directly and naturally resulting from the buyer's breach. If the seller has to store the goods, then the cost of storage will be part of the damages. If the goods must be re-routed or returned to the seller's place of business, then the cost of transportation is included: as would handling costs, legal costs and any costs of seizure by a bailiff or sheriff. If the seller resells the goods, any cost of effecting the new sale will be part of the damages directly and naturally resulting from the buyer's breach. If, as an alternative to re-sale, the seller must return the goods to a supplier, then the cost incurred in doing so will be considered as damages.

CASE 15   FROLICK v. DAVIDSON

Davidson refused delivery of goods purchased from Frolick who, after making several demands for payment, advised her that he intended to find another buyer and sue for the loss, if any. Frolick flew to Davidson's city, found a buyer that day, sold for what he could get and brought an action for damages. He included his plane fare, lunch, cab fare, a substantial amount equivalent to his loss and interest on the entire amount from the date of non-acceptance by Davidson. Davidson claimed the expenses were not relevant; no interest should be charged; and the sale to the new buyer was reckless and resulted in a needless loss. Try to decide who is right before reading on.

Like all legal issues this presents certain difficulties and defies a pat answer. If you followed the procedure for analyzing sales problems, the issue will certainly have been clear to you. Frolick's actions appear to have been impetuous. If the goods were perishable and speed was absolutely necessary, his conduct would have been understandable. If market conditions were such that quick action should be taken, it would have been justified. For example, if the goods were summer clothing in large quantities and it was late in August at the time of default, in such cases the expenses of the quick sale would be considered as costs to be included as loss directly flowing from the buyer's default. If the circumstances were different and there was no urgency and an available means to effect a sale, the cost would be considered too remote and could not be recovered. In asserting his rights a seller is expected to be responsible and act as a reasonable, prudent person might in his position.

*Wertheim v. Chicoutimi Pulp Co. (1911) A.C. 301.

The claim for interest is a triable issue. In most provinces this type of award would not be allowed unless the contract provided the right to calculate interest. If the parties concluded this contract in Prince Edward Island, Saskatchewan, Alberta, Northwest Territories or the Yukon the interest claim would be allowed. Frolick would not collect if he brought this action in one of the other provinces.

On the facts, Frolick sold "for what I could get." On the balance of probabilities Davidson has a legitimate grievance on this point. Frolick may have been reckless in settling on a new buyer too quickly. If he did, he can't very well expect Davidson to bear the loss so established. The rule is that a seller has a duty to mitigate or lessen resulting damage and any loss that can be attributed to the seller's negligence cannot be collected from the buyer. Frolick's argument in this case was that it was necessary for him to act quickly to avoid further loss. How to resolve this conflict? The rule in the Act referring to the current market price of similar goods must be used. If Frolick sold for an amount roughly close to the usual price, he will prove to have been a prudent man of business worthy of an award for loss. If the new sale price falls grossly below the current price, the loss will be attributed to his negligence and he may collect either nothing or only that part of his loss that could be considered to have arisen naturally from Davidson's default.

Seller's rights to retain goods

Sellers who have sold goods, but still have possession of them, have a duty to deliver them. In certain cases the seller is given the legal right to delay the physical delivery of the goods to ensure payment by the buyer. If the seller has possession and the goods have been sold without reference to an extension of time for payment (credit terms), the seller may keep the goods until he is paid. If credit has been extended and the seller still has possession when the time limit for the extension is up and no payment has been received from the buyer, the seller may keep the goods until payment is made. If the seller learns that the buyer is insolvent or bankrupt before possession is given up, the seller has the right to retain the goods.

These are sensible rules to protect the seller who has good reason to believe collecting the price after transferring physical possession will be difficult. In all other cases (except those listed below) the seller has a duty to comply with the terms requiring the giving up of possession.

The right of the seller who retains the goods is in the nature of a lien. Therefore, it should not matter whether or not title has passed to the buyer. If title has passed, the seller is merely holding the goods on behalf of the buyer-owner and claiming a lien against them. In doing so the seller's right is based on possession, not ownership. A lienholder has the right to retain the goods until he is paid; if he is not paid to sell them to a third party; and if there is a deficiency to sue for the difference. A seller-lien claimant is entitled to the difference between the original price (together with the cost of sale) and the amount recovered on sale to the third party.

This right to lien is available to the seller up to the time the goods are delivered to a carrier for the purpose of transporting them to the buyer, or the buyer otherwise gets possession. At this point the lien is lost.

The insolvent buyer

If the buyer becomes insolvent, the seller may retain the goods if he is still in possession of them. But what if the goods have been loaded on a transport and are on their way to the buyer when the seller first learns of the insolvency? The Act gives such a seller the right to stop the goods in transit and retake possession until the purchase price has been paid. The carrier must be instructed to hold onto the goods, divert them to another destination, or return them to the seller. If the purchase price is not paid, the seller has the right to sell to another buyer.

If, at any stage of transit, the buyer obtains possession, or takes delivery through some other legal means, the seller loses the right to stop the goods and regain possession. For example, if the carrier of the goods advises or informs the buyer that the goods have arrived, this is considered a sufficient delivery to deprive the seller of the right to retake the goods.

How sellers assert other rights

It is usually the seller who prepares the sales contract. In doing so the shrewd seller incorporates in the "fine print" terms which he feels are needed to protect him. As the prime principle of sales is that the parties are free to make their own contracts, the seller is restricted only by the limits of his creative imagination and the ordinary rules of contracts.

The *Sale of Goods Act* provides that the parties to a sales contract may, by express agreement, vary the sales rules or ignore them entirely. Sellers who

do not wish to be bound by the awkward, old-fashioned Act include *exclusionary clauses* in contracts to negate or vary those sales rules which are most troublesome.

CASE 16   PICKERING v. LeCRON

Pickering discovered too late that purchased goods were not suitable for her business requirements. She complained that LeCron had made statements leading her to believe that the goods would suit her needs. LeCron recalled some discussions but claimed that Pickering had an opportunity to examine samples while at his factory, and should have identified the deficiency before she signed a contract. The agreement contained this clause, "This agreement shall constitute the entire agreement between seller and buyer and there is no representation, warranty, collateral agreement or condition affecting this agreement or the goods, otherwise, than as expressed herein in writing." Consider this case from the point of view of the defendant LeCron.

The Act makes it clear that the parties may make their own agreements if their intention is expressed definitely and clearly. We must look to the agreement before we apply the rules under the Act. The exclusionary clause effectively excludes any warranty or condition which is not in the written contract. We must examine the contract to see what reference, if any, is made to define the quality of the goods required by the buyer. The contract contains nothing to identify the standard that the goods must meet to be acceptable to the buyer. We have evidence of oral statements about quality and they must represent either a warranty of fitness or a condition of fitness to be of any use to Pickering; but the contract specifically excludes all warranties *and* conditions unless written into the contract. Pickering must lose her right to set up the oral statements and her action will fail. This is the type of windfall result that LeCron had hoped for when he drew up the contract. He had one nervous eye on the implied condition as to fitness rule contained in the Act.

CASE 17   LEE v. ROGERS

(This case did not get to court but was discussed in a lawyer's office.) Lee ordered a new car from Rogers fifteen weeks ago but it had not yet been delivered. Lee wanted to get his deposit back and buy a car that could be delivered right away from another dealer. The contract read in part, "I will accept delivery of the motor vehicle at the seller's place of business, ordered herein, within forty-eight hours after I have been notified that it is ready for delivery. Failure on my part to accept the goods will result in the forfeit of the deposit . . . ."

Under the *Sale of Goods Act* the seller must deliver the goods on the day specified or, if no deadline is given, then within a reasonable time. If the Act applied to establish whether Rogers is in breach of his duty to deliver on time, it would be necessary to determine whether 15 weeks is more than a reasonable time. The Act, however, permits the parties to make their own rules and in this case the seller's contract, which the buyer signed, delays the obligation to deliver until the goods are actually in the seller's possession and still further until the seller gets around to notifying the buyer that the goods are available.

Sellers have become masters of drafting exempting clauses such as those in the two cases above. In this age of the pre-printed contract which includes blank spaces to fill in specific names and details, but not much room to write in a great deal, such clauses are extremely effective. So devastating are most seller's contracts that purchasing agents for companies often refuse to sign the seller's contract, preferring to prepare their own purchase orders which they deliver to the seller and give him the choice of either accepting or rejecting the deal as expressed in the purchase order.

Sellers have a tremendous advantage. In drafting their contracts they can put what they like in them. Can sellers make their own "laws" with impunity? They could, except for the regulating power of the courts, which take the position that the advantage secured by the seller must in some measure be counterbalanced by an advantage to the buyer. The courts do this by interpreting the clauses of exclusion strictly against the seller. If the clause is at all vague or ambiguous, the courts are not likely to find in favour of the seller. If the clause doesn't fit precisely the facts in issue, the courts are likely to decide in favour of the purchaser.

CASE 18   CONWAY v. SAYLOR

Conway purchased a mini-computer for business and personal use. He indicated to Saylor that he knew little about computers and simply wanted an inexpensive one that would perform certain functions which would be useful to him. Saylor recommended a model which soon after purchase

proved hopelessly inadequate. Conway now seeks to rescind the contract and buy a different model. The sales contract read in part, "There are no statements, representations, warranties, guarantees (other than manufacturer's guarantee) or other agreement other than as appears in this written contract." Conway argued that the effect of this clause was to exclude liability on any statement made before the contract was signed and which was not included in the written contract.

Conway made known to the seller the purpose for which he required the goods in such a manner as to demonstrate that he was relying on Saylor's judgment. Therefore, as the computer was of a type ordinarily sold by Saylor, there was an implied condition that the goods were suitable for the use required by Conway. The exclusionary clauses did not exempt the seller from conditions expressed or implied and as Conway's argument relied on a condition of contract, the court ruled in his favour. The goods were unfit. The seller was in breach of a condition which entitled the buyer to rescind and required the seller to return the purchase money.

Additional limitations on exclusionary clauses

Some provinces have passed laws limiting the use of exclusionary clauses in retail sales transactions in which goods are sold to a consumer in the ordinary course of the seller's business. The British Columbia Legislature amended its *Sale of Goods Act* by adding a section making terms or clauses in a retail sales contract attempting to negate or vary any condition or warranty relating to the goods absolutely void and of no effect. Manitoba and Ontario accomplished the same results by passing a new law embodied in their *Consumer Protection Acts* which, in effect, invalidate exclusionary clauses which would negate or diminish the recognized conditions and warranties relating to goods for sale. Be careful! These new laws apply only to *retail sales* and do not apply to the many other types of sales such as a sale by a wholesaler to a retailer (who intends to resell to consumers); sales by a manufacturer to a retailer (who intends to use the goods in his business as opposed to re-selling them); sales by trustees in bankruptcy; sheriff sales; or sales by anyone out of the ordinary course of business. It is most probable that other provinces will pass similar legislation to restrict the impact of the exempting clauses.

We have attempted in these three units to deal with aspects of sales which are basic and which are likely to be with us for a long time. However, in recent years the trend in lawmaking has been to provide more protection to the consumer at the expense of the seller. There is no reason to believe that this trend will not continue through the eighties. What, then, is the future of Sale of Goods? We are likely to see many changes. Sale of Goods is likely to be a dynamic area from now on, so do keep abreast of developments.

KEY TO YOU ARE THE JURY

IN RE FLYNN   The trustee loses (in fact this case was settled out of court). The dealings between these "old" contracting parties make it clear that property in the goods had passed to the buyer and that the seller, having loaded the tires onto the transport for delivery to the buyer, had lost his right to retain the goods. The key to this case is the fact that Flynn was identified as an insolvent person before he received possession of the goods. The Act provides that in the event of the insolvency of the buyer the seller has the right to stop the goods during the course of transit up to the time the buyer takes possession of the goods or delivery by operation of law. Flynn advised the transport company before such time and therefore is legally entitled to retake possession. If the trustee wants the goods, the purchase price will have to be paid; otherwise the seller may resell them and, if there is a deficiency, claim against the bankrupt estate for the loss. In this case you should note that the action of the creditors in putting Flynn into receivership is evidence of his insolvency under the *Bankruptcy Act of Canada.*

Unit IV Special business transactions

YOU ARE THE JURY

IN THE MATTER OF CHAPMAN AND KING HONG

An oriental supplier negotiated the transfer of human hair wigs with Gardner who ran a wholesale business in Ontario. "We can ship the wigs by the end of the month," said King. "Our usual arrangement is F.O.B. our warehouse."

Gardner replied, "I expected the shipment to be C.O.D. our warehouse. That's the only reason I'll buy at that price."

"I'll tell you what I can do," replied King. "We'll split the insurance and freight with you and ship C.I.F. your warehouse. Or we can send them to you on consignment."

Gardner agreed to take the goods on consignment and they were shipped on that basis to the Ontario firm. When Gardner failed to pay for the goods under the consignment arrangement, King investigated and found that Gardner had sold the entire lot of wigs in bulk to Chapman and absconded to parts unknown.

Define and consider the effects of each of the delivery terms F.O.B., C.O.D., and C.I.F. Define and consider the effects of delivery of goods on consignment. Will King succeed? Give reasons for your answer.

OBJECTIVES

- to be able to list the special types of agreements used in business transactions.
- to be able to identify the elements of the F.O.B., C.O.D. and C.I.F. quotations.
- to be able to identify the advantages and disadvantages of F.O.B., C.O.D, C.I.F., C & F, and Consignment quotations.
- to be able to identify the legal rules relating to sales in bulk and sales by auction.

LEXICON

Bill of Lading   A written document prepared by a shipper of goods outlining the terms of transportation. Its delivery to the receiver represents a transfer of title or ownership to the goods.

Consignee   A person who receives possession of goods from an owner (for the purpose of sale to third parties) in the capacity of an agent.

Consignor   An owner of goods who parts with possession of goods (but not ownership/title) to a mercantile agent usually for the purpose of sale to third parties.

Contract of Carriage   An agreement made with a shipper, railway or transport company to transport or convey goods from one place to another.

Mercantile Agent   A business person who receives possession and custody of goods owned by another. He has the responsibility to sell or dispose of the goods according to agreement, maintain records, pay owner the price of goods "consigned" and provide owner with an accounting of the sales or dispositions.

Premium   The amount charged by an insurance company as the consideration for insuring property for or on behalf of the person with an insurable interest.

We now have an opportunity to apply our knowledge of contract and of sale of goods to several special business transactions common in Canada. We will build on the concept of "change of ownership" by investigating methods of making commercial contracts which avoid the unsatisfactory rules established by the provincial *Sale of Goods Acts* by using special agreements. These agreements specify the time when title will pass; who will bear the risk of loss; who has the obligation to insure and to transport; and they provide details of terms of delivery designed to anticipate most problems which might arise.

In the Chapman case, the seller and buyer carried on business on different continents. It is not unusual for buyers and sellers of commercial goods to live some distance from each other. These situations magnify ordinary contractual problems and create some new ones. Buyers will want to receive goods and examine them before paying for them. They will want the sellers to bear the risk of loss and the cost of shipping. Sellers will want to receive payment before giving up possession of goods, and want to shift the burdens of ownership to the buyers at the earliest possible moment. These conflicts are resolved through negotiation and settled most commonly by F.O.B., C.I.F., or C.O.D. quotations.

F.O.B. contracts

The F.O.B. contract is expressed in the form of a quotation which links the designation F.O.B. (free on board) with the name of a place in order to identify the place at which title or ownership

(Name of issuing Carrier)

Carrier's No. _____

Vehicle No. _____

Shipper's No. _____

Bill of Lading – Original – Not Negotiable

(Issued in accordance with the Regulations made under the Public Commercial Vehicles Act)

At _____ Date _____
(Point of Origin)

Shipper _____

Received at point of origin on this date from the shipper, the goods herein described, in apparent good order, except as noted (contents and conditions of contents of packages unknown) marked, consigned, and destined as indicated below, which the carrier agrees to carry and deliver to the consignee at the destination if on its own route, otherwise to deliver to another carrier on the route to the destination.

It is agreed as to each carrier of all or any of the goods over all or any portion of the route to destination, and as to each party at any time interested in all or any of the goods, that every service to be performed hereunder shall be subject to all the conditions, whether printed or written, herein contained, including conditions on back hereof, which are hereby agreed to by the shipper and accepted for himself and his assigns.

Consigned to _____ At _____
(Destination)

Street Address _____ Route _____
(Province or State)

No. of Pieces or Quantity	Description of goods and special marks	Weight (Subject to Correction)	Rate	Amount	Freight Charges
					PREPAID ☐
					COLLECT ☐
					Freight charges will be collect unless *marked* Prepaid.
					When goods move under CLASS "C" authority – freight charges will be paid by

1. Any agreement covering transportation of the goods described herein with other than due despatch, or for specific time, must be endorsed on this bill of lading and signed by the parties hereto.

2. When a shipment is at "owner's risk", the words "AT OWNER'S RISK" must be entered and initialled by both parties thereto.

C.O.D.
AMOUNT $ . . . .

FEE $ . . . .

C.O.D. FEE   C.O.D. FEE
PREPAID   COLLECT

(Receipt of goods at destination)

Received in apparent good order (except as noted), from _____
(Name of Carrier)

at _____ the goods described herein.

_____ Consignee. __ Date _____

DECLARED VALUATION $_____ MAXIMUM LIABILITY $1.50 PER POUND
UNLESS DECLARED VALUATION STATES OTHERWISE
(See Condition 10 on back)

Shipper _____ Carrier _____

Per _____ Per _____

(This Bill of Lading is to be signed by the Shipper and Carrier)

Bill of Lading.

passes to the buyer, and to define the respective responsibilities of both the seller and buyer.

The quotation *F.O.B. seller's warehouse* means that the buyer has agreed to become "owner" of the goods and to assume full responsibility for the risk of loss or damage the moment they are put into the hands of an agent designated by the buyer to transport them to the buyer's place of business. The buyer must arrange for insurance protection and pay for shipping charges. The buyer must also inform the seller of the desired method of transportation and must specify the name of the shipper, railway company or other carrier. If the goods are lost or damaged in transit, the buyer must bear the loss subject to any claim which may be available against the insurance company or the carrier.

The seller must make arrangements to transfer the goods to the buyer's shipper and must pay the cost of transport up to that point; and, of course, he continues to bear the risk of loss or damage until the transfer is completed. The seller also has an obligation to advise the buyer when these things have been done so that the buyer will be "put on notice" of the transfer of ownership and risk and the need to insure against loss.

A contract quotation designating delivery as *F.O.B. buyer's warehouse* means that the seller has agreed to retain title to the goods and to consequently bear the risk of loss or damage until the goods have been deposited safely at the buyer's place of business. The seller will bear the risk of loss or damage to the goods while in transit. The seller must provide insurance coverage and will be responsible for shipping arrangements and charges.

C.I.F. contracts

The C.I.F. contract is expressed in the form of a quotation which links the designation C.I.F. (Cost, Insurance, and Freight) to the name of a place, as a means of identifying the point in time and the place at which title or ownership passes to the buyer and of defining the respective duties of the seller and buyer.

The quotation *C.I.F. buyer's warehouse* means that the seller will handle all shipping and insurance arrangements. C.I.F. refers to a total "price" to be paid by the buyer which is equivalent to the actual price of the goods themselves, the amount of the insurance premiums required to insure the goods in transit and the cost of transportation. While it is the seller's responsibility to insure and transport, the cost of these services is passed on to the buyer.

In the *C.I.F. buyer's warehouse* procedures, the seller has a duty to do the following:

- produce or obtain the quantity and quality of goods ordered by the buyer.
- obtain adequate insurance on behalf of the buyer and pay premiums to insurer.
- arrange contract of carriage directly with a shipper, railway, or transport company and pay transportation costs.
- obtain a bill of lading from shipper.
- prepare invoice (charging "total price" to buyer).
- forward invoices, insurance policies and bill of lading to buyer (usually through a branch of the seller's bank in buyer's city).

When the seller has completed these steps, the buyer pays the total price to the seller's banker in exchange for the seller's documents. The buyer then receives the goods.

From the moment the C.I.F. sales contract is made, the goods are treated as though title had passed to the buyer. If loss or damage occurs during transit and the insurance coverage is adequate, neither the seller nor the buyer will experience loss because the seller is entitled to be paid in any event, and the buyer has a claim against the insurance company.

In the event the seller, by oversight, fails to insure or insures for an inadequate amount and the buyer's goods are damaged, lost or destroyed, the buyer has a claim against the seller for breach of contract and may recover damages to compensate for loss. Some buyers are reluctant to trust the insurance coverage to the seller and prefer to bargain for a C & F (cost and freight) total price. This leaves the buyer free to place the insurance coverage himself.

The C.I.F. contract is a mixed blessing for the buyer. On the one hand, it is convenient for him to pay one total price for the services provided by the seller (who must arrange insurance coverage and a proper means of transportation) particularly when the goods must travel a great distance from a foreign land. On the other hand the buyer pays for the goods (on the delivery of documents) before they arrive (indeed, whether they arrive or not) and therefore does not have the usual right to examine the goods before making payment. However, the right of examination is merely postponed until the goods do arrive, at which time the buyer may reject them if they are not in the right quantity or of the proper quality. The buyer may reject them and claim against the seller for the return of the money paid.

C.O.D. contracts

The C.O.D. (cash on delivery) contract requires the seller to deliver the goods to the buyer's place of business, warehouse or an alternative place designated by the buyer. Ownership and risk remain with the buyer until the goods arrive safely at the designated place. From the buyer's point of view this is a most desirable procedure because it eliminates risk and insurance and transport costs until the goods are under his control. It also provides the buyer with an opportunity to examine the goods to determine their quantity and quality before paying for them. Goods which are damaged or fail to answer the description of the goods ordered may be rejected by the buyer.

Bulk sales

CASE 19 IN RE SWANSON ET AL

The Lily Company, an electronics and television retailer, owed various creditors and suppliers over $20 000 in unsecured debts. The company entered into a contract with Swanson to sell her all its "stock-in-trade business fixtures" together with a list of specified chattels used in the business (i.e., cash register, desk, calculator, furniture) for $80 000. Swanson closed the deal by paying the full contract price in return for a bill of sale for the inventory, fixtures and goods. She opened her own business, "The Computer Store," at the same location adding micro-computers as the major sales product of the new firm. Two months after the Lily deal, Popovich, an agent for one of the Lily creditors, learned of the deal and demanded that Swanson pay the creditors' outstanding account. Swanson replied she had never heard of them and refused to pay. Consider the implications of this case. Assume that the Lily Company has no assets and that its officers have absconded with the firm's cash. What rights do the creditors have?

This is a classic case because both Swanson and the creditors are "innocent" parties (the villain is beyond reach). If the creditors are to have any recourse, it will be against the other "innocent" party. The analysis of bulk sales below will illustrate the type of exercise available at law to ensure that the "*least* innocent of two competing parties" will bear the risk of loss.

All Canadian provinces have enacted acts called the *Bulk Sales Acts* to protect unsecured creditors in the event their business debtors sell all or substantially all their stock-in-trade out of the ordinary course of business without making adequate provision to see that the creditors are paid out of the proceeds of sale. Such sales are known as bulk sales and include in addition to unusual sales of inventory:

- substantial sales of business fixtures, assets, chattels and goods which seriously impair either the ability of the business to carry on or the business' ability to repay the creditors.
- sales of the entire business operation as a going concern.

Each of the provincial acts anticipates the problems arising out of bulk sales by legislating that the responsibility to see the creditors paid falls to the bulk sale buyer, rather than the bulk sale seller. The buyers must take certain steps to see that the seller's creditors are informed of the proposed bulk sale in order to ensure that no fraud is perpetrated against the creditors.

The Act requires the buyer to demand from the seller a sworn statement listing creditors' names and addresses together with the amounts owing to each. Before any substantial part of the purchase price is paid by the buyer, the seller must arrange to pay the creditors out of the proceeds of sale. This is usually accomplished on the understanding of the seller's lawyer to take "custody" of the purchase price, pay the creditors first, then give the balance (if any) to the seller. The waivers are in the form of a release of interest by the creditors in the assets purchased by the buyer and must be given to the buyer before the seller receives the purchase price.

It may not always be practicable to pay all of the creditors at once, particularly when the seller insists on carrying on business in some form despite the bulk sale and the creditors after all, may not be concerned enough about their accounts to demand immediate payment. In this case the buyer must demand that the seller obtain written waivers of rights from a substantial majority of the creditors. This consent from the majority then relieves the buyer from responsibility to *all* creditors and the bulk sale may be completed without penalty to the buyer.

It may be that the proceeds of the sale will be insufficient to satisfy all the creditors and that, at the same time, it is not possible to obtain the necessary waivers. Under these circumstances, the buyer may complete the transaction but the proceeds of sale must be paid to a trustee who distributes the funds to the creditors on a pro rata basis. Further, this procedure relieves the buyer of responsibility to all the seller's creditors and will avoid any remedy the creditors may have under the relevant provincial *Bulk Sales Act*.

In order to ensure immunity from creditors' claims, the bulk sale buyer must register a written document outlining the details of the sale with the county or district court having jurisdiction in the place where the business is located within a matter of days of the completion of the bulk sale. The buyer who complies with the bulk sale procedure and conforms to the requirements will successfully effect a bulk purchase without risk of loss.

It is obvious that the Acts are designed to prevent civil fraud by establishing business creditors as a "privileged" group entitled to extraordinary protection. The theory behind the statutes is that usually businesses are operable only as long as creditors and suppliers are willing to extend credit or supply stock. If the debtor defaults, creditors and suppliers are entitled to rely on the business assets of the debtor for ultimate payment; and the business debtor has a duty not to put these assets beyond the reach of its creditors. It is unusual for business creditors to take specific security for amounts owing to them from time to time and they are, accordingly, vulnerable to loss.

In the bulk sale, the privileged status provided for creditors discriminates against the buyer. This is a reasonable procedure; however, it would be unreasonable to extend rights to creditors without imposing any time limit for action. The provincial Acts provide that creditors must institute legal proceedings against the buyer promptly. In Ontario, creditors lose any claim they might have under the Act six months after the bulk sale. In Saskatchewan the limit is two months, and in Prince Edward Island four months. In effect the bulk sale transaction is voidable against the creditors and will be treated in law as void when one or more creditors acts within the time limit. If no creditor takes action in time, all creditors lose their rights.

In practice, one creditor commences a "class action" on behalf of itself and all other creditors. This action asks for a court order declaring the sale void and a judgment against the buyer personally in an amount equivalent to the bulk sale purchase price.

Bulk sales procedure is relatively expensive for both buyer and seller. The provincial Acts contain provisions allowing a judge to grant an order, in proper cases, exempting a particular sale from the requirements and consequences of the Act. The order allows the buyer to pay the purchase price to the seller without risk.

Each Act automatically exempts certain sales. For example, Ontario exempts sales where the total dollar value owed to unsecured creditors does not exceed $2 500 (and the value of debts to secured creditors is less than $2 500). Ontario also exempts the sale when the seller provides the buyer with a sworn statement that he has paid all his creditors in full or that adequate security for payment in full has been made. In each of these cases the buyer is entitled to rely on the seller's information and may proceed to complete the sale without further compliance with the Act and without risk if the statement later turns out to be incorrect or fraudulent.

Sale by auction

The classified advertisement sections of newspapers dramatically underline the importance of sales by auction in Canadian business. They announce sales of everything from factories, buildings, lands, business fixtures and assets, chattels and stock-in-trade to the contents of farms or old homes. Auctioneers specify that sales are "with reserve" or "without reserve" and subject to the right of sellers to engage in the bidding. The special features, quirks and terminology of these sales procedures merit careful examination before one makes a decision to either sell by auction or attend as a bidder.

Auction sales formula

The following visual formula may be helpful:

Auction Sale = general contract law + sale of goods law + special provincial *Sale of Goods Act* rules + special common law rules.

The auction sale

Five persons may make a decision to sell by auction: a person with the right to dispose of assets; the owner; an auditor who has obtained the property in foreclosure; a trustee in bankruptcy acting on behalf of creditors generally; or an executor of the estate of a deceased owner. The auctioneer is engaged as an agent.* The auctioneer takes possession of the goods, settles the extent of authority to sell, advertises the sale for an appointed time and place, and processes sales to high bidders.

In advertising the sale, auctioneers announce, on behalf of the "principal," an *intention* to hold an auction. This does not amount to a warranty that an auction sale will actually take place and therefore there is not a legal obligation to the public to carry through with an advertised sale. The owner who has a change of heart may, up to

---

*For an analysis of the rights and liability of auctioneers one should refer to Chapter Eight, Unit Two which deals with the rules of agency.

the time of the auction, cancel the sale without being liable to prospective bidders.

Auction procedure requires the auctioneer to present property as individual items or as "lots" by way of an invitation to participants to purchase through bidding. This amounts only to an invitation to buy (or "treat") and does not amount to a *contract offer*. Therefore the auctioneer has the legal right to withdraw and refuse to sell any item until the procedure reaches a final stage. If bidding is sluggish or grossly inadequate, and the auctioneer considers it good business to remove an item rather than accept an unsatisfactory bid, participants have no legal right to object.

In order to put the bargaining process into operation, participants are required to bid on each item or lot by bids which are equivalent to definite, legal contract offers. Each succeeding bid acts in the same way as a counter-offer. It replaces the previous offer so that only the last and highest bid remains "alive." As a contract offer cannot stand alone and is only one-half of a mutual agreement, a high bidder may legally withdraw an offer/bid up to the moment of *acceptance* by the auctioneer. The auctioneer will then have to consider the previous high bid as "alive" and may encourage further bidding by others; but he has no legal recourse against the withdrawing bidder.

The auctioneer signifies *contract acceptance* by the fall of a hammer or in any other customary manner. After he does this, it is too late both for a high bidder to repudiate and for the auctioneer to withdraw the property from the auction. The sale is complete. There is a legally binding contract.

Reservations and fraud by sellers

The obvious danger in sale by auction is that property may be sold for grossly inadequate sums. To prevent this, sellers may establish "reserved or upset prices" and instruct the auctioneer to hold a sale "with reservations." The auctioneer must notify participants that the sale is subject to a reserve price or prices, and that if the bids do not match or exceed the price, the property will be withdrawn. Participants are not told the actual amounts of the reserved prices; they are known only to the seller and the auctioneer. In this case, if the highest bid is below the reserved amount, the bidder will not be able to claim the goods.

In the "with reserve" procedure, sellers may also reserve the right to bid on the goods either personally or through any one person acting on their behalf. The auctioneer must notify the participants that the seller has this right and may be bidding against them. Otherwise the rule is that sellers cannot bid at their own auction.

If a seller or seller's agent participates in auction sales without express reservation and notification, the sales are voidable at the option of the successful highest bidders whose offers have been accepted. Such bidders may reject the goods and refuse to honour their bid. If they have the goods and have paid the purchase price, they may return the goods and receive a refund.

When an auction sale is expressed to be *without reserve*, or where no express notice is given that the sale is *with reserve*, the property may be sold to the highest bidders without the need to match or exceed a pre-determined figure. If the sale is expressly described as "without reserve," then the sellers, either themselves or through an agent, are forbidden to participate in the bidding. If they do so, there is a breach of contract and the highest bidders have a right to sue for damages. Usually such actions are brought against the auctioneer who is considered responsible for the "fraud," and the amount which may be recovered should be sufficient to compensate the bidder for any direct loss.

Buyers' fraud

Competitive bidding is the key advantage obtained by auction sellers. Remove this element and the auction will be a failure. Buyers who get together to agree not to bid against themselves or not to bid beyond a certain price effectively destroy the value of this important business tool. These "knockout" agreements are in fact illegal pursuant to S338 of the *Criminal Code of Canada*:

> Everyone who by deceit – or other fraudulent means – with intent to defraud, affects the public market price of merchandise, or anything offered for sale to the public is guilty of an indictable offence.

Thus, any sale tainted by a "knockout" agreement will be invalid and unenforceable because it was obtained through criminal action.

Sales on consignment

CASE 20 IN RE OLIVETTI

Sforza, a Montreal dealer in diamonds, negotiated an arrangement with Olivetti, a retail jeweller in Winnipeg, by which Sforza was to ship a quantity of high quality diamonds "on consignment" on the understanding that Olivetti would deal exclusively with Sforza for diamond needs in the future. The property or title to the diamonds was to remain in Sforza, but Olivetti was to have possession for the purpose of sale to consumers. Olivetti was to pay on the basis of diamonds actually sold by him. He was to remit funds on a monthly basis and was required to provide an accounting identifying the diamond sales transactions. Olivetti was to keep the "mark up" as profit and he had the privilege of returning all or part of the diamond consignment to Sforza at any time. After several months of satisfactory payment, Olivetti suddenly failed to pay or give the required accounting. Sforza learned that the sheriff had seized the inventory and assets of Olivetti's business to satisfy judgment creditors. Sforza said, "I want my diamonds back." The sheriff replied, "They were in the store and we'll be keeping them for the creditors." Who is right? What remedy is available to Sforza?

This case represents a typical consignment transaction. Consignment refers to a transaction in which goods are forwarded to a "mercantile agent" for the purpose of ultimate sale to a third party or other disposition agreed to in advance by the owner/shipper and the "agent." Consignment arrangements are common when a retailer does not have the funds to make outright purchases from suppliers or when suppliers are concerned about the ability of the retailer to pay for the goods and an extension of time for payment is practicable. If goods are sent on consignment, and the retailer has financial difficulties, a consignor may always take back the goods because title has not passed.

The contract here was one of consignment, not sale of goods; therefore neither provincial *Sale of Goods Act* would apply. In the contract the parties clearly expressed the intention that title would not pass to Olivetti until a sale to an ultimate consumer had been made. Ownership remained in Sforza, and the sheriff must give up the diamonds to Sforza. The only legal right Olivetti had was the right to possession as long as the agreement with Sforza was being honoured. The sheriff claiming on behalf of creditors through Olivetti can have no greater right than the consignee Olivetti.

The procedure involved here is not equivalent to a sale because title to the goods remains with the consignor who merely gives up possession to the consignee so that they might be commercially dealt with at a local level. The consignee has possession but no title; yet he is authorized to appear as an owner and to deal with goods as an owner as far as third parties are concerned. Usually, the consignee is expected to sell the goods to third parties, pay the consignor an agreed sum, and retain the balance.

Consignees, such as Olivetti, are business agents for consignors such as Sforza. These agents owe their consignors a duty to keep records, report, remit proceeds as agreed and give a true accounting of sales or dispositions. As the consignee receives funds, they legally become trust funds in the hands of an agent and must be accounted for even if obtained in the course of the consignee's business.

KEY TO YOU ARE THE JURY

IN THE MATTER OF CHAPMAN AND KING HONG   F.O.B. means "free on board." When a sales contract gives delivery as "F.O.B. seller's warehouse," it is understood that the seller's responsibility is to load the goods on a truck, railway car or ship at the seller's location and that from then on they are the responsibility of the buyer. If the goods are damaged after they are loaded, the loss falls on the buyer. Therefore the buyer must bear the risk of loss and if insurance protection is needed the buyer must purchase it.

C.O.D. means "cash on delivery." In a C.O.D. sale the seller takes the responsibility for delivery to the buyer's place of business as well as the risk of loss from damage in shipping.

C.I.F. means "cost, insurance and freight." A shipment "C.I.F. buyer's warehouse" means the seller will handle all the shipping arrangements and will obtain the insurance. If insurance coverage is adequate, neither the seller nor the buyer will suffer loss. If the insurance coverage is inadequate, the loss falls to the seller.

The effect of the consignment was to give Gardner authority to re-sell and pass title to purchasers who bought in good faith and without any notice of any claim by King as original owner. In this case Chapman acted in good faith and had no notice of King's ownership. King could not reclaim the goods themselves from Chapman. In his capacity as creditor King applied for an injunction to prohibit the sale of the wigs by auction and moved to set aside the sale from Gardner to Chapman, arguing that the transaction was a sale governed by *Bulk Sales Act*. As Chapman had not followed the procedures established by the Act, the Gardner sale was voidable against the creditors. Chapman was compelled to deliver the wigs to the sheriff in trust for creditors of Gardner. The wigs were sold at a sheriff's sale and the proceeds were divided among Gardner's creditors, thus giving King substantial relief at the expense of Chapman.

Review: Special business transactions

1. GIORDANO v. SING Giordano, a Canadian retailer, had for several years purchased human hair wigs from a supplier in the far east on a F.O.B. seller's warehouse delivery basis. The established procedure was for Giordano to place the order specifying quantity, quality and method of delivery. Sing would then make delivery and Giordano would deposit a cheque for the price in a local bank account maintained by Sing. Payment was usually made after Giordano had inspected the goods but on occasion Giordano made payment when the goods arrived at Canada Customs. When advised that a new shipment had arrived, Giordano made payment but later when the goods were inspected discovered that they were infested with lice. Customs impounded the goods and refused to release them. Giordano stopped payment on his cheque. An investigation revealed that the goods were fine when they left Sing's warehouse and had become infested on the transport ship. Sing sued for payment. Should Sing succeed?

2. List the obligations of a seller when a sales contract contains "C.I.F. buyer's warehouse" delivery terms.

3. What is meant by C. & F. delivery terms?

4. RADIC v. GUINNESS Astro-Equip Corp. sold 85% of its inventory to Guinness, providing her with the documents required to register such transactions including sworn declarations from the president of the company. Several weeks after the purchase price had been paid in full, one of Astro's creditors discovered the sale and objected. Guinness had no prior knowledge of the existence of the creditors and contended that the Astro company had fraudulently concealed information and its president had sworn a false affidavit. Assume that she is correct. What steps do any or all of the creditors have the right to take? What specific source of law would apply? What are the chances of the creditors succeeding under these circumstances?

5. KUBIC v. LYNCH Shannon Alicia Lynch purchased a china cabinet from Brooke Kubic. An order form was prepared which included a $15 delivery charge. When asked how she wished to pay for the item, Shannon signed the order form and wrote across its face "C.O.D." Brooke indicated that was acceptable and explained that it was store policy to make delivery the following day by Pronto-Presto, an independent delivery service. The following day the truck delivering the cabinet was struck by a hit-and-run motorist who was entirely responsible for the accident. The cabinet was badly damaged and Shannon refused delivery. Neither Brooke nor Pronto-Presto would admit responsibility for the damage. When Shannon refused to acknowledge invoices sent by Brooke over the next three months, Brooke sued for the price. Should Brooke succeed?

6. What is meant when an auction is advertised as being "with reserve?"

7. ASHDOWN v. GLOW AND PAQUIN ET AL Glow retained an auctioneer, Paquin, to sell all of his business equipment, furnishings, fixtures and stock in trade at a public auction. Paquin received no specific instructions on the method of conducting the sale and proceeded to advertise it as a sale "without reserve." At the sale Ashdown was outbid on an antique desk by Lightfoot, who had been asked by Glow to bid on his behalf if it appeared as though the desk would go at a sacrifice price. Later, Ashdown learned certain facts that led her to believe that she had been outbid by an agent of the owner. Deal with this matter and decide what remedies, if any, are available to Ashdown.

Checklist: Sale of goods

This checklist is designed to cover the purchase of multiple items but is useful as well in single item purchases.

1. Contract in Writing   Write out terms in writing as you would a contract under the Contract Checklist in Chapter Three. Parties should sign. Deposit usually required.

2. Representations, Warranties   All representations and warranties given by parties must be written into contract (to avoid parole evidence rule and exclusionary clauses). Comprehensive list includes: statement seller has right to sell; description of physical condition of the goods; specifications that no liens or encumbrances against goods; and buyer to have quiet (peaceable) possession. Other oral undertakings, statements of quality also included.

3. Conditions Precedent   Write in conditions which must be met by the parties; undertakings to put goods in a deliverable state. Specify how notice to be given buyer when condition has been met. Specify title not to pass to buyer until condition met and buyer notified. Specify deposit (if any) to be held in trust until title passes.

4. Parties   Describe specific individuals. Proper legal names and status (sole proprietor; partnership; corporation). Consider other person's capacity to bind (authority). If dealing with agent, ask to see authority in writing or make reasonable inquiries into agent's actual authority to bind a principal. If dealing with partner, has partner authority to bind the firm? Make inquiries.

5. Financial Responsibility   If dealing for substantial item or price on ongoing basis, check financial stability of other party through lawyer, credit agency, bank, Dunn and Bradstreet.

6. Identify Items   Describe fully. Serial numbers. Distinguishing features. Quality required. Exact quantity ordered. Location of items at time of contract.

7. Title   Negotiate contract which provides most advantageous transfer of title terms possible. F.O.B., C.I.F., C.O.D., sale or return. Express intention regarding transfer of title from seller to buyer to avoid problem of interpretation under provincial *Sale of Goods Act*.

8. Delivery   Define delivery for purpose of this contract. Specific terms. When to be made. When to arrive. How to be made. Form of delivery i.e., by Bill of Lading, physical delivery of goods or making available for collection by buyer at specified point.

9. Purchase Price   Specify amount; time to be paid; effect of non-payment on time. If purchase price based on sales or net profits, define clearly. If based on appraisal, set out in detail method of selection of appraisers; limits on appraisers in determining value. Specify when payment to be made. If to agent, agree agent's receipt will be a sufficient, good release.

10. Allocation of Purchase Price   If purchase in bulk will result in tax implications for buyer and seller, allocate price to specific items. Get advice from accountants.

11. Pre-printed Contracts   Sellers have firm lawyers review standard pre-printed contracts if problems with buyers occur. Buyers read sellers contracts carefully; particularly fine print and sections headed "Exclusionary Clauses." Sellers attempt to limit responsibility and legal liability through such means. Strike out objectionable clauses or refuse to sign seller's purchase orders. Most sellers will deal on basis of buyer's written confirmation of material terms. Look for strenuous objections. If necessary, deal elsewhere.

12. Cancellation Clause   Insert cancellation clause in contract to cover foreseeable risks. Provide for cancellation of agreement in event goods substantially damaged, other party becomes bankrupt, there is failure to fulfil conditions precedent, failure to deliver by specific date, failure to pay purchase price as agreed, etc.

13. Default   Specify what you expect to happen if other party defaults. Try to estimate damages (liquidated damages). Alert other party to any special loss that might occur as result of default.

Review

1. Define a contract of sale.

2. What are the rules relating to the risk of loss of goods?

3. WEATHERBED v. LODGE BYKES
Weatherbed, a college student, gave Lodge a cheque for the price of a motorized bike. Lodge was to oil and grease the bike and prepare it for the road. Lodge did the required work and cashed the cheque. Several days later Weatherbed returned to the store and was advised that the bike was ready. Weatherbed said, "I didn't come here for the bike. I came to get my money back. I thought the cheque was just to hold the bike. I didn't expect you to cash it. I've had some personal problems so I didn't come back; but I want my money back now. You can sell it to someone else, can't you?" What can Weatherbed do if Lodge refuses to refund the money?

4. BIKINI VILLAGE v. NER-SHRINK SWIMWEAR   A clothing store purchased a quantity of women's swimsuits described as "unshrinkable." The bathing suits were delivered and accepted by the store which quickly sold out at a special sale. The swimwear shrunk drastically when immersed in water and proved unsuitable to customers. Can the store recover the price from the supplier?

5. IN RE YU   A supplier of television sets agreed to deliver 20 sets to Yu, an appliance retailer. Yu was to pay for the sets in 30 days. The sets were delivered to Yu's place of business. The following day a trustee in bankruptcy shut down the business on behalf of certain creditors and claimed title to all goods on the premises, including the recently delivered television sets. Who had title to the goods at the time of seizure? Was the trustee correct?

6. AGOSTINO v. ZIMMER   Agostino, a wholsesale furniture dealer, contracted with a manufacturer to manufacture end tables according to an Agostino design. Terms in the contract gave Agostino the right to examine the goods and accept them only if they were satisfactory. Agostino examined several samples of the tables, found them to be satisfactory, directed that they be crated in pairs and undertook to send a transport truck the following morning to pick the goods up. The goods were crated that afternoon. Late that evening an explosion in premises next door occupied by another manufacturer destroyed Zimmer's premises. The end tables were damaged beyond repair. Agostino refused to pay for the goods and Zimmer sued for the price. Will Zimmer's action succeed? Give reasons for your conclusions.

7. CANNON v. VAN PELT   Cannon purchased furniture from Van Pelt C.O.D. Van Pelt loaded several items of furniture destined for various customers, including Cannon. All deliveries were made except the shipment to Cannon when the truck was involved in an accident with another transport. The furniture was damaged as a result of the accident. Cannon refused to accept delivery and refused to pay for the goods. Can Van Pelt force Cannon to accept delivery and pay for the goods?

CHAPTER 5

Consumer Law

YOU ARE THE JURY

STEVENSON v. GENERAL MOTORS ET AL

Rhodes, an independent car dealer, retails General Motors products in a large Canadian city. The vehicles come with a new car warranty against defects and defective parts. General Motors limits its liability to repairs and replacement of parts.

Stevenson purchases a Cadillac from Rhodes which proves to be defective. Complaints include constant stalling, sagging front springs, noisy wheel bearings and leaking rear axle seals. All attempts to fix the vehicle satisfactorily fail.

Stevenson sues the manufacturer and the dealer for the return of the purchase price. The dealer goes out of business at this time. Therefore the only effective remedy is against General Motors, which argues that Stevenson has a contract with Rhodes, the dealer, and not with GM, the manufacturer, and accordingly has no remedy. In the alternative, GM argues it has limited its warranty liability to repair and replacement. "If it can't be fixed it can't be fixed," their lawyer argues. Stevenson argues that a contract that attempts to change the law relating to obligations arising out of latent defects is null and void. How will the case be decided?

OBJECTIVES
• to list the governmental and non-governmental organizations which regulate or participate in consumer law.
• to define prohibited business practices under federal and provincial statutes.

LEXICON

Combines   An alliance of companies designed to form a team and severely restrict competition. The *Combines Investigation Act* prohibits combinations which unduly lessen competition in the production and distribution of goods and services.

Merger   The joining of business firms to form a monopoly. This is illegal if it lessens competition to the detriment of the public and others dealing in the particular goods or services involved.

Consumer law developed in the 1960s as a result of consumers' numerous complaints of shoddy merchandise, poor service, unscrupulous sellers and misleading advertising. Governments were encouraged to enact laws to restrict and punish abuses against the public in the marketing of goods and services. Both the federal and provincial governments responded, and continued to do

so through the '70s. No doubt this response will continue into the 1980s.

There are many reasons for this rise in "consumerism," as it is called. In addition to the dissatisfaction with goods and services, the Canadian consumer is more sophisticated and better educated than ever before in our history. Consumers also have more discretionary time in which to complain, and they are supported by a number of consumer associations and independent research bodies which are capable of investigating and exposing marketing practices detrimental to the public. Governments in recent years have been quick to enact legislation to protect the public and to restrict unfair trade practices.

As a result, in the climate of the 1980s business must conduct its commercial operations within the framework of our Canadian consumer laws. The Stevenson case quoted in the "You Are The Jury" section of this unit is a prime example of a manufacturer's desire, in conflict with the general laws of the country, to limit and restrict liability. As such, it indicates that a working knowledge of consumer law is of great value to both the business person and the consumer.

Structure of consumer law in Canada

The *British North America Act* divides the responsibility for trade and commerce between the federal government and the provincial governments. The federal authority rests with the Ministry of Consumer and Corporate Affairs which maintains a Bureau of Competition Policy, a marketing branch, and an Information and Public Relations branch. Through the Ministry and its various branches, the federal government is able to regulate and prosecute businesses for fraud and deception. The government also regulates products which are hazardous to health and safety by establishing standards of quality and levels of safety. In general, then, the federal system of consumer law is designed to provide the consumer with assistance, information and advice.

The provincial laws are designed to compliment the federal system. All of the provincial governments have authority to regulate trade and commerce within their borders. Each of the provinces has enacted consumer protection legislation establishing consumer protection bureaus which are able to utilize both the provincial and federal laws.

In addition to government agencies, there are a number of independent associations which have a profound effect on the way business is run in

Canada. Here is a list of five of the more important of these organizations and their functions:

- Consumers' Association of Canada
  studies consumer problems; informs public; publishes *Canadian Consumer.*
- Better Business Bureau
  in all major cities and towns; assists business and consumers; checks on ethical practices of businesses in community; checks media advertising (newspapers, television, radio); attempts to resolve complaints from business and public; maintains records on reliability of businesses.
- Canadian Standards Association
  a private testing organization designed to test products and give independent opinion on fitness and suitability of goods.
- Consumer Council
  an independent organization designed to advise the federal Ministry of Consumer and Corporate Affairs.
- The Retail Research Foundation of Canada
  tests products submitted to it by Canadian industry for independent opinion and endorsement.

Combines Investigation Act

For the purposes of Canadian consumer law the most important piece of legislation is the federal *Competition Act* (*Combines Investigation Act*) which is designed to prohibit unfair trade practices. It is enforced through the Bureau of Competition Policy which maintains an investigative branch, a marketing practices branch and an information branch. The Act lists and defines prohibited business conduct and provides the necessary authority for officers of the government to receive complaints, investigate them and act upon them. It also provides substantial penalties for non-compliance with the law.

Price Discrimination

Suppliers who sell goods to a number of customers who are all in competition with each other have a legal obligation to charge all such customers who purchase the same quality and quantity of goods the same price. It is still legal for the supplier to offer discounts for quantity purchases, provided that all buyers who are in competition with each other for resale are advised of the opportunity to purchase at a discount. If a supplier and a customer enter into an arrangement by which the customer is to receive preferential treatment in pricing, then both the supplier and the customer may be prosecuted and fined under the provisions of the Act.

Promotions and Allowances

It is a common business practice for suppliers of businesses to reduce prices by offering rebates and discounts. This practice remains lawful under the Act provided that these rebates and discounts are offered to all customers who are in competition with each other for resale of the goods on the same terms and without preferential treatment.

Predatory Pricing

The federal Act makes it an offence to offer goods for sale at unreasonably low prices designed to drive out competition. For example, for many years it was the practice of a famous Canadian manufacturing company to reduce prices severely each time a new competitor entered the market, and continue with the price reductions until the competitor was forced out of business. Then the manufacturer, having regained its monopoly, raised its prices substantially.

Misleading Price Advertising

The Act provides penalties for misleading the public with respect to the price of items. Retailers who quote a regular price to dramatize the savings of a new price must have in fact sold goods at the regular price mentioned in the usual and ordinary course of their business.

CASE 1   R. v. THE WALKER BOYS' T.V. AND APPLIANCES LTD.

The accused retailer advertised a microwave oven on sale for "$297.00 - regular $469.00." It was established that the accused had not previously sold the oven at the advertised regular price, and that the ordinary selling price of the oven was less than the retailer's advertised regular price. The retailer was prosecuted under the Act and convicted.

Retail Sales Maintenance

It is an offence under the Act for manufacturers and wholesalers to include a term in the contract of sale to a retailer which requires the resale of the goods at a minimum selling price. The objective of this provision is to prevent manufacturers and wholesalers from controlling the amounts at which retailers will offer goods to the public.

False or Misleading Advertising

Canadians who have been victimized by deceptive marketing practices may effectively lodge consumer complaints with the federal government through its Director of Investigation and Research. The Director has been given broad powers to investigate complaints, enter business premises, examine books of account, interview witnesses and prose-

cute business offenders through the courts. Over sixty-five per cent of all complaints brought to the Director's attention deal with advertising which falsely describes the quality of goods or which misleads consumers to believe that goods are being sold at a special low price. Such business practices are of concern not only because the advertiser is attempting to take advantage of consumers, but also because he is attempting to obtain an unfair advantage over his competitors. It should not be surprising to note that many of the complaints laid before the Director originate with the advertisers' competitors who are very prompt in reporting complaints to the Director. Convictions convey to the consumer a sense of justified power, while at the same time warning business to be honest in its dealings with the public.

CASE 2   R. v. CHARLES R. CLARK

Clark carried on business as Clark's TV in London, Ontario. He published a series of advertisements in a local newspaper offering for sale Chrysler Airtemp, 5000 BTU air conditioners for $59.00. A complaint came to the attention of the Director and an investigation was launched. It was established that, in contravention of section 37 of the Act, during the period that the advertisements were published the accused did not have a reasonable quantity of the advertised model in stock. Clark was convicted on six separate charges and fined $2 000.00 on each.

CASE 3   R. v. LISTOWELL TROPHIES LTD.

The accused company's catalogue contained the statement that "you are entitled to a 33⅓ per cent discount off all items in this catalogue." It was shown not only that the catalogue prices were not the regular prices at which articles were sold, but also that the prices were not specifically represented therein to be the regular or ordinary prices.

The company argued that the representations were true as it did in fact discount the catalogue price by 33⅓ per cent. The government prosecutor argued that the word "discount" gave the impression of a bargain price which, in fact, was no discount at all because it involved a reduction from a fictitious price. The judge applied a general impression test: "The statement conveyed a general impression that was false and misleading. Consumers were in fact misled or deceived by the promised discount which was not a bargain as the statement implied." Thus, a statement which was literally true was found to be misleading in the context of the entire advertisement.

CASE 4 R. v. NATIONAL UPHOLSTERING MFG. LTD.

In advertising furniture for sale National represented that the furniture was manufactured in their factory and that the purchaser would therefore receive "big factory to you savings." The Director investigated and found that most of the furniture advertised was not manufactured by National and that savings to the customer would not have been as great as he might have anticipated. National was prosecuted and convicted under section 36 of the Act.

CASE 5 R. v. CLAUDE ARBOUR INC.

A retailer advertised a photocopier at a special price of $2 995. A customer interested in the "bargain" found that the photocopier was indeed on sale for that price, but that the price did not include the cylinder which was an important part of the copier. It would have to be purchased separately. Consequently, the court found the advertisement misleading and convicted the retailer.

In advertising products for sale retailers often use terms such as "reduced," "special," and "on sale." If they do so and a complaint is made or the Director uncovers such advertising in the course of a routine investigation, they must justify the terms as being factual descriptions of what actually happened. Otherwise, they may be prosecuted by the Director. The term "on sale" may only be used if the sale price is actually lower than the usual selling price of the same goods.

Court decisions also make it clear that once the goods are placed on sale, the period of the sale must be limited.

CASE 6 R. v. RED CIRCLE SHOPS

Goods which had sold regularly for several months at $200 each were put on sale at a price of $179 each. The goods remained tagged "on sale" for a period of 18 months. Was this a contravention of the *Competition Act*?

The court decided that 18 months was not a reasonable time for the goods to remain on sale and that the tags represented a false and misleading statement. While the court agreed that the goods could be sold at the lower price, it concluded that the designation "on sale" would have to come off in a reasonable time.

Bait and Switch

In the past unscrupulous sellers have advertised certain makes or types of goods at low prices in order to attract customers. When customers inquired about the advertised goods, they were shown such goods, but the sales person discouraged the person from buying the goods by describing them as inferior and attempting to divert the customer to another make or model which sold for a higher price. The Act now makes such tactics unlawful.

Under the Act, sellers who advertise products for sale must maintain on hand a reasonable quantity of the goods offered at the sale prices. However, retailers will not be liable for prosecution if they can establish they were unable to obtain a reasonable quantity of the goods to be on hand at the time of the sale because of events beyond their control – for example, strikes, damage to goods in transit, and suppliers' failure to deliver. Retailers who have made an honest mistake may also avoid prosecution under the Act by providing consumers with a "rain check" on request. The retailer then orders the out-of-stock item for delivery at a later time but still at the advertised price.

Correction Notices

The Act attempts to protect the honest businessman who has inadvertently made a false or misleading statement in an advertisement. The honest retailer may avoid prosecution by immediately publishing a correction notice intended to bring the correct information to those who might have read the original advertisement. The correction must be published as soon as practical after the error or misstatement is detected, and it must be placed conspicuously so as to be likely to come to the attention of consumers who may have seen the advertisement. Prosecution may only be avoided if the advertiser acted in complete good faith in placing both the original ad and the subsequent correction. Dishonest persons who deliberately place false advertisements and then attempt to avoid liability by placing corrective ads on, for example, the back page of the newspaper long after a sale has been concluded will not be protected from prosecution and conviction.

Promotional Contests

The Act requires that businesses which conduct promotional contests must select winners by random choice or contestant's skill and distribute prizes without undue delay. Businesses are also required to disclose to contestants the number and approximate value of the prizes. They must also publish or display any factual information which would materially affect the chances of winning.

CASE 7   R. v. ANDREAS PIZZA MILL LTD.

Andreas Pizza Mill distributed entry forms to its customers, all of whom were eligible to win a trip to Greece "all expenses paid." The forms did not show a date for the drawing and did not contain any facts which would disclose to a consumer the chances of winning. The business was convicted under the *Combines Investigation Act.*

Misrepresentation of Product Quality

The Act makes it an offence to falsely advertise the quality of goods and to advertise the quality and capabilities of the goods without having conducted "adequate and proper tests." The Act requires that the testing be conducted by an independent public agency or by the National Research Council of Canada. The onus is on the advertiser to establish that advertised claims have in fact been established by tests.

Restriction of Competition

The Act also prohibits business conduct which tends to restrict free competition in the market place and establishes procedures for investigating combines, mergers, monopolies and unfair trade practices.

CASE 8   R. v. GARGUNTA SUPPLY LTD.

A company with an exclusive licence to distribute a new and valuable product entered into arrangements with its retailer-customers which required them to buy other products in addition to the goods over which it maintained a monopoly. The court held that this was a "tying arrangement" which was generally prejudicial to the welfare of the business community.

Provincial Consumer Protection Acts

Each of the provinces has enacted legislation which regulates businesses and protects the consumer. The provinces administer their consumer protection laws through consumer protection bureaus which attempt to resolve disputes between businesses and customers. The usual procedure is for the consumer to lodge a complaint in writing to the bureau, which in turn communicates with the business in question and attempts to mediate a settlement of the dispute. If the complaint and attempt to settle reveal that the merchant has been guilty of sharp practice or deceit, the bureau will refer the matter to the government agency which licences the business. The agency has the power to deal with and decide the matter and may revoke or suspend the business' registration licence, penalize it by fines ranging from $2 000 to $25 000, imprison offenders or obtain restraining orders through the courts to prohibit further objectionable activities.

Unconscionable transactions statutes

Each of the provinces has enacted legislation which gives the courts the power to review transactions which, having regard to all the circumstances, are unconscionable or grossly unfair. An unconscionable transaction has been described as a contract which no reasonable, honest person would require another to perform and one which no reasonable, prudent person would agree to perform unless compelled to do so under great stress. The conduct of one of the parties must be seen to be excessive or unprincipled. There must be some evidence that unfair advantage was taken of the other party. The victim may have such a transaction judicially reviewed. If the court finds the transaction is in fact unconscionable, it has the power to remedy the situation by varying or amending the terms.

CASE 9   MUNDY v. MUNDY

Herman and Kaye Mundy were husband and wife, and partners in a retail children's clothing business. Alleging cruelty, Kaye separated from her husband. She had great difficulty in adjusting to the separation and suffered a nervous breakdown. She found further participation in the business was intolerable and consented to Herman's offer to buy her out. After a short period of negotiation, Kaye agreed to sell her business interest to her husband at a fraction of its real value. Two years later, fully recovered and adjusted to her new life, Kaye thought better of the transaction and applied to the court to have it set aside. What do you think was the result? Give reasons for your answer.

How to lodge a consumer complaint

Any person who wishes to inform the Director of Investigation and Research of any matter that may involve advertising or marketing practices can do so by writing to the Marketing Practices Branch, Ministry of Consumer and Corporate Affairs, at one of the following addresses:

Montreal Towers
6th Floor
5151 George Street
Halifax, Nova Scotia
B3J 1M5

Pacific Centre Ltd.
P.O. Box 10059
700 W Georgia Street
Vancouver, British Columbia
V7Y 1C9

6th Floor
4900 Yonge Street
Willowdale, Ontario
M2N 6A6

855 Ste. Catherine Street E.
12th Floor
Montreal, Quebec
H2L 4N4

Room 201-206
St. Mary Avenue
Winnipeg, Manitoba
R3C 0M6

Information may also be obtained from the Complaints Officer, Marketing Practices Branch, Bureau of Competition Policy, Consumer and Corporate Affairs Canada, Ottawa/Hull, K1A 0C9. In order to assist Canadian consumers in obtaining information and lodging complaints of a general nature, the federal government has established a clearing house known as "The Consumer" which may be contacted at Box 99, Ottawa, Ontario K1N 8P9. Consumers may write to this address either to obtain any consumer information they desire or to provide the federal government with information on any matter of consumer concern.

KEY TO YOU ARE THE JURY

STEVENSON v. GENERAL MOTORS ET AL

The court rejected arguments by General Motors that Stevenson's remedy was limited to an action against the dealer. The warranty against defects which the manufacturer gives to a dealer is transferred to a buyer who may look directly to the manufacturer for a remedy in the courts. Manufacturers are liable for latent defects in their products and cannot, under the pretext of the contract, avoid their responsibility or limit their liability. A judgment was given against GM requiring it to repay Stevenson an amount equivalent to the selling price of the vehicle.

Checklist: Consumer law

COMBINES

Director of Investigation and Research, Combines Investigation Act, Ministry of Consumer and Corporate Affairs, Place du Portage, Ottawa/Hull K1A 0C9.

Restrictive Trade Practices Commission, Box 336, Station A, Ottawa, Ontario.

CONSUMER PROTECTION

Information Branch, Ministry of Consumer and Corporate Affairs, Place du Portage, Victoria Street, Ottawa/Hull K1A 0C9.

For information regarding restrictive trade practices, consumer complaints, hazardous products:

Ministry of Consumer and Corporate Affairs, 10065 Jasper Ave., Edmonton, Alberta.

British Columbia Ministry of Consumer and Corporate Affairs, Parliament Buildings, Victoria, B.C.

Manitoba Consumer Bureau, 307 Kennedy Street, Winnipeg, Manitoba.

New Brunswick Consumer Bureau, Provincial Secretary, Box 6000, Fredericton, New Brunswick.

Newfoundland Ministry of Provincial Affairs and Environment, Elizabeth Towers, Elizabeth Avenue, St. John's Nfld.

Nova Scotia Department of Consumer Affairs, Box 998, Halifax, Nova Scotia.

Ontario Consumer Protection Bureau, Ministry of Consumer and Commercial Relations, 555 Yonge Street, Toronto, Ontario.

Prince Edward Island Provincial Secretary, Box 2000, Charlottetown, Prince Edward Island.

Quebec Consumer Protection Bureau, 800 Place d'Youville, 7th Floor, Quebec, Quebec.

Saskatchewan Consumer Affairs, 11th Floor, Saskatchewan Power Building, Scarth and Victoria, Regina, Saskatchewan.

Review

1. What role does the federal government play in consumer protection? From the information in this chapter, prepare a schematic diagram tracing the flow of federal authority from the *British North America Act* to the various government branches created to protect the consumer. List one or more functions of the various branches or bureaus which appear in your diagram.

2. What is the role of the provincial *Consumer Protection Acts* and bureaus?

3. What is the *Combines Investigation Act?* What purpose does it serve? List the practices that the statute is designed to regulate.

4. What is the Better Business Bureau? List its functions.

5. List the non-governmental organizations which are designed to protect consumers. Identify the functions of each.

6. REGINA v. LIBIS Libis, a supplier, consistently gave Farmer a discount although Farmer

was not a high volume buyer. Libis did not advertise availability of discounts, neither did he give any to other customers other than high volume dealers. Farmer appreciated the discounts but was not aware he was receiving "preferential treatment." Have either Libis or Farmer committed any offence? If not, give reasons. If so, identify the offence and the probable consequences.

7. REGINA v. CROSS Duggan complained to the Ministry of Consumer and Corporate Affairs that he had been driven out of business unfairly by Cross. Duggan claimed that Cross, who had been in the sheet metal business in a small community for years, had dramatically reduced prices when Duggan opened a competing shop. Unable to compete, Duggan was forced to close his doors and Cross promptly raised prices to new highs. Duggan claimed that he had evidence that Cross had eliminated competition in the past by similar practices. In fact, no other person had been able to maintain a competing business for over ten years. "This is free enterprise," Cross claimed.

"When I can afford to give customers a good deal, I do it. The customer benefits and if others can't complete what has that to do with me?" Has Cross committed an offence? Consider the issues and consequences.

8. You run an honest business. You are close to the line, but solvent. You are disturbed by the content of ads that have been appearing in the local newspaper. On the basis of your experience you are satisfied that the ads, which have been placed by a competitor, are deceptive. Your complaints to the publisher go unanswered. What steps might you take to deal with the matter and what results would you hope to accomplish? Consider the consequences to your competitor should you be right.

9. Define retail sales maintenance. Is it a legitimate business practice or an offence?

10. An examination of an advertisement you have just placed in the local newspaper actually promises more than you can deliver. Your sale, which will last two days, starts tonight. The next edition of the newspaper will be on sale tomorrow evening. What steps, if any, would you consider necessary under the circumstances?

11. How can a consumer register an effective complaint with the federal government?

CHAPTER 6

Employment Law

Unit 1 The relationship between employers and employees

YOU ARE THE JURY

CRUMP v. PROUDFOOT

Walter Proudfoot, an executive with one advertising company, lured Martha Crump away from her employment with another company in a distant city by offering her a fantastic salary. Martha quit her job, left her friends and relatives and set up a new home in the strange city. Martha learned that, in addition to good pay, each member of the staff who was on the payroll as of December 31st of each year received a substantial bonus.

After 18 months of creating innovative and imaginative scripts and copy, Martha advised Proudfoot that she was pregnant and while she would ask for maternity leave, she definitely intended to continue working. Shortly after this conversation Proudfoot became unusually critical of Martha's work. One day, without advance warning and in the presence of several other workers, Proudfoot shouted, "Your work has lost its sparkle. I can't afford to carry deadwood around here. You're fired. I want you to disappear. Tell us where to send your things." When Martha returned to the office the following day she was stopped by a fellow employee. "Sorry, Martha, I've got orders not to let you in here. You know what he's done? He's hired that "Whiz Kid" just out of college for half of your salary." Martha realized with horror that in addition to the degrading way she was discharged, she wouldn't be around to collect the year-end bonus. She sought comparable positions in the city, but could find none. It became clear that in order to find work which would utilize her talents, she would likely have to move again.

This case presents several issues. Can you identify them? See if you are able to identify Martha's rights.

OBJECTIVES

- to define the legal relationship between employers and employees.
- to identify the method by which a contract of employment may be legally terminated.
- to list employee activities that will warrant the employer dismissing for cause.
- to analyze employer conduct in dismissing an employee which may lead to an action for wrongful dismissal.

LEXICON ~~ON Test~~

Dismissal for Cause Justified firing of an employee *without notice* for undesirable conduct; employee to leave instantly.

Master and Servant A branch of law (more properly defined today as *Employment Law*) in which an employer is referred to as *Master* and an employee as *Servant*.*

Negligence The act of doing something improperly, or failing to do something which one has a duty to do which results in damage or injury to another person or the property of another person.

Notice A statement of intention to terminate employment at a specified future date; may be given either by the employer or the employee.

Quantum Meruit So much as it is worth.

Vicarious Liability Employer's legal responsibility for damage or loss suffered by a third party as a result of the negligence of an employee.

Wrongful Dismissal Improper firing of employee without proper notice and/or without justifiable reasons.

In this chapter we deal with rights and duties of employers and employees and, to a lesser degree, with the rights of customers or clients.

Employment is based on a contract of hiring and service in which the essential elements we discussed in Chapter Three are coloured and varied by the special rules of the Law of Employment. We may find that the employment contract has been expressed by spoken words only; in a formal written document; or that the ingredients of the contract are implied mainly through the conduct of the parties – that is, the way in which they behaved towards each other during the course of employment. Any of these possibilities or a combination of them creates a valid contract of employment.

*In reading texts or cases it may help to mentally convert Master to Employer, Servant to Employee. When looking up reference material, include both of the headings Master and Servant in your search.

The federal and provincial governments have attempted to establish regulations and minimum standards to assist workers. Therefore it will be necessary during the course of our discussion to examine the impact government laws have on the relationship between employer and employee.

General relationship rules

The employer has a legal obligation to pay agreed wages as they fall due. Employees who are paid hourly wages are entitled to be paid only for the time actually worked. The hourly rates are subject to laws regarding minimum wages and overtime.

Salaried workers are entitled to their salary which must be paid at the times agreed to in the employment contract. It is usual for an employer to pay full salary to an employee even though the employee has been away for short periods either because of illness or personal or family requirements. This is particularly true if the employee is of long standing and is considered a valuable asset to the business. However, the employee does not have any legal right to such payment. If the employer decides to withhold some pay in this situation, the employee receives pay on a percentage or quantum meruit basis.

The employer must provide safe equipment and a safe place to work. Otherwise, the employee has the right to refuse to attend work until the dangerous situation has been remedied.

The employer is entitled to issue only lawful orders to an employee. If an unlawful order is resisted by an employee, the employer cannot insist that the thing be done. If the employer does insist, the employee is justified in refusing to comply and has the right to resign.

The employer must reimburse the employee for any authorized disbursement or expense incurred out of the pocket of the employee in the performing of necessary services for the employer. If the expenses are reasonable, they must be paid even though the employer argues they were not specifically authorized.

The employer does not have any claim on the employees after work time has been completed. The employer cannot prevent the employee from taking a part-time position with another employer unless the part-time work represents a conflict of interest – for example, an employee working for a competitor – or unless the part-time work interferes with the full-time job – for example, the employee is too tired from part-time work and therefore represents a hazard to himself and others in the operation of machinery.

The employer is required to make available work of the type for which the employee was hired, and to provide an adequate opportunity for the employee to perform such work and to maintain skills.

The employee is required to perform the services contracted for without negligence; comply with lawful orders; conform with the system; act honestly; be truthful and loyal; come to work on time and as often as required by the contract. If the employee consistently fails to do these things, the employer has the right to dismiss for cause.

How to end employment with notice

No-one has a life contract to work for any business. Neither may any employer expect to hold employees in bondage forever. Statistics show that workers will change jobs five or more times during their working careers. Often new positions take employees to another employer. The likelihood of such turnovers in the labour force makes the rules governing the proper termination of an employee's contract for services extremely important.

Some contracts specify that the employee will be hired for a certain period of time or until a certain job has been completed. At the end of the term or job, the employment comes to an end automatically, without the need for either employer or employee to give formal notice. From the beginning of the contract each is considered to have notice of its termination.

But suppose that either the employer (say, Gowan) or the employee (say, Pryor, a young college graduate) desires the termination of the employment before the time period specified in the contract expires. Perhaps Pryor feels she could profit from five years' employment, and Gowan feels that is just right for his purposes. If they sign an employment contract for a five year period, at the end of the term Pryor would be free to leave Gowan to pursue other goals.

Once Pryor starts working, either she or Gowan may find that things are not working out. Gowan may find he has to cut back because of financial restraints. He may find that Pryor is, after all, not suited to the position. Pryor may find that she is not being given the type of work opportunity she was promised, and therefore she may not want to continue in a dead-end job.

It is for reasons such as these that parties will frequently insert in their contracts a clause permitting either of them to terminate the employment on giving the other notice. The details of giving notice would be written in the agreement.

If Pryor wishes to quit before the term is up, she must do so by strictly complying with the requirement in the contract for giving notice. In her case, probably three to six months' notice would be adequate. She will continue to work for the three or six months, and then be free to leave. If Gowan wishes to release her, he may do so by giving her proper notice advising that her employment has been terminated, but he must keep her on staff until the time in the notice has expired.

But this kind of situation is less pervasive than the existence of formal contracts. Most people are hired on an on-going basis and are paid weekly, bi-weekly or monthly. Usually these contracts do not contain any statement indicating how much notice must be given by either party to terminate employment. By means of precedent in such cases the law inserts into the contract an implied term that the parties must give reasonable notice of termination. What is reasonable notice depends on the peculiar circumstances of each case.

The general rule is to look to the pay period as a guide. If the employee is paid by the week, one full week's notice must be given before the employment can be legally terminated by either the employer or employee. If the employee is paid bi-weekly, two weeks notice is required; if monthly, one full month's notice is needed.

This general rule may be varied by circumstances. There are customs in certain trades that dictate how a notice is to be given and how much notice is required. Everyone in these businesses knows what the customary rules are and if a question of notice comes before a court, it will likely follow the custom of the trade or business as it has been established by the employers and employees themselves.

A second circumstance which may cause the general rule to be varied involves situations in which the conduct of the parties clearly indicates they anticipated a long term relationship when the contract of employment was made. Employees such as administrators, accountants, engineers, supervisors and administrative assistants are hired to work on the long range goals of the business. Traditionally, these people are valuable and cannot be quickly replaced. Similarly, if released it may take them a considerable time to locate a comparable position elsewhere. For these reasons the pay period test is inappropriate and there is an implied term incorporated into the employment contract of such employees that reasonable notice will be three to six months. But executives and other highly placed personnel are entitled to anywhere from six to twenty-four months' notice.

Mid-management personnel are entitled to three to six months' notice. If a key employee holds a particularly important position or has been with the firm for a sufficient length of time, the reasonable amount of notice has been held to be nine months to one year.

You should keep in mind that the above rules relating to notice apply equally whether the termination occurs by the employer discharging the employee or the employee quitting.

CASE 1   IN RE THE WILSON CORPORATION

Bell, a valued employee of long standing, requested that he be permitted to resign his position immediately because of a serious family situation. Bell was paid by the month. A clause in his contract stated that either he or the company could terminate the contract by giving six months' notice. The company felt it important for Bell to stay with them until a suitable replacement could be trained. They estimated this would take more than six months.

This case presents an interesting contrast between the needs of the employee on the one hand and of the employer on the other. When Bell negotiated his employment contract with Wilson, he agreed to give the company at least six months' notice before leaving and he had an assurance from the company that he could not be dismissed without a similar notice. As the contract stood in law, Bell had to give six months' notice and stay on for at least that period. Why, then, did Bell and Wilson try to change the terms of the contract? They did so because, as we discovered in Chapter Three, the parties to a contract may enter into any new, mutually agreeable arrangement they can negotiate. In this case, the solicitor for the company urged it to let Bell leave immediately and drew up a fresh agreement which permitted Bell to leave as he requested. The advice was well-founded because soon afterward Bell's personal life disintegrated around him. He would not have been able under the circumstances to continue as an employee of the company. The moral of this case seems to be that when an employee wants to leave, the employer should not insist on "the letter of the law" regarding proper notice in the employment contract.

If an employee is terminated without proper notice he may sue for an amount equivalent to the pay he would have received if he had been given proper notice and had continued to work to the last day of the termination term. The employee is also entitled to sue for benefits which would have accrued up to and including the last day.

If an employee leaves his employment without giving proper notice, the employer need pay only to the date of leaving. He also has cause for action against the employee for damages for breach of contract. The employer would be able to collect for all loss which results directly from the improper action of the employee (i.e., the cost of advertising for and hiring a replacement).

How to end employment for cause

If working conditions or the employer's conduct are such that prudent employees could not reasonably be expected to continue in employment, the employee may resign without giving notice and may sue the employer for breach of contract.

If an employee's conduct justifies dismissal for cause, the employer may summarily fire the employee without giving notice. The employee is entitled to be paid, including any accumulated benefits, to the date of dismissal. If the conduct for which the employee has been discharged causes the employer a loss, the employer may sue to recover damages.

The employee may be dismissed for cause for any of the following reasons: negligence, incompetence, non-compliance with lawful orders, disgraceful conduct, disloyalty, dishonesty or other circumstances that render it impossible for him to effectively comply with a contract of service.

Negligence

An employer has the right to expect from an employee the quality of work of a reasonably diligent and careful person who normally performs services under similar circumstances. The employee has a duty to the employer to live up to the standard of an average careful employee. If the employee's conduct falls below that standard and the employer suffers loss as a result, the employer has the right to discharge without notice.

CASE 2   MCLEOD v. THOMPSON

McLeod sued her former employer for wrongful dismissal. Thompson claimed that although McLeod had worked satisfactorily in his office for five years, she had seriously exceeded her authority in drafting a document which resulted in his being sued by a client.

A single act of negligence which results in loss may entitle the employer to discharge an employee. The conduct of the employee must be of a serious nature and must result in a recognizable loss to the employer. In this case, Thompson not only lost a client, he became the defendant in a

court action. He was justified in dismissing his employee. Thus we see that one negligent act can wipe out several years of good, solid work.

Incompetence

An employee is expected to provide the degree of skill which is normally provided by persons in comparable positions working for equal pay. An employee who continually turns in substandard work provides evidence of incompetence. If people cannot or will not do the work for which they were hired, the employer may discharge without notice. However, upon identifying the faults in the work, the employer must bring them to the attention of the employee and provide a reasonable time for improvement. The employer must do what reasonably can be done to assist. The employee is then expected to bring the work up to standard. If he does not do so within a reasonable time, the employee may be discharged.

CASE 3   DEANE v. NATIONAL COLLEGE BOARD

Deane, a tenured professor, was discharged by a university which claimed that he consistently failed to show up for classes, failed to conduct tests according to standard departmental procedures and had failed to complete any significant research project. Deane sued for wrongful dismissal claiming that he expected students to be able to work on their own and that no-one had pointed out to him that his testing procedure did not conform. At the hearing, he produced a large quantity of unpublished notes which he claimed was his research. Student evaluations over the years had consistently rated his performance as among the poorest in the department. Deane had been warned about his ''no show'' record and demands were made on him to conduct required research. What do you think was the result?

Compliance

The employee must obey the lawful orders of the employer. The employee breaches this condition of the employment contract by refusing to perform the task outright or by simply neglecting to do the task without actually refusing. Both actions amount to insubordination which can lead to dismissal without notice. Employees are also expected to conform to the system by attending meetings, completing forms in a certain way and following established procedures. Certain individuals are not able to conform substantially to rules of the establishment. The results for the non-conformist may be legal discharge without notice.

114

Disgraceful behaviour

The conduct of the employee is of vital concern to the employer. Outrageous behaviour on the part of the employee may justify dismissal for cause. Grossly immoral conduct which is likely to disrupt work or affect the morale of other employees is behaviour which will warrant dismissal. The offence may take place anywhere. Reports of it at home or in public may result in dismissal, but dismissal is much more likely if the offence occurs on the job.

An employee who is convicted of a serious crime may be summarily dismissed. However, not every conviction will entitle the employer to fire. In order to be justified in the firing of an employee on the grounds of conviction, the crime must be of such a nature as to show the employee guilty of immorality. Common examples include convictions for theft, embezzlement or forgery. But there have also been dismissals under special circumstances: a conviction for impaired driving led to the dismissal of a beer salesman; a conviction for indecent assault resulted in the justified dismissal for cause of a male counsellor in a home for young female offenders; and a taxi driver was discharged after being convicted of theft of an automobile.

Misconduct

An employee may be discharged for cause for general misconduct at work. Examples of this include consistent tardiness in arriving, consistent absence from work or from an assigned work area, rudeness towards the employer, co-workers or customers. The employer is also entitled to the complete loyalty of the employee. For example, a secretary who persistently attempted to undermine the credibility of her immediate supervisors was justifiably fired by the firm for disloyalty.

The basis of the relationship between employer and employee is trust. If the employee proves untrustworthy, the employer is entitled to discharge. An executive, fired on the spot for lying to his superior during the course of a meeting sued for wrongful dismissal. The court held that deliberately lying to the employer broke down the trust which was essential to continue the business relationship. An employer has no legal obligations to keep an untrustworthy person on staff.

Disability

If events occur which render it difficult or impossible for the employee to carry on his duties, the employer may be justified in terminating the

employment even though the employee is not responsible for any wrongdoing. If, because of illness or accident, an employee becomes permanently disabled and is unable to perform all of the services required under the terms of the employment contract, the employer may consider the purpose of the original working arrangement as having been frustrated and may dismiss the employee for that reason.

CASE 4   MYERS v. PETERS

Myers, who had worked for Peters for twenty years, was dismissed after contracting an illness which kept him away from work fairly regularly. His physician advised that with the exception of being periodically incapacitated, Myers was perfectly normal. The illness was considered permanent, but Myers argued Peters should have kept him on and hired periodic part-timers to fill in when he was sick. "I have a business to run. I hate doing this to Harry, but I need someone I can count on," said Peters. Who is right?

Employee's right to leave

Just as the employer has the right to dismiss for cause the employee has a right to leave employment for cause.

The employee is justified in leaving employment immediately, for cause and without giving notice, in the following circumstances:

- There are dangerous premises or equipment likely to cause injury and which the employer refuses or neglects to rectify. The employee must return if the employer rectifies or if correction is undertaken within a reasonable time.
- The employer persistently requests the employee to do an unlawful act. The employee must refuse.
- The employer makes an unreasonable demand. Employee may refuse.
- There is non-payment of salary, wages, commission or other earnings.

If such circumstances force an employee to quit, he has a right to sue his former employer for damages for breach of contract.

Wrongful dismissal

CASE 5   GIFFORD v. STONE

Gifford, the president of Stone's business company, was first advised that his services had been terminated one day before a public announcement

was made that he had "resigned" and would be succeeded by another person. The surrounding circumstances of the dismissal were highly embarrassing. Stone had the firm's accountant calculate three months of Gifford's salary and the amount of his earned benefits. Stone presented Gifford with a cheque for the resulting amount and demanded that he surrender all office keys and leave immediately. Instructions were given to bar the former president from the premises. His personal effects were sent on by courier. Gifford sued for wrongful dismissal.

Instead of giving notice, an employer is entitled to pay a reasonable sum of money to a dismissed employee and then insist that the employee leave the premises immediately. The payment must be for an amount equal to the salary and benefits to which the employee would have been entitled during a period of proper notice. The payment takes the place of proper notice and puts the employee in the same position as if notice had been given and the employee had worked to the end of the notice period. In the Gifford case, no notice was given. If Gifford's contract calls for three months' notice, Stone's calculations provided adequate compensation for loss of employment. If Gifford's contract did not specify a minimum period of notice, it would be a question of fact whether or not the calculation represented reasonable compensation.

While an employer's inherent right to dismiss is recognized, he will not be allowed to run roughshod over employees he wishes to terminate. Employees who are wrongfully dismissed have the right to sue their employers for breach of contract. Unless the basic work agreement is part of a collective union agreement that contains a provision that employees who are wrongfully dismissed shall have their jobs back, the employer is not entitled to be reinstated. The employee's only remedy is a claim for damages for wrongful dismissal.

In *Bardal v. Globe & Mail Ltd.* McRuer C.J.H.C. laid down the basic formula (known as the Bardal test) which is followed in Canada today:

> The contractual obligation is to give reasonable notice and continue the servant in employment. If the servant is dismissed without reasonable notice he is entitled to the damages that flow from the failure to observe this contractual obligation, which damages the servant is bound in law to mitigate to the best of his ability . . .
>
> There can be no catalogue laid down as to what is reasonable notice in particular classes of

116

cases. The reasonableness of the notice must be decided with reference to each particular case, having regard to the character of the employment, the length of service of the servant, the age of the servant and the availability of similar employment, having regard to the experience, training and qualifications of the servant.

Damages are designed to put injured parties back to the same position they would have been in had there been no breach. An award of damages includes losses which are a direct and natural result of the employer's breach, i.e., lost salary for the period of time for which the employee should have been given notice; lost benefits calculated to the end of the notice period, and reasonable costs of seeking new employment.

An employee who is dismissed wrongfully is not entitled to any compensation for injured feelings or damage to reputation. Presumably if the employee wins the action, this is proof enough that the employer acted badly. The victory in court should repair any damage to one's good name.

In the case discussed above, Gifford received no compensation for the cavalier manner in which Stone let him go. Gifford was a highly placed specialist. The court held that reasonable notice in his case would have been 21 months. Damages in lieu of notice were assessed at $166 000 plus the rather considerable expenses incurred by Gifford in his effort to find other employment. This judgment included lost salary, the cost of equivalent pension, disability and life insurance and medical and dental benefits during the notice period.

Mitigation

Employees who have been wrongfully dismissed have an obligation to make a sincere and dedicated effort to obtain other employment. If an employee declines an opportunity for suitable alternate employment, the court will reduce the amount of the employee's damages by the amount that might have been earned during the required term of notice.

Vicarious liability of employer

The employer is liable to third parties for harm caused to them or their property as a result of the negligence of his employees in performing activities in the course of the employer's business.

Suppose a customer is seriously injured on the premises of a business. If it can be established that an employee's act resulted in the injury, the employee will be liable to compensate the customer. If the customer can prove further that the employee was performing duties for the employer at the time, the customer may sue the employer as well.

Employers who are successfully sued under the vicarious liability principle may in turn have a good claim against negligent employees. In such cases the steps of the litigation would be:

- third party sues employer and worker.
- judgment to third party against both.
- employer claims in same action against employee.
- third party collects from employer.
- employer collects (amounts paid to third party) from employee.

CASE 6   BETTGER v. SCHWARTZ ET AL

Bettger was struck by an object thrown from the roof of a construction site by an employee of Schwartz. On several previous occasions Schwartz had warned employees not to throw debris to the ground. A written directive had been posted in the main office prohibiting this method of discarding material.

Schwartz was liable. An employer continues to be liable for acts of employees even though the employer had no knowledge of the act and actually prohibited the type of behaviour that led to the injury. The employer continues to be liable even though the act complained of may have occurred in a distant location over which the employer could exercise little or no control.

CASE 7   SPETZ v. SINGH ET AL

Spetz was injured by a truck driven by an employee of Singh. The driver had finished his duties early but instead of returning to the shop, detoured to visit a girlfriend in another part of town. The employer denied liability, claiming that she had not authorized the side trip, had no knowledge of it, and had given strict instructions to return to the office as soon as deliveries had been completed. Spetz claimed this should make no difference: "All I know is I seen this name, Singh, written all over the truck so if she's not responsible, who is?"

The court held that the driver had left the course of employment and had embarked on an individual enterprise, "a fun and frolic of his own wholly unconcerned with his employer's business." The employer was not liable. Spetz had a cause of action only against the negligent driver.

Baxter sued both a bartender and the owner of a lounge for injuries resulting from an assault. Baxter had been critical of the bartender's national origin, and the assault took place after a violent argument on this matter. The owner denied liability, claiming that while the bartender was on duty in his lounge he did not pay him to argue with customers, particularly on racial matters. The employer further claimed that the customer was the author of his own misfortune because he taunted the powerful barman beyond a point at which self-control would be possible.

Is the owner liable to pay damages to the customer? Suppose the argument raged around the quality of liquor served on the premises? Would this affect your answer?

KEY TO YOU ARE THE JURY

CRUMP v. PROUDFOOT   The main issue is whether or not Martha was wrongfully dismissed. The aspect of law to apply is the common law rules that define an employer's right to discharge an employee with or without notice.

The contractual obligation of the employer is to give reasonable notice of dismissal and either retain the employee for that period or pay the employee a reasonable sum for the privilege of demanding instant departure. Having failed to give any notice at all, Proudfoot breached the employment contract. Martha is entitled to damages for wrongful dismissal.

The court held that six months would have constituted a reasonable notice period, and Martha therefore recovered an amount equal to six months' salary plus compensation for expenses incurred in her job search. The six months' notice period found by the judge to be adequate would not have taken her to the end of the year; therefore the bonus question was not resolved. However, on the basis of previously decided cases, she probably would not have been entitled to claim the bonus. She was also not entitled to any damages for the embarrassment or hurt feelings which may have been caused by the manner of dismissal, nor to any amount for damage to reputation.

The maternity issue is a secondary one in that Martha could not prove on the balance of probabilities that Proudfoot fired her because of her pregnancy. If she was able to prove such discriminatory motives, they would constitute another ground for her claim of wrongful dismissal.

Proudfoot's only defence was that Martha was incompetent. The overriding evidence was that her work was superior. His last-minute criticism of her work carried little weight at the trial.

Unit II Federal and provincial legislation relating to employment

YOU ARE THE JURY

IN RE NAPOLEON PRESS LIMITED

Hardy is the principal shareholder and a director of an incorporated printing and publishing business. His wife and the firm's accountant hold the balance of the shares and are also directors.

The company employs seven men and three women. Although the women perform the same work as some of the men, they are paid less. Although they complain that Hardy should give equal pay for equal work, nothing is done to adjust their wages. To complicate matters, for the past several months Hardy has been having difficulty meeting his payroll with the result that the workers are frequently paid a week or so late. Four weeks' wages are now in arrears, but Hardy has assured his workers that a big contract is about to be signed and "everything will be alright." The workers feel frustrated and foolish, that they are "working for nothing," but are concerned about quitting and desperately need to be paid.

What issues are raised by this case? Assume that Hardy's position will not improve. Plan a strategy for these workers to collect their pay. Consider all the legal remedies you believe are available to them.

OBJECTIVES

- to list and describe the various procedures by which an employer may be compelled to pay wages.
- to identify statutory rules against discrimination in hiring, work conditions, promotion and training.
- to list rules designed to promote equality in employment.

LEXICON

Garnishee The legal attachment of wages or other debts owing to a debtor.

Human Rights Rights of all human beings which have been established by the common consent of western civilization and which are legally established in Canada by federal or provincial government legislation. This legislation is designed to outlaw discrimination on grounds of sex, marital status, age, national origin, race, colour or religion by establishing commissions with investigative powers, the authority to deal with and decide issues, and powers to penalize.

Collection of wages

The employer has a duty to pay the salary, wages or commission agreed to under the contract of employment. If the employer fails to pay them, they constitute a debt owing to the employee and he may collect them by an ordinary law suit. This is a cumbersome and at times lengthy procedure. There are more expeditious means of compelling the reluctant employer to pay.

Master and servant applications

In Canada, an employee who has not been paid may lay a complaint (charge) through the local police. The police will arrange to have a justice of the peace summon the employer to court, and the case can generally be heard within a week or so. The procedure is simple and there are no costs to the employee.

The justice of the peace (or provincial judge) hears evidence given under oath and has the power to order that any wages up to an amount of $500 proved to be due and unpaid be paid to the employee within eight days. If payment is not made, the justice may instruct a bailiff to seize assets of the employer under a "warrant of distress" which secures payment. In some cases the justice may issue a warrant to arrest the employer.

The employee must bring the court action within six months from the date the wages fell due or else the right to this procedure is lost. If the employer can prove that the wages were not paid because the employee owed money to the employer, the court is entitled to set off any such amount and reduce the employee's claim accordingly.

Director of Employment Standards as collector

The employee who has not been paid may notify the Director of Employment Standards of the province, usually by letter, that the employer has neglected or refused to pay wages. The Director has the power to attend at the employer's place of business, examine the books and determine the amount owing. The employer becomes liable to pay an amount equivalent to unpaid wages plus a penalty upon receiving written notice from the Director. The amount of the unpaid wages is then paid to the wronged employee, and the amount of the penalty is retained by the Director.

If the employer fails to pay within the time specified, the Director may garnishee or attach any debt owing by a third party to the employer by sending a registered letter to the third party. On receipt of this written notice the third party must pay the amount specified by the Director up to the amount owing by the third party to the employer.

CASE 9   IN RE JORGER

Jorger, an employer, failed to pay $1 000 (including penalty) in overdue wages to the Director after being given a written demand to do so. The Director then forwarded a garnishee letter to a customer, Czura, who owed Jorger $5 000 for goods received. Czura paid the $1 000 demanded to the Director and paid the balance of $4 000 to Jorger. The entire debt owing by Czura was paid in full in law even though the original creditor Jorger received only $4 000. The Director then paid the wage portion to the employee and retained the penalty.

Since the employer failed to comply with an order of the Director, he is also liable to be prosecuted and fined.

Mechanics' liens

Any person who does any work which improves property may claim a lien against the title to such property to secure unpaid wages. A lien claim must be filed against the title to the property within 45 days from the last work done; otherwise the lien claim will lapse. The effect of filing the lien is to make the owner of the property liable for all (or in some cases a percentage) of the unpaid wages. In the event of non-payment, the workers have the right to sell the premises through the court to satisfy their claims.

The corporate employer

It may happen that an incorporated company does not have sufficient assets to pay its employees. The directors of the corporate business are personally liable for up to six months' unpaid wages and accrued vacation pay. The employee must first sue the company within six months after the wages fell due, then obtain a judgment from the court and make an effort to collect on the judgment through the sheriff or bailiff. If the employee still has not collected, an action may be brought against one or more company directors who will be liable to pay the wages personally.

Which remedy is best?

Employers who are unable to pay wages are in deep financial trouble. Therefore the employee must act quickly while there are still assets available and before the time limits operate to prevent collection. The best method of attack usually depends on the particular type of employer involved. If the employee is in construction, the mechanics' lien action is a powerful weapon. The prudent business person will probably fear the prospect of a "police court hearing" under a Master and Servant application. An application to the Director of Employment Standards often results in a speedy, inexpensive recovery. Employers may expect knowledgeable employees to try to apply the "heat treatment" by taking several of the steps suggested above simultaneously.

Discrimination in employment

Human rights

Part IV of the *Unemployment Insurance Act of Canada* prohibits discrimination on grounds of sex or marital status. The National Employment Service, which has the responsibility to place unemployed persons, is charged with the responsibility of keeping prospective employers honest. The federal *Fair Wages and Hours of Work Act* prohibits discrimination in the hiring and treatment of employees on grounds of age, sex, marital status, race, colour, religion and national origin.

Each of the provinces as well as the Northwest Territories and the Yukon have passed Human or Individual Rights Codes which prohibit sex, marital status and age discrimination in hiring, conditions of employment, advertising, training, promotion, and seniority.

Newspapers are not permitted to accept advertisements specifying job qualifications which would eliminate women or the elderly from competition. Employment agencies are not allowed to act for a client whose instructions are discriminatory.

The provinces oversee anti-discrimination laws through Human Rights Commissions which have wide investigative powers to gather evidence, make findings and take effective action against an offending employer.

CASE 10   IN RE HERRINGTON

Herrington advertised for drapery makers. A young man aged 18 applied for the position. Herrington advised the applicant to get a hair cut and, "find a man's job. Men can't do this work. Women can. Besides, you are too young." The applicant complained to the Ontario Human Rights Commission.

The commissioner conducted a formal hearing at the court house and concluded that Herrington had discriminated against the applicant on grounds of both sex and age within the meaning of the *Human Rights Code of Ontario*. The commissioner ordered Herrington to pay the young man damages equivalent to the wages he would have earned working for Herrington from the time he was rejected to the time he obtained employment. Herrington was also ordered to pay the cost of the hearing.

Employers do not have to give any reasons for rejecting an applicant. In spite of the best laws in the country, there may always be discrimination based on personal feelings. Only employers who are open about their prejudices run the risk of being penalized by the law.

Equal pay for equal work

The *Canada Labour Code* prohibits differences in wages between men and women when they are employed in the same establishment, performing the same (or similar) work which requires the same skills, effort and responsibility. The *Human Rights Codes* and *Labour Standard Acts* of the provinces, the Northwest Territories and the Yukon provide for equal pay for men and women who perform substantially the same work.

The anti-discrimination law with respect to equal pay permits a person alleging pay discrimination to file a complaint with the Ministry of Labour which has broad investigative and remedial powers. In British Columbia, Alberta, Quebec, Ontario and Newfoundland the complaint must be lodged with the provincial Human Rights Commission. The Ministry or the commissions have the power to calculate any difference in pay wrongfully withheld, treat it as unpaid wages which may be recovered from the employer on behalf of the victimized employee through formal notice to pay, and to apply garnishment and fines for non-compliance with orders. Field officers also have the power to make routine checks of business records and payrolls to make certain that companies do not discriminate overtly regarding wages.

CASE 11 IN RE JONES

A woman employee lodged a complaint with the Employment Standards Branch of the Ministry of Labour alleging that a male employee who did substantially the same work received twice her salary. An investigation revealed that the male employee had been with the institution eight years longer than his counterpart; his output exceeded hers in both quantity and quality; and that the institution based its salary increments on seniority and merit.

It was held that where the evidence establishes that a difference in rate of pay is based on objective factors other than sex, such difference is justified and does not amount to discrimination.

Maternity leave

The *Unemployment Insurance Act* provides for benefits to be paid to an employee in the event of maternity. The rules are flexible enough to permit the mother to claim benefits both before and after her confinement.

The *Canada Labour Code* and provincial legislation in most provinces provide all women employees maternity leave without pay for varying periods before and after the date of confinement. The Acts prohibit employers from dismissing employees because of pregnancy. Provided the employee returns to work within the time limit prescribed by the Acts, the employee is entitled to have her old job back, or be given a comparable position, with no loss of seniority and accrued benefits.

Bill of rights

The *Canadian Bill of Rights* recognizes that in Canada fundamental human rights "continue to exist without discrimination by reason of race, national origin, colour, religion, or sex." You will find a copy of the Bill in any library or government bookstore. The effect of these statutory rights should also be considered in assessing the relationship of employers and employees.

KEY TO YOU ARE THE JURY

IN RE NAPOLEON PRESS LIMITED Two issues are raised: equal pay for equal work and non-payment of wages.

At first glance, the equal pay issue seems simple enough but consider the IN RE JONES case and the implication it has for the women working for this company. If the complaint of the workers is justified, a complaint may be lodged with the provincial Ministry of Labour which has the power to conduct an investigation and order an adjustment to equalize the workers' pay.

The worker's decision to remain on the job will be a personal not a legal one. The legal remedy most immediately available to them is to bring a Master and Servant Application to the courts through the local justice of the peace or police office. A hearing will be available before a judge or justice of the peace who will have the power to order the arrears of wages to be paid forthwith. A second remedy is to lodge a complaint with the provincial Director of Employment Standards who has powers of investigation and collection. If the corporate employer is unable to pay because it is insolvent, the directors of the company are personally liable for wages. If the workers have been unsuccessful in attempts to collect against the company, they may sue the directors or any one of them for the amount of their wages.

Checklist: Employment contract

Note: Employers wishing to attract, make best use of and retain employees from administrative assistants and supervisors to high ranking executives must base contracts of employment on terms which provide for mutual benefits and rewards in a comprehensive written form. The following is a list of essential points for such contracts. Other employees may be hired on a less formal basis and employees belonging to a union will be governed by a collective agreement.

Duties

1. List specific and general duties. For executive positions, prepare comprehensive list including responsibilities (if any) for planning, production, sales, budget, market studies.

2. Agree on areas in which employee will work independently and those in which employee must cooperate with others.

3. Discuss extent to which employer may modify duties as business changes or expands.

Time exclusivity

4. Agree on whether employee will devote full time to employment.

5. Agree on whether employer will have exclusive right to employee's services or if employee may engage in outside work.

6. Provision preventing employee from conflict of interest activities.

Inventions; ideas

7. Decide whether employee obliged to disclose to employer all work-related ideas and development and details thereof.

8. Decide whether employee's inventions and developments belong to employer and agree on any exceptions. Apply this clause to inventions and developments of employee during employment and for stated period thereafter.

9. Provision that employee will sign Patent applications and assign to employer (unless invention within exception).

10. Decide whether employee to receive royalties or bonus for work resulting in significant developments or Patents used by employer.

11. Provision restricting employee from disclosing trade secrets, confidential information, customer lists, special plans.

12. From point of view of employer the agreement should cover the following matters:

(i) if inventions relate to the employer's business and are to be developed during employment, provide that they should be owned by the employer;
(ii) compensation arrangements for developments should be worked out to provide adequate reward to employee (provide continuing inducement to best efforts) based on sales, net profits, bonus, or percentage of savings of costs.
13. From point of view of employee, consider the following points:
(i) employee's right to exploit the invention if employer does not utilize it within a reasonable time, including right to apply for Patent if employer fails to do so;
(ii) reasonable compensation for inventions, ideas, developments of exceptional value based on percentage of sales, net profits, savings or bonus;
(iii) in the event employment terminated, the right to continue above benefits.

Compensation

14. Fix compensation or base it on percentage of sales (define ''sales'' carefully) or percentage of net profits from operation (define ''net profits''); how to be paid (weekly, monthly).

15. Adjustments in salary at stated times; inflation clause; any agreement to increase salary based on performance.

16. Consider an agreement to continue salary in whole or in part in event temporary or permanent disability.

Fringe benefits

17. Consider benefits which will attract and retain competent employees, including:

(i) pension, stock option or bonus plans;
(ii) group life insurance;
(iii) hospitalization, medical, dental coverage;
(iv) salary continuation plan in event of illness;
(v) use of vehicle;
(vi) death benefits to spouse;
(vii) vacations with pay.

Non-competition clauses

18. Restriction on competition of employee during term of employment contract.

19. Non-competition of employee after termination of employment for stated time and geographic areas (because this involves "restriction of trade," it is enforceable only if reasonable).

Duration of agreement

20. Agree on length of time of employment:
(i) month to month; year to year;
(ii) terminated by specific notice? Identify method by which notice to be given; length of required notice.

Termination of agreement

21. Agree on provisions under which the rights of the parties under agreement may be terminated, for example:
(i) substantial non-performance of duties by employee;
(ii) employee misconduct;
(iii) failure of employer to pay as agreed;
(iv) disability rendering employee unable to perform substantially as contemplated;
(v) change in employer's position (i.e., going out of business);
(vi) substantial breach of contract by either party.

Review

If you were the jury how would you decide the following and on what grounds?

1. NEEDHAM v. SLOAN   Needham, an employee, pressed his employer, Sloan, for one month's back wages. The employer discharged him without payment. What are Needham's remedies?

2. GRONER v. STE. MARIE   An employee, Groner, was immediately dismissed during a meeting with his employer and several others after he disagreed with and abused his employer with extremely colourful language. When the employer refused to reinstate him, Groner sued for wrongful dismissal. The employee who took over his duties discovered that Groner had falsified expense accounts and misused company credit cards. The employer was not aware of these matters at the time of the dismissal. Is Groner entitled to be reinstated? Is Groner entitled to recover damages?

3. LALONDE v. CRAVEN   A lawyer, Craven, was surprised to learn that a secretary in his office was working part time, one evening a week, for another law firm in the same city and that she worked occasionally on weekends as a waitress. The secretary, whose work was otherwise satisfactory argued, "We've never discussed this. No-one should be able to tell me what to do with my free time. If Bob paid me more, I wouldn't have to do these things." If the lawyer fired her, would she have a good case of wrongful dismissal?

4. STOKES v. MORTON AND SPENCE   An employer, Spence, asked an employee, Morton, to deliver a package "after work on your way home." She agreed, but while in the process of making the delivery she struck and injured a pedestrian, Stokes. Assume she was driving her own vehicle at the time and that she was negligent. Stokes sued both Morton and Spence. Will Stokes recover against Morton? Morton and Spence? Spence only?

5. QUESTIONS
(a) List the legal obligations of an employer to an employee which arise in the ordinary course of employment.
(b) List the legal obligations of an employee to the employer which arise out of the ordinary course of employment.
(c) What is the meaning of the phrase "vicarious liability"? Can you create a set of facts which will result in an employer being vicariously liable?
(d) List and explain the obligations of an employer as required by the provincial and federal Human Rights Codes.
(e) List and briefly explain the type of torts an employee might commit during the course of employment.

CHAPTER 7

Insurance and Business Risks

Unit I Structure of Canadian insurance law

YOU ARE THE JURY

PARR ET AL. v. MOHAWK METAL WORKS LTD.

Mohawk, a prosperous eastern Canadian metal work manufacturer, rented premises from Parr in an industrial block occupied by two other manufacturer-tenants. Mohawk retained Black, an insurance broker, to place insurance coverage. Black negotiated coverage in the sum of $100 000 which he believed would be adequate to cover the firm's equipment, machinery and stock.

Mohawk maintained a 48 gallon tank of varsol on the premises. Employees were required to turn off a nearby flame when drawing off varsol from this tank. An employee forgot to turn off the flame during this process and the resulting explosion ignited a large vat filled with paint, thereby destroying machinery, stock belonging to customers and causing damage to the building, the premises of the other tenants and their equipment and stock.

The insurance policy contained a term that the insured was not to keep more than 5 gallons of petroleum products on the premises and the insurance company therefore refused to pay on its policy. The landlord, Parr, claimed $100 000 as compensation for damages to the building and premises. Vitali, the tenant next to Mohawk, sued for damages to his machinery, equipment and stock and the tenant next to him sued for damages in the amount of $20 000. Mohawk's customers also threatened to sue for the loss of their property in Mohawk's possession at the time of the fire.

What is the role of an insurance broker? Decide whether or not the insurance company is entitled to withhold payment? What are the probable results of each of the actions and claims made against Mohawk? List the kinds of policies which should have been obtained by Mohawk to avoid the problems which actually occurred.

OBJECTIVES

- to identify the essential elements of insurance as a special contract.
- to prepare you to work with an insurance agent or broker to obtain suitable insurance protection.
- to define policy, application and renewal of insurance coverage.
- to list the steps in the settlement of an insurable business loss.

LEXICON

Actuaries   Accountants qualified to perform mathematical calculations which define probable risks of loss for insurance companies (e.g., mortality tables; statistics of accidents involving certain age groups).

Endorsement   A separate paper attached to an existing insurance policy on which the parties change a term of the insurance contract.

Exclusionary Clauses   Clauses in a contract of insurance which identify the circumstances in which the company will not be legally liable to pay for losses suffered by an insured.

Insurance Adjuster   An expert in the appraisal of losses who offers services to insurers for a fee to establish liability of insurer to pay claims and the amounts to be paid.

Insurance Agent   A person who acts as an agent for an insurance company (principal) to sell insurance contracts to third parties.

Insured   An individual or company which offers to pay a premium to transfer a risk of loss to an insurer.

Insurer   An insurance company authorized by government to carry on the business of an insurance company.

Premium   The price an insured pays to transfer the risk of loss to an insurer.

Rider   Additional clauses added to a standard insurance policy providing insured with additional coverage for a further premium.

Statutory Conditions   Conditions of contract set out in the provincial *Insurance Acts* which by law must be printed on and form part of the contract. These conditions cannot be varied, omitted or altered.

Subrogation   The right of an insurer which has paid a claim to an insured to collect against a third party who caused the loss or damage.

Underwriter   An insurer who underwrites or signs an insurance policy, thereby indemnifying an insured person against losses referred to in the policy. It is the underwriters who sell insurance through a system of insurance agents or brokers.

Risk of loss is part of living and carrying on business. A person in business must be able to list the hazards which might reasonably arise in the future and be able to work out a protection plan that will control the chance of loss by transferring the risk to an insurance company.

Insurance is a type of contract to which the ordinary rules of contract described in Chapter Three apply. The objective of the insurance contract is to permit one person (the insured), in consideration of the payment of a price (premium), to transfer the risk of loss to another person (called an insurance company or insurer) which accepts and agrees to indemnify the insured or a named beneficiary in the event of loss covered by the contract.

Risk of Loss

The concept of the transfer of the risk of loss is the key to understanding insurance rules, regulations and procedures. The insurance industry must provide protection which the Canadian business community considers essential and desirable, and it must do so at a reasonable cost. It anticipates that there will be losses for which it will be ultimately responsible, and therefore every insurance company must take care to arrange its affairs so that earned premiums and profits will exceed claims. Companies which fail to do so soon go out of business. Prudent insurers accomplish this necessity through the use of actuaries; insuring average risks based on acturial tables; using standard pre-printed contract forms limiting liability; incorporating exclusionary clauses in their contracts; paying only for actual loss where possible; using insurance adjusters and proof-of-claim forms to keep insured persons honest; and taking advantage of the principles of subrogation.

Insurance contracts require the utmost good faith (*uberrimae fide*) on the part of the insured who is required to be both honest and accurate in his representations to and dealings with the company. If the insured fails to meet this standard, the insurer may be able to deny liability to pay a claim. Using all of the above techniques, insurers are able to control their own risk of loss, make decisions as to who they will or will not insure, charge an appropriate premium and stay in business.

The insurance industry in Canada

Jurisdiction over insurance law is divided between the federal government and the provinces with the greater, more immediate control being administered by the provinces.

The government of Canada exercises a degree of authority through *The Canadian and British Insurance Companies Act* and *The Foreign Insurance Com-*

panies Act. Through these statutes insurance companies wishing to carry on business in Canada are compelled to register with the federal government. In their registration these companies are required to provide evidence of financial responsibility, to limit the securities in which they may invest to those authorized, maintain prescribed assets in Canada and to follow the prescribed legal procedures by which an insurance company may be incorporated in Canada. The main purpose of the federal government in Insurance Law is to protect the public from the possibility of an insurance company becoming insolvent and therefore unable to pay claims against it.

Each province has enacted an *Insurance Act* together with other statutes that regulate the insurance industry. Each province appoints a Superintendent of Insurance to administer provincial insurance rules and to licence and regulate insurers and other individuals providing insurance services. The Superintendent is the watchdog of the insurance industry. He oversees the activities of licenced insurers, agents, brokers and adjusters; handles consumer complaints; and investigates the finances of insurance companies carrying on business in the province.

The provincial *Insurance Acts* are designed to protect the consumer by:

- requiring certain terms to be mandatory parts of every insurance contract (statutory conditions).
- incorporating into every insurance contract *implied terms* when the parties have not expressed a contrary intention.
- defining the effect of misrepresentation on the contract.
- limiting the effect of suicide on a contract of life insurance.
- defining and limiting the effect of honest nondisclosure or error in applications for insurance.

Standing just outside this rather elaborate structure are the business persons who wish to obtain insurance protection. They will deal through agents or brokers and must therefore keep in mind the rules of agency (see Chapter Eight, Unit Two) as a way of doing business. They will ultimately obtain from the insurance company an acceptable agreement in the form of a contract and must therefore also consider the rules of contract (Chapter Three).

The agency aspect of insurance

One of the objectives of this unit is to prepare you for working with an insurance agent or broker to obtain suitable insurance coverage. As the consumer, you will deal directly with either one and therefore it is important to examine their role in insurance coverage.

Many insurance companies employ agents who work as employees. Their primary loyalty is to their employer, and they are limited in the services they are able to provide to those offered by their company. It must be kept in mind that they are agents for their company, *not* for the consumer.

Insurance companies also retain independent insurance agents, who operate as independent contractors and often represent a number of different companies. The independent agents maintain their own businesses separate from those of the companies they represent. They are in a better position to provide advice and provide the consumer with an opportunity to select appropriate coverage from among the policies of different companies. However, independent agents are also agents for the insurance company and are not agents for the consumer. As a general rule, this separation from the consumer must be appreciated.

A broker, on the other hand, is an insurance specialist who may be retained by the wise business person or industrialist to analyze needs and risks and offer truly independent advice. The broker endeavors to obtain suitable coverage at the lowest cost. He is an agent for the insured, not the insurance company with which the coverage is eventually placed.

The application for insurance

Through its agents, the insurer invites the consumer to do business. The consumer must make a contractual offer to buy coverage and the company may then accept the offer or reject it. In order to assist in its decision, in each case the company requires the consumer to complete an application form containing information it considers material to the risk to be assumed.

As the intended insurance contract is one involving the utmost good faith, the insurance company is entitled to know the full extent of each individual risk it undertakes. The consumer (insured) has a legal duty to be honest and accurate, and to make full disclosure of facts which may be material to the risk.

The information required on the application varies according to the type of insurance coverage requested. Thus, information required may range from informal fact-finding for some types of property insurance such as fire and automobile, to detailed and reaching inquiries for life insurance. Whatever the form of the application, the intended insured must keep in mind the seriousness of making an inaccurate statement on the application. The duty is on the insured to make certain the information received by the company is accurate. If full and accurate disclosure is made on the application and the company accepts it, the resulting contract will be valid and enforceable by the insured. He will be in a position to compel the company to pay for an insured loss. If the application contains a fraudulent misrepresentation (deliberate misstatement of facts) and the company accepts, the resulting "contract" will be voidable at the option of the insurance company. The insured will not be able to compel the company to pay for a loss covered by the policy.

If the applicant for insurance fails to disclose a material fact which should reasonably have been disclosed in the application and the insurer accepts, then the resulting "contract" will be voidable at the option of the insurer. If the insured suffered a loss covered by the policy, the insurer could not be compelled to pay indemnity for the loss. If the non-disclosure was considered fraudulent, the contract remains forever voidable. If the non-disclosure was an innocent oversight, the provincial *Insurance Acts* come to the assistance of the honest insured who inadvertently erred by rendering the contract voidable for only two years from the date of the application. If such an insured maintained insurance in force for more than two years, paid the premiums, and then suffered a loss, the contract would be considered valid in spite of the original inaccuracy.

CASE 1   BROOS v. STERLING INSURANCE

Broos, the owner of a legal courier service which filed and served papers for lawyers, applied for insurance coverage for a fleet of three vehicles. In the application form Broos was required to list the names and ages of the persons who would be driving the vehicles. One of the questions on the application form was, "Has any user lost driving privileges in the last five years?" Broos responded, "No." Unknown to Broos one of his drivers, Susan Thompson, had lost her licence for six months during the period in question. Sterling Insurance Company placed the insurance and Broos paid the required premium. Six months later Aucoin, another driver, caused a serious motor vehicle accident in the course of his employment. The insurance adjuster retained to process the claim discovered the error regarding Thompson and advised the company to refuse to pay for the damage. Broos claimed he had no knowledge of Thompson's loss of driving privileges and argued that, even if he was mistaken, as the accident was caused by another employee the mistake had no bearing on the risk of loss assumed by the insurer.

Broos lost; the company did not have to pay. It did not matter that Broos was unaware of the Thompson conviction. The company conceded that Broos was honest and had made no attempt to deceive. However, what was important was that the application contained an error in a fact that would be material to the risk to be undertaken. The company had the right to know and, as an insurance contract places a duty on the applicant based on the principle of utmost good faith, even an honest error was fatal. It also made no difference that the eventual loss was totally unrelated to the actual misstatement of fact contained in the application. Finally, the fact that the accident happened only six months after the application was signed did not allow the saving provisions of the provincial *Insurance Act* to operate.

CASE 2   FALCONBRIDGE v. UNITED

United Insurance Company declined to pay for a loss, claiming that Falconbridge had made an inaccurate answer to a question on a written application form. Falconbridge argued that she had given the right answer but the secretary for the insurance agency who asked the questions and then typed the answers on the form had made the error.

Falconbridge's argument was no defence; the company did not have to pay. By signing the application, the insured became responsible for its contents. It made no difference who prepared the form or how the error occurred.

The lesson to be learned from these two cases is that the insured must take great care to be both honest and accurate in making an application for insurance, or else run the risk of creating a voidable contract.

The insurance contract

An insurance contract is created by an insured person making a legal *offer* to pay a premium price to transfer the risk of a foreseeable possible loss to an insurer who accepts and agrees to indemnify the insured against losses defined and listed in an insurance policy. The policy is the written evidence of the insurance contract to which the ordinary rules of contract apply.

The insurance companies prepare standard pre-printed policy forms designed to cover average risks for certain groups or segments of the business community and for which they are able to charge a reasonable premium. In order

to do this they limit their liability by including *exclusionary clauses* which restrict their obligation to paying only for definite listed hazards. This weighs the risk factor in favor of the insurer. For these reasons it is essential for a potential insured to require the agent to explain the actual hazards for which the insurer will bear the risk of loss and to take the time to examine the policy with care.

Two factors correct most of the unfairness that might arise from the standard insurance contract. First, each of the provincial *Insurance Acts* require that *statutory conditions* of contract be part of insurance contracts. These conditions must be printed on each policy, and examination of the policy will clearly disclose these conditions and alert the insured to the present state of the law which may affect any claim he may make. Secondly, in interpreting contracts prepared by one party, the courts require terms to be set out in clear, unambigious language. If the term is vague or uncertain, the courts will interpret it in the most favourable way possible for the other party.

Riders are available for the insured who requires additional coverage to that contained in the standard policy. In consideration of the payment of an additional premium, the company may accept the additional risk required and prepare a separate writing evidencing the agreement which it affixes to the policy.

If the parties agree to amend or vary the terms of a policy of insurance after it has been prepared, this may be done by typing an *endorsement* on the back of the policy or by typing the required amendment on an "endorsement form" and attaching it to the policy. For example, if Smith wanted to increase her public liability insurance from $100 000 to $500 000, this could be done by endorsement instead of by writing up an entirely new policy.

Insurance policies often contain *deductible clauses* which specify amounts that insured persons will pay themselves in the event of loss. For example, if Jones' policy was an automobile policy with a $200 deductible clause, and damage in the sum of $150 occurred, Jones would be responsible for the entire amount of the loss. If the loss exceeded $200, the insurance company would be liable only for the excess of that amount.

The objective of an application for insurance is to have the insurer accept and thus create a mutually binding contract. In order to avoid unnecessary and perhaps dangerous delays in giving its acceptance, many insurers have given the insurance agents who process the applications the authority to bind the insurer. These agents have the power to sign on behalf of the insurer, deliver policies and renew the insurance as required from time to time. When such an agent accepts on behalf of an insurer, a *binder* is prepared. It is a written memo setting out the coverage required, name of insured and the date and time the coverage was put into effect. The copy of the memo is then sent to the insurer at the end of the day's business. As all agents do not have this authority, it is important for a person buying insurance to inquire to make certain that there will be no delay in coverage. If the agent does not have such authority, appropriate action must be taken by the insured to ensure that coverage is in place before any potential loss occurs.

Renewal of insurance contracts

Insurance contracts contain an expiry date at which time the coverage purchased comes to an end. The contract may be renewed from time to time. The insurance agent prepares and forwards a renewal policy which is, in effect, an offer by the insurer. The insured is then free to accept the contract for the renewal by paying the bill for premium which invariably accompanies the insurer's offer, or by otherwise communicating acceptance to the insurer or its agent. The insured is also entitled to reject the insurer's offer by advising it that further coverage is not required. This may be done by returning the offer with an appropriate note attached.

The agent sends the offer because it is good business to do so, not because it is legally required. The onus is *always on the insured* to keep the policy in force and to arrange to renew before the expiry date of the coverage. For this reason it is important for the insured not only to calendar the date of renewal but also to be certain he takes all steps necessary to ensure continued coverage.

Cancellation of insurance

Most insurance policies may be cancelled at any time by either the insured or the insurer. The policy will contain a condition setting out the procedure to be followed. Usually the insured must surrender the policy to the insurer with a request for cancellation (which may be done by simply writing the word "cancel" on the back of the policy together with the date and signature). If the insurer wishes to cancel, he is usually required to send a cancellation notice by registered mail. The notice provides the insured with a specified number of days of continued coverage before the contract is actually cancelled. The insured may then make other arrangements for suitable alternate coverage. The most common cause for cancellation of policies is the non-payment of premiums.

Assignment of insurance

An insured person may assign an insurance contract to a third party. For example, a life insurance contract may be assigned to a bank as security for a loan. The insured signs an agreement that, in the event of his death the bank will be entitled to claim sufficient proceeds to pay off the loan. If the policy has a cash surrender value, the agreement may also authorize the bank to cash the policy if the payment of the loan has not been made, and to apply the proceeds against the loan. Such an assignment may be made without the consent of the insurer, but it is entitled to notice of the assignment. Neither is it usually necessary to obtain the consent of a beneficiary named in the policy (except if the beneficiary is an irrevocable beneficiary).

Property insurance such as automobile and home or fire insurance policies are also transferable. If a car or home is sold, the owner may assign the insurance coverage for the unexpired term to the buyer in consideration for an amount equivalent to the paid-up premiums for this period. However, such a transfer is not valid until consented to by the insurer because substituting a new owner may materially alter the risk. Attempting to transfer one's interest in property insurance is dangerous for both the seller and the purchaser of property. It is far better for purchasers to place their own insurance and for sellers to cancel their coverage and receive a rebate of unearned premium from the insurer.

CASE 3   IN RE BEST

Best took over the insurance coverage on the assets of a business he purchased. He received a copy of the policy and a written transfer of insurance from the previous owner. Best mailed the transfer to the insurer for its approval. Before the transfer was delivered, the premises were damaged by fire. The company then refused to consent to the transfer.

The insurer was not obligated to consent to the transfer and, under the circumstances, was not obliged to make the loss good to Best. The original owner had no further insurable interest in the property, and there was at the time of the damage no contractual relationship between Best and the insurer. How could Best have avoided this loss?

Notice of change in risk

The insurance company makes its decision to insure or not and settles the terms of coverage on the basis of the information it receives at the time of the application. It follows that if any material change in the risk occurs, the insurer is entitled to notification of such change. The rule is that insured persons have a duty to notify insurers of any changes in the material risk within their control and knowledge. Such notification provides the insurer with the option to continue coverage (perhaps at an increased premium) or to cancel the policy. If the required notice is not given, the contract becomes voidable at the option of the insurer which cannot be compelled to indemnify the insured for loss. Insured persons were unable to collect from their insurers when they failed to report the following events:

- part of basement converted to part-time furniture finishing business requiring storage of paint and petroleum products (home insurance).
- driver's licence suspended for six months for reckless driving in spite of opportunity to report this when policy renewed (auto insurance).
- hired ex-offender with history of theft convictions; serious loss through theft occurred (theft insurance).

Notice of loss

The insurer is entitled to a prompt notification of loss. If an insured does not notify the insurer of a loss covered by the policy and which is within the insured's knowledge, the insurer will be relieved of liability to indemnify the insured for such loss.

CASE 4   MANIX v. SILVER

Silver, a lawyer, failed to file a writ of summons on time thus depriving a client of a right to sue and collect damages from a third party. Silver admitted her error and attempted to negotiate a settlement with her client over a four-month period. The client retained another lawyer who issued a writ against Silver. At that stage Silver reported the matter to the insurer that carried her malpractice insurance. The company refused to pay on the grounds that it was entitled to prompt notice of the Manix claim. Silver was thus deprived of indemnity against the amount she would have to pay her client in damages.

How to make an insurance claim

The time to consider the possibility of making a claim against the insurer is when the insurance coverage is obtained. The loss has not yet occurred, but it can be anticipated. If sufficient time and considerable thought are devoted to real needs, the best coverage the insurer will give may be obtained and used when the loss does occur. There are eight steps to take in the event of an insured loss.

1. Identify all things that must be done to minimize the loss and take action.
2. Notify the insurance company promptly of the loss and its surrounding circumstances.
3. Document the events leading up to the loss, details of the loss and steps taken after the loss. Keep meticulous and complete records.
4. Co-operate with the insurance adjuster retained by the insurance company to investigate the loss. The adjuster will first examine the application for insurance, the policy and renewals, if any. The investigation will include checking the ''facts'' in the application and giving an opinion on the validity of the policy. If grounds are found to deny liability, the adjuster has a duty to advise the insurer. The adjuster is entitled to take a statement from the insured and to conduct an investigation of the facts surrounding the loss. If grounds are found to deny liability, the adjuster again has a duty to advise the insurer. On the basis of the adjuster's report, the insurance company decides whether it will indemnify the insured for the loss.
5. Presuming the company agrees it is liable to indemnify, the adjuster assesses the actual loss in terms of dollars. The adjuster may negotiate this amount with the insured or the insured's lawyer. The adjuster receives instructions from the insurer and its claims investigator.

    While the adjuster and claims investigator endeavour to be fair, their primary obligation is to the insurer. An insured involved in a loss in excess of $1 000 should therefore retain a lawyer to assist in a fair settlement.
6. The insured is required to complete a ''proof of loss'' form which details loss or damage and the amounts claimed. This form is signed by the insured and has the same effect as a statement made under oath in court. If false information is given, the claimant is guilty of perjury and is liable to prosecution.
7. The insured and the adjuster settle on the amount the insurer must pay by way of indemnity. The adjuster reports the settlement to the insurer's claims examiner who reviews the file, approves the settlement and arranges for a cheque to be issued to the insured.
8. In consideration of the payment of indemnity agreed upon, the insured signs a release accepting the funds in full settlement of the claim.

KEY TO YOU ARE THE JURY

PARR ET AL. v. MOHAWK METAL WORKS LTD. The insurance broker was an independent agent retained by Mohawk as an insurance specialist to analyze insurance needs and place appropriate coverage at the lowest premium.

The policy itself prohibited more than 5 gallons of petroleum products on the premises as a condition of coverage. As Mohawk maintained substantially more on the premises, this may have been a good defence for the insurer to avoid payment. However, the courts strictly interpret standard contract terms against the insurer in favour of the insured. Having regard to the nature of Mohawk's business, it could be argued that the insurer was not mislead. In this case the insurer agreed to pay 80% of the policy coverage ($80 000).

All claims against Mohawk were valid. The types of insurance which should have been carried were:

- fire insurance on equipment, stock, furniture.
- insurance to cover loss or damage to the premises owned by Parr.
- liability insurance to cover loss to other parts of building.
- bailee insurance to cover loss of stock stored on premises belonging to others.
- business interruption insurance, covering loss of profits, wages, ongoing expenses.

This case illustrates the serious consequences that flow from failure to plan insurance protection and provides a preview of problems discussed more fully in Unit Two.

Unit II Types of insurance

YOU ARE THE JURY

VANCE v. IMPERIAL-SOUTH INSURANCE

Vance and Perron carried on a prosperous business consulting firm. An agent of the insurer approached them encouraging them to purchase insurance on each other's lives. The agent worked with the firm's accountant and lawyer to help draft a partnership agreement in which each partner agreed to take out a policy of insurance on the life of the other. As part of this arrangement Vance took out a policy on the life of Perron which named Vance as beneficiary. The premiums were paid quarterly. Two years later Perron agreed to dissolve the partnership. Signed documents completed the dissolution process. Two weeks later Perron died. Vance produced her copy of the paid-up policy of insurance requesting payment of its face value of $85 000. The insurer declined.

Is the insurance company entitled to refuse payment? Take some trouble to review what you know about insurance law. Apply this information to these facts. Make a list of the issues raised for which you have no workable solution.

OBJECTIVES

- to define the term "insurable interest."
- to list the various types of insurance useful to and needed by business.
- to list essential information required to enable you to make informed insurance decisions.

LEXICON

Indemnity Compensation paid by an insurer to an insured for loss or damage covered under the terms of the insurance contract.

Term Insurance A type of insurance policy which requires the insurer to pay only in the event of an actual loss and which does not include any provision for savings or investment.

Insurable interest

In order to shift the risk of loss to an insurer, the insured must have an insurable interest in the property or in the life insured. The insured must have a legal or equitable interest therein such that he will clearly be seen to benefit from the safety of the subject matter of the contract and be just as clearly prejudiced by its loss or damage to it. Thus, one has an insurable interest in one's own life; the life of a spouse; the life of a partner or key person in the business; or in the life of a debtor. A property owner has an insurable interest in the premises owned whether it be mortgaged or not. The person who holds a mortgage on the premises likewise has an insurable interest.

Take away this key element of "insurable risk" and what's left? A gamble, pure and simple; and the law will not enforce a contract based on a gamble or wager. When placing insurance, then, the insured must always be the person (or all the persons) with the insurable interest, otherwise the insurance contract will be void and unenforceable against the insurance company.

CASE 5 ZORBA v. ATLANTIC INSURANCE

Two brothers owned a business block which they placed in the name of an uncle by a registered deed. The uncle placed fire insurance in his own name. A fire destroyed the building. During the course of investigation the adjuster discovered that the uncle was not the true owner of the premises and, as the insurer had no "contract" with the owners, it was advised to deny liability. The uncle argued that he was a trustee for his nephews and should be recognized as an "owner" or agent of an owner. The insurer argued that only those with a clear legal or equitable interest in property are entitled to insure it and that because ownership is material to the risk, it was entitled to know the identity of the true owner before it accepted the risk. The court agreed. The insurer did not have to pay.

CASE 6 ZEPPACOSTA v. POWER INSURANCE LTD.

A father made a graduation gift of a new automobile to his son. On the advice of a friend the father had the son transfer the ownership to him so he could place insurance on the vehicle at a lower premium rate. In the application the father listed himself as owner and the son as a "casual driver." In fact, the son continued to drive and use the car almost exclusively and to be responsible for its repair and licencing until he and several people in another vehicle were killed in an accident. The accident was caused by the negligence of the son, but the insurance company refused to pay under the terms of the policy claiming the father had no insurable interest and on the basis of misstatements of fact contained in the application.

Fire insurance

The standard fire insurance policy provides coverage for loss to buildings, furniture, fixtures, equipment and merchandise. Coverage must be extended by endorsement to cover losses arising out of such hazards as earthquake, collapse, flood, rain, snowstorm, wind or hail. The fire insurance policy defines the losses covered and does not cover the following:

- books of account, receivable records, business papers.
- cash, money in other forms, securities, bonds.
- business papers, plans, designs.
- other person's property stored or on the premises at the time of a fire (bailee).
- fire caused by deliberate act of owner (arson).
- loss of profits.
- theft during the fire.
- fire caused by heating system or industrial process (i.e., fireplace, furnace, boiler).

These excluded coverages may also be purchased by special endorsement and the payment of a higher premium.

Business interruption insurance

The insured may wish to transfer the risk of loss which would naturally arise if damage to business premises required a shut-down or serious curtailment of the business operation. The objective of the insured is to maintain the same position he would have been in if the damage had not occurred. This objective may be achieved by purchasing business interruption insurance which will provide:

- funds equivalent to net profits before taxes for a stated limited period or until the business is operational once more.
- funds to pay continuing expenses, rent, taxes.
- extra expense endorsement to cover cost of getting back into business.
- (possibly) funds to cover wages and salaries of key personnel and other essential workers.

Interruption coverage may be obtained as a supplement to fire insurance coverage and may be available on request for such other hazards as malicious damage, riots, falling aircraft, water damage from a faulty sprinkler system.

Co-insurance

The most immediate concern of the insured is the amount of the premium which must be paid for insurance coverage. While it is reasonable for the consumer to attempt to obtain the best coverage for the least premium, it is a dangerous practice to permit the actual cost of the coverage to be the prime factor in making a decision to insure. For example, a business with sound, safe buildings will easily appreciate that total loss is impossible. It will then only consider the risks of substantial losses, and may decide to insure the property for less than its true insurable value. The reasoning is valid but it alters the risk of loss for the insurance company which in turn realizes that people will attempt to cut corners in this way. To protect themselves the insurers may insert a co-insurance clause in the policy requiring the insured to maintain coverage equivalent to a minimum stated percentage of the actual cash value of the insured property. A typical co-insurance clause reads as follows:

> It is part of the consideration of this policy upon which the rate of premium is fixed that the insured maintain insurance . . . to the extent of 80 per cent of the actual cash value of the insured property and if the insured fails to do so, the insured shall be a co-insurer and shall bear his share of the loss.

CASE 7   IN RE ZINN ENTERPRISES INC.

Zinn owns a warehouse, equipment and fixtures having an actual cash value of $200 000. The amount of insurance carried is $90 000. The policy contains a co-insurance clause and the premiums paid to the insurer have been calculated on the amount of insurance carried. Damages to the premises caused by fire is $10 000. Zinn expects to recover the full amount of the loss from the insurer as it is well within the limits of the policy. Is this expectation justified?

The co-insurance clause means that Zinn and the insurer are "partners" in an enterprise in which the risk of loss is to be borne by each. Let's say the minimum percentage of coverage was 80% of the actual cash value. Zinn should have carried $160 000 insurance (80% of $200 000) but he carried less. Therefore Zinn is a co-insurer and the liability for the loss must be divided on the basis of the following formula:

$$\frac{\text{Actual amount of insurance carried}}{\text{Minimum coverage required by co-insurance clause}} \times \text{Amount of loss}$$

$$\frac{\$90\ 000}{\$160\ 000} \quad \times \quad \$10\ 000 \quad = \quad \$5\ 625$$

or

In this case Zinn must absorb $5 625 of the loss and will collect only $4 375 from the insurer.

Depending on the circumstances, the percentage of actual cash value will vary from 50% to 90%.

If a policy is to contain a co-insurance clause, the prudent business person must weigh the saving of premiums now against the responsibility of bearing a large portion of a potential loss. The clause encourages businesses to insure at the required amount or at an amount very close to it. It also encourages businesses to conduct annual evaluations of insured property to keep insurance coverage in line with the fluctuations of actual cash values.

Glass (plate glass)

Fire insurance includes the breakage or damage to plate glass only if the damage is caused by a fire. Many businesses display merchandise in large, glassed areas and advertise their business names or services by lettering on the glass. Replacing broken plate glass store windows is an unacceptable risk, and businesses purchase replacement cost insurance (often as a separate rider on the fire policy) in the event of damage by hazards other than fire.

Theft, burglary, robbery

Theft, burglary and robbery insurance are designed to cover different risks in which the property of the insured may be wrongfully stolen. Theft insurance is the most comprehensive: it includes burglary and robbery. Coverage includes money, securities and most items of personal or moveable property. Because theft insurance is the most comprehensive of the three types of coverage under this heading, it is also the most expensive. Further, it is the riskiest for the insurer: it hedges on its liability by limiting the amount for which it will be liable for the theft of articles which are easily stolen or by placing a substantial deductible clause in the policy. Thus, businesses are encouraged to take proper security measures to preserve their property.

Burglary coverage insures against loss when thieves gain access to the premises by forcible, unlawful entry, and covers the loss of inventory, money, equipment, moveable property, furnishings and safes.

Robbery coverage insures against theft of property by force or threats of violence, and covers the same type of property.

Machinery insurance

A special form of insurance is available for expensive machinery which is vital to the operation of a business. It covers losses arising out of breakdown or damage to such machinery as boilers, air conditioning systems, engines, generators, electric meters and computers, and includes coverage for damage from explosion.

Automobile insurance

The provincial *Insurance Acts* regulate the insurance coverage of loss arising out of motor vehicle ownership and use. Each provincial Act clearly states the importance of honest, full disclosure of material facts in the application for insurance. Every application for motor vehicle insurance must be in writing and the policy negotiated must provide the coverage requested in the application. In all provinces both documents must contain a prominent clause which reads as follows:

Where the applicant gives false particulars of the described automobile to be insured to the prejudice of the insurer, or knowingly misrepresents or fails to disclose any fact required to be stated in the application or where the insured violates a term or condition of the policy or commits fraud or makes a deliberate false statement with respect to a claim, then a claim by the insured to recover indemnity is invalid.

The *Insurance Acts* also set out the law relating to prohibited uses of vehicles; carrying passengers for hire; notices (such as changes in risk and occurrences which result in a loss) to be given the insurer; and the proper way in which to process claims.

The automobile insurance coverage available to business is as follows:

- bodily injury.
- property damage indemnity liability for damage to property resulting from an automobile accident.
- accident benefits indemnity, medical benefits, disability, death of applicant, driver, passenger of applicant's vehicle.

- collision coverage (subject to deductible clauses) compensates for damage to applicant's vehicles resulting from collision.
- comprehensive coverage extends collision coverage to such perils as fire, explosion, malicious damage and theft.

Life insurance

Life insurance plays an important role in business as a means of providing capital in the event of the death of a sole proprietor, partner or key person. Term insurance is the most practical and inexpensive type of coverage. The business person decides how much money will be needed quickly to control the loss which will occur by death, and the insurer matches this with an appropriate premium and covers the risk. Premiums are then paid periodically to maintain the coverage. They are kept by the insurance company and lost forever to the insured because the insurer pays nothing unless the insured dies.

A second type of life insurance used in business is one which has a cash surrender value. Premiums paid are "saved" by the company for the insured and at the end of a fixed term represent an investment: if the insured survives, the insurer will pay back an amount agreed upon. In addition to this savings aspect, the insurer will pay the face value of the policy in the event of the death of the insured during the period of coverage. The advantage lies in the savings aspect; the disadvantage in the correspondingly higher premiums which are charged.

Sole proprietor

Life insurance is important to the sole proprietor who "is" the business. Should the proprietor die what would become of the business? Would it continue to operate or cease to be carried on effectively? Insurance provides the proprietor's beneficiaries with capital to keep the business viable, hire a manager to assume the work of the deceased and to maintain the business as a going concern. Usually the proprietor consults a lawyer and accountant for advice on this matter at the time the business begins and from time to time as the business increases in value.

Partnership

The death of one partner terminates a partnership business. Surviving partners may be required to wind up the business and pay the deceased's share to the estate, perhaps at a financial loss for all. Partners recognize the need of surviving partners to carry on without interruption. They en-

sure this in part when they take the trouble to prepare a written partnership agreement that contains terms avoiding termination and winding-up of the business in the event of death. The financing of this arrangement is accomplished through partnership insurance. The agreement provides that the survivors will buy out the beneficiaries of the deceased by paying an agreed amount which will be either a predetermined lump sum or a sum to be determined by accounting procedures establishing the fair value of the deceased's share at the time of death. Each partner agrees to carry life insurance on the life of every other partner. This arrangement is designed to provide the surviving partners with the funds required to pay for a deceased partner's share in the firm.

Guarantee insurance

This type of insurance includes:

- "fidelity insurance," which insures against loss resulting from unfaithful performance of duties by a person in a position of trust, and is designed to guarantee the performance of a person holding any office.
- "surety insurance," which guarantees the performance of a contract or undertaking, usually providing for the payment of a sum of money calculated to indemnify the insured for the default of another party to a contract.

For example, an accounting firm might take out fidelity insurance against the possibility that a junior clerk, who has the responsibility to handle and bank money for clients, may misappropriate it. An architect who was given an undertaking to have a shopping plaza ready for occupancy might take out surety insurance against the possibility that the general contractor will not have the construction work completed on time.

Guarantees

A contract of guarantee is an agreement to perform the obligation or discharge the liability of another person if that person defaults. The person giving such a guarantee is known as the guarantor. In any contract of guarantee there are three essential parties:

- principal debtor, the person primarily liable.
- creditor, the person to whom the obligation is owed.
- guarantor, the person who, in consideration of some promise or act of the creditor, promises the creditor to discharge the debtor's liability *if the debtor defaults*.

Guarantee must be in writing

Each Canadian province has enacted a statute known generally as the *Statute of Frauds* which requires guarantees to be in writing and signed by the guarantor (or an authorized agent) in order to render the guarantor liable. Any form of writing will be sufficient as long as it clearly identifies the parties and includes all of the essential terms of the agreement. An oral promise to guarantee a debt of another is unenforceable by action in the courts and for all practical purposes is uncollectable from the "guarantor."

Legal consideration

Like any contract, a guarantee must be supported by valuable consideration moving from the person most benefiting from the contract, usually the creditor. The mere fact that the debtor owes money is not sufficient. There must be "new consideration" given by the creditor. This need not benefit the guarantor. In fact, in the typical case the guarantor derives no tangible benefit. It is sufficient if the creditor gives a benefit to the debtor *at the guarantor's request*. Examples of benefits which will amount to good consideration are:

- creditor extends credit to debtor at guarantor's request.
- creditor supplies goods to debtor at guarantor's request.
- creditor advances funds to debtor at guarantor's request.
- creditor extends time for payment at guarantor's request.
- creditor forbears lawsuit against debtor at guarantor's request.
- creditor withdraws an action already commenced or refrains from legal collection from debtor at request of guarantor.

Discharge of guarantor

The guarantor's obligation is a fragile arrangement for the creditor who must take steps not to do anything which would prejudice the guarantor's rights. The guarantor will be legally let off the hook under the following circumstances:

- debtor pays in full or otherwise obtains valid discharge from the creditor.
- creditor changes the debtor's position after the guarantee is given without the knowledge and consent of the guarantor by agreeing with the debtor to extend the time for any payments, changing the terms of the guarantee, or by changing the terms of the transactions between the creditor and the debtor.

CASE 8   THE TORONTO-DOMINION BANK v. GRENVILLE

Grenville signed a guarantee with the bank to guarantee a loan secured by her partner to obtain funds to buy Grenville's interest in the business. The terms of the transaction required the partner to sign a promissory note requiring monthly payments of $500 each and to pay off the balance in five years. Grenville then retired while her former partner carried on the business alone. During the course of the business the bank extended further credit several times, each time preparing new promissory notes in various amounts to replace the old ones and increasing or decreasing the monthly payments according to the needs of the business. Eventually, the business failed and the debtor was unable to pay the bank. The bank's lawyers were instructed to demand payment from Grenville.

On examining the situation the lawyers concluded that Grenville was no longer liable to the bank on the guarantee. The original note evidencing the loan guarantee had been "retired" and no longer existed. Grenville had never been consulted and the bank had never obtained her consent to the many changes made by the creditor and debtor.

KEY TO YOU ARE THE JURY

VANCE v. IMPERIAL-SOUTH INSURANCE

The insurance company had to pay. In order to succeed it was necessary for Vance to establish that she had an insurable interest in Perron's life. At the time of the making of the insurance contract, Vance and Perron were partners. Partners, for obvious business reasons, benefit by the continued existence of their associates and are prejudiced by their deaths. Vance argued that the test of whether she had an insurable interest is satisfied if she had such an interest at the time of the purchase of the insurance. The insurance company argued that while Vance may have had an insurable interest when the insurance was taken out, she had no such interest in Perron's life at the time of death as the two were no longer partners, their affairs had been successfully resolved, and the dissolution documents had been signed. Vance, according to the company, could no longer claim any benefit from Perron's continued existence. The court ruled that, with respect to life insurance coverage, the insured must have an insurable interest in the life insured at the time the contract is made, but it is not essential to have such interest at the actual time of death.

Checklist: Insurance

FIRE INSURANCE

1. Consider need to control risk of loss by fire. Outline desirable coverage. List possible hazards.
2. List exact names of owners of property to be protected (insurable interest).
3. Consider need for additional coverage to cover money, account receivable records, securities.
4. Record exact post office address and brief legal description of premises (from deed or lease).
5. Review present coverage. Consider inflationary factors; whether coverage should be increased.
6. Will policy be subject to co-insurance clause? Obtain coverage at least to this value.
7. Consider need to add endorsement to cover loss to property of others in your custody (bailee insurance).
8. Consider whether policy limits amount of petroleum products which may be on the premises.
9. Consider endorsement to provide rent insurance.
10. Request an automatic renewal clause.
11. Request premium reduction cost by offering to take coverage for a period of years (three years instead of one).
12. Consider cost of adding additional coverage for hazards not covered by standard policy (theft of merchandise during fire; fire caused by heating system; perishables under refrigeration damaged by heat).
13. If premises rented, include coverage for damage to landlord's building through negligence of employee, insured.
14. If others occupy same building, include coverage for damage to premises or property of neighbouring business.
15. If property mortgaged, include mortgage clause.
16. If premises will be vacant for more than 30 days at a time, obtain vacancy permit to avoid voiding of contract.
17. Record and calendar expiry date of policy to remind you to renew before policy expires.
18. Record replacement value of property; review once a year regarding adequate coverage and co-insurance requirements.
19. Maintain insurance policies, receipts, documents, correspondence, memos regarding telephone conversations with insurer in safe place. Examine policies, noting exclusionary clauses, limits of liability, duties imposed.

20. On application for insurance, have all the facts been complete, honest and accurate? Have the agent explain the policy, limitations, exclusions.
21. Shop for coverage. All companies are not equal. For extensive coverage retain insurance broker not agent.
22. Review Insurance and Business Risks in this book several times a year. Read other material.

AUTOMOBILE INSURANCE

1. Record facts concerning vehicles, drivers. Consider need to control foreseeable risk for your type of business. Correct description of vehicles.
2. Check records of all drivers. Duly licensed? Traffic offences? Loss of driving privileges? Experience?
3. Include coverage of injury to passengers.
4. Consider any no-fault insurance regulations in force in your province.
5. Include coverage for theft and resulting loss of use.
6. Will policy permit carrying of passengers for hire (if part of anticipated operation)?
7. Add endorsement to cover damage by fire, explosion, civil insurrection, riot, hail, wind, tornado.
8. Compare premiums for various amounts of coverage. Purchase maximum public liability allowable for reasonable premium.
9. Five or more vehicles? Request lower fleet rate.
10. Consider suitable deductible in relation to reduction in premium.
11. Request coverage to extend to vehicles rented for term or from time to time.
12. Consider coverage for personal medical expenses of driver, of passengers.
13. Shop around. Insurers' services, coverage and rates vary.
14. Choose comprehensive collision coverage desired.
15. Application. Check facts out. Be honest, accurate. Descriptions accurate? Representations accurate? Read printed portions over before signing. If possible, complete application yourself rather than having an employee of the agent fill in the answers.

LIABILITY INSURANCE

1. Document ownership of property (insurable interest); legal description of premises; civic address.
2. Examine existing policies, limitations, exclusions.
3. Prepare broad statement of operation and business activities carried on both on and off the premises. Request coverage for these including off-premises operations.
4. Consider loss or damage to property of others in parking lots operated or under control of the business.
5. Request coverage for liability arising out of negligence of owner, agents, employees, independent contractors working for owners.
6. Compare with automobile insurance coverage. Complement to cover liability arising out of operation of every type of motor vehicle operated by the business.
7. Include coverage for damage caused by motorized equipment other than motor vehicles and trucks.
8. Cover medical costs whether liability will arise or not.
9. Examine policy amounts. Adequate? Increase? Review once a year.
10. Review policies, coverage once a year. Re-examine limits, exclusions.
11. Lower premium costs by offering to maintain insurance coverage for a term of years (three instead of one).
12. Application is completed honestly, accurately.
13. Calendar expiry date. Renew before coverage expires.

Review

If you were a jury how would you decide the following cases and on what grounds?

1. McVITTY v. SOUTHWINDS EQUITY LIFE

The widow of Murray McVitty claimed to be entitled to the proceeds of her husband's life insurance policy after he was killed in a traffic accident. In the application for insurance McVitty stated that he had not had any disturbance of the heart and blood vessels and no coronary heart disease. In fact, before applying for insurance McVitty had suffered a serious cardiac problem and he had been in hospital to have a tube inserted in his heart. Southwinds elected under the circumstances to refuse to pay on the grounds that McVitty deliberately failed to disclose his condition truthfully and accurately.

2. PETRONELA v. STERLING INSURANCE COMPANY

When Petronela and Marcellus purchased a motor vehicle, the vendor completed a number of forms including an application for insurance coverage. Petronela is described as the owner and Marcellus as an occasional driver. Petronela signed the application and the company issued a policy of insurance. Six months later Petronela was involved in an accident and applied to the company for insurance proceeds. The application shows the answer "No" to the question "has any driver (user) lost driving privileges in the last five years?" In fact, Marcellus' licence had been suspended for three months during this period. The company refused to pay. "What does that have to do with my accident," said Petronela. "I had the accident, not Marc, and besides I was never asked that question. The girl in the office simply typed that in on her own. She should have asked."

3. HUDSON v. UNIVERSAL LIFE

Hudson had insured his home with Universal for years and had never made a claim. Several months ago Hudson retired and began trying his hand at furniture finishing in his basement for fun and profit. He carried on a business in a small way and gradually began purchasing more tools, paint and finishing liquids. An accidental fire, unrelated to the business, started in a bedroom and damaged the second floor extensively but left the downstairs and basement relatively untouched. The company refused to pay. "Hudson should have told us about the business he started," the company claimed. Hudson replied, "Nonsense. None of their business. That had nothing to do with the fire. It's just their cheap way of getting out of paying me after all these years."

4. ZACH v. O'HAGAN

Rogers asked O'Hagan to assist him in obtaining merchandise on credit from Zach. O'Hagan went with Rogers to see Zach and during the discussion Zach expressed willingness to deal with Rogers if O'Hagan would sign a guarantee. "You know me and paper. Don't care for the stuff, but if you'll give my friend credit I'll see you paid." Rogers got her credit but her business failed and she was unable to pay. Zach sued O'Hagan.

5. HENNESSY v. MINTY   Minty signed an agreement to guarantee Scrimshaw's debt of $5 000 to Hennessy. During the course of the loan Hennessy reluctantly accepted instalment payments in an amount less than called for from Scrimshaw on his undertaking to double up future payments when things "pick-up." Apparently they never did because Scrimshaw was unable to do so and did not have the money to pay the balance of the debt when it fell due. Hennessy agreed to give Scrimshaw a further 30 days in which to pay the debt. After the extended time Scrimshaw still had not paid. Hennessy sued Minty. Can Hennessy recover from Minty?

6. QUESTIONS

1. The insurance agent hands you a printed copy of your business insurance policy and says, "You're fully covered." Why wouldn't you accept this statement even though you had great trust in your agent?

2. Consider the reasons why the law requires applicants for insurance to act in "utmost good faith." List the probable consequences when an insured fails to live up to this standard.

3. Define robbery, burglary and theft insurance. Which is the most expensive to purchase and why?

4. Suppose you are the owner of a business and you are in the process of an annual review of your insurance coverage and needs. List five important things you would consider.

5. Is an insurance company justified in making it a condition of its liability to pay that the insured report loss within a very short time after the event? Write down reasons for your answer.

CHAPTER 8

Legal Forms of Business Organization

Unit I Sole proprietorship

YOU ARE THE JURY

IN RE NORTHERN LIGHTS

Blunden, the sole proprietor of an unregistered light fixture retail business known as Northern Lights (Ontario), was unable to meet his business obligations as they arose. Personal debts on his home, car, purchases and a bank loan were kept up-to-date. Business creditors appointed a Trustee in Bankruptcy to force Blunden into involuntary receivership.

Blunden was the only owner of the business and, at the time owned the store premises, fixtures, equipment, vehicles, inventory and accounts receivable. He also owned his home, a cottage, personal car, savings bonds and he had a personal savings account. All of his business and personal assets were combined but were insufficient to see the creditors paid in full.

Will the trustee be able to force Blunden into bankruptcy or are the creditor's rights limited to the business, "Northern Lights?" List the assets which will be subject to seizure for the general benefit of creditors.

OBJECTIVES

- to define the sole proprietorship form of business organization.
- to identify the advantages and disadvantages of sole proprietorship as a form of business organization.
- to identify the extent of liability of sole proprietors.

LEXICON

Bankruptcy (Receivership) A procedure by which the assets of an individual or corporation may be liquidated for the general benefit of creditors through a trustee in bankruptcy licenced by the federal government. Receivership is a form of bankruptcy in which creditors, through a trustee in bankruptcy, take over a debtor's assets to satisfy their claims.

Sole Proprietorship The form of business organization in which all business assets are owned by one person who is ultimately responsible for all business decisions.

A perusal of the yellow pages of the telephone directory will dramatically demonstrate that Canadians carry on business under a variety of legal forms of commercial organization. We discover sole proprietors, partnerships and corporations operating under a rich assortment of names and designations. What motivated each to select a particular form over another? What advantages does one form provide over another? What are the disadvantages of a particular form?

There are four legal forms of business organization in Canada. They are:

1. Sole Proprietorship.
2. Partnerships.
3. Limited Partnership.
4. Limited Company.

Each form brings with it advantages and disadvantages. It is important for people going into business to effectively choose one form over another by shrewdly weighing the advantages against the disadvantages for their own business purpose. It is also important for businesses, manufacturers and suppliers dealing with a business to be able to recognize its organizational strengths and weaknesses so they can govern themselves accordingly.

Organization

An individual may carry on business subject to registration and licencing requirements. The individual as sole owner of the business is directly responsible for the performance of all contracts and for all liabilities. Such an owner cannot separate business assets from personal assets. In the event of business failure, everything owned by the proprietor is subject to seizure by creditors to satisfy unpaid debts. The advantages and disadvantages of this type of business form are set out in the Checklist to this unit.

Income taxes

In the hands of sole proprietors, income from all sources is considered to be personal income. Income tax must be paid on total income because the business is not a separate legal entity. This can be a decided disadvantage as income of individuals is taxed at a progressively escalating rate to a maximum of over 60% (including provincial rates). Profits earned by corporate organizations are taxed at lower rates and Canadian-owned private corporations may be entitled to small business deductions not available to the sole proprietor. The result is that the sole proprietor will pay more total tax.

If the spouse of a sole proprietor works in or provides services to the business, any remuneration paid to the spouse is included in the income of the proprietor. Thus, the total is taxed at a substantially higher rate and results in more tax payable. If spouses are partners in a business, they might be able to report their own income separately; but the Minister of National Revenue has the power to add the income of one spouse to another in order to assess a higher rate of tax. If the business is incorporated and the spouses are shareholders, their income from the business (and from dividends) is considered as separate and may be taxed separately resulting in lower overall taxes being paid.

Name of business

Canadian sole proprietors are permitted to carry on business under various names, styles and designations. These include:

- proprietor's own name (William Psynischny Bakery).
- name other than proprietor's name (Psynischny uses William Piper as a business name).
- name of a place or object (London Bakery).
- coined words (Port-a-Po, name of a portable toilet business).
- foreign words (Allbergo Benvenuto).
- generic names (Gorden Fruit Market).
- name combined with the word Company or Co.
- name combined with words that suggest more than owner (i.e., Group, Associates, and Sons, etc.).

Sole proprietors must demonstrate good faith in choosing names other than their own. They are not allowed to deliberately mislead the public. Neither will the use of a name be permitted if it is likely to confuse the public as to who it is dealing with.

CASE 1   IN RE BLAKE-ROBERT'S MOTORS

York, whose given names were Blake Robert, named his used car business Blake-Robert's motors. At the time a man named Blake Roberts, an elected official, was the attorney-general of the province. An action to restrain York from using the name succeeded.

The court held that York deliberately chose the name to take advantage of similarity to mislead the public.

Sole proprietors are not permitted to use the designations Corporation, Limited, Ltd., Incorporated, or Inc. as part of their business name. These words may be legally used only by limited companies incorporated under provincial or federal legislation.

If sole proprietors use a name other than their own or names which suggest more than one owner, the name must be registered pursuant to the provincial law.

Registration

Each province requires that all persons engaged in business for trading, manufacturing or mining purposes who use business names other than their own, or which suggest plurality of ownership (such as Pilgrim and Daughters; Pilgrim and Associates) must register in a central registry office operated by the provincial government, a written declaration revealing the identity of the true owner, address of the business and the date the business was first commenced.

If sole proprietors do not comply with the registration requirements, they are liable to be fined. Ontario and Nova Scotia provide additional penalties which provide that if the business is not registered, the proprietor is not allowed to sue any person in respect to any contract made in connection with the business.

CASE 2   SUZUKI v. ZELLER

Zeller signed a contract to pay $900 by installments for a specified number of lessons in the martial arts with Suzuki who carried on business in Ontario under the name Hop Ky Doo Studios. Zeller paid the first installment of $25, took one lesson and never returned. He refused to pay the balance and Suzuki sued. A search of the registry office revealed that the business had never been registered.

Zeller was able to raise non-registration as a technical defence and did not have to pay. Ontario law denies access to the courts to sole proprietors who fail to register.

Registrations of businesses become part of the public record. Any interested party may obtain

the information contained in such public records by requesting them from the provincial government registration office and paying a small fee. Creditors use such information to check on the true ownership of a business. Those who intend to bring legal action against a business are required to accurately identify the owner by proper name; therefore the registration particulars are invaluable. For example, the author was instructed by a creditor to collect an outstanding debt owing by a business known only to the client as the "CandyWoman Variety." A check of the provincial business registration disclosed the owner to be Peter Meir. The court papers then named the defendant as "Peter Meir, carrying on business under the name and style of CandyWoman Variety."

KEY TO YOU ARE THE JURY

IN RE BLUNDEN   As a sole proprietor, Blunden was entitled to carry on business under the name and style of Northern Lights. However, in doing so he did not create a legal entity separate from himself. A sole proprietor is fully liable for business debts and financial obligations to the full extent of his total assets, including personal assets. All of his assets are subject to seizure and liquidation in order to pay creditors. The fact that the business was not registered is irrelevant because the consequence of non-registration is a penalty by way of fine (and in Blunden's province denying his business the right to sue for any business debt or contract). Non-registration does not prevent the sole proprietor from being sued by others and gives no protection from actions of creditors asserting their rights.

All of the assets listed may be seized and liquidated for the general benefit of creditors. (For details on the method of seizure and distribution see Chapter Ten, Creditors' Rights.)

Checklist: Sole proprietorship

1. Consider advantages and disadvantages of sole proprietorship as an organizational form in relation to partnership or incorporation (see item 15 and Partnership and Corporation checklists).
2. Consult accountant for advice on tax matters, business deductions, record keeping, availability of government grants. Consult business lawyer for legal advice arising out of interview with accountant.
3. Choose in good faith business name which will not be likely to confuse or mislead the public. Name will become a saleable asset as part of goodwill, so this is an important step.
4. If business other than own or suggests plurality of ownership, inquire at the nearest provincial or court building for particulars of registration requirements and fees. Complete forms. Register business. Note expiry date.
5. Inquire at municipal offices about procedure for obtaining business licences.
6. Inquire at nearest federal and provincial offices about procedures; obtain any necessary licence.
7. List personal assets. Consider transfer to spouse or another to protect from seizure by creditors in event of business failure. Legal if done while still solvent and if no intent to defraud (see Creditors' Rights – Bankruptcy for fraudulent

conveyance rules).
8. Consult insurance agency for details on *insurable business risks* (life, theft, burglary, robbery, business interruption, premises, public liability). See Chapter Seven.
9. At intervals review existing and potential legal business problems. Identify dangers. Don't pursue service, products, sales, profits, to such an extent that potential risks go unnoticed.
10. Consider key employees' positions with company. Consider motivating through profit share or buy-sell agreement. Consult lawyer and accountant. Review possibilities carefully.
11. At intervals review status of personal and business assets. Consider need to protect personal assets by legal transfer to spouse, a corporation or other person.
12. Business year-end is a good time for review of business affairs and to establish sound tax planning.
13. Consider change in organization to partnership or limited company to overcome disadvantages of sole proprietor form.
14. Keep up to date on business law, government statutes, regulations and requirements.
15. Advantages and disadvantages.

Advantages	Disadvantages
(i) Responsibility: Answer to no other. Total control. Sole right to decide.	Absolute responsibility limits sole proprietor's effectiveness to areas of strength; limits in area of weakness.
(ii) Liability: None.	Absolute liability. Need to take great care to insure against most risks. Need to transfer personal assets may result in loss of control to another.
(iii) Profit: No need to share profit.	Total liability for loss which can't be shared by others.
(iv) Organizational Form: Inexpensive. Standard, uncomplicated system for operation. Costs limited to registration and licencing fees. Only standard government forms to complete.	Unlimited liability. Too much responsibility. Possible lack of prestige when dealing with "big customer."
(v) Taxation: None.	Income from all sources is personal income for tax purposes. If spouse employed in business, no tax advantage if paid a salary.

(vi) Grants:

A few government grants may be available.

Most government grants restricted to limited company organization.

(vii) Borrowing:

None.

Most difficult organizational form to borrow larger sums.

(viii) Expansion:

Sole decider on need to expand.

Degree of expansion limited to effectiveness and liability of one person.

(xi) Sale of Business:

Sole decision-maker on terms of sale.

Corporation form may carry more weight in sale. Partners' joint decisions may be more effective in getting best deal on sale.

(x) Death:

None.

May result in forced sale at loss. Sole decision-maker now a disadvantage procedure.

Unit II Agency

YOU ARE THE JURY

SHERMAN v. SILVER

Alicia Sherman was permanently injured in a motor vehicle accident and retained Sterling Silver to sue Gurofsky, the other driver, for damages. Gurofsky defended the action. Silver and Gurofsky's lawyer made repeated attempts to settle the case out of court without success. Silver reported to Alicia on a regular basis, bringing her up-to-date on progress and the efforts to negotiate a settlement. During the course of the trial Silver negotiated a settlement in the sum of $150 000. The lawyers exchanged written memoranda as evidence of settlement. "I retained you to fight for me, Mr. Silver, not sell me out. My claim must be worth more than that. I'm sorry, you should have got my permission before you signed that paper." Gurofsky's lawyer insisted that Alicia recover no more than the settlement figure. Silver claimed he did his best. Valid legal opinion will demonstrate that damages of at least $250 000 would be awarded by the court.

Is Alicia bound by the settlement? List the problems suggested by this case. Identify the apparent remedies available to the parties. Consider the probable results.

OBJECTIVES

- to define agency as a method of carrying on all or part of the affairs of a Canadian business.
- to identify the duties and responsibilities of principals, agents and third parties.
- to distinguish between express authority and apparent authority and examine probable legal consequences when either type of authority is present.

LEXICON

Estoppel   A law that prevents a person from setting up the true state of facts against an innocent third party who has relied on the conduct of that person.

Indemnity   Compensation for trouble, expense or loss incurred. A principal undertakes to indemnify the agent for payments made or expense incurred by the agent on behalf of the principal.

Agency is the employment of one person (the Agent) by another (the Principal) for the purpose of making contracts between the principal and third parties. The relationship of agency arises whenever the agent has *Authority Express or Implied* to act on behalf of the principal, and consents to so act. The key to understanding the legal consequences of appointing an agent lies in carefully defining this concept of delegated authority.

Canadian business organizations could not function without the use of agents. Manufacturers appoint sales agents in various parts of the country to obtain purchasers for their goods. Businesses employ courier, transport and railway companies as agents to transport their goods. They use telegraph companies and postal services as agents to transmit their messages. They retain outside engineers, architects, lawyers, auditors and brokers on a fee or commission basis to transact part of their business. Partners in a business conducted for profit are agents for all other partners; their acts will bind the firm. Business corporations cannot conduct any business whatsoever except through its officers and other agents.

This unit examines the special rules that relate to agency situations such as those listed above. The law is uniform across Canada, with some minor differences in the law of Mandate (agency) as it relates to Quebec.

How an agency is created

Agents are appointed by means of employment contracts in which they are delegated authority by their principals to perform specified tasks on the principal's behalf. Principals will be legally bound by all acts done by their agents *within the limits of the authority delegated*.

It is common business practice to make the appointment by means of an agency contract in which the task to be performed is identified, the authority of the agent is defined and the fee or commission to be paid for services rendered is fixed. The ordinary rules of contract apply to such agreements. Some such agreements must be in writing (i.e., those which will take more than one year to complete and contracts with real estate brokers to pay commission) but others may be created by an oral agreement.

The agent's authority may be express or implied. *Express authority* is that list of delegated duties or powers actually given to the agent by the principal through specific instructions contained in the written or oral agency agreement. *Implied authority* is that which is created by the conduct of the principal. Whenever principals act in such a way as to give third parties the impression that their agents have the power to act for them in certain matters, they are bound by all acts done by their agents even though the acts are beyond the actual, real or express authority delegated. The agents are said to have acted within the scope of their *apparent authority.* This policy of law was developed in order to assist third parties who might otherwise be materially misled and who usually do not have access to the private agreements between principals and their agents.

CASE 3   ROBB v. GILCHRIST

Gilchrist, a shoe retailer, authorized an agent to make bulk purchases on his behalf. Gilchrist provided purchase order forms to be used and authorized the agent to sign the contract forms on his behalf. The agent purchased shoes from Robb (with whom he had dealt in the past) completing and signing one of the forms. Gilchrist refused to accept the shoes, arguing that the instructions he gave the agent were to include a term that the contract was not to be binding on him, as principal, until he approved samples. Nothing had been said to Robb about this fact. Robb sued for the price of the order.

Gilchrist himself provided the forms which were to be signed, and held the agent out as his representative. The agent had no actual or real authority to bind Gilchrist but if Robb had no notice of the limitation on the agent's authority, he would be entitled to hold the principal, Gilchrist, liable for the price on the grounds that the agent had been "clothed with" sufficient apparent authority.

Estoppel

The decision in the *Robb v. Gilchrist* case is an important one because it illustrates a useful principle of law (which should be committed to memory and applied as the occasion arises). The rule may be stated as follows:

> *Those who by their conduct or words cause others to believe that certain things are "facts"* and *those others are induced to act on that belief to their detriment* then *those responsible are estopped (prevented) from setting up the true facts as a defence.*

Notice that the term *estoppel* contains within it the word *stop,* and use this as a trigger for review of this rule.

Three-way analysis

A review of Canadian cases dealing with agency matters reveals that a reasonably comprehensive study can be undertaken by examining the rights and duties created between:

1. Principal and Agent.
2. Principal and Third Party.
3. Third Party and Agent.

Principal and agent

A principal has a duty to his agent to:

- pay for services rendered.
- complete the resulting contract with third parties.
- indemnify agent against loss or liability incurred by agent when acting within express authority.

The duties of agents to their principals are to:

- act within express authority.
- exercise reasonable care and skill (having regard to all the circumstances).
- be honest; act in good faith.
- disclose all relevant information (full disclosure).
- not represent both principal and third party without express consent of both.
- keep accurate accounts.
- not accept any secret commission or bribe.
- have no interest conflicting with principal's interests.
- perform the agency contract.

CASE 4   LAYCOCK v. FRASER

Laycock purchased a commercial building through Fraser, a real estate agent, and engaged Fraser to manage it and collect rents. After an accidental fire partially damaged the premises, Fraser offered to buy the building. Laycock sold it to Fraser thereby realizing a profit of a few hundred dollars. Fraser subsequently made a profit of several thousand dollars. At all relevant times Fraser knew (but did not tell Laycock) that a highway extension would substantially increase the value of the building. What do you think was the result?

CASE 5 GRADY v. QUICK AND SLY

Grady retained Quick, a realtor, to sell her summer home. A third party, Sly, submitted an offer to buy through the realtor and promised to pay a "bonus of $1 000" if the offer was accepted by the owner "without alteration or amendment." After the transaction had been closed, Grady discovered the existence of the bonus. She brought an action to rescind the contract with Sly and for damages against both Quick and Sly.

Sly was ordered to return the title to the property to Grady. Damages were awarded against both defendants; Quick was ordered to pay back the full amount of the commission paid by Grady $1 000 bonus. Damages equivalent to Grady's out-of-pocket expenses and legal fees totalling $915.55 were awarded in addition against both defendants.

If an agent receives payment from a third party without the principal's knowledge and consent, such payment amounts to a bribe for which both the agent and third party may be prosecuted under the *Criminal Code of Canada*.

CASE 6 McMURCHIE v. HERRICK

McMurchie instructed Herrick to act as agent to effect the sale of a ship which had several latent defects. McMurchie instructed Herrick to bring those defects to the attention of prospective buyers. Herrick deliberately misled the eventual buyer who, on discovery of the defects, successfully set the contract with McMurchie aside. McMurchie sued the agent for (1) the return of the commission paid (2) damages arising out of the aborted sale.

McMurchie succeeded. The court held that agents *warrant* (i.e., legally promise) that they will act within the scope of their actual real authority, and that failure to do so amounts to a "breach of warranty of authority" which will entitle the principal to the remedy of damages.

Principal and third party
The duties of principals to third parties are to:

- complete contracts made by agents which have been expressly authorized.
- complete contracts made by agents which have

not been expressly authorized but for which the agent has apparent authority.

The duties of third parties to the principal are to:
- take reasonable steps to satisfy themselves as to the actual scope of the agent's authority.
- complete contracts made by the principal's agent.

CASE 7 HATT v. NORTHWINDS MOBILE INC.

Northwinds, a manufacturer of mobile homes appointed Saint as an independent sales agent. Saint was to receive commission on the sale of new units and had authority to take and dispose of trade-ins. The agency contract read in part, "It is further understood between the parties that all sales must have the final approval of Mr. Dickie (President) and/or Mr. Mamo before being considered final."

Hatt agreed to purchase a new mobile home through Saint for a price of $20 000 to be paid $7 000 cash together with a trade-in of his old unit for which he was to receive credit in the sum of $13 000. A contract was drawn up but not signed. Hatt knew that the contract would not be valid without the approval of Mr. Dickie. Saint had made that clear and had read over the contract form. When Hatt did not hear back from Saint, he advised that he could wait no longer and would deal elsewhere. That afternoon Saint advised Hatt that he had now obtained approval "from head office, so if you still want to go through with this come in right away." Hatt signed at the bottom of the contract. The place for the company's signature took the following form:

NORTHWINDS MOBILE INC.

``

Not valid unless Signed and Accepted by an officer of the Company

"By _____
Approved subject to acceptance of financing by bank or finance company"

In the document, Saint had signed his name on the first line below the corporate name, and a person designated as a witness had signed on the second line. Hatt delivered the keys to his old unit and understood that the new one would be delivered from Northwinds' plant within 30 days. When the unit failed to arrive, Hatt contacted Dickie and was advised that no-one at the plant knew anything about the contract; that he at no time had approved or accepted it; and that Saint's

agency contract had recently been terminated by the company. A subsequent investigation by Dickie showed the "trade-in" had a value of only $7 000. Northwinds refused to accept it as a trade-in but offered in settlement to sell a new unit to Hatt for $20 000 cash. Hatt sued Northwinds for breach of contract.

The question which the court had to determine was whether the representation by Saint that he had approval for the sale from head office (when in fact no approval had been obtained) bound the company so that his signature to the document validated the contract. In this case the court found no evidence that the company at any time held Saint out as an officer of the company for the purpose of signing and validating contracts. Neither was there any evidence that the company had in any way modified the limitation on Saint's authority. The court said that it was unable to attribute to Northwinds "a holding-out" that Saint was authorized to inform Hatt in effect that he, by his own signature, could bind the company. The court said:

> It is undoubted that a person who deals with an agent, whose authority he knows to be limited, does so at his own peril, in this sense, that should the agent be found to have exceeded his authority his principal cannot be made responsible.

The court dismissed Hatt's action with costs of the court case assessed against him.

Third party and agent

The duties of agents to third parties are to:
- act within express authority.
- be honest; act in good faith.
- not represent both principal and third party without consent of both.
- not mislead; to honestly respond to legitimate inquiry but not otherwise volunteer information even if relevant to the transaction.

The third party owes no duty to the agent. There should be no contractual relationship between the agent and the third party because their objective is to make a contract between the principal and third party.

CASE 8 HATT v. SAINT

Hatt unsuccessfully sued Northwinds as principal on the facts outlined in *Hatt v. Northwinds Mobile Inc.* above. Hatt subsequently sued Saint personally for damages, claiming that Saint had knowingly acted without real authority and breached a duty owed by him as agent to Hatt as third party.

The court held that Saint's misrepresentation of his authority amounted to the tort of deceit and that Hatt was entitled to recover such damages as could be shown to have been the direct foreseeable result. On the evidence presented at trial the judge fixed the damages at $2 900 and entered a judgment against Saint for that amount.

It should be noted that Hatt should have joined Saint as a defendant in the first action. Lawyers usually advise clients to sue all of those who might reasonably be responsible in one action. If the action then fails against one defendant, it might be successful against a second. In this way all issues will be resolved without the necessity of bringing more than one action.

Precautions when dealing with agents

The fact that persons act as agents for others implies that the power they have to bind their principals may be limited. Therefore third parties should make reasonable efforts to ascertain the precise scope of an agent's authority. Agents should have readily available evidence of their authority, and if they do not, no important transactions should be entered into through them.

It is dangerous to pay money to an agent. If the agent has no real or apparent authority to receive funds, they cannot be later recovered from the principal. It is best to make payment directly in favour of the principal. Some agents (such as realtors) are bonded and, if funds are misappropriated they may be recovered through insurance.

When dealing with an unknown principal through a responsible or trusted agent, it may be wise for the third party to require the agent to be personally liable for the resultant contract.

KEY TO YOU ARE THE JURY

SHERMAN v. SILVER Sherman is bound by the settlement. Gurofsky (the insurance company) is entitled to rely on Silver's *apparent authority* as legal agent for Sherman to conclude a settlement on her behalf.

While Silver had no *real authority* from his principal, Sherman, nevertheless Sherman will be estopped from setting this lack of authority up as a defence against Gurofsky.

Gurofsky's lawyer, as the third party, had an obligation to be reasonably satisfied that Silver had authority to act and if, during the course of the various attempts to settle it would have been clear to a reasonable and prudent person that Silver had to have the consent to any settlement from Sherman, she may have been able to rely on the failure of the third party to make reasonable inquiries. This however is not the case here.

Sherman has the right to sue her agent, Silver, for damages for breach of authority and will recover the difference between the amount Gurofsky is now committed to pay and the amount she would likely have recovered if the matter had been decided by the court.

Gurofsky must pay $150 000 into court and will not be responsible for the excess.

Checklist: Agency

1. Principal makes decision to do all or part of business through an agent.

2. Consider agent's reputation, honesty, competence, and experience. Make deliberate, careful choice. Make independent inquiries.

3. Prepare written agency contract of appointment: explicit full instructions; identify express (real) authority; establish clear limits to delegated authority; fix fee or commission; set out in clear terms things that must happen before agent entitled to be paid.

4. Consider incidental powers agent must exercise to accomplish goal; if likely to incur substantial disbursement liability to principal or expose principal to risk, include limits in agency contract.

5. Agent must consent to act: agent reviews to see if legal requirements for written agreement (i.e., more than one year needed to complete; real estate sale; contracts to be made under seal).

6. Agent must act honestly, in best interests of principal, within limit of authority and exercise degree of skill expected of an agent with similar background and experience.

7. Agent must maintain careful accounting.

8. Agent must make full disclosure if transaction created conflict of interest: make principal aware of all relevant facts.

9. Agent must receive no payment other than from principal without knowledge and consent of principal and third party: unauthorized payments considered bribes (which offend both civil and criminal law: See Canadian *Criminal Code* – Secret Commissions).

10. Agent must obtain ratification, consent of principal at soonest possible time.

11. Third party must make reasonable inquiry to satisfy self that agent has authority to bind principal; may bargain with agent for personal liability of agent to guarantee performance.

12. Principal and third party must complete transaction.

13. Principal must pay agent.

14. Agent acts without authority or exceeds authority. Principal reviews remedies available. May include refusal to complete transaction; power to ratify; damages against agent (breach of warranty of authority); damages against principal for failure to complete.

15. Principal wishing to limit authority of agent considers impact, consequences of apparent authority; makes limitations known to all agents dealt with in past (and potential third parties if practicable).

16. Principal terminating agency relationship considers who has to know about it to avoid consequences of agent's apparent authority.

Review

1. DIONISI v. HAMMOND A merchant, Hammond, instructed a clerk (agent) to purchase several items of office furniture from Dionisi, who delivered the goods which were paid for by Hammond. Several weeks later the clerk ordered two typewriters from Dionisi without any instructions. She pawned the typewriters, and concealed the transaction from the merchant for several months by making small installment payments until she was discovered. Hammond refused to pay the account arguing that the purchase had never been authorized. Dionisi sued Hammond. Result?

2. KAY v. McLAY McLay authorized an agent to purchase specified goods. The agent actually purchased goods which were of a different quality. They were delivered to McLay, who refused to accept them. Kay, the seller, sued McLay for the price of the goods. Would Kay succeed?

3. SUZUKI v. BORBRIDGE Borbridge, the owner of a motel which had been damaged by fire, made Short his agent to repair and renovate. Short arranged to purchase lumber from Suzuki, which was to be charged to Borbridge. As the work progressed Borbridge, alarmed over his agent's "extravagance," prepared a written memorandum to Short limiting his authority to make purchases. This limitation was never brought to the attention of Suzuki, who continued to supply lumber. Suzuki sued Borbridge for the unpaid portion of his account. Was Suzuki entitled to do so?

4. FORBES v. MOSES Moses listed several properties with Rogers, a real estate broker. Moses entered into a contract to sell one of the properties to Forbes. Later, Moses discovered that Forbes was an employee of the realtor and refused to close the transaction. Forbes sued for specific performance, to compel Moses to close. What would be the probable result?

5. LOVELACE v. KNIGHT A farmer (Knight) listed his land with an agent (Lovelace) for sale. The agent agreed to purchase the land, advised the farmer he was purchasing on his own behalf and drew up the necessary contracts which were signed. Lovelace was aware that a developer, Scotti, was in the process of purchasing land in the area but did not reveal this fact to Knight. Knight learned that Lovelace had signed a separate contract to re-sell to Scotti at a price which would give a substantial profit. Knight refused to complete the contract and to deliver the necessary deed of land to Lovelace. Was Knight entitled to refuse?

6. CALHOON v. YEOMAN Yeoman, the manager of a company, misunderstood instructions from his head office. He honestly believed that he had been authorized to sell its local assets and to engage an agent for this purpose. An agent effected a sale of all the assets and it later became clear that the company had not authorized a sale. The third party buyer (Calhoon) sued the manager for damages. Result?

7. GORSKY v. ALCOTT The owner of a building (Alcott) listed it with an agent for sale. The property was sold to Gorsky. The agent agreed to place fire insurance on the building for Gorsky who gave the agent a cheque to pay the premium. The agent did not place the insurance and the building was later damaged by fire. Gorsky sued Alcott for damages to the extent of the insurance that the agent should have placed. Discuss. Result?

Unit III Partnership

YOU ARE THE JURY

QUIGLEY v. APPLEBY

Quigley and Appleby entered into a business under the firm name "Quality Data Systems." Quigley advanced $10 000 to get the business started and Appleby contributed $5 000. It was understood he would pay an additional $5 000 into the business as soon as he was able.

They did not have a written agreement nor did they bother to discuss the business organization in any detail. That was to be done later. Quigley worked effectively and built up a respectable clientele. Appleby generated only a few clients but he put in an average of 12 hours a day 6 days a week.

Each drew $200 a week from the business for their personal use. After the first year of operation their accountants advised that they had earned a good profit:

Profit (before draws/taxes)	$40 000
Quigley draws	10 400
Appleby draws	10 400

Quigley realized that she had billed twice as much as Appleby and that she had contributed twice as much capital investment. She told Appleby that she should get more of the profit of the firm and suggested a split of profits as follows:

Quigley	Appleby
$30 000 share of profit	$10 000 share of profit
- 10 400 drawn	-10 400 drawn
$19 600 balance due	$ 400 overdrawn

Appleby disagreed and demanded half of the profit. He pointed out he put in 12-hour days and also, because he kept the books and records of the firm, that he should be reimbursed for his time and service acting as bookkeeper. He suggested an additional $1 000 would be sufficient.

How should the profit be split? Is Appleby entitled to remuneration for his bookkeeping services? Can Quigley demand that Appleby forthwith pay a further $5 000 into the business to even out the capital contribution?

OBJECTIVES

- to identify the legal rules that apply to partnerships.
- to define the legal relationship between a partnership firm and third parties.
- to define the legal relationship between or among partners.
- to identify ways in which partnerships are created and terminated.

LEXICON

Business   Any trade, occupation or profession carried on for profit by two or more persons who are not incorporated.

Firm (Firm Name)   A legal term by which a partnership business identifies partners as a group but which does not give the group any separate legal existence apart from the partners themselves. The name given to the business by the partners is known as the firm name.

Partnership Agreement   A legal contract signed by all of the partners in which they establish rules and regulations, duties and rights which form the legal basis for their business organization.

Pledging Credit of the Firm   Borrowing money and giving the creditor a security against partnership property.

Quigley and Appleby did not deliberately set out to create a business organization to which partnership laws would apply. However, that is just what they did. This unfortunate alliance provides an example of how people enter into partnerships. Their major concern is to establish contact with suppliers and customers. They do not seem to understand that before too long they may be caught in a trap of their own design. In this unit we examine the legal rules that apply to partnerships; the relationship of a partnership firm to third parties; the relationship of partners to each other; and how partnerships are created and terminated.

Nature of partnership

Subject to minor variations, the law relating to partnerships is uniform across Canada. You will find the law of your province set out in the *Partnership Act*, the *Limited Partnership Act* and the *Partnership Registration Act*. These statutes accurately represent the law of partnerships as it exists today in clear, comprehensive, well-drafted written form. Those wishing to seriously study these subject areas should obtain copies of the statutes from their provincial government offices. In Quebec, the rules are set out in the *Civil Code*.

Organization

A partnership is the relationship that exists between persons for the purpose of jointly carrying on business for profit. The associates are called partners. The partners are known collectively as a "firm" and the name under which they carry on business is called the "firm name." The three key words in this definition are *persons, business* and *profit*. The organization must consist of two or more owners who may participate in management. Business is defined as including every trade, occupation and profession. An objective of the venture must be profit. If *any* of these three elements are missing, the enterprise is not a partnership and partnership laws will not apply to it. A list of those organizations to which partnership laws do not apply is set out at the end of this unit.

Relationships of partners to persons dealing with the firm

Every partner is an agent of the firm and the other partners for the purpose of the business of the partnership. The acts of every partner in the *usual* course of business of a kind carried on by the firm will bind the firm and all of the partners *unless* the partner so acting has in fact no authority to do the act *and* the other party either knows the partner has no authority or does not know of the partnership relationship that exists between the partner and the firm.

Every partner of the firm is liable jointly with all of the other partners for all debts and obligations of the firm incurred while he is a partner.

CASE 9   WHATLEY v. DIXEY

Harold Dixey, a partner in a firm known as Dixey Drugs, was an avid photographer who had over the past year begun promoting the sale of photographic accessories in one area of the store. Harold's partners did not approve but raised no objection because this "sideline" did bring in a modest profit and contributed to the goodwill of the business. However, the other partners became furious over a contract Dixey signed (without their consent) with Whatley, a camera wholesaler, for a quantity of expensive cameras. They wanted the order cancelled. Whatley knew the business was being operated as a partnership.

The main issue is whether or not the purchase for resale of the cameras was part of the usual business of the kind carried on by the firm. A secondary, but important issue, is whether Whatley was aware of any lack of authority to sign the contract on Dixey's part.

The bulk of the business done by the firm was the sale of drugs, cosmetics, paper products, hygienic and baby supplies. While film and camera accessories accounted for one per cent of the sales of the business, it had never actually sold *cameras* and had no available space to display such merchandise. It was held that the firm was not bound by the contract signed by Dixey because camera sales were not "in the usual course of business of the kind carried on" by the partnership.

A second defence raised at the trial on behalf of the firm was that Dixey had no authority to sign the Whatley contract. While the partners were successful in the action, this argument failed. To succeed in this defence, the partners would have had to be in a position to prove facts which would show that Whatley knew or ought to have known that Dixey had limited authority. In the absence of such facts, Whatley was entitled to rely on Dixey's apparent authority as an agent of the firm. There were no such facts upon which they could rely. In the alternative, it would have been necessary to prove that Whatley was not aware that he was dealing with a partnership and in this case the facts were against them because Whatley knew he was dealing with Dixey as a partner of a firm.

Dixey set up a defence of lack of genuine intention based on misrepresentation which failed. The court held that while he had no real or apparent authority to bind his partners, he was nevertheless personally liable on the contract to the same extent he would have been as a sole proprietor. Whatley was awarded damages against Dixey for breach of contract. This amounted to $3 850 plus costs.

CASE 10   PHILPOTT INC. v. COSTELLO AND VALENTINE

The two partners of a firm known as "Costello and Valentine Stationery" had a written partnership agreement providing that no partner acting alone had the authority to enter into contracts on behalf of the firm in excess of $500 without the signature of the other. During the course of negotiating the bulk purchase of an expensive item identified as "The New World Globe Light,"

Valentine informed a sales agent of Philpott Inc., "Costello's through. We're splitting up at the end of the week. You can deal with me directly from now on and, by the way, you can expect some pretty big orders with me in charge." Costello did withdraw at the end of the week. When advised that an order of this magnitude would not go through head office on Valentine's signature alone she signed it, "Costello and Valentine Stationery: per Wilma S. Valentine." But the lights did not sell and Philpott, in due course, sued both Costello and Valentine for the price.

Review the applicable law, establish the issues and consider the results.

If, while carrying out a task in the usual course of the business, a partner acts so negligently as to cause a loss or injury to a third party, the firm and all of the partners are liable.

CASE 11   ELIAS v. TYSON AND UNDERHILL

Tyson, a non-stop sales type, was in the habit of demonstrating a portable gas barbeque to friends and neighbours. Tyson was proud of the number of sales these demonstrations produced for his business. During one such demonstration, Elias was injured by an explosion. She sued Tyson and his partner, Underwood. "Nonsense," said Underwood. "It was Sunday and Tyson was having a party in his backyard. If he was careless, he should pay. But that has nothing to do with me or the business." Do you agree? Take care to identify the proper issues.

CASE 12   ROEBUCK v. DAME AND MITCHELL

Ferguson, a partner in an auto sales firm, received $5 000 in cash from Roebuck in payment for an automobile to be delivered the following day. Ferguson absconded with these and other funds. Roebuck sued Dame and Mitchell as partners when they refused to deliver the vehicle. At trial, the partners said, "We didn't authorize Ferguson to steal so he acted beyond the scope of his authority. Roebuck should find Ferguson and sue him, not us."

The important thing to bear in mind in this case is that as a partner Ferguson had the apparent authority to receive money from customers on behalf of the firm. If a partner misappropriates funds so received, the firm and all of the partners are liable to make good the loss. However, the same rule does not apply to the misappropriation of funds received by a firm *in trust*.

CASE 13 SHAPIRO v. THORPE AND CRISPPE

Shapiro deposited $5 000 with a real estate partnership firm Wilde, Thorpe and Crisppe to the credit of the firm's trust account. The money was to be used as a deposit on property Shapiro wished to buy. Wilde, a partner, misappropriated the funds to his own use and left the country.

If Thorpe and Crisppe had no knowledge of the theft of these trust funds, they would not as partners be liable. The rule relating to trust funds is that, should a partner improperly misapply trust property, no other partner is liable to the person beneficially entitled unless it can be shown that the partners had notice of the breach of trust or that they still maintained possession of or control over the funds.

The liability of partners to third parties begins when they become partners. They are not responsible for debts which were incurred before their admission to the partnership. Partners are liable for debts that are incurred while they are partners and they continue to be liable for debts even after they withdraw from the partnership and cease to be partners unless they do these three things:

- cause a dissolution of partnership to be filed.
- notify creditors and others with whom they have dealt that they are no longer partners.
- file public notice that they are no longer partners with the provincial partnership registration office (see Dissolution of Partnership).

When partners retire from a firm it is also possible for them to contract out of liability for debts incurred while members of the firm. This is done by agreement with the remaining partners (as newly constituted) provided that existing creditors have knowledge of the agreement and expressly consent or infer consent from their conduct towards and dealings with the firm as newly constituted.

Partners may delegate the power to bind the firm to employees by expressly authorizing them to deal with third parties on matters relating to the business or by assigning to them duties which usually involve such authority. When third parties deal with the firm through such employees, the acts done or the contracts made will bind the firm and all the partners to the same extent as acts or contracts made by one of the partners.

Employees of a partnership firm to whom wide powers have been delegated must take care that third parties do not believe they are members of the partnership. All persons who, by words or conduct, represent themselves as partners are liable as partners to any misled third party who provides credit, goods or services to the firm.

CASE 14 QUINCEY LIMITED v. RHODES AND SCOTT

Rhodes was the sole proprietor of a business known as Dusty-Rhodes and Company. In conversation, Rhodes frequently referred to Scott as "my partner." The firm letterhead showed the name and address of the business, and the names J. R. "Dusty" Rhodes and Walter M. Scott appearing one below the other. When the business failed Quincey, a supplier, sued both men. Scott proved that he was merely an employee drawing a salary; that Rhodes put his name on the letterhead without consulting him; and that he (Scott) never told anyone he was a partner. "I was just the manager. Dusty called me "partner" as a term of affection. I never imagined anyone would take it as any more than a joke." Quincey replied, "On the contrary I always thought of Scott as a partner."

The court held that Scott had a duty to take care that there was no mistake about his status as an employee. He could have pointed out to third parties that Rhodes' references to him as "partner" were in fun and he could have negated the implication that he was a partner or associate by qualifying his signature by such a word as "manager." Scott permitted himself to be held out as a partner and as such was liable to all those who advanced credit to the business at a time when they believed him to be a partner. Quincey succeeded against both Rhodes and Scott.

CASE 15 REDRUPP v. DEL PAPPA AND MANTELLO

Mantello, the sole proprietor of a construction company, was unable to pay a substantial debt to a radio station. In an effort to keep the business going and to secure the debt, Del Pappa, the owner of the station, provided Mantello with business advice and assistance. Gradually Del Pappa became more involved: he assisted in negotiations, drew up contracts and obtained the authority to co-sign cheques. Del Pappa was not an employee, paid agent, proprietor or partner of the business. Nevertheless, he was sued by Redrupp for the unpaid balance of a business contract he helped negotiate for Mantello. Result?

Partnership Agreement

A Partnership Agreement is a contract made by persons carrying on or who intend to carry on business as partners. It is a contract in which the parties record the objectives of the business; define the authority of the partners and the responsibility of each; state the duration of the partnership, the entitlement to profits and liability for losses; establish procedures for settling disputes; and provide for dissolution and retirement of partners as well as those terms that the partners consider necessary to avoid the arbitrary rules of the *Partnership Act*. A checklist at the end of this unit lists the matters to be considered in a partnership contract.

Partnership registration

Every Canadian partnership which carries on business for profit in trading, manufacturing or mining must register with the provincial government by filing a declaration signed by all of the partners stating:
- full name and residence of each partner.
- firm name.
- date of commencement of partnership.
- nature of the business.

The time limits and place of registration are established by each province in the *Partnership Registration Act* or its equivalent. Partnerships which fail to register are subject to substantial fines. In Ontario and Nova Scotia partnerships which fail to register will be denied the use of the courts to collect debts or resolve disputes.

The registration system is designed to provide essential information to members of the public dealing with the partnership business. Creditors may search the records to determine the names and addresses of all of the partners and those wishing to bring an action against the firm may use the registration record to make certain that they sue all of the persons who are liable as partners.

Each provincial Act also provides a system for registering notices of dissolution of partnerships. When partners withdraw from a firm or dissolve a firm it is important to register such a notice to correct the public record. Otherwise the partners may continue to be liable for future debts of a reconstituted firm.

CASE 16   SHORE v. CANTWELL

At the time a partnership commenced an action, it did not hold a certificate of registration. The *Partnership and Business Registration Act* of the province provides that, "unless and until a partnership holds a certificate of registration . . . the partnership shall not be capable of bringing or maintaining any action . . . ." The defendant raised non-registration as a defence and succeeded in having the action struck out (in effect, dismissed).

The limited partnership

At times Canadians invest in partnership businesses but do not wish to take the great risks involved in being general partners. This type of business investment is permitted through the *Limited Partnership Acts* of each province (except Quebec, which accomplishes the same results through its *Civil Code*).

A limited partnership is one composed of one or more general partners who control and manage the business and one or more limited or special partners who contribute money to the capital of the firm. The limited partners must not participate in management. They must not permit their names to be used in connection with the partnership and they must not hold themselves out to be general partners.

Limited partners are not liable for the debts of the firm beyond the amounts that they contribute to capital. They may give advice and counsel to the firm without losing the privilege of limited liability.

Limited partners are investors in the business. They are not permitted to withdraw their investment in any form during the life of the limited partnership (usually five years). Limited partners are entitled only to a share of the firm's profits or interest as specified in a written partnership agreement.

A limited partnership must be registered before the commencement of business by filing in the provincial registry office a declaration designated for the purpose, signed and sworn by all of the general and limited partners before a notary public, stating:
- firm name.
- name and residence of each general partner.
- name and address of each special partner.
- date of commencement of partnership.
- date partnership arrangement is to end.

In each province, limited partners become liable as general partners if:

1. The partnership is not registered as provided above.
2. The partnership continues on beyond its expiry date without a renewal certificate being filed showing the intention to extend the agreement.

3. Any false or misleading statement is given in obtaining a certificate.
4. A limited partner takes part in the management of the affairs of the business.
5. A limited partner's name is used in conjunction with the firm name or in the event a limited partner holds himself out as a general partner.

Dissolution of a limited partnership is governed by the same rule as those for a general partnership.

Relationship of partners to each other

In Canada, persons wishing to use the partnership form of business organization have the authority to establish their own rules for their business operations. This is most effectively done through a written *Partnership Agreement* drafted with the assistance of an accountant and a lawyer, and signed by all partners. If parties form a partnership business but do not have a written agreement, they may still establish their own rules by the manner in which they conduct their business over a period of time.

But if neither a written agreement nor the conduct of the parties clearly reveals the intention of the partners with respect to operational rules, it then is necessary to examine the rules governing the relationship between partners which are created by the provincial *Partnership Acts*. You will need a system to assist you in your analysis of problems arising among partners. Here, in general terms, is a practicable checklist gleaned from the Acts:

- Does the organization consist of two or more people carrying on business jointly with a view to profit? If so, is it a legal partnership to which partnership laws will apply?
- Do the partners have a written Partnership Agreement signed by the partners? If so, disputes may be resolved by applying the express terms and rules set out in the Agreement.
- If there is no written agreement (of if a written agreement does not contain terms relating to specific problems) examine the manner in which the partners carried on business. Do the "facts" consisting of words and conduct reveal the intentions of the partners to create clearly identifiable partnership rules? Disputes may be settled by examining the way the partnership has been run by consent in the past.
- If the written agreement does not cover a point in dispute (or if there is no written agreement) and the conduct of the business does not clearly demonstrate that the partners have created their own partnership rules, examine the applicable *Partnership Act* for implied terms or rules which

apply to all partnerships. Disputes may be resolved by applying the statutory rules listed below.

1. Partners have the first right to create for their own business organization a "constitution" of mutual rights and duties. It is only when they fail to do so that the government rules contained in the Act may be used to resolve disputes among partners.
2. All partners are entitled to share equally in the profits of the business.
3. All partners must contribute equally towards losses.
4. All partners are entitled to share equally in the capital of the business.
5. Every partner who had personally paid any firm debt or disbursement is entitled to be reimbursed for such payment if made in ordinary and proper conduct of the business of the firm.
6. Every partner may take part in the management of the partnership business.
7. No partner is entitled to remuneration for acting in the partnership business.
8. No new partner may be brought into the firm without the consent of all existing partners.
9. Any difference arising as to ordinary matters connected with the partnership business may be decided by a majority of the partners.
10. No change in the nature of the partnership business may be made without the consent of all existing partners.
11. The partnership books are to be kept at the principal place of business of the partnership and every partner may have access to and inspect them.
12. In the absence of an express agreement, no majority of the partners can expel any partner.

Apply the system and rules set out above to the *Quigley v. Appleby* case at the beginning of this unit. You should now be in a better position to define the problems between partners and to arrive at probable conclusions. In doing so note the undesirable consequences first from Quigley's point of view, then from Appleby's. Try to determine how the problems could have been avoided by a proper Partnership Agreement or otherwise.

CASE 17   IN RE TNT PRINTERS

Thatcher and Tiffany carried on a commercial printing business as partners for several years. Thatcher wanted to bring in a third partner to ease the workload and obtain fresh capital. Tiffany consistently refused. Eventually, after a great deal of pressure, Tiffany consented and

Chance was admitted as a partner. Thatcher was responsible for sales and worked outside. Tiffany and Chance worked inside. Tiffany refused to permit Chance to see any of the business records which were kept under lock and key. Chance began making managerial decisions which conflicted with the way Tiffany wanted things run. Both complained to Thatcher who refused to take sides. After 18 months, relations among the partners had deteriorated to the point that Tiffany consulted a lawyer. Tiffany told the lawyer that he had no choice but to admit Chance to the partnership and that at no time had any partnership agreement been signed.

The introduction of a new partner is the most common cause of disagreement which drives people to a lawyer's office after years of tranquil operations. In this case, because there was no partnership agreement the terms of the *Partnership Act* apply. They provide that Tiffany did not have to consent to the admission of a new partner. Once having agreed to the new partner "to keep peace in the family," her proper course of action would have been to have insisted on the preparation of a comprehensive Partnership Agreement which would have spelled out for the parties the extent of the authority of each and would also have provided a mechanism for resolving internal disputes. Under the *Partnership Act*, Thatcher had no obligation to act as a tie-breaker and Chance had every legal right to participate in management. In cases such as TNT the only practicable solution a lawyer can recommend is for one of the partners to dissolve the partnership and have the partners go their separate ways.

Dissolution of partnership

The termination of a partnership is called "dissolution." By their very nature business partnerships are not intended to last forever. Partners of successful businesses find it wise to incorporate. Partners of unsuccessful businesses find it necessary to discontinue. Others find that personality conflicts with partners are not worth the aggravation, and still others seek a way out of an arrangement that has "married" them to incompetent, dishonest or unproductive partners. These are the main reasons for which it is necessary to provide Canadian partnerships with escape hatches which provide the mechanics for effective dissolution and winding-up of a partnership business.

The *Partnership Act* provides rules for dissolution on the happening of certain events. These rules provide for rights of creditors and others; rights of partners to partnership profits and assets; and the general mechanics of the winding-up process.

The rules set out in the *Partnership Act* apply if the partners have not expressed a contrary intention in their Partnership Agreement. Most well-drafted Partnership Agreements do in fact provide exact procedures for dissolution, including a formula for identifying circumstances leading to dissolution; legal steps to follow; method of notifying creditors and others; methods of establishing values of partnership assets, paying debts of the firm and distributing the remaining assets and profits among the partners. In such agreements the partners may establish any lawful procedure they see fit.

In the past five years only twenty per cent of those firms seeking dissolution in Canada were able to rely entirely on dissolution rules set out in a written agreement. The remaining eighty per cent had to rely on one or more of the following statutory rules.

Fixed term/Single venture

When partners express an intention to maintain their business for a fixed period of time, the partnership is automatically dissolved at the end of that period. At times people will enter into a partnership to complete one transaction or undertaking. They cease to be partners on the completion or abandonment of the venture. For example, a physician, an accountant, and a real estate broker pooled their financial resources to purchase a parcel of land in order to develop it. While the development was still in progress, they sold it to a construction firm for a profit. They ceased to be partners when the profits were split.

No time limit partnership

If a partnership is formed for the purpose of doing business on an ongoing basis and the partners have not expressed any specific time limit, *any* partner may give notice to the other partners of the intention to terminate the partnership business. In this case the partnership is dissolved as of the date set out in the notice. If no specific date is mentioned in the notice, the partnership is dissolved as soon as the notice has been delivered to the other partners. No special form is needed. However, to be effective such notice must be in writing and establish a reasonable time period for dissolution to permit an orderly winding-up of the business. The partner seeking dissolution should take care to document evidence of the actual delivery to the others and to establish the delivery date.

Death of a partner

Partners must consider the legal consequences of

the death of a partner. The partnership firm has no *real* existence apart from the partners themselves, and the death of one partner dissolves the partnership by operation of law. It is possible to avoid the agony of forced dissolution by providing for continuation of the partnership by the remaining partners on the condition that they buy out the deceased. That is, the remaining partners pay the deceased's share of the value of the business to his estate.

Insolvency of a partner

If one partner is unable to meet personal and business financial obligations generally as they arise to such an extent as to be insolvent, the partnership is dissolved on the same terms as on the death of a partner described above.

Pledging credit of firm

A partner who uses partnership property for personal gain not connected with the firm's ordinary course of business is said to pledge the credit of the firm. If the partner has not been specially authorized to do so by the other partners, the firm is not bound and is not responsible for such acts to third parties. If in doing so the partner puts his share of the partnership property up as security for a separate personal debt, the partnership may be dissolved at the option of the partners.

Illegality of the business

A partnership is, in every case, dissolved by the happening of any event that makes it unlawful for the business of the firm to be carried on or for the members of the firm to carry it on in partnership.

CASE 18   BUCHAN v. PIERCE

Two partners sold printed material through a mail order business which depended on a pyramidic sales scheme. A change in the law made such schemes unlawful unless licenced by the government. Buchan and Pierce applied for a licence but were refused. Buchan then wanted the firm wound up, but Pierce wanted them to continue by getting into other lines.

Buchan's argument that the main purpose of the business had been frustrated was successful. The court confirmed that the partnership had been dissolved by operation of law and gave directions for its winding-up and distribution.

Court order

Under certain circumstances it is not possible for the partners to effectively or legally dissolve the partnership. In such cases a partner may make an application to the courts for an order declaring the partnership dissolved and for directions as to how the partnership property should be distributed. On such an application a court may order a dissolution of a partnership:

1. When one partner is found to be mentally incompetent or is shown to the satisfaction of the court to be permanently of unsound mind. In either case, the application may be brought by a partner or by the personal representative of the incapacitated partner.
2. When one partner becomes in any other way permanently incapable of performing necessary duties and responsibilities in the partnership.
3. When one partner has been guilty of such conduct as, in the opinion of the court, prejudically affects the carrying on of the business. The court must consider both the seriousness of the partner's actions and the nature of the business.
4. When a partner wilfully and persistently breaches the terms of the partnership contract or demonstrates by conduct relating to the partnership that it is not reasonably practicable for the other partners to tolerate such conduct and continue in partnership.
5. When the business of the partnership can only be carried on at a loss.
6. When circumstances have arisen so that, in the opinion of the court, it would be just and equitable to dissolve the partnership.

Notice of dissolution

Dissolution of a partnership is a serious business. The partners have an obligation to give notice to those with whom they have dealt in the past and the public generally of the fact of the dissolution. This is particularly true if, after the dissolution, the old firm is re-constituted into a new business organization to be carried on by one or more of the old partners. Where the newly constituted firm continues to do business with third parties who in the past have done business with the old firm, these third parties are entitled to hold all members of the old firm liable on the new contracts until they have notice of the dissolution or change. A partner who is out of the business may obtain protection by sending a notice of dissolution to all persons who dealt with the firm in the past and who are liable to continue to deal with the newly constituted firm. As the number of third parties is probably great, it may only be possible to notify important creditors and suppliers to whom there may be a high risk of liability. Publication of the dissolution in local newspapers and the provincial gazettes will be effective to avoid future liability to others. But the partners should also comply with provincial law requiring them to file a Notice of Dissolution with the provincial government pursuant to the *Partnership Registration Act*.

CASE 19   FORMBY v. RYAN AND PICK

Pick withdrew from a partnership known as Royal Penguin Supplies, thus dissolving the partnership. Ryan, who continued on under the old firm name, began doing business with Formby. After extending credit to the firm, Formby checked the registration records and, because no dissolution notice had been filed, found Pick to be an apparent partner. After several months Formby sued for the balance of his unpaid account and added Pick as a defendant. Pick claimed she was not liable and set up the earlier dissolution as a defence.

While Pick was able to present a fairly respectable defence, the overriding consideration was the failure of the former partners to register the necessary dissolution notice. Pick was held liable for holding herself out as a partner.

Authority after dissolution

After dissolution, each of the partners has the authority to bind the firm insofar as is necessary to wind up the affairs of the partnership and to complete transactions begun but unfinished at the time of the dissolution. But the partners do not have authority to transact other business on behalf of the firm.

Partnership property

On the dissolution of a partnership the partners have a duty to apply partnership funds and assets to the payment of the debts and liabilities of the firm. If a surplus remains, the debts and liabilities owing by the firm to any partner may be paid. After such payments, any surplus may be used to repay capital. The balance, if any, may be divided among the partners in the same proportion in which profits were divisible.

The near partnerships

Every activity through which associates anticipate a profit does not create a legal partnership. The consequences which may flow from a legal partnership are so serious that it is essential to be able to identify those arrangements to which partnership law may not apply.

1. Non-profit organizations   Business in partnership law is restricted to every trade, occupation and profession carred on for a profit. Therefore, partnership laws cannot be applied to charitable organizations, non-profit associations and public boards.

2. Joint ownership of property   Joint or common ownership of property does not of itself create a partnership even though profits are shared.

3. Gross profits   Gross profits in themselves do not create a partnership, regardless of whether the persons sharing such returns have or have not a joint right or interest in any property from which or from the use of which the profits are derived.

4.   In certain circumstances a non-partner may receive a share of profits without becoming a legal partner of the business (i.e., a creditor receiving payment of a debt out of profit; an employee receiving remuneration by way of a share of profits; the estate of a deceased partner under an agreement by which the firm pays from its profits the purchase price of the deceased partner's share).

KEY TO YOU ARE THE JURY

QUIGLEY v. APPLEBY   Quigley and Appleby carried on business in common with a view to profit under circumstances which created a legal partnership organization to which partnership law applied.

They had no written contract. An examination of the way in which they conducted their business does not reveal any express intention to establish rules for sharing profits or to establish remuneration, wages or salaries for work done for the firm. Therefore the rules in the *Partnership Act* will govern this situation.

Quigley must share profits equally with Appleby. On the other hand, Appleby cannot demand remuneration for the services he provided to the firm. He will not be entitled to any payment for the extraordinary amount of time he spent ''on the job'' nor will he be entitled to any payment for bookkeeping services.

Quigley may demand that Appleby pay the additional $5 000 capital into the firm. Appleby may be able to delay this payment on the ground that he still is not financially in a position to pay.

Quigley may not insist that the payment be made out of the profits Appleby will receive. Appleby is absolutely entitled to those. Quigley's only real remedy is to give notice of dissolution, wind up the business and start anew on her own or with a more competent partner.

Checklist: Organization of a partnership

1. Advantages and Disadvantages Consider advantages and disadvantages against sole proprietorship, limited partnership or corporation. (See item 21.)

2. Accountant/Lawyer Consult accountant on tax matters, business deductions, record keeping, accounting principles for valuation purposes, availability of government grants. Consult lawyer for legal advice and preparation of Partnership Agreement.

3. Associates Partnership organization is only as good as one's associates. Reconsider advisability of going into business with others. Consider others' reliability, responsibility, qualifications and competence to conduct business and participate in management.

4. Select Firm Name Check possible conflicts with trade names now in use by similar businesses in the locale in which you wish to operate. Check city and telephone directories. Search provincial business records offices and companies branch. Search Trade Marks Office, Ottawa. Consider impact, attractiveness of name. It should contribute to goodwill value of business. Consider name appropriate for later incorporation.

Review *Partnership and Business Registration Acts* (*Civil Code* for Quebec firms) registration requirements, time limits, procedure. Obtain necessary documents. Complete and submit to provincial registration office with required fee to comply with provincial law and to preserve right to use of the name in the future.

Name of partner to be used in firm name? Get written consent, consider consequences if partner withdraws or dies. Establish terms for continued use of such name.

Establish terms restricting partners from use of firm name for other than firm business.

5. Usual Business Of Firm Define intended business of the firm in detail. Limit partner's authority to usual scope of business. If one partner is engaged in other business, define competition limitations. Avoid conflict.

Establish terms for anticipated expansion; how decisions to be made; state whether consent of all or majority needed.

6. Capital Contributions Determine amount and nature of capital to be contributed by each. Cash? Other property? Services?

Define extent of each partner's contribution. State deadlines for making contribution and consequences of failure to make necessary contribu-

tion on time.

Fix values to contributions if other than cash. Consider potential need for additional capital. Include terms obliging partners to make future contributions to capital by amount or percentage of partnership share.

7. Profit/Loss Determine whether partners will draw "salaries" and if so exclude amount of salaries so paid as an expense in calculating profits.

Determine how profits to be divided. Consider guarantee of minimum profit to any partner. Fix time to distribute profit (i.e., usually after required audit).

Determine how losses (if any) to be shared. Determine any internal limitations on liability for losses among partners.

Provide terms for periodic review of criteria or basis for share of profit and loss and establish mechanism to revise.

8. Partner's Duties State duties of each partner. Fix time to be devoted to firm business (i.e., full-time, part-time). If some partners are part-time and others are full-time, provide for fair compensation by way of payment of wage or salary.

Provide for remuneration paid as wages or salary to partners as an expense of the business before calculation of profits.

Identify who is in charge of sales, administration, production. Unless otherwise agreed, all are entitled to participate in management.

List what can be done by any partner on own without consent of others. List types of contracts which may be signed by any partner without prior approval of others.

Include terms to prevent withdrawing partner from competing with the business for specified time (non-competition clause).

9. Books/Accounting Identify nature of records to be kept; type of statements to be provided to all partners on regular basis.

Choose outside auditor and provide for independent audit at required intervals.

Establish provisions for partners to examine books, records.

Fix accounting period; fiscal year-end.

10. Banking Arrangements Choose bank and identify types of accounts to be operated. Complete banking forms.

Name partners authorized to sign cheques (usually more than one for larger amounts). Provide procedure for changing authority to sign. Stipulate authority for making usual relatively small disbursement by partners.

11. Meetings   Design format for calling meetings to consider partnership matters, making and recording decisions. Provide for regular meetings; keep minutes; record major decisions. Too frequently misunderstandings occur when decisions are not recorded.

12. Prohibited Acts   Generally powers of partners are broader than those of shareholders in corporate organizations. It is necessary to list forbidden activities including:

- competition in any other business (except as expressly authorized).
- ownership of interests in competing business (except as expressly authorized).
- assignment of partnership interest to third party.
- hiring/firing without express approval.
- making purchases beyond an agreed sum without express approval.
- acting beyond the scope of actual authority in such a way as to bind the firm or make the partners responsible to a third party.
- disclosing trade secrets, processes, or confidential information of the firm.
- use of the partnership name after withdrawal from or dissolution of the partnership.

13. Life Insurance   Consider purchase of life insurance on the life of one or more partners either as ''key-person'' insurance or to provide funds for a purchase/sale agreement among the partners. This is useful in event of the death of a partner resulting in the need of those remaining to purchase deceased partner's interest from estate.

14. Withdrawal   May a partner withdraw at any time? Such a right is not to be permitted lightly because it creates a burden on remaining partners. If partner to be permitted right to withdraw, establish conditions for the eventuality including: right of remaining partners to buy withdrawing partner's share; terms of purchase; method of fixing values; method of payment. Terms should be heavily weighted in favour of remaining partners and provide extended time for payment of purchase price on favourable terms.

Consider accounting procedure to be used to value partnership share of withdrawing partner (i.e., value at cost, market or depreciated value).

Provide right of remaining partners to carry on business without dissolution and giving right to goodwill including right to continue use of firm name.

15. Death/Retirement   A partnership dissolves on the death of a partner unless otherwise provid-

ed in the Partnership Agreement. Provide for continuation of business without dissolution on death of any partner at option of the remaining partners as well as a formula for the purchase of the deceased partner's share by remaining partners. Terms of purchase should be more flexible and generous than those for partner who voluntarily withdraws.

Purchase life insurance to fund purchase of deceased partner's share.

Retirement (as opposed to withdrawal) involves the same basic consideration as death of a partner situation.

16. Duration   Establish and record date of commencement of partnership. Specify length of time firm is to remain in business. Consider short period (at first) to avoid being obligated to carry on business in event disagreements result in inability to work effectively together.

Provide automatic continuance or renewal clause to permit partners to carry on business beyond fixed term without having to take additional steps. Provide continuance (after expiry of fixed term) from year to year until one partner provides termination notice.

17. Expulsion of Partner   Unless expressly agreed, partners cannot get rid of any one partner without dissolving the partnership. Consider terms for expelling a partner for cause (without dissolution) on vote of majority.

18. Admission of New Partners   Provide for admission of new partners by majority vote (if desirable). Establish mechanics for entry, payment for share.

19 Arbitration of Disputes   Establish rules for internal resolving of disputes by democratic process. Establish mechanism to resolve disputes which cannot be resolved by partners by method other than court action. Usually this means establishing auditor or some other trusted outsider as final, unappealable arbitrator of dispute. An alternative method involves submitting dispute to single arbitrator appointed under Arbitrations legislation of the province. That decision is final, but the procedure is expensive.

20. Internal Management Rules   Instruct lawyers to provide other terms for consideration including drawing arrangements, valuation methods, non-competition clauses, grounds for dissolution, options to purchase, partnership property, provincial law applicable, additional insurance provisions and mechanics for future amendment to Partnership Agreement.

21. Advantages and Disadvantages.

Advantages	Disadvantages
(i) Responsibility: Discussion with associates likely to lead to effective decisions; fewer errors.	Potential areas for dispute leading to disagreement causing delay, procrastination.
(ii) Liability: Losses shared with others.	Personally liable for firm debts. Potential risk greater with more people involved in business. Possible liability for mistakes, fraud, torts of other partners.
(iii) Profit: Greater potential for earnings.	Profits must be shared with others. Hardest working, greatest earner may have to share disproportionate amount of profits with less productive partners.
(iv) Organizational Form: Need for Partnership Agreement leads to greater appreciation of legal and accounting consequences.	Need for Partnership Agreement leads to formal structure, legal and accounting expense. Registration requirements more stringent. Need to register notice of dissolution.
(v) Taxation: None.	Income from partnership is personal income in hands of partner.
(vi) Government Grants: Some grants available.	Many grants available only to corporate businesses.
(vii) Borrowing: Increased borrowing power.	Must be personally liable for sums borrowed by the firm.
(viii) Expansion: Some increased ability to expand by taking on new partners into an existing partnership organization.	May need consent of all partners or majority of partners to expand.
(ix) Death: Can avoid dissolution by proper Partnership Agreement.	Unless expressly avoided by Partnership Agreement, death of a partner results in dissolution of partnership.

Review

1. JOLLY v. MARTINUK AND OTHERS

Martinuk, Drake and Parsons carried on a business as partners. Martinuk contacted Jolly to advise that his partner Drake had died and he intended to carry on business at the same location as Parsons who had never been particularly active in the business and had decided to retire. Martinuk then placed an order for goods on an old piece of firm letterhead showing Martinuk, Drake and Parsons as owners and partners under the firm name. When Martinuk failed to pay, Jolly sued Martinuk, Parsons and the personal representative of the deceased Drake. Would you permit Jolly to recover against all or any of the defendants?

2. MARS MOTORS v. HILL AND OTHERS

A partnership was dissolved by mutual consent. Two of the partners decided to carry on business as a new firm. The partnership assets were sold, the firm's liabilities were paid in full and the funds left over were divided among the old partners. Hill, one of the continuing partners, bought a motor vehicle in the name of the firm (which was identical to the name of the old firm). When Hill defaulted in payment, Mars sued all of the partners of the old firm. What would you decide?

3. PATTON v. MacARTHUR

Patton and MacArthur were partners. Patton took a leave of absence from the business for health reasons and was away for six months. In that time MacArthur decided to draw a salary of $300 a week. On her return Patton demanded an accounting and demanded that MacArthur repay the amounts drawn for salary claiming that he was not entitled to anything over profits for doing all of the work. Would you agree with Patton?

4. LARSON v. BLACK, BROWNE AND GREENE

Browne and Greene are partners in a firm desperately in need of outside sales contracts. Recognizing Black's expertise in this field, they offered him a one-third interest in the firm, if Black agreed to attend to outside marketing. They further agreed that Black was not to be responsible for firm debts or losses. Several months later Larson, unaware of the arrangements, sued all three for a considerable firm debt. The evidence at the trial was that no record was ever made of the arrangements exempting Black from firm debts or losses. However, the arrangement was not disputed. Would you give judgment against Black as well as Browne and Greene?

5. Questions

a) Define a partnership.

b) What purpose is served by a written Partnership Agreement?

c) What does the partner of a firm have in common with an agent?

d) What is the practical effect of the *Partnership Act* of your province?

Unit IV   Corporations

YOU ARE THE JURY

CATALANO CORP v. HESTER DEVELOPMENTS INC.

Twelve people incorporated a business to purchase country lands for development and resale as ''cabin lots'' for skiers and hunters. Blackacres, a large tract of land, was offered for sale to the corporation but the majority of the directors voted not to purchase it. Three of the directors (Hester, Holland and McBain) resigned, formed their own company and made an offer on the property which was accepted. During the course of reorganization the original company re-considered the decision on Blackacres and decided to buy it after all. On discovering that the land had already been sold to Hester and her group, the Catalano group had its lawyers write a letter demanding that the property be turned over to it at the price originally quoted by the owner of Blackacres. ''Not on your life,'' replied Hester. ''You had your chance and turned it down. We formed our own corporation and now we own the property and intend to keep it.''

What role do directors play in a limited company? What are the duties of directors? Does an obligation owed by a director survive the director's resignation? Consider these issues and decide whether or not Catalano Corp. has any claim on Blackacres.

OBJECTIVES

- to identify the requirements for formation of a Canadian limited company.
- to identify the methods by which a limited company is organized.
- to identify the methods by which a corporation carries on business.
- to define the duties of a board of directors.

LEXICON

Articles of Incorporation   The document that is both an application for incorporation for a federal (or Ontario) company and a permanent ''constitution'' of basic rules for the corporation.
By-Laws   General rules which establish the methods by which the business will be run as a corporation. They are passed by the directors and form part of the constitution of the corporation.
Letters Patent   The document under provincial seal by which a company is incorporated in Manitoba, Quebec, New Brunswick and Prince Edward Island.
Memorandum of Association   A document filed with the provincial government by applicants for incorporation which sets out the fundamental terms of the proposed corporation. It is required for registration in British Columbia, Saskatchewan and Alberta.
Shares   A method of describing the proportionate legal interest held by an ''owner'' of a corporation share certificate. A formal certificate issued by a corporation to a person as evidence that that person is the legal holder of a specified share in the corporate undertaking.

A corporation or limited company is a business organization which has a separate legal existence from that of its members. It has the power to enter into contracts and sue in its own name. It may in turn be sued directly by others. It is recognized as the legal owner of the assets of the business. A corporation executes documents in its own name through authorized signing officers who act as agents. In the case of formal documents, these agents affix the official corporate seal as well.

The creation of this separate legal entity gives the corporation most of the legal rights and powers of a person and makes the corporate organizational form fundamentally different from those of the sole proprietorship and partnership. A partnership has no existence separate from the partners themselves. Partners in a firm own the assets personally and are personally liable for the debts and obligations of the firm. A corporation becomes owner of the assets which are acquired in its name and its shareholders are not personally liable for its debts.

Those corporations whose operations and property are in one province only usually will incorporate under that province's legislation. But nothing prevents a business which will operate in one province only from incorporating under the federal statute. This is done when the company intends to obtain foreign financing. It is also done to obtain the extra prestige that federal incorporation appears to provide. If a business intends to extend its operation to one or two other provinces, it still may incorporate under provincial law and

<table>
<tr><td>

**CANADA BUSINESS
CORPORATIONS ACT**
FORM 1
ARTICLES OF INCORPORATION
(SECTION 6)

</td><td>

</td><td>

**LOI SUR LES CORPORATIONS
COMMERCIALES CANADIENNES**
FORMULE 1
STATUTS D'INCORPORATION
(ARTICLE 6)

</td></tr>
</table>

1 – Name of Corporation	Nom de la corporation

2 – The place in Canada where the registered office is to be situated	Lieu au Canada où doit être situé le siège social

3 – The classes and any maximum number of shares that the corporation is authorized to issue	Catégories et tout nombre maximal d'actions que la corporation est autorisée à émettre

4 – Restrictions if any on share transfers	Restrictions sur le transfert des actions, s'il y a lieu

5 – Number (or minimum and maximum number) of directors	Nombre (ou nombre minimum et maximum) d'administrateurs

6 – Restrictions if any on business the corporation may carry on	Restrictions imposées quant aux entreprises que la corporation peut exploiter, s'il y a lieu

7 – Other provisions if any	Autres dispositions s'il y a lieu

8 – Incorporators — Fondateurs

Names – Noms	Address (include postal code) Adresse (inclure le code postal)	Signature

FOR DEPARTMENTAL USE ONLY — À L'USAGE DU MINISTÈRE SEULEMENT

Corporation No. – No de la corporation	Filed – Déposée

CCA-1385

Section 6 of Articles of Incorporation under the *Canada Business Corporations Act.*

obtain extra-provincial licences to maintain such operations.

Unlike sole proprietorship, business through agency and partnership, the corporate organizational form is available only after formal permission to use it has been obtained from the federal or provincial governments. The statutes under which such permission may be granted are:

The Canada Business Corporations Act and the Ontario Business Corporation Act   Incorporation under these Acts is automatic if the incorporators submit documents in proper form. Incorporators submit Articles of Incorporation, submit the proposed name of the corporation and pay a prescribed fee. The government then issues a Certificate of Incorporation (in effect the birth certificate of the limited company).

Provincial Letters Patents Acts   Incorporation under these Acts is not automatic. Incorporators submit a Petition for Incorporation to the provincial government. The minister in charge of incorporations for these provinces has a wide discretion to consent to incorporation or withhold consent. If the minister consents, the provincial government issues under its seal a document called Letters Patent. This procedure is available in Manitoba, Quebec, New Brunswick and Prince Edward Island.

Provincial Registration Acts   Incorporators are required to register a Memorandum of Association which sets out the agreement of the incorporators and operates as a constitution for the corporation to be formed. On payment of the required fee the corporation is registered under the authority of the provincial government. Provinces in which the registration system is in use are British Columbia, Saskatchewan and Alberta. The system is also used in the Yukon and the Northwest Territories.

How to form a Canadian business corporation

As the *Canada Business Corporations Act* is the most comprehensive and modern business corporations legislation, we'll make best use of our time by analyzing the incorporation procedures it sets forth. (The Ontario rules are similar but other provincial Acts provide alternate procedures.) Under the CBCA, any one or more persons may apply for incorporation of a business by signing and filing Articles of Incorporation in duplicate with the federal government together with the required fee. The articles will be the basic constitution of the company and must identify the intend-

ed corporate name, head office, corporate objects, authorized capital and share structure, names and addresses of the incorporators, number of shares to be issued to incorporators and the number of directors.

If the intended name is "unobjectionable," the corporate objects are lawful and the Articles in proper form, the federal government must issue a *Certificate of Incorporation*. The certificate is signed by a designated government official, given a reference number and dated. The company has full powers to carry on business as of the Certificate date. The Certificate is attached to one copy of the Articles and returned to the incorporators. Copies are retained in Ottawa and are available to any member of the public.

Following incorporation the company is organized under the direction of its accountant and lawyer. Shareholders purchase shares in the enterprise. Officers and directors are elected; by-laws and resolutions are passed. Shareholders enter into a shareholders' agreement which defines the corporation's duties to them and their respective rights and duties toward each other. If an existing business venture has been incorporated, the proprietors of the old business transfer the assets of the business as "a going concern" to the corporation in consideration for shares in the corporation or other value. If the corporation is a new venture entirely, it simply commences its operation and acquires business and assets as it goes along.

Corporate name and seal

Incorporators of a federal business corporation must obtain the consent of the federal government to the use of a name. A corporation will not be permitted to use any name which is so similar to that of another corporation, proprietorship, partnership or person likely to mislead or confuse the public. Incorporators apply for a name clearance and approval before submitting their application. In doing so they often submit several alternate names in order of preference in the event that one or more submissions prove objectionable. For some businesses the name is unimportant. In such cases the incorporators may ask that the corporation be assigned a "designated number" or a "corporation name number" to avoid difficulties in obtaining name approval.

If a corporation comes into existence with a name that is in fact objectionable, the federal government has the power, on discovering the error, to direct the corporation to change its name within 60 days.

The word "Limited," "Limitee," "Incorporated," "Incorporee" or "Corporation" or the abbreviation "Ltd.," "Ltee.," "Inc." or "Corp." *must* be used as the last name of every corporation. On the other hand, it is unlawful for any business which has not been incorporated by the federal or provincial governments to use such designations as part of its name.

The provincial rules with respect to corporate names are similar. Federal and provincial operations must clearly set out their authorized corporate names in all contracts, invoices, cheques, other negotiable instruments and orders for goods and services issued or made by or on behalf of the corporation.

Each corporation must have a corporate seal which must be impressed on all share certificates, bonds, by-laws, deeds or other documents requiring the affixing of a seal and on all *formal* contracts entered into by the corporation. The authorized signing officers usually witness the "sealing" by affixing their signatures.

Organization of a corporation

By-Laws
Once incorporated, all business corporations in Canada are required to prepare and maintain at the designated head office a minute and record book containing:

- the Articles (or Letters Patent), by-laws, directors' resolutions and copies of unanimous shareholder agreements.
- minutes of meetings and shareholders' resolutions.
- copies of all notices required by the *Corporation Acts.*
- a shareholders' register showing names and addresses of each person who is or has been a shareholder, a record of number of shares held by each; date of the issue and transfer of shares.

The directors must first pass *By-laws* to establish fundamental rules to govern the operation of the business. By-law Number 1 is a general comprehensive by-law that establishes the method by which meetings are called, notices are given, officers are elected or appointed, documents are executed, directors are removed, quorums are established and other matters that affect the long term operation. This first by-law is in effect a "rulebook" of procedures that must be followed in order for business to be conducted properly and fairly in the best interests of the corporation and

its shareholders.

Other by-laws are passed to establish banking and borrowing arrangements and other procedures. Standard forms of by-laws are available in procedural books which may be obtained in a library or purchased from legal stationers. It is usual for the "Secretary" of the company or the company's solicitor to prepare these by-laws.

Resolutions
Other business such as election of officers, allotment of shares, declaration of dividends, and approval of financial statements is done by *Resolutions* passed by a majority of the directors. Shareholders who have the ultimate authority to approve the by-laws, elect the directors and appoint the auditors do so by passing resolutions. In this case, too, the majority rules.

Substantial business decisions may be made by *Special Resolutions* which are resolutions passed by the directors and confirmed by two-thirds or more of the shareholders. Special resolutions are required to sell the business or a substantial part of the business, amend the Articles (or Letters Patent) or amalgamate with another corporation. It is usually necessary for a meeting to be called to transact business that requires the passing of by-laws and resolutions. However, federal (and Ontario) business corporations have the power to do so without calling a meeting if all of the directors or all of the shareholders entitled to vote at a meeting consent in writing.

Shareholders' agreements
Many corporations are really partnerships which have incorporated on the advice of their lawyers to obtain tax relief, limited liability and other advantages. In these circumstances incorporators still have need of internal rules and terms similar to those in their Partnership Agreements. Therefore a *Shareholders' Agreement* is entered into which identifies the rights, duties and responsibilities of the shareholders as between themselves and in relation to the corporation. The Shareholders' Agreement includes terms which:

- restrict transfer of shares to strangers: shareholder who wishes to sell or retire must sell shares to existing shareholders at price and terms fixed in agreement.
- give right of first refusal to existing shareholders in event one shareholder becomes incapacitated or dies.
- give right to a shareholder to sell shares to outsiders if existing shareholders fail to purchase ("Put up, Shut up" clause).

- allow the company to agree to employ shareholders (or named ones), set term of employment, salary, duties, non-competition clauses.
- establish procedure for settling disputes i.e., identify specific person such as auditor of firm to act as tie-breaker in disputes; or agree to single arbitrator procedure under provincial *Arbitration Acts.*

Share capital

Every business corporation has a certain amount of authorized capital which consists of one or more classes of shares which it is entitled to issue. The number of shares of each class and the amount for which they can be issued must be set out in the Articles of Incorporation. On the incorporation of the company, the incorporators are issued shares. Subject to the requirements of the Act, additional shares are issued from time to time for money, services or other consideration as circumstances require.

Classes of shares

As indicated above, the capital of a corporation may be divided into one or more classes of shares. Each corporation must have at least one class of shares called "common shares." In addition, the corporation may have "special" or "preference" shares. The share structure of the corporation is determined by the Articles of Incorporation.

The corporation issues share certificates to its shareholders. The shareholders keep the certificates in their possession as evidence of their legal interest in the corporation. The corporation in turn maintains a shareholders' register which must accurately record the names, addresses and exact holdings of each of its shareholders. A corporate share is a type of personal property which not only represents the legal interests of the shareholder in the undertaking of the corporation, but also establishes the extent of shareholders' liability and identifies the proportion of the corporation's net worth or equity that they "own."

One may become a shareholder in a corporation in one of three ways:

(a) by incorporating a corporation and having shares issued on incorporation;
(b) by entering into an agreement with an existing corporation to give value in consideration for the corporation issuing shares and recording the transaction in the shareholders' register;
(c) by obtaining the transfer of issued shares directly from an existing shareholder and having the transfer recorded in the shareholders' register.

Dividends

A corporation may distribute all or part of its profits to its shareholders in the form of dividends. The directors declare that the corporation has excess profits and direct the corporation to pay dividends to those shareholders whose share holdings contain such a privilege. This privilege is printed on their share certificates and authorized by the Articles of Incorporation.

Conduct of corporate business

Powers distributed

Since a corporation is an artificial person, it can only act through its servants or agents. The most senior of these are the directors of the corporation and the day-to-day control of the corporation is in their hands. The various corporation Acts identify the activities which are under their control and define their general functions. The Acts provide that "the board of directors shall manage or supervise the management of the affairs and business of the corporation." The directors of small corporations are usually those persons who hold the majority of the shares. The board of directors of larger firms often include persons with special expertise or connections who are elected to sit on the board for those reasons rather than actual substantial share holdings.

Election of directors

Every corporation must have a board of directors. A majority of the board must be Canadian citizens ordinarily resident in Canada. The directors are elected by the shareholders in a general annual meeting. Each share held entitles its holder to one vote for each position to be filled in the board. In this way the majority shareholders may control the elections of directors. However, the Articles of Incorporation may change this pattern by extending the term of office of directors and giving greater voting rights to minority shareholders.

Duties of directors

Once elected, directors become representatives of the corporation and are considered to hold positions of trust. The *Business Corporation Act* of Ontario (Section 144) best describes what is expected of them:

> Every director and officer shall exercise the powers and discharge the duties of office

honestly, in good faith and in the best interests of the corporation, and in connection therewith shall exercise the degree of care, diligence and skill that a reasonable, prudent person would exercise in comparable circumstances.

The official position of directors is one of trust. As to third parties directors are agents; as to the corporation they are chargeable as trustees. The judgment of the directors must be unwarped by personal conflict of interest. They must not accept any outside remuneration for the performance of their duties. If they do accept payment from outsiders for the discharge of their duties as directors, such remuneration belongs to the corporation. In such cases the corporation may not only hold directors liable for breach of their fiduciary duties, but may also hold third parties liable for inducing directors to breach their duty.

CASE 20   PROUDFOOT INC. v. ROSS AND CUMMINS LTD.

Wheeler, a director of the Proudfoot corporation, received $5 000 from the Cummins company for inducing Proudfoot to award a certain contract to Cummins. On discovering the facts Proudfoot removed Wheeler from office and sued both Wheeler for breach of trust and Cummins for inducing breach of trust. Proudfoot recovered damages in the sum of $5 000 being an amount equivalent to the bribe.

General supervision and the actual conduct of a corporation's affairs by its directors is exclusive; that is, they are not subject to outside interference. Even shareholders owning a majority of the shares of the corporation may not override or interfere with the direction and control of the board of directors, so long as they hold office. As one judge put it, "If the action of the board of directors does not express the will and wish of the majority of the shares of stock, the majority has its remedy by retiring the directors . . . at the regular time for the election of directors." Neither will the courts interfere with the judgment and discretion of directors except for fraud or arbitrary conduct contrary to the best interests of the corporation. Even the courts cannot compel directors to act wisely, although they have the power to compel them to act honestly.

Directors, as has been pointed out, stand in a position of trust to the corporations they serve. Directors are therefore disqualified from voting at a meeting of the board if they have any personal interest in a matter before the board. Neither can their vote in such cases be counted in making up a quorum (minimum legal number required to transact business at a meeting). If a director with a personal interest in a matter does cast a decisive vote, the decision of the board can be set aside by a person having an interest therein. It is customary for directors who have personal interests in a matter under consideration by the board to note on the minutes that they refrained from voting in respect to the matter. Such directors should also record that they made a full disclosure of their personal interest to the board in keeping with their status as trustees.

Directors, like agents, are liable to the corporation for loss sustained by it through their negligence in office.

CASE 21   MEREN CORPORATION v. BELL AND CHALMERS

A resolution of the Meren Corporation provided that all cheques were to be signed by the treasurer and countersigned by the president or a director. By a series of ingenious excuses, the treasurer from time to time obtained counter-signatures by directors Bell and Chalmers, of cheques payable to cash, then misappropriated the proceeds and disappeared. Upon discovering the thefts, the corporation brought an action in negligence against the two directors. The court found the directors liable in tort: "Bell and Chalmers failed to exercise that degree of care and skill which a reasonable and prudent person would have exercised under the circumstances."

When a majority of the board of directors adopts a resolution that some directors believe to be wrong, the latter should see that their dissent from the resolution is noted in the minutes. The trend of recent cases calls for more strict liability against directors. It is not longer possible for directors to simply hold office and play a passive role in the company. The duty to act honestly and as a reasonable, prudent person requires directors to be active and informed. Even if directors are absent from a meeting at which a decision is made they may not be safe. If such directors wish to avoid liability, they must inform themselves as soon as possible of the business transacted and as soon as practicable have their dissent put on record if they disagree.

Directors are also personally liable for unpaid wages (up to six months per employee) which employees are unable to collect from the corporation.

Powers of shareholders

The shareholders elect the directors and in this sense have ultimate control over the affairs of the corporation. Directors must call an annual meeting of shareholders at which the shareholders are entitled to vote, review the financial affairs of the company, elect directors and generally review the stewardship of the directors over the past year. Each shareholder is entitled to receive a copy of the financial statement and the auditor's report in advance of this meeting. Shareholders also have the power to appoint the auditors of the corporation and to fix their remuneration. The auditors, then, are responsible to the shareholders. By-laws passed by the directors during the previous year must be submitted to the shareholders for ratification. Shareholders are entitled to vote in person or to give their right to cast votes to another by a form called a proxy. They have no liability for corporate debts beyond the amount they have paid for their shares, and they are entitled to dividends as declared by the directors.

KEY TO YOU ARE THE JURY

CATALANO CORP. v. HESTER DEVELOPMENTS INC.   The court ordered the Hester corporation to convey Blackacres to Catalano at the price offered by the original owners. Directors stand in a fiduciary position, that is one of complete loyalty to the corporation they serve. Directors must rigidly refrain from taking advantage of corporate opportunities. The judge said, "Even where the corporation rejects a transaction, directors though acting ostensibly in good faith and with the best of motives must not avail themselves of the transaction thus rejected. If they do they will be open to the suspicion that they rejected the transaction on behalf of the corporation so that they could take advantage of the opportunity themselves. Fiduciaries cannot be permitted to assume a position in which their individual interests might conflict with those of the corporation. Nor can they shed their obligation of trust by resigning their directorship and forming a new company."

Checklist: Corporations

1. Consider: advantages/disadvantages over present organizational form; substantial uninsurable risk; need for uninterrupted operation (perpetual existence) and estate/family business planning needs; government grants; tax advantages; business deductions. (See item 18.)

2. Study corporation information available from government offices, texts, manuals, library. Obtain advice from associates, experienced business people.

3. Consult accountant and/or corporate lawyer. Be selective. Retain best, most qualified. Inquire into competence. Select for long term relationship/benefits.

4. Where to incorporate? Federal business: other countries, several or all provinces. Provincial business: one to three provinces only.

5. Firm name. Check trade names used by similar businesses in locale for conflicts (see trade, telephone, city directories). Have lawyer search names. Search Trade Marks Office, Ottawa. Consider impact of name on goodwill.

6. Select head office location and address.

7. List objects, what corporation is supposed to be able to do. List broad comprehensive objectives. Cover all potential activities.

8. Consult banker to establish working relationship. Advise type of accounts to operate; bank services; loan policies.

9. Share structure. Establish authorized capital limits. Special shares par value; special shares no par value; other classes preference shares; common shares par value or no par value.

10. What amount of capital is needed now and in future for expansion?

11. Identify preferences; rights; restrictions on transfer; dividends; cumulative; non-cumulative; priority of dividends; power to redeem; special provisions.

12. Establish voting rights for common shares and preference shares.

13. List number of incorporators and their names and addresses.

14. How many directors needed? List their names, addresses and what offices to be held (i.e., president, vice-president, secretary, treasurer, manager). Establish quorum for voting required for valid meeting.

15. Tax advantages/liabilities. Advantages should at least exceed cost of incorporation.

16. Obtain estimate of legal costs and disbursements of incorporation and additional accounting fees, other charges and fees. General rule: tax advantages must be equal to or exceed costs.

17. Decide whether to proceed to incorporation. If yes, follow advice of corporate lawyer on post-incorporation organization, shareholder agreements, issue of shares, transfer assets to corporation.

18. Advantages and Disadvantages

Advantages	Disadvantages
(i) Responsibility: One-person control same as sole-proprietor.	Control by board of directors; potential area of dispute leading to disagreement, delay, procrastination.
(ii) Liability: Shareholder limited to investment in corporation and personal guarantees; creditors limited to corporate assets. Great advantage when business activity produces high uninsurable risk (i.e., large trade bills, torts of employees, damage and loss claims).	Banks, creditors usually take personal guarantee from shareholder who will be liable to this extent and investment in business.
(iii) Profit: None except if several work together (similar to partnership potential for profit increases).	Minor difficulty converting profits to salary, wages, dividends, other types of earnings in hands of shareholder. If several shareholders, profits must be shared.
(iv) Organizational form: Prestige. Streamlines operation. Separates management from ownership; better management specialization.	More expensive. Legal/Accounting cost range $600 to $2 000. Costs continue after incorporation as need greater legal/accounting assistance to maintain and use organization. More complex. Need additional government forms, reports.
(v) Taxation: Less income tax possible. Lower percentage rate of tax. Spouse and other family member employees draw salary for services deducted for corporate expense tax purposes.	If new corporation suffers loss shareholder may not write loss off against income.
(vi) Government grants: More government grants available than any other form.	None.
(vii) Borrowing: Increased borrowing potential. Structure permits borrowing through sale of shares, issuing debentures or bonds.	None.
(viii) Expansion: Easy system to transfer or issue shares simplifies expansion by allowing new shareholders to buy into company.	May need consent of directors, or other shareholders (according to shareholders agreement) may oppose expansion plans.

Review

1. List the steps which must be taken to form a federal (Canadian) limited company.
2. Identify the steps which are taken after incorporation to organize a Canadian corporation.
3. Identify the two major internal means by which a corporation transacts important matters of business.
4. What is the purpose of the Corporate Seal?
5. What are the duties of the Board of Directors of a corporation?
6. Distinguish the term "Articles of Incorporation" from "Certificate of Incorporation."
7. What particular problems are encountered in naming a corporation to be formed and what is the recommended procedure for obtaining a corporate name?
8. What is the purpose of the "Shareholders' Agreement"?

CHAPTER 9

Industrial and Intellectual Property

Unit I Patents, trade secrets, industrial design

YOU ARE THE JURY

IN RE KOZAK

During the course of interviewing a full-blooded Indian chief Kozak, a reporter, learned the mechanics of building an ingenious folding kayak which the chief had perfected and used many years before. Kozak modified the design slightly, substituted plastic hinges and made plans to market this marvellous craft. In order to prevent unscrupulous competitors from stealing his "invention," Kozak retained a patent agent to assist him in obtaining a patent (Letters Patent).

What advice do you believe the patent agent will give Kozak? Should Kozak be able to patent the device? Give reasons for your answer.

OBJECTIVES

- to define the protection provided by Letters Patent.
- to list what may be patented and what may not be patented.
- to identify persons who may apply for a patent.
- to list the steps required to obtain Letters Patent.

LEXICON

International Convention for the Protection of Industrial Property A group of countries which gives citizens who are parties to the convention similar patent rights. Some members are Canada, the United States, United Kingdom, Austria, France, Germany, Italy, Japan and Spain.
Invention Any new and useful process, machine, manufacture or composition of matter, or any new and useful improvement thereof.
Letters Patent A certificate issued by the federal government to an inventor giving an exclusive right to make, use or sell an invention in Canada for a period of 17 years.
Patent The legal right granted to the first inventor to exclude others from producing, manufacturing and offering a device for sale for a period of 17 years.
Patentee An inventor who has successfully applied for patent rights (i.e., has been granted Letters Patent by the Commissioner of Patents).

Patents, trade secrets, industrial design, copyright and trade marks are all part of the law of In-

dustrial and Intellectual Property. Each is a form of property which may be "owned" exclusively by one person who has a monopoly on production, sale or use which may be enforced by the courts. The purpose of this kind of law is to provide a substantial incentive to artistic and technical development by granting the creators or inventors an absolute priority over other persons. Industrial property law provides certain persons with the right to construct legal protective fences around their property. Patents permit an inventor to build a fence around a new and useful device. Copyright entitles an author to build a fence around a literary or artistic work. Trade marks build a fence around an identifying symbol. Outsiders who attempt to copy, use or misappropriate protected industrial property are trespassers. They may be sued for damages and the courts have the power to order them to cease activities which conflict with those of the protected industrial property holders. To continue the fence analogy, if an outsider is found within one of the legal fences, he may be ejected from the premises and sued for damages.

One judge who was considering an industrial property case (Patents) put it this way:

> By his claims [patents][1] the inventor puts fences around the fields of his monopoly and warns the public against trespassing upon his property. His fences must be clearly placed in order to give the necessary warning and he must not fence in any property that is not his own. The terms of a claim [patent] must be free from avoidable ambiguity or obscurity and must not be flexible; they must be clear and precise so that the public will be able to know not only where it must *not* trespass, but also where it may safely go. If a claim [patent] does not satisfy these requirements it cannot stand. The inventor may make his claims [patents] as narrow as he pleases within the limits of his invention but he must not make them too broad. He must not claim [patent] what he has not invented for thereby he would be fencing off property which does not belong to him. It follows that a claim [patent] must fail if in addition to claiming [patenting] what is new and useful it also claims [patents] something that is old or something that is useless.

---

1. *Note*: a "claim" is a special clause in a Patent which defines the scope of the monopoly.

Patents

In Canada the legal rules for patents are contained in a federal statute called the *Patent Act*. The law is administered by the federal Ministry of Consumer and Corporate Affairs. It has established a Bureau of Intellectual Property which has as one of its branches a Patent Office in Ottawa/ Hull operated by a Commissioner of Patents.

On filing an application with the Commissioner of Patents and on compliance with the regulations of the *Patent Act*, an inventor may obtain a patent granting an exclusive property in an invention which is useful and a novel improvement over what was previously known. The Commissioner issues a Letters Patent bearing the signature and seal of his office and recording the date the patent was issued.

Patent rights give the inventor the exclusive right in Canada to produce and sell an invention for a period of 17 years. After the expiry of that time, the inventor's monopoly expires and the invention becomes public property.

What may be patented

A device that qualifies as an invention not previously known may be patented. The *Patent Act* defines an invention as:

Any new and useful art, process, machine, manufacture or composition of matter

or

Any new and useful improvement in any art, process, machine, manufacture or composition of matter.

Note that the definition encompasses five terms and contains the qualification that the invention must be both novel (new) *and* useful.

- "Art" means a method of accomplishing a desired result. It is an act or series of acts which effect a desired change in an object.
- "Process" means a method of obtaining a chemical action by applying a force of nature to produce a desired result.
- "Machine" means any mechanical device or combination of mechanical powers and devices which performs a function to produce a desired result.
- "Manufacture" means anything that can be made and includes the method of making it.
- "Composition of Matter" means all compounds and substances produced by chemical reaction or by mechanical mixture.

In order to qualify for patent protection the invention must be both useful (that is, have some

practical value), and new (in that it was not previously known). Section 28 of the *Patent Act* establishes a novelty test which provides that the Commissioner of Patents may grant an "exclusive property in an invention to the inventor" provided that it was:

(a) not known or used by any other person before he invented it;
(b) not described in any patent or in any publication printed in Canada or in any other country more than two years before presentation of the petition; and
(c) not in public use or on sale in Canada for more than two years prior to his application in Canada.

CASE 1   IN RE MONTEITH

While on a visit to an Asian country, Monteith examined a unique set of ancient knives which he had never seen before and which were unknown in the Western world. On his return to Canada Monteith prepared a detailed specification of the knives and attempted to apply for a Canadian patent. Should Monteith succeed?

CASE 2   IN RE DEAN

After many years of hard labour, Dean perfected a new type of tool which performed significantly better than anything else he had seen. Dean travelled to the United States to obtain financial backing and discovered that the same device was on sale there. Should Dean apply for a Canadian patent? If he does, what objections would be raised to his application?

CASE 3   IN RE BOYER

Boyer invented a device and successfully marketed it in Canada for 10 years. As business prospered she established an extensive mail-order campaign in which her device was illustrated and described in detail. On discovering that a competitor was planning to manufacture and sell the same device Boyer decided to patent her invention. Can she?

Review the You Are The Jury case for this unit in light of what you have learned about patents.

What may not be patented

It is clear that certain inventions are not patentable. Here is a list of what may not be the subject of a patent application:

- device described in a prior patent.
- device in public use more than 2 years.
- device on public sale more than 2 years.
- device known or used by another person (S28(a)).
- device used for medical purposes.
- device which has no practical, functional use.
- business systems or plans.
- industrial designs, trade marks and copyrights.
- device which only changes existing device (i.e., in terms of size, shape, material).

Who may apply for a patent (Who is entitled to build the fence)?

The inventor or the legal representative of an invention which is both useful and legally novel may apply for Letters Patent. The *Patent Act* recognizes only the *first* inventor who conceived and developed an original idea to the point that it could be made useful and who produces definite plans and specifications for the public record.

In the event that several persons contribute their time, talent and energies to a joint project, all of them are considered the "inventor" and all must apply for a patent. If all of the joint inventors fail to join in the patent application, it will fail unless the circumstances are extraordinary. Section 33 of the *Patent Act* provides:

> Where an invention is made by two or more inventors and one of them refused to make application for a patent or his whereabouts cannot be ascertained after diligent inquiry, the other inventor or his legal representative may make application and a patent may be granted in the name of the inventor who makes the application on satisfying the Commissioner that the joint inventor has refused to make application or that his whereabouts cannot be ascertained after diligent inquiry.

Application may also be made by the legal representative of the inventor. If an inventor dies before an application for patent has been made, it may be made by that person's executor, estate administor or heirs. If an inventor does not wish to apply for patent, the rights to the invention may be assigned to another person in writing. The "assignee" may then make the application.

The employee-inventor

When the inventor responsible for a novel, useful device is an employee of a firm, it is often difficult to identify the legal owner because the firm may claim the legal right to the patent the device.

CASE 4   IN RE WILLIS AND QUINTO INC.

Willis (the marketing manager for a firm which manufactured and sold a variety of chemical products) invented a novel, useful and inexpensive device to measure the moisture needs of indoor plants. Willis admitted that he did much of the experimental work with the plants which were in his office. His employer argued, "Willis did this on our time so the invention belongs to the company." Willis disagreed, "I'm in sales, not development. I did this instead of taking coffee breaks so I want my Willisometer." Try to decide who is right before reading on.

First, when the inventor is also an employee it is necessary to look to the contract of employment. If the employment is not governed by an express contract that deals with ownership of patent rights, it is necessary to apply the appropriate general rules that have been established by the courts or by common law:

- if the invention was created in the usual course of employment, it is the property of the employer. This is true if, on examining the employee's job description, one can identify a duty to create.
- if the inventor-employee is employed to perform certain duties and the invention is unrelated to those duties, the patent right belongs to the employee regardless of the time and place of inspiration or development. This may be true even if the employee uses the employer's facilities for development purposes.
- if the employee was hired to develop and invent, inventions related to the type of work required belong to the employer regardless of the time and place of inspiration or development. This may be true even if the employee makes the discovery at home or on his own time.

In the circumstances of this case, the employer is the owner and can compel the inventor/employee to assign his invention.

How to apply for a patent (How to build the fence)

Once an inventor solves a longstanding problem by the creation of a useful device previously unknown, a decision must be made to patent it, assign the legal rights to another or to maintain the solution as a trade secret. In Canada there are certain professionals who practice as patent agents. Usually they are also lawyers. Patent agents must pass examinations set by the Commission of Patents and are then registered. No decision to patent or not to patent should be taken without consulting a registered patent agent. A list of all registered patent agents may be obtained from the Commissioner.

Usually inventors contact their own lawyers first in order to obtain general information about costs and procedures. At this stage the inventor is required to divulge sufficient information so that preliminary opinions can be given as to usefulness, novelty and probable patentability of the invention. The lawyer will assist in retaining a registered patent agent to engineer the actual building of the patent fence. At this stage, the inventor is required to make full disclosure to the lawyer and the patent agent to permit the work to proceed. The inventor must trust the lawyer and agent implicitly if the desired results are to be obtained.

The patent agent will cause a search to be made at the Patent Office in Ottawa for particulars of all previously filed patents for similar devices. If no conflicting patent is on file, the agent will recommend a search at the Patent Office for the United States. These searches are relatively inexpensive and they effectively disclose the "known." On the basis of these searches the patent agent will advise the inventor whether or not the invention is sufficiently new to be patented.

The next step is to file an application with the Commissioner of Patents in Ottawa/Hull. The application consists of:
- a petition.
- specifications disclosing claims, description, drawings.
- the filing fee ($50).
- models, specimens (if required by Commissioner).

Section 36 of the *Patent Act* requires that:

(1) The applicant shall in the specifications, correctly and fully describe the invention and its operating or use as contemplated by the inventor, and set forth clearly the various steps in a process or the method of constructing . . . or using a machine, manufacture or composition of matter, in such full, clear, concise and exact terms as to enable any person skilled in the art or science . . . to make, compound or use it; in the case of a machine explain the principle thereof and the best mode of application of that principle; in the case of a process explain the necessary sequence, if any, of the various steps, so as to distinguish the invention from other inventions; particularly indicate and distinctly

claim the part, improvement or combination which is claimed as an invention.

(2) The specification shall end with a claim or claims stating distinctly and in explicit terms the things or combinations that the applicant regards as new and in which is claimed an exclusive property or privilege.

The application is reviewed by an examiner. If it is deficient, the Commissioner may reject the application, notify the applicant and provide an opportunity to correct it. If the application is not corrected within three months (or within one year of the date of application, whichever is later) the application is considered to have been abandoned.

If the application is in order, the Commissioner requires a further, substantial fee to be paid and then signs and seals Letters Patent, then dates, numbers and forwards it to the applicant's patent agent. The Commissioner of course maintains a copy on file in the Ottawa office. From this day on, any person can purchase a copy of the patent for $2.

It can now be said that the applicant has revealed his invention to the world in exchange for being given an exclusive period of 17 years in which to produce and market it in Canada.

How patented products may be identified (Where are the fences)?

Every person who offers a patented device for sale must, if possible, stamp or engrave on each patented article a notice of the year of the date of the patent, i.e., PATENTED 1980. If the article cannot be stamped, the patentee must clearly indicate on the packaging or accompanying literature a notice that the article has been patented. Failure to do so may result in a fine or imprisonment.

Similar but stiffer penalties are established by the Act for any person who marks any article for sale in Canada with any notice suggesting that it is patented when, in fact, no Letters Patent have been issued.

Patent pending

Frequently one observes on an article for sale the words PATENT PENDING. These words have no legal significance. They indicate that a person who supplied the articles has made an application for patent which is still in progress. As such applications are secret up to the point of granting Letters Patent, there is no convenient way of obtaining information on pending applications.

The International Convention for the Protection of Industrial Property

An applicant for a Canadian patent can only obtain exclusive rights to the use, production and sale of articles in Canada. Individuals and corporations in foreign countries are not bound. In order to obtain international protection, an inventor must apply for a patent in every country in which protection is necessary. However, because this may be impracticable, many Canadian inventors obtain both Canadian and American patents to provide a North American fence of significant proportions.

Both Canada and the United States belong to an international convention of nations which recognizes the special status of the first inventor. The Canadian inventor who files an application for patent in Canada is given a one-year priority for his invention over all other applicants in every country which belongs to the convention. He must file an application in each foreign country within the year.

CASE 5   IN RE FRANK JUSTICE

On September 9th, Justice (a Canadian) filed an application to patent an invention with the Canadian Patent Office. In December of the same year he filed an application in the American Patent Office. He subsequently discovered that an American inventor had filed an application for a similar device in October. As the United States is a member of the convention, the Canadian's application was given priority and Justice succeeded in obtaining an American patent on the strength of the earlier Canadian application.

If foreign inventors whose countries belong to the convention apply for a Canadian patent within one year after they applied for patent in their own country, their Canadian application has the same effect as if they had filed in Canada on the date of filing in the foreign countries.

Infringement (Trespassers caught inside the fence)

The *Patent Act* provides that if any person other than the patentee attempts to make, use or sell the invention without the patentee's consent within the 17 year period, that person may be sued for damages for infringement and an injunction may be obtained to restrain him from further unauthorized acts.

Trade secrets

Despite all we have said so far, inventors are not *required* to seek patent protection. Some devices and processes are incapable of protection and some are not patentable. In any event, patent rights automatically expire after 17 years. Inventors who choose not to disclose their inventions may maintain them as "Trade Secrets" or "Confidential Information." The formula for Coca-Cola is an example of a trade secret. No disclosure of the formula has ever been made and there has never been any application for a patent. Yet the confidential formula has effectively given an Atlanta-based corporation a world-wide monopoly over the production and sale of "Coke."

The owners of a trade secret have an absolute monopoly forever. They never need to be concerned about time limitations and they have no obligation to reveal the secret to the public. However, they do run the risk of having another person who is working independently discover the same secret or formula; if this happens, the new discovery may be used immediately in competition.

A trade secret may consist of any formula, pattern, device or compilation of information which is used in one's business and which gives an opportunity to obtain an advantage over competitors who do not know or use it. It may be a formula for a chemical compound, a process for manufacturing, treating or preserving materials, a pattern for a machine or other device, or a list of customers. Trade secrets also include "know-how" – that is, valuable information developed by a business regarding techniques of manufacture which allow increased production at lower cost. It may include mailing lists, customer information or advertising schemes.

Industrial design

The appearance or shape of an object cannot ordinarily be patented and, because it is available for all to see, it cannot be kept as a trade secret. Yet the design or shape of an object may be so distinctive that it may be essential to attempt to protect it. Examples include the characteristic shape of a "Princess" telephone or a pattern applied to wallpaper. The *Industrial Designs Act* of Canada permits Canadians to legally build fences around designs which are purely ornamental and which have no particular functional value.

To obtain protection for a design the owner must submit an application together with formal drawings or photographs of the design to the Commissioner of Patents in Ottawa. Under Canadian law the design must be registered within one year of its first appearance in a publication or the first public display in Canada. Note that registration must be *complete* within the year. It is not sufficient simply to apply within the year. The Patent Office conducts a search of previously registered designs to make certain the design does not closely resemble one already registered. If the design appears to be visually unique, a Certificate of Registration will be issued which is valid for five years and can be renewed for a further five. Once the Certificate is issued, each of the articles produced and sold must be marked with the letters RD followed by the year of registration and the name of the design's owner. If these markings do not appear on the articles, the owner loses the design protection and is subject to a fine under the Act.

Once a design has the protection of a Certificate, no-one is permitted to copy the design and use it on similar articles offered for sale. The registered owner of a design has the right to sue for damages and apply for an injunction to prohibit further infringement and competition.

KEY TO YOU ARE THE JURY

IN RE KOZAK   Kozak should not be granted Letters Patent. Only the first, true inventor may apply for a patent and the first inventor here was the Indian chief. An invention must be the product of a patent applicant's own mind and work. It is not possible for a person who hears of an invention from another to claim to be the inventor. Section 28 also requires that the invention must not have been previously known or used by any other person in order to qualify as an invention. As the chief has used a similar device for many years, the device was not patentable.

Unit II Copyright

YOU ARE THE JURY

GOLDSMITH v. EATON

Goldsmith prepared an original pamphlet advertising a unique concept of providing secretarial support service to small businesses. She spent several days composing the material and adding photographs and artistic touches. She printed and distributed the brochure. The resulting business attracted by the advertising pamphlet exceeded her expectations. However, she took no steps to protect her work. Neither did she affix any special markings or warnings against copying her work. Goldsmith later discovered that Eaton, a competitor, had begun distributing a brochure which was substantially the same as hers with the exception of a word here and there and the photographs. Eaton's pamphlet was marked "copyright EATON 1979." Goldsmith consulted her lawyer because she felt Eaton had no right to copy her work. Although a reasonable, prudent person would come to the conclusion Eaton did copy the Goldsmith brochure, Eaton argued that the similarities were "just coincidence and Goldsmith didn't protect her rights the way I did. I marked mine 'copyright' and registered it with the Copyright Office. I have a certificate of copyright. Goldsmith doesn't." What remedies are available to Goldsmith?

OBJECTIVES

- to identify when copyright arises in Canada and the United States.
- to define the "owner" of a copyright.
- to identify the extent of copyright protection.
- to list the remedies for copyright infringement.

LEXICON

Certificate of Registration   A certificate provided by the Registrar of Copyright as evidence that an applicant has filed an application for copyright in the Copyright Office of Canada. The certificate does not in itself create copyright.
Convention   Most developed countries belong to one of two international copyright groups (called conventions) which, provided the Canadian owner has followed their rules, recognize Canadian copyright owners world-wide.

Fair Dealing   A system whereby a person may quote short excerpts of a copyrighted work for private study, research, criticism, review or newspaper summary without liability to the copyright owner.
Infringement   Knowingly copying all or a substantial part of a work protected by copyright with the intention of using, producing or selling it without the consent of the copyright owner.
Plagiarism   Knowingly and deliberately copying another person's literary, artistic, scientific or musical work in whole or in part without consent.

Copyright means that the author or originator of a literary, scientific, dramatic or musical work is the only person entitled to legally copy, produce, reproduce, publish or perform such work. This right includes the legal power to prevent any other person from copying an originator's work without permission. For copyright purposes a work may be defined as original, uncopied material and includes books, pamphlets, brochures, printed matter, advertisements, directories, catalogues, magazines, drawings, photographs, maps, plays, poetry and musical compositions. Copyright law is designed to encourage originators to produce and profit from their inspiration and labour without fear that others will steal their work.

In Canada copyright arises automatically as soon as a work is produced in concrete form by an author. No formalities must be observed and there are no registration requirements except those explained further on. The legal copyright fence is erected in place immediately.

Copyright Act

The basic rules of copyright law are found in a federal statute called the *Copyright Act*. The Act is under the direction of the federal Minister of Consumer and Corporate Affairs and is administered through a copyright office (Place du Portage, Hull, Quebec) which is run by the Commissioner of Patents and a Registrar of Copyright. In it public records are maintained.

Copyright conventions

Canada, like almost all developed countries in the world, belongs to the Berne Convention. In effect all member countries have agreed that a Canadian craftsman, author or composer will automatically have copyright protection in each country as

soon as the work is produced in concrete form without the need for any formality, procedure or registration.

However, many countries, including the United States and Soviet Union, belong to the Universal Copyright Convention. In order to obtain copyright protection in these countries, Canadian authors must follow the rules of this second convention by placing a copyright notice in the required formal style on all copies of the work. The procedure involves placing at the beginning or end of the work the word "copyright" or the letter "c" in a circle followed by the name of the copyright owner and the year of first publication, sale or distribution.

This book, of course, contains the copyright sign. It can be found on the reverse side of the title page. It conveys the information that Copp Clark Pitman Inc. has the sole legal right to reproduce the content of this book and that it first produced and offered this book for sale in 1980. The legal reason the copyright is not in the author's name is discussed under the heading "Assignment and Licencing."

Copyright ownership (Who may build a copyright fence?)

The *Copyright Act* defines those individuals who are entitled to build copyright fences. Section 12 of the Act provides as follows:

(1) Subject to this Act, the author of a work shall be the first owner of the copyright therein.

(2) Where, in the case of an engraving, photograph, or portrait, the plate or other original was ordered by some other person and was made for valuable consideration in pursuance of that order, then in the absence of any agreement to the contrary, the person by whom such plate or other original was ordered shall be the first owner of the copyright.

(3) Where the author was in the employment of some other person under a contract of service or apprenticeship and the work was made in the course of employment by that person, the person by whom the author was employed shall, in the absence of any agreement to the contrary, be the first owner of the copyright.

CASE 6   MAY v. JORJOVICH

May, a Dean of Business, hired a professional photographer to take his picture with Prince Philip during a recent royal visit to Canada. The Dean was displeased with the results. He felt the

183

unusual camera angles made him appear somewhat comical. The photographer advised May he intended to produce copies for exhibition. May objected. Who is the owner of the copyright?

Ordinarily, the photographer as author would be the legal owner of the copyright. However, in this case, May paid to have the photograph taken. Therefore he is the owner of the copyright and has the right to prevent the photographer from reproducing, exhibiting or using the photograph without permission.

CASE 7   ANDERSON v. BURGHARDT

Burghardt snapped Anderson's picture as she was getting on a bus downtown. Burghardt intended to use several photographs, including this one, in an advertisement promoting mass transportation. Anderson objected. Who is the owner of the copyright? What issues does this case raise? Would Anderson be able to restrain the intended use of the photograph?

CASE 8   PETERSON v. PIONEER COLLEGE

Under the direction of their immediate supervisor, several teachers planned, developed and created a unique office simulation package for use by students at the college. After several years of use the college decided to market the entire package to other similar institutions across Canada. One of the teachers, Peterson, objected to such reproductions and sales unless he was paid royalties based on his contribution and involvement in preparation. Is Peterson entitled to royalties? Who is the probable owner of the copyright?

Length of protective status (When the fences come down)

Copyright in Canada exists for the life of the author plus 50 years following the author's death. However, there are exceptions to this rule. They are:

- Photographs. 50 years after making original negative.
- Records. Tapes. 50 years after original made.
- Government work. 50 years after first publication.
- Joint authorship. 50 years after death of last survivor.

Registration of copyright (Building a better fence)

The *Copyright Act* provides a formal procedure for registering copyright. While registration does not create the right to copy, registering under the Act does provide a Certificate of Registration from the government which may prove valuable if the copyright is challenged. The author produces the work, completes and signs an application form, forwards the form to the Copyright Office together with a certified cheque or money order for $10. payable to the Receiver General of Canada. The work itself is not submitted. The Registrar of Copyright records the information in Registers of Copyrights which contain the names or titles of works and the names and addresses of authors. The Registrar then issues a Certificate of Copyright which is evidence of ownership of copyright and may be used in court to help establish authorship and ownership of the work. While it is not necessary to submit a copy of the work to the Copyright Office, authors of books published in Canada must send two copies to the National Library, Ottawa, Ontario.

Another method of obtaining evidence of copyright, originality and authorship is for the author to place a copy of the work in a self-addressed envelope and mail it by prepaid registered post. When the envelope is delivered by the Post Office, the author signs for it and stores it *unopened* in a safe place. If authorship is challenged in the future, the author has proof that the work was complete and in existence as of the postmarked date on the envelope.

Assignment and licencing

Authors are often not in a position to publish or profit from their own work without the assistance of others. The *Copyright Act* provides the author with authority to assign or licence copyright to others for all or part of the allowable term. The assignment must be in writing and must be signed by the author. He thereby transfers legal ownership of the work to the other person who will register it with the Copyright Office to provide public notice of the transfer of legal ownership and prevent the author from attempting to sell, assign or licence the right to any third party. The author licences copyright to another in this way usually in consideration of being paid royalties. The ordinary rules of contract apply to such licencing agreements.

In addition to private agreements to licence, the *Copyright Act* may permit compulsory licencing

FORM 9
(Formerly FORM I)

APPLICATION FOR REGISTRATION OF COPYRIGHT IN A PUBLISHED WORK

I,(we) _____
Here insert full name and full address of proprietor(s)

_____

_____

hereby declare that I am(we are) the owner(s) of the Copyright in the original

_____ work
(Here insert: literary, dramatic, musical or artistic, as the case may be)

entitled _____
Here insert title only (no descriptive matter).

_____

by _____
Here insert full name and full address of author(s)

_____

_____

and that the said work was first published by the issue of copies thereof to the public on the

_____day of _____ 19 _____
month

in the _____ of _____
(city, town)   (province, state, country)

and I(we) hereby request you to register the Copyright of the said work in my(our) name(s) in accordance

with the provisions of the Copyright Act.

I(We) forward herewith the fee of $25.00 for the examination, registration and issue of a certificate of re-

gistration of copyright.

Dated at _____ this _____day of _____ 19__
city, town   month

_____
Signature(s) (See Rule 33)

The Commissioner of Patent
The Copyright Office,
Hull, Canada,
K1A 0E1

CCA-776 (9/78)

Application For Registration of Copyright In A Published Work.

under certain limited circumstances. For instance, any person may apply to the Minister for a licence to print and publish in Canada any book wherein copyright subsists, if the owner of the copyright fails to print the book or fails to supply enough copies for the reasonable demands of the Canadian market. On condition that a royalty be paid to the owner on the retail selling price of every copy, the Minister has the discretionary right to issue a licence to the applicant giving the sole right to print and publish such books in Canada for five years.

Copyright infringement (What to do with the trespassers inside the fence)

The *Copyright Act* provides that if any person attempts to reproduce or use copyright material without the consent of the owner, that person may be sued for damages for infringement; an injunction may be obtained to restrain further unauthorized use; the offender may be prosecuted and fined; and, in the event of a second offence, he may be imprisoned. Infringement consists of unauthorized copying of all or substantial parts of copyright material. The owner of copyright need not prove that the offender made an exact copy. It is sufficient to prove that the copy is so similar to the original that, on the balance of probabilities, the other person deliberately plagiarized the owner's work.

It may be difficult to prove plagiarism of protected material. Therefore authors often set traps for thieves by including in their work false data. For instance, the compilers of directories will insert fictitious names or addresses in their work. If another person blatantly copies their work and includes the false information, this is strong evidence that material was "lifted" from the original list of the author. In one famous case the author of a biography of an American hero included an entirely imaginary and highly colorful activity at an Indian village. He later sued the producer of a movie claiming plagiarism. The movie-maker claimed his motion picture was substantially similar to the book because he used similar sources for his script. But he was unable to explain the source of a ten-minute segment which graphically depicted the totally fictitious encounter at the Indian village.

The probable damages which may be awarded in cases of infringement are similar to those which might be awarded for fraudulent misrepresentation as discussed in Chapter Three. The owner should reasonably expect to recover damages for any actual loss sustained as well as a further sum equivalent to the unjust profit earned by the other party.

There are some instances in which a non-owner of copyright may make limited use of copyright material without fear of infringement. Section 17 of the Act provides exemption for the following:

(1) any fair dealing with any work for the purpose of private study, research, criticism, review or newspaper summary. (Note: The intention here is to permit a person to quote or reproduce excerpts consisting of a few lines or short paragraphs for the purposes mentioned.)
(2) short passages from published literary works for the use of publications for schools. The source of the passages must be acknowledged.
(3) newspaper reports of a political address delivered at a public meeting.

KEY TO YOU ARE THE JURY

GOLDSMITH v. EATON   Goldsmith succeeded in obtaining an injunction to restrain Eaton from further distributing his brochure or one substantially similar to it. She recovered damages for infringement of her copyright based in part on loss of business.

Goldsmith did not have to take any steps to protect her copyright in her brochure as her "right to copy" arose the moment she produced her writing in a concrete form. Registration of the work would have given her no greater rights in Canada.

It was necessary for Goldsmith to prove that she was the originator of a work which had been substantially copied by Eaton. It was not necessary for her to prove Eaton's work was an exact copy.

Eaton copied the work of another and did not gain any legal rights by inserting the copyright sign on his work or by registering it with the Copyright Office.

Unit III   Trade Marks

YOU ARE THE JURY

KIRK v. UNGER

Kirk, the manufacturer and distributor of fans in your province registered with the federal Registrar of Trade Marks in Ottawa a trade mark which consists of a picture of a fan partially circled by the designation "FAN-TASTIK." Kirk decided to extend his operation to another province and in doing so discovered the existence of another manufacturer there using the same trade mark. Unger, the president of the other company said, "We've never heard of you. We just thought this was a great idea and everyone out here knows of us as the "FAN-TASTIC" company. We spell ours with a 'C'. You've never done business out here and they don't know you. So if you're going to ask us to change our name we're not going to do any such foolish thing." Kirk admitted he had never done business outside your province before but claims a prior legal right because his trade mark was registered before Unger began using his mark.

Assume all of the above facts are correct. Does Kirk have a legal right to prevent Unger from continuing to use his trade mark?

OBJECTIVES

- to be able to identify marks and symbols which may be registered as trade marks.
- to be able to list the classes of persons who have the legal right to apply to register trade marks.
- to identify the steps which must be taken to register a trade mark.
- to identify the rights of holders of unregistered trade marks.

LEXICON

Infringement   An interference with the property rights of another who claims a prior legal right usually by using the same name or mark or one so similar as to cause confusion to the public as to the source of goods or services.

Onus   The burden or responsibility of proving a case. In the case of trade marks the responsibility of proving infringement rests with the person who claims a legal right has been infringed.

In Canada the law of trade marks is governed by the federal *Trade Marks Act* and administered by the Ministry of Consumer and Corporate Affairs which maintains a Trade Marks Office in Ottawa/Hull.

A trade mark is a word, symbol, design, shape, picture, drawing, special colouring or striping or any combination of these used by a manufacturer or business to distinguish its products or services from those of others. It is a type of industrial property that grows in value through use in the marketplace. It contributes to the saleability of products because people tend to buy "brands." The more distinctive and effective the mark, the more likely the public will select goods so marked over those of a competitor.

Examples of trade marks in use are:

- the plaid marking on scotch tape (3M).
- "Coke" as used in connection with Coca-Cola.
- "Kodak" or "Polaroid" cameras and accessories.
- distinctive colours used on the marquee signs of Holiday Inns.
- shape of standard size Coca-Cola bottle.
- distinctive stripes on Adidas footwear.
- penguin in a circle (Penguin Books).

In addition to these national brands, regional and local manufacturers, retailers and businesses are using distinctive "logos" in an attempt to provide their products or services with a higher public profile. For example, one small publishing company, Napoleon On The Hill Press, uses a silhouette of a Napoleonic figure standing on a hill as its mark. You've probably never heard of them; but someday their distinctive symbol may be as recognizable as Penguin's.

Trade mark rights generally arise out of their use in Canada but registration of the mark in the federal Trade Marks Office provides a legal protective fence which will guarantee exclusive use to the owner for many years.

What may be registered as a trade mark

Any mark or symbol used or made known in Canada may be registered, provided that it is sufficiently distinctive and

- does not closely resemble the symbol or emblem of any charitable or government agency.

- does not closely resemble or imitate a mark which has already been registered so as to likely confuse the public.
- does not falsely suggest a connection with any living individual.
- is not primarily merely the name or the surname of an individual who is living or has died within the preceding thirty years.
- is not the portrait or signature of any individual who is living or has died within the preceding thirty years.
- does not contain any scandalous, obscene or immoral word or device.
- is not comprised primarily of words which are descriptive of the quality of the goods.

The *Trade Marks Act* of Canada establishes a system for protection of trade marks through registration with the Registrar's office in Ottawa. In the words of Chief Justice Jackett, of the federal Court of Canada:

> The registration system under the *Trade Marks Act* is a means for protecting business people generally, and the public, from dishonest business people who would "defraud" the public by taking advantage of the good reputations of established competitors. The basic scheme is the providing of legal protection to those who have brought about situations whereby certain marks distinguish their wares from the wares of others. They may register such marks and, having done so they are entitled to protection against infringers. It is however essential to the scheme that such persons are only entitled to protection in respect of marks if they do, in fact, distinguish their wares from the wares of others.[1]

CASE 9 IN RE JOSEPH HILL

Dr. Hill forms a corporation to market various products grown on his farm. He applies to register three separate trade marks: (1) the words DOKTOR JOE in a circle which also depicts a caracture of himself; (2) the words DELISIOUS APPLES; (3) and the words SHAKESPEARE PRODUCE linked to a drawn likeness of William Shakespeare, the playwright. What consideration should be given each application?

The DOKTOR JOE symbol probably would be registerable because, first, Hill is not attempting to secure exclusive use of a common surname (Hill) and secondly, he proposes to limit his need

---

[1.] Marketing International Ltd. v. S.C. Johnson 3 B.L.R. 298.

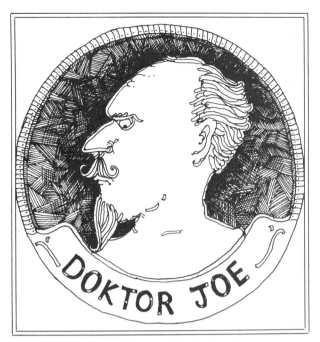

to protect the given name "Joe" by the combination with DOKTOR which appears to make it distinctive enough. The caricature of himself may give him some trouble because it is close to "a portrait" of a living person. But as long as he consents to its use, this part also is probably registerable.

In spite of the deliberate misspelling, DELISIOUS APPLES would not be registerable because the word "delicious" is a commonly descriptive word (particularly of a type of apple) and lacks any distinctive features.

SHAKESPEARE PRODUCE would probably be acceptable. The use of the picture of the long dead English writer seems a clear enough attempt to identify the product with an historical figure. This should be acceptable particularly because today the use of Shakespeare as a surname is relatively rare. In any event, the two "acceptable" proposed marks would have to be checked against already registered marks to make certain they are not so similar to others that they are likely to cause confusion in the minds of the public.

Who may apply for trade mark registration

The first person to use a trade mark in Canada or make it known in this country has the right to register the mark. A mark is made known in Canada if it is used in a foreign country and has become well known in Canada by reason of the advertising of wares or services in printed publications or by television or radio broadcasts. This basis for registration makes it possible for foreign applicants to acquire rights to their trade marks in Canada before there has been any actual sale of a product or performance of a service in this country. The intent of this provision is to prevent piracy of an internationally known trade mark before the owner of the mark acquires rights by actual use in Canada. Section 16 (1) of the *Trade Marks Act* defines those persons who are entitled to make application to register a trade mark:

(i) any person who has used a trade mark in Canada in association with wares or services;
(ii) any person who has made known a trade mark in Canada in association with wares or services;
(iii) any person who has registered a trade mark in a foreign country and has used it in association with wares or services; and
(iv) any person who intends to use a trade mark in Canada in association with wares or services, provided the mark is so used within six months of the application.

How an application is made

An application in a form found in the Trade Mark Regulations is completed. It:

- lists the goods or services the mark is associated with.
- gives date of first use in Canada. or
- gives date first made known in Canada. or
- states intention to use in Canada within 6 months.

The application must be supported by formal black and white drawings and three specimens (unless the mark consists only of words which are not distinctively drawn or represented) and a certified cheque or money order for $35.00 payable to the Receiver General of Canada. The application material should be forwarded by pre-paid registered mail to the Registrar of Trade Marks, Bureau of Intellectual Property, Consumer and Corporate Affairs Canada, Place du Portage, Hull, Quebec.

The Registrar may reject any mark which is prohibited by the Act. He will cause a search to be made of the Register which contains information on all registered marks in Canada and may reject the mark if it is so similar to a previously registered mark that it is likely to confuse or deceive the public. Notice of the application and a description of the mark is advertised by the Registrar in the *Trade Marks Journal,* a magazine designed to give sufficient public notice to those who

may object to the registration. If an objection is made, the objecting party must file a Statement of Opposition with the Registrar within one month. If the objection has merit, the Registrar has the power to reject the application; if it does not, the Registrar may proceed. Either party may appeal the decision to the Federal Court of Canada.

This entire process may involve several months to a year. However, once a trade mark is registered it gives the owner the exclusive right to use it throughout Canada for fifteen years. This right is renewable for further periods of fifteen years each upon application. A renewal application must be made before the expiry of the preceding 15-year period.

Infringement of trade mark

The onus is on the owners of registered trade marks to prevent others from ''infringing'' or trespassing on their protected area. If other persons adopt, steal or substantially copy an existing registered mark, and use it in association with or sale of goods and services, the owner of the original right must consider taking legal action.

The true legal owner must be in a position to prove a prior legal right to the mark and that the infringing mark is so similar as to be likely to confuse the public as to the source of the goods – that is, the general impression given by the two marks is that they symbolize or represent goods or services from the same source. It is not necessary for the true owner to prove cases of actual confusion. Nor is it necessary for him to prove that the two marks are identical in every way. It is only necessary to establish, on a general comparison of the two marks, that a substantial part or an important feature is the same. If the second mark does in fact amount to an infringement, the owner may obtain an injunction to prohibit and restrain the infringer from further use of the offending mark.

The owner may also obtain a court order requiring the destruction of labels, containers and packages bearing the offending mark. In serious cases, the court has the power to require the infringer to destroy the actual goods still in his possession and control to which the mark has been affixed.

The owner may be able to prove that actual direct damage was caused by the infringement. In such cases, the court may award monetary damages similar to those discussed in relation to contracts in Chapter Three.

In the alternative, if the owner is not able to establish serious and direct loss, a claim for accounting may be made. If this claim is granted, the infringer must reveal the profits he earned through his use of the offending mark. The court award may include an amount equivalent to all or part of the unjust profit so earned. The successful owner will also be entitled to court costs.

Protection for unregistered trade marks

While it is advisable for owners of trade marks to properly register them, some measure of protection is given to people who have not registered but who have nevertheless built up property in goodwill from the use of such a mark in the marketplace. Section 7 of the Act provides that:

> No person shall direct public attention to his wares, services or business in such a way as to cause or be likely to cause confusion in Canada at the time commenced so to direct attention to them, between his wares, services or business and the wares, services and business of another.

This section codifies the common law rules for a "passing off" action. It prohibits one person from using a trade mark the same as or similar to that of another person provided the person complaining can establish that:

- the original trade mark was in fact distinctive of the victim's wares, services or business in the mind of the public; and
- the trade mark of the second person is likely to cause the public to be confused.

In such a passing-off action the court must consider both the similarity of the wares, services and business of the parties and the similarities of the trade marks. It must be satisfied from its analysis that there is evidence which discloses that members of the public are likely to confuse the two. It is therefore often difficult to succeed in an action for passing-off.

KEY TO YOU ARE THE JURY

KIRK v. UNGER   Kirk obtained a legal advantage by registering the symbol and name as a trade mark. Registration with the Trade Marks Office in Ottawa provides a protective "fence" across Canada. The question for the court was simply whether or not there likely would be confusion if the products were on the market in the same area or province. It was necessary for Kirk to establish that the infringing mark "FAN-TAS-TIC" was substantially similar so as to be likely to cause confusion between the two products when examined generally or casually by an average consumer. The general impression created by the two marks was that they represented goods from the same source. Kirk succeeded in obtaining an injunction prohibiting Unger from marketing fans bearing the "FAN-TASTIC" trade mark.

Checklist: Industrial and intellectual property

A. PATENT

1. Solve longstanding problem. Develop novel improvement over the "known" leading to useful device or process.
2. Consider application for patent. Obtain copy of *Patent Act* from Commissioner of Patents, Ottawa/Hull or a government bookstore. Examine Act.
3. Consider implications of public sale or publication before patent obtained (2 year time limitation).
4. Reduce information to writing, sketches, plans sufficient to discuss with lawyer.
5. Attend on lawyer for general information, advice on whether subject matter patentable, limitation periods, costs. He will advise most practicable ways to do so safe market studies.
6. Satisfy self of market which will warrant expense and trouble of patent application.
7. Decide whether to abandon project, develop further, maintain as a trade secret, or apply for patent.
8. If decision to patent, lawyer will refer you to patent agent. Confirm estimated costs of each step. Arrange appointment.
9. You will receive letter from patent agent with list of information needed for interview.
10. Prepare written description clearly identifying subject matter, operation, use, steps in process, method of construction, and claims you wish to protect.
11. Attend with prepared material on patent agent. Review opinion on probable success of application, steps and costs. Deal with agent and decide whether to proceed further. If decision to proceed, follow steps 12-19 below.
12. Instruct patent agent to run "search" in Canada and/or the United States patent offices.
13. If no conflicting patent on file, instruct patent agent to prepare application, specifications, drawings, specimens and claims.
14. Examine application documents. Be prepared to discuss with patent agent if in doubt about a point. Sign application and deliver to patent agent.
15. If presently manufacturing or producing the commodity, consider marking items or packages with "Patent Pending" designation.

16. Consider need or advice to patent in other jurisdictions i.e., the United States, United Kingdom and remember one year limitation period.

17. Receive Letters Patent giving exclusive right to produce and sell for 17 years.
18. Mark each article or package with word "Patent" and year patent issued.
19. Decide whether to produce commodity yourself or licence rights out to others in exchange for royalties.

B. TRADE SECRET

1. If decision not to patent but to maintain device or formula as trade secret, follow these steps.
2. Arrange business so few have access to information or manufacture or "know how" in production.
3. Instruct lawyer to prepare employment contract prohibiting employees or agents from disclosing to others any part of secret obtained during course of employment or from using it outside course of employment with your firm.

C. COPYRIGHT

1. Obtain copy of *Copyright Act* and bulletin from Copyright Office, Ottawa/Hull, Quebec or a government bookstore.
2. Consider ownership of work to be produced. If done as part of employment, who is owner? Employer? Employee? Discuss and reach agreement on ownership.
3. Obtain written agreement with employer, employee, customer or client clearly establishing your interest or ownership of copyright in the work.
4. Prepare original uncopied manuscript, advertisement, brochure, catalogue, drawing, magazine, photographs, music, etc. in concrete form.
5. Do not copy from other sources except as
• fair dealing, in study; credit source.
• quote of short passage in reference; credit source.
6. To prevent competitor copying your work, include items of false data, words or numbers which will characterize the work as yours and expose subsequent plagiarism.
7. Forward copy of completed work in self-addressed, stamped envelope by prepaid registered mail; sign for envelope when delivered. Keep sealed as record of date of work in case of dispute.
8. Copyright automatic in Canada (Berne Convention) but to obtain wider copyright protection

(i.e., the United States, Universal Convention) place symbol ''c'' followed by name of copyright owner and year at front or end of work.

9. Publish work or assign to another in exchange for royalties. Must sufficiently meet needs of Canadian market. For assignment cross-refer to Contract Checklist (Chapter Three).

10. Consider registration of copyright. Forms available free. Write Copyright and Industrial Design Branch, Bureau of Intellectual Property, Consumer and Corporate Affairs Canada, Place du Portage, 1 Victoria Street, Hull, Quebec K1A 0E1. Complete application. Sign. Submit by registered post. Include cheque for $10.00 payable to Receiver General of Canada. Receive Certificate of Copyright.

11. If there is infringement by others of your work, review your work and documents. Onus on you to prove other work is copy of yours. Prove other had opportunity to copy; similarities not due to coincidence, common source; copy is substantially similar to yours. Prove competitors work confuses consumers by similarity. Seek injunction and establish loss. Have competitor account for profit earned as direct result of copying.

D. TRADE MARK

1. Obtain copy of *Trade Marks Act,* Regulations and Registration Application forms from
   Registrar Trade Marks,
   Bureau of Intellectual Property,
   Consumer and Corporate Affairs,
   Hull, Quebec.

2. Examine *Trade Mark Journal* and consult lawyer or professional agency for advice.

3. Create design, logo, symbol, etc. to distinguish products, business or services. Do not simulate substantially copy marks of others or those of charitable or government agencies.

4. Obtain consent of living persons whose names or likenesses are used.

5. Put mark into use or decide to put into use within short period of time.

6. Prepare black and white drawings and three specimens.

7. Complete application. Prepare certified cheque to Receiver General of Canada. Forward by prepaid registered mail to Registrar.

8. Receive Certificate of Registration giving monopoly use in Canada.

Review

If you were the jury, how would you decide the following cases and on what grounds?

1. DOKUMAT v. SHEARING   A supervisor (Shearing) for a retail firm which sold and serviced office equipment worked on an invention for cleaning typewriters during slack intervals on the job. She obtained a patent which her employer claimed belonged to him because it had been developed by an employee during working hours. Is the employer entitled to any rights in the invention?

2. SMIT AND ASSOCIATES v. SCHROEDER
Smit brought an action for infringement against Schroeder proving that his device and one being sold by Schroeder were identical. Smit produced his Letters Patent in support of the claim. Schroeder argued that he had begun manufacture and sale of his device 18 months before Smit had applied for his patent and that he had used ''know how'' he acquired in Germany where, he contends, similar devices have been in production for over 12 years. Will Smit succeed?

3. SHREDDED WHEAT CO. v. KELLOG
After the plaintiff's patent for the manufacture of what it described as ''shredded wheat'' expired, it registered ''shredded wheat'' as a trade mark for its breakfast cereal. Six years later Kellog of Canada manufactured the identical product and described it as ''shredded whole wheat.'' Can the plaintiff restrain Kellog from manufacturing and selling the product? Can it successfully claim Kellog must stop using the name ''shredded whole wheat'' on the grounds of infringement of trade mark? Give an opinion on whether Kellog will be liable to pay damages.

4. HAY v. SAUNDERS   Hay brought an action for infringement of copyright in the plans and building of a house known as ''Belaire.'' He asserted that he had made plans and sketches and that in building the home Saunders had copied his plans. Evidence showed that the houses of both parties were practically identical; of the two Hay had in fact been first to plan and construct this type of home; and that the plans of both contractors resembled designs of homes built elsewhere by others. Is this properly the subject matter of copyright? If so, should Hay succeed?

5. ELDON v. RELIABLE TOY   A businessman obtained a sample tow truck from Eldon. Later, the businessman agreed to supply a Canadian oil company with a number of such toys and he arranged with Reliable to manufacture them. Reliable copied the design but did not use the same colour and substituted the oil company's insignia for that on the sample truck. Eldon sued for infringement of industrial design, copyright and trade mark. Should it succeed on any of the three counts?

CHAPTER 10

Creditors' Rights

Unit I Collection of debts

YOU ARE THE JURY

WALSH v. GRANT

Richard Grant is the sole owner of Grant Realty. He owes Walsh $22 000 on an unsecured promissory note he signed 3 1/2 years ago.

Richard has office space in a building owned by his wife Joan. He transferred the title to this property to her five years ago. His office is elaborately furnished and decorated with several expensive oil paintings. He has the usual amount of office equipment and is modestly successful. His office closes several real estate transactions a month and, on each closing, he is able to transfer earned commission by way of profit. Richard maintains a business trust account and a general account. He has in addition a savings account having a present balance of $900.50.

Richard purchased a Lincoln motor vehicle worth $19 000 which is subject to a conditional sale contract in the sum of $16 000. Richard uses his car for his business and makes monthly payments on the contract from his business income.

Three months ago Richard transferred the ownership of another vehicle valued at $5 000 to his wife Joan. She drives the car but he pays for the expenses and licence.

What assets might be available to satisfy a judgment in Walsh's favour? What problems could he expect to encounter in attempting to collect?

OBJECTIVES
- to be able to list the remedies available to creditors to preserve and enforce their rights.
- to be able to define execution and list the steps a creditor may take to force payment of a debt after an execution writ has been filed with the sheriff.
- to define a fraudulent conveyance and distinguish it from other conveyances and transfers.
- to identify the legal rules of foreclosure.

LEXICON

Colour of Right   To do an act under the mistaken but honest belief that one has the legal right to do it.

Replevin Order   An order of the court directed to the sheriff, giving authority to the sheriff to seize and take into possession goods from the individual who has possession of them when the right to such possession is challenged by a third party.

Writ of Execution   A certificate registered with the sheriff of a county or district which orders that goods or property of a judgment debtor be seized and sold to satisfy a judgment given by a court in favour of a creditor.

Once a business creditor determines that an outstanding debt cannot be collected in the usual way, he must make a decision whether to collect the debt through legal process or not. If the creditor has knowledge that the debt is virtually uncollectable, it may be advantageous to write it off as a bad debt. If it appears that the debt is collectable, then collection is possible through a collection agency or the courts. If the debt is small, it may be possible to collect it directly through a provincial small claims court without the necessity of retaining an agent or lawyer.

Larger debts which are to be collected through the courts are processed by lawyers. The obligation of the creditor is to gather up all of the pertinent information concerning the debt, invoices, correspondence and business records. These are photocopied and forwarded to the lawyer with instructions to collect. If the documentation is adequate, the lawyer proceeds by forwarding a collection letter to the debtor. The objective of the letter is to provide one final opportunity for the debtor to pay and to confirm that the debtor is still at the address given by the creditor. The lawyer then elects the appropriate court in which to bring an action in order to obtain the necessary court judgment against the debtor.

Execution

The court judgment provides the creditor with several new avenues of collection. Once it has been obtained, the lawyer will file written evidence of it with the sheriff with instructions to enter the judgment as an execution against the property of the debtor within the county or d' The effect of the execution is in the na' lien against any such property. The e serves as public notice of this. In the the debtor subsequently attempts to buildings, inventory in bulk or su' amounts of equipment, the purc' the records of the sheriff's offic'

196
land relatives

discovers an outstanding writ of execution in the hands of the sheriff, the purchaser is legally bound to require the debtor to settle the obligation with the judgment creditor before the sale can be completed.

CASE 1   IN RE MARTIN

Martin purchased lands from Fleming. There were outstanding executions against Fleming in the hands of the sheriff. However, Martin failed to make a search of the sheriff's records. A judgment creditor instructed the sheriff to seize and sell the lands now in the name of Martin. Much to Martin's surprise, he found that he had taken the property subject to the lien of the execution creditors and to avoid the seizure it was necessary for him to pay them off.

Executions in the hands of the sheriff are usually valid for a period of six years but may be renewed from time to time for further periods of six years each.

After an execution has been on file with the sheriff for twelve months, the sheriff can sell lands and buildings owned by the debtor. The terms of the sale are supervised by the court.

The sheriff also has the power under the authority of an execution to seize goods owned by the debtor (such as inventory, automobiles and equipment). The sheriff may also attach debts owing by third parties to the debtor by giving notice to such third parties to pay the amount of such debts directly to the sheriff's office.

Fraudulent conveyances

A fraudulent conveyance is a transfer of ownership of either real or personal property by the debtor to another person with the intention of defeating or delaying the payment of money owing to the debtor's creditors. Each of the provinces has passed fraudulent conveyance statutes which provide that any such transfer is null and void as against creditors. Creditors may have such transfers (or conveyances as they are called) set aside if they can establish that the transfer of ownership was made with intent to defeat or defraud creditors, and that the purchaser was aware that the conveyance was made with this intention.

The real intent of the transaction must be to remove the assets from the clutches of the creditors and this is unlawful. But it is not unlawful for a person to anticipate that a business might fail at some time in the future and to make transfers of [...] for little or no consideration to close friends, [...] or associates. Such transfers are protected as long as at the time of the transfer the individual is solvent and meeting debts generally as they arise. Even though this person subsequently becomes insolvent, the original transfer will be protected if it was made in good faith. For example, in the Grant case Richard Grant transferred the title of a building to his wife Joan five years ago. If the transfer was made by Grant in anticipation that he might possibly in the future get into financial difficulty, and if he was solvent at the time, the transfer will not be considered an unlawful preference. However, the transfer of the vehicle was made at the time when Richard apparently was not meeting debts as they generally arose and therefore it is suspect and may be set aside as a fraudulent preference.

The creditor must first have information that the debtor has transferred assets to another person for inadequate consideration. He must also be able to prove that the debtor was insolvent – that is, was not meeting debts generally as they arose at the time of the transfer; and that the transfer was made in order to defeat or defraud him. Some knowledge of this intention must be attributable to the person to whom the property was transferred. If all of these elements are present, a creditor with a judgment may apply to the courts to have the transaction set aside. The effect of this is to return the title to the debtor for seizure by the sheriff, and sale and distribution of the proceeds among the creditors.

Absconding debtors

The legal process for collecting a debt is a lengthy one. It is effective as long as the debtor is available, has assets in the community and has some form of income which may be attached. Frequently, however, debtors in trouble will attempt to liquidate everything and quickly leave the jurisdiction. Such debtors are referred to as absconding debtors. Each of the provinces has passed absconding debtors' legislation which provides creditors with quick access to courts which have the authority to issue orders for the immediate seizure of assets about to be removed from the jurisdiction and to prevent the debtor from quickly absconding from the area. In one Ontario case the solicitor for a creditor obtained an order under the provincial *Absconding Debtor's Act* and seized a young German national on a boat docked in a Canadian harbour on its way to Hamburg. The young man had failed in business, quickly liquidated all his tangible assets and converted them into cash. He was found with $15 000 in cash, all of which was seized and distributed among the creditors.

Replevin orders

A person who owns goods in the possession and control of another person who unjustifiably refuses to give them up may retake them by applying for a replevin order. The applicant must be the true owner of the goods or have a sufficient "colour of right" in them to be entitled to possession. The property must be in the possession of another person without authority or permission and that person must have refused to deliver up possession after a demand has been made. The owner, through a legal representative, may appear before a judge immediately to establish the fact of ownership and wrongful taking or possession. This evidence is usually provided by filing an affidavit with a court. No notice need be given at this stage to the other party. The judge need only be satisfied that, on the balance of probabilities, the applicant is the owner or the person entitled to possession and that possession cannot be obtained in any other practical way. The judge will then issue an order directed to the sheriff of the county in which the goods are situate requiring the sheriff to seize the goods and hold them under security until a formal hearing is held to determine the entitlement to possession of the goods. The sheriff is then required to attend upon the person in possession with the written order and instruct that person to

give up possession. Compliance must be immediate. If the order is refused, the sheriff has the power to seize the assets by force and to break into any enclosure in which the goods are kept. The sheriff then takes the goods and keeps them under security. An arrangement is then made for the respective parties to attend upon the judge to present formal evidence. The judge hears both sides and makes a decision as to the person entitled to possession. Finally, he directs the sheriff to deliver up the goods to that person.

Foreclosure: Real property

Creditors who hold mortgages against real property consisting of land or lands and buildings receive a mortgage contract. This is a document which transfers the legal title to the legal creditor while leaving the possession of the property and right to use it to the debtor. The contract requires the debtor to perform certain obligations and to repay the mortgage loan. If the debtor defaults, the creditor has the right to take possession and sell the legal title to the property by way of foreclosure. To do this, the creditor prepares a writ of foreclosure and serves it on the debtor. The writ provides an accounting and establishes a balance owing by the debtor. The writ requires the foreclosure of all the right, title, and equitable interest of the debtor in the property. If the debtor does not give up possession, an order of foreclosure is signed by the court declaring the creditor to be the sole owner of all the legal and equitable interests in the property and giving the creditor the right to evict the debtor. The creditor then takes steps to remove the debtor from the premises by instructing the sheriff to act on the order. Then the creditor has full control of the property and may occupy it, lease it or sell it.

Every mortgage document signed by a debtor contains a personal promise that the debtor will be responsible to repay all of the principal and interest outstanding under the mortgage contract. This is a personal liability. In addition to foreclosing the property, the creditor is also entitled to include in the action a claim against the debtor on the personal covenant to pay. If the foreclosure includes a personal judgment against the debtor, the creditor may, in addition to retaking possession of the property and acquiring legal title, collect on the mortgage through garnishee or other process. The creditor may continue to collect upon the personal judgment as long as the property itself is not sold to another person. If the creditor elects to sell the property to liquidate the debt, the personal judgment is lost.

CASE 2   IN THE MATTER OF BROCK

Brock defaulted on a mortgage contract in favour of Aloe. At the time, the outstanding balance of principal and interest was $52 000. However, the secured property had depreciated to $48 000 in value. The mortgagee, Aloe, decided to foreclose but found that the legal cost for foreclosure would be $1 500 and the cost to resell the property would be another $2 500. Aloe elected to sue for foreclosure, hold on to the property, obtain a personal judgment against Brock and attempt to collect further sums from Brock by way of garnishee or other attachment on the judgement debt. Thus he could bring the outstanding balance owing down to the point where the property could be resold without any financial loss.

In a foreclosure action, the debtor has the right to apply to the court for relief against foreclosure by entering an appearance to the writ and giving an undertaking to the court to bring the defaulted payments up to date and to pay all court costs. On the basis of that undertaking, the court may give an order allowing the debtor an additional six months in which to put the mortgage into good standing and to pay the legal costs of the action. If within the six-month period the debtor does put

the mortgage into good standing and pay the court costs, the foreclosure action must be abandoned and the parties continue on as though there had been no default. During the six-month period the debtor is entitled to remain in possession of the property on terms fixed by the court. These usually require the debtor to pay a monthly sum equivalent to rent to the mortgage creditor. If at the end of the six-month period the debtor fails in the undertaking, the creditor may proceed with the foreclosure as outlined above.

It is possible to put second and third mortgages on property. Creditors who hold such mortgages have similar rights of foreclosure except that any person with a previous mortgage will have priority.

The second mortgagee usually decides to take a foreclosure procedure. The first mortgagee has a prior claim and therefore has control. The second mortgagee must therefore approach the first to make a deal. Usually the second mortgagee asks for permission to have "carriage of the action," which means that the second mortgagee will retain a lawyer and will process a form of foreclosure which will protect the interest of both mortgagees. The objective of the arrangement is to put the creditors back into a regular position. The property may be sold and both mortgages paid off in full; or it may be sold under terms on which the purchaser will pay off the second mortgage but take over or assume responsibility for the first mortgage. The second mortgagee has the advantage of being paid off and the first mortgagee has the advantage of having the mortgage investment intact on a regular basis. A third arrangement might provide for a sale of the property under which the prospective purchaser pays money down, pays an amount sufficient to put both mortgages back into a current position and then assumes all further responsibility to discharge all obligations under both mortgages.

Power of sale

In addition to the foreclosure privilege, most mortgages contain a right of power of sale. This reserves to the mortgage creditor the right, on default, to sell the property under a court order. When the mortgage debtor goes into default, the mortgage creditor has an option to foreclose or sell under the power of sale. There are many advantages to selling rather than foreclosing, particularly when the actual cash value is less than the outstanding balance on the mortgage.

The creditor who decides to exercise the judicial power of sale prepares a notice which includes an accounting resulting in a statement of the outstanding balance of the mortgage. The debtor is directed to make full payment of the outstanding balance within a specified number of days. If the debtor fails to make the payment within the required time, the creditor will obtain a court order allowing the forced sale of the property. This order is deposited with the sheriff with instructions to obtain possession of the property under the order and to proceed with the sale. The property may be offered for sale through the regular channels or it may be advertised and sold by auction. In any event, the sheriff effects a sale and pays the proceeds to the mortgage creditor.

If the proceeds of sale are less than the outstanding balance and legal costs, the creditor establishes the deficiency (the difference between the debt owing and the net amount actually received from the sheriff) and is entitled to sue the debtor for that amount on the basis of the debtor's personal covenant to pay which was contained in the mortgage contract.

The advantages of the power of sale procedure lie in the quickness of the remedy and the ease with which the debtor may be sued for the deficiency after the sale.

Reconsider the Brock case and decide whether sale procedures would have been more effective for Aloe than foreclosure.

Foreclosure: Personal property

Personal property such as furnishings, equipment, inventory and motor vehicles may be secured under a mortgage called a chattel mortgage. Such mortgage contracts contain a creditor's right to retake possession on default of payment or other undertaking contained in the contract. If the debtor defaults and the creditor is satisfied that the most practical remedy is repossession, the creditor retains a bailiff to attend upon the debtor and seize the assets. They are then sold by advertisement or public auction. If the creditor does not fully realize the outstanding balance under the mortgage contract and the necessary costs, he may sue the debtor for the deficiency. If the creditor recovers from the sale more than the funds owed plus costs, the creditor must pay the excess sum to the debtor.

KEY TO YOU ARE THE JURY

WALSH v. GRANT As the debt owing to Walsh is based on an unsecured promissory note, he is not entitled to look to any particular asset

for collection purposes. Nor is he entitled to take any effective steps himself to collect the outstanding amount on the note. He must first institute an action through the courts claiming to be entitled to the outstanding amount of the promissory note. If he is successful in this action, he will obtain a judgment in writing from the court. His next step would be to conduct an examination of Grant as judgment debtor to obtain information as to the assets now owned by him, the disposition of any assets in the past and the possibility of obtaining fresh assets in the future.

The office building transferred to Joan five years ago should be considered. If Joan paid full value for the building, the transaction is protected. If Joan paid inadequate consideration or no consideration, the transfer was a preference. The question now becomes whether or not it is an unlawful or fraudulent preference under the provincial *Preferences Act.* If Grant was insolvent – that is, unable to meet debts as they generally arose at the time – and if it is obvious from the facts that the intention was to defeat creditors, then the transaction was an unlawful preference and may be set aside through court action to satisfy Walsh's debt. Some evidence would also have to be available that Joan Grant was aware of the intent to defeat the creditors.

While furnishings are generally exempt from seizure, the more elaborate or luxurious items of office furniture (such as the oil paintings) which had considerable value could be seized by the sheriff under writ of execution. Household furniture, on the other hand, and necessities of life could not be seized.

The expensive automobile driven in the course of employment under the Grant circumstances would not be considered a tool of trade and could be seized. While it is a valuable asset, it is encumbered by a substantial conditional sale contract. The sheriff will not seize it unless instructions are given by Walsh to do so. In view of the expenses involved in seizure, the large amount owing under the conditional sale contract and the uncertainty as to how much could be obtained on a sale, it is highly unlikely that a seizure of this automobile will yield any money to satisfy the debt. For practical purposes this vehicle should not be seized.

The circumstances surrounding the transfer of the second vehicle suggests strongly that this is an unlawful preference. The vehicle should be available for seizure to satisfy part of the debt.

The commissions earned by Richard in the business provide a source of income that may be attached by garnishee.

Unit II   Bankruptcy

YOU ARE THE JURY

IN RE ESTATE OF CHECKETS, IN BANKRUPTCY

Checkets, a businessman, declared personal bankruptcy by way of an assignment for the general benefit of his creditors. Checkets undertook to pay one of his creditors, who was also a good friend, in full after the bankruptcy proceedings were complete. The bank with which Checkets dealt discovered at the first meeting of creditors that Checkets had failed to disclose his true financial situation at the time of his final loan from the bank several months preceding the bankruptcy. Three months before he declared bankruptcy Checkets paid a debt to a close relative in full. The trustee appointed by the creditors to investigate Checkets' affairs was able to determine that some of his assets had disappeared. While Checkets was unable to assist the trustee in locating the assets, the investigation revealed that Checkets had deposited $5 000 in cash into a savings account in the name of his wife and that a piece of equipment worth approximately $10 000 had been given to a creditor named Bedard as settlement for an outstanding debt of $7 000. Consider the implications of each of the transactions in relation to the bankruptcy assignment.

OBJECTIVES

- to be able to identify circumstances in which an insolvent may make an Assignment for the General Benefit of Creditors (Voluntary Bankruptcy).
- to be able to list bankruptcy offences which will entitle a creditor to petition a debtor into bankruptcy (Receiving Order).
- to be able to identify the elements of a proposal as an alternative to bankruptcy.

LEXICON

Assignment for General Benefit of Creditors A document by which an insolvent debtor transfers all rights and title to assets and property to a trustee in bankruptcy with authority to the trustee to liquidate them for the benefit of creditors.

Bankrupt   A person or corporation declared by the court to be unable to meet debts generally as they arise.

Bankruptcy Offences   A list of unlawful activities which constitute offences under the *Bankruptcy Act* of Canada and for which creditors may force a debtor into bankruptcy.

Insolvent   A person or company not yet declared by a court as bankrupt but which is unable to meet debts generally as they arise. Includes those who have committed bankruptcy offences.

In Canada bankruptcy laws are uniform throughout the provinces and most of the law is to be found in a federal statute called the *Bankruptcy Act.* This Act was comprehensively revised in 1979. Under the *Bankruptcy Act* it is possible to take three types of proceedings:

- voluntary assignment by a debtor.
- petition by a creditor resulting in a receiving order.
- proposal by a debtor either with or without bankruptcy occurring.

Bankruptcy involves the transfer of title of assets from the debtor to trustee and the eventual distribution of the proceeds to the creditors.

The trustee in bankruptcy is licenced by the Superintendent of Bankruptcy under the authority of the Ministry of Consumer and Corporate Affairs. The trustee is usually a chartered accountant in public practice. In each bankruptcy the trustee is appointed by the creditors and receives authority from them subject to certain responsibilities which are imposed by the *Bankruptcy Act.* In effect, the trustee becomes an agent for all of the creditors for the purpose of liquidating the assets of a debtor, converting them into money and distributing the funds so obtained among the creditors.

Voluntary assignment by a debtor

Sometimes called "voluntary bankruptcy," this occurs when a debtor who is insolvent voluntarily files an Assignment for the General Benefit of Creditors and turns over all his property to a licenced trustee for distribution among the preferred and unsecured creditors. There are a number of matters which should be considered before a voluntary assignment in bankruptcy is filed. Some of these are as follows.

Extent of indebtedness

A debtor must owe at least $1 000 before he can make an assignment. The difficult question is to determine how much in excess of $1 000 should be owing to utilize the voluntary assignment. It would seem that a rough rule of thumb would be that anything in excess of $10 000 will likely require bankruptcy and if less than $10 000 is owing, there may be hope for using some other solution.

Number of creditors

Again, a rough rule of thumb would suggest that if there are more than ten creditors, an assignment will likely be the only answer.

Garnishees and other proceedings

If the debtor is having his salary attached by a number of creditors, this will be a strong reason for considering an assignment. If the debtor is being harrassed by his creditors, being constantly examined and having other proceedings taken against him, bankruptcy may be his only means of obtaining relief.

Debtor's desire to work out of insolvency

To most people, bankruptcy is a great disgrace. Rather than go bankrupt, a debtor who has a large burden of debts may decide against taking advantage of the *Bankruptcy Act*. Commendable as this attitude is in principle, it may be unrealistic.

Costs of assignment

If the debtor has assets, the question to be determined is whether these assets are sufficient to pay the usually substantial trustee's fees and legal fees. On the other hand, if the debtor is not a corporation and if the realizable assets of the bankrupt after deducting the claims of secured creditors will not exceed $500, he may be entitled to use the services of the federal trustee who charges a nominal fee of $50.

Debt obtained by fraud

Any debt obtained by fraudulent means cannot be discharged by bankruptcy. Fraud in this instance means both criminal and civil fraud. For example, a loan obtained by fraudulently misrepresenting one's true financial situation either by over-inflating assets or failing to disclose existing indebtedness is considered a debt obtained by fraud. The creditor is entitled to refuse to participate in the bankruptcy and sue the debtor in the ordinary courts for the full amount of the debt without having to submit the claim to the trustee and stand in line with all other creditors.

CASE 3   IN THE MATTER OF THE ESTATE OF TAGGART, IN BANKRUPTCY

The sales manager of Miller Machine Limited was induced to sell a quantity of machine equipment on credit to Taggart. In order to obtain credit Taggart submitted a balance sheet showing a net worth of $200 000. Actually Taggart was insolvent. Thirty days later Taggart was adjudged a bankrupt and a trustee was appointed to take title to and control of Taggart's assets. Miller demanded the return of the equipment from the trustee who declined suggesting that Miller was entitled only to prove as an unsecured creditor in the bankruptcy. The trustee intended to sell the equipment and divide the proceeds along with the balance of funds available among all of the creditors. For Miller, proving in the bankruptcy meant receiving 30 cents on the dollar. What arguments can be raised on Miller's part?

Miller refused to prove in the bankruptcy and brought an action in replevin against the trustee. The court decided that Taggart's conduct in producing a false statement was to induce Miller to turn over assets. This amounted to a fraudulent misrepresentation in contract which entitled Miller to rescind and be put back into the same position it was in before the contract. In effect this meant Miller was entitled to have the equipment returned. The court specifically found that as the property was obtained by fraud it was not the proper subject for transfer by an assignment in bankruptcy and the trustee therefore had no title to the equipment.

Powers of trustee in bankruptcy

Once an assignment has been made, the trustee becomes an agent for the creditors and must therefore act in their best interest and not that of the debtor. As a result the trustee has the duty to fully investigate the activities of the bankrupt. An investigation is conducted by the trustee with the assistance of a lawyer retained by the trustee. It is designed to review transactions entered into by the bankrupt prior to the assignment and to make certain that all of the assets of the debtor to which the trustee may make a legal claim are included in the bankrupt estate. The following rules assist the trustee:

- The debtor is required to report under oath to the trustee all facts relating to the debtor's affairs and make all books and records available.
- Any transaction entered into between the debtor and a third party is voidable against the

trustee if made within three months of the assignment. The trustee is entitled to a court order setting such transactions aside unless the third party can prove that the transaction was made in the ordinary course of business, in good faith and for valuable consideration. The transaction may also be set aside if it is shown that the other party received an unlawful preference.

- The trustee is entitled to review any transaction entered into by the debtor for a period of 12 months preceding the bankruptcy and is entitled to a court order setting aside those transactions not made in the ordinary course of business, or not made in good faith or made for no consideration. Transactions can be set aside also if it can be shown the other party received an unlawful preference.
- The trustee is further entitled to examine settlements or transfers of assets to relatives made within a five-year period prior to the bankruptcy. If they were made at a time when the debtor was insolvent, the trustee is entitled to order that the asset be turned back to the estate for the benefit of creditors.
- In all cases where transactions are set aside the other party is ordered to transfer the asset back to the estate or pay an equivalent value to the trustee.

CASE 4 IN THE MATTER OF THE ESTATE OF REGINALD WELLINGTON, IN BANKRUPTCY

Over the years Wellington had borrowed over $40 000 from his mother to help him keep his business going. While he had never repaid any of this sum to her, it was understood that he would do so when business improved. On April 1st Wellington gave his mother a mortgage on his buildings and lands and a chattel mortgage on his equipment as security for her "loans" in the principal sum of $40 000 with interest at 6% and no payment due under either document for five years. Four months later Wellington made an Assignment in Bankruptcy. After investigation the Trustee instructed Mother Wellington to release the assets so they could be sold. She said, "No. These were loans and I have all my receipts. They total $40 000." Who is right and why?

Petition by a creditor resulting in a receiving order

Involuntary bankruptcy occurs when a creditor files a petition which asks the court to issue a re-

ceiving order against an insolvent debtor. A debtor may be petitioned into bankruptcy by any creditor or creditors having claims against the debtor of at least $1 000 and where the debtor has committed what is called an "act of bankruptcy." The most common acts of bankruptcy are:

- where the debtor makes a fraudulent conveyance or transfer of property.
- where a debtor exhibits to a meeting of his creditors any statement of his assets and liabilities which shows he is insolvent or if he admits in writing at such meeting that he is unable to pay his debts.
- where the debtor gives notice to his creditors that he has suspended or is about to suspend payment of his debts.
- where the debtor defaults in any proposal made under the *Bankruptcy Act.*
- where the debtor ceases to meet his liabilities generally as they become due.

There are a number of matters which creditors should consider prior to petitioning a debtor into bankruptcy. Some of these are as follows.

Possibility of doing debtor a favour
If you petition a debtor who has no assets, you may do the debtor a favour because you will be paying the legal and trustee's fees which should have been the obligation of the insolvent.

Bankruptcy court is not a collection agency
Creditors are expected to collect debts through the ordinary courts before applying for a Receiving Order. A bankruptcy court views such applications as final remedies available only to those creditors who have demonstrated honest attempts to satisfy their claims by other means. As one judge put it:

> A bankruptcy court is not to be used as a collection agency. The court must carefully scrutinize the motives of the petition-seeking creditor. Receiving Orders must only be granted in cases in which applicants establish that debts cannot be reasonably collected by traditional methods or that some urgent reason exists to prevent a debtor from disposing of assets to defeat the creditors.

Attacking preferences and fraudulent transactions
A petition is a proper remedy if a debtor has given a fraudulent preference to one of his creditors, or has fraudulently disposed of his assets. By means of bankruptcy, the debtor's assets can be frozen, thus preventing their further disposal.

Putting competitor out of business

A petition must not be filed for the purpose of getting rid of a trade competitor. If one is, it will be dismissed.

Method of ascertaining loss

If you have a large claim, you may wish to petition in order to clarify your position – that is, to determine your loss and finalize the situation.

Preventing further waste of assets

If a debtor who is in financial trouble is put into bankruptcy before it is too late, it may be possible to salvage sufficient assets to at least pay creditors a percentage of their outstanding claims.

Costs of petitions

If there are assets which will produce sufficient funds to satisfy the trustee's fees and legal fees, you will not have to worry about costs.

Proposals

The *Bankruptcy Act* allows a person or corporation who is insolvent but wishes to continue in business to offer a proposal or plan to his unsecured creditors. This proposal is designed to permit him to carry on his business, and it provides a greater recovery to the creditors than they would likely obtain in a bankruptcy proceeding.

The debtor may offer his unsecured creditors equity in the business; payment of claims in full after an extension of time; partial payment of existing debts; or any combination of these. In return, the creditors agree not to liquidate his business in bankruptcy proceedings. In such cases a licenced trustee is required to conduct an investigation; to report to the creditors on the merits of the debtor's proposal; and to act as referee to ensure that the terms of the proposal are complied with and that the claims of the creditors are properly recognized. The proposal can be made either without bankruptcy occurring or after an assignment in bankruptcy or a receiving order has been made.

The following matters should be considered in determining whether or not a debtor should make a proposal.

Desire of debtor to meet obligations

If the insolvent is anxious to work his way out of his difficulties and to either pay his creditors in full or make some reasonable settlement with them, then a proposal is worth considering.

Extent of indebtedness

If the amount of money which is owed by the debtor is completely out of proportion to his assets, it may not be practical to offer a proposal.

Desire of creditors to work with debtor

If the debtor has been guilty of fraudulent conduct and the creditors are suspicious of him, then a proposal will not likely be accepted.

Costs of proposal

Since a proposal involves a good deal of work both for a lawyer and the licenced trustee, a substantial expense will have to be incurred to complete it.

Will the proposal offer more to creditors than could be obtained in a bankruptcy?

The usual rule is that creditors should receive something more in a proposal than they would in a bankruptcy.

Effect on secured claims

Under a proposal it is not possible to bind creditors who have secured claims.

Distribution by trustee

The trustee is required to pay preferred claims as soon as funds are available from the realization of assets. The order of preference is set out in the *Bankruptcy Act.*

If the creditors are paid in full, any surplus is used to pay interest on the claims of creditors at 5% from the date of bankruptcy to the date of payment. Any surplus after payment of creditors' claims and interest is returned to the bankrupt.

Preferences and fraudulent transactions

It is a common practice of debtors to attempt to provide certain creditors – such as friends, relatives and those persons in business who have been particularly helpful to the debtor – with preferential treatment prior to filing for bankruptcy. Usually these desires are prompted by feelings of loyalty and responsibility. It is not uncommon as well for debtors to attempt to fraudulently conceal or protect certain assets by putting them out of the reach of the creditors. This is usually accomplished by making some form of transfer to a third party. The debtors always have an advantage because they are usually the first to know that they have become insolvent and unable to meet their debts generally as they arise. In order to protect the creditors, the *Bankruptcy Act* has established certain rules, the more important of which are outlined in the paragraphs below.

Trustees are given wide authority to conduct investigations into a bankrupt's affairs. This authority includes access to all books and records and the right to retain a lawyer and such other specialists as may be necessary to disclose the true state of a bankrupt's affairs and uncover assets which may have been hidden.

When assets have been transferred or deposited with persons closely related to the bankrupt, the trustee is given the authority to review all transactions made by the debtor within the past five years. The bankruptcy laws of Canada treat such transactions as voidable, provided the trustee is able to show that at the time of the transfer the bankrupt was technically insolvent and was not meeting debts generally as they arose.

All transactions entered into by the bankrupt within three months of the bankruptcy are void unless the person with whom the bankrupt dealt is able to establish that the transaction was made in good faith for valuable consideration and without the knowledge that an unlawful preference was being given by the bankrupt.

The bankruptcy laws prohibit the bankrupt who is about to declare bankruptcy or to be put into bankruptcy by the creditors to give preferential treatment to any one single creditor or small groups of creditors to the prejudice of other creditors or the estate.

Each of the provinces has passed a *Fraudulent Transactions Act* which further inhibits a debtor's ability to transfer assets to third parties unless this is done at arm's length for valuable consideration. When these statutes are combined with the federal *Bankruptcy Act,* it becomes unlawful for a debtor when he is insolvent and not meeting obligations generally as they arise to attempt to transfer assets to a spouse or other close relative, friend or associate in order to put the assets out of the reach of the creditors.

Discharge of bankrupt

The making of a receiving order or the filing of an assignment (except in the case of a corporation) operates as the application for discharge of the bankrupt. However, it is necessary to obtain an appointment from the court for the date on which the discharge will be heard. The trustee is required to apply for an appointment for the hearing of the discharge not earlier than three months and not later than 12 months after the bankruptcy.

Corporations cannot apply for a discharge unless they have paid their creditors in full.

A creditor has the right to oppose the application for a discharge. Conditional upon certain terms being met by the bankrupt, the court has the power to grant or refuse an order of discharge or to suspend the operation of the discharge for a given period of time. Normally, the court will grant the discharge if no facts are reported under section 143 of the *Bankruptcy Act*. Some of these include the following:

- the assets of the bankrupt are not of a value equal to 50¢ on the dollar on the amount of the unsecured liability.
- the bankrupt has continued to trade after knowing himself to be insolvent.
- the bankrupt has admitted to keeping such books of account as are usual and proper in the business.
- the bankrupt has failed to account satisfactorily for any loss of assets.
- the bankrupt has brought on or contributed to his bankruptcy by rash and hazardous speculation or by unjustifiable extravagance in living, gambling, etc.
- the bankrupt has put any of his creditors to unnecessary expense by a frivolous and vexatious defence to any action.
- the bankrupt has given an undue preference to any of his creditors.
- the bankrupt has on any previous occasion been bankrupt or made a proposal to his creditors.
- the bankrupt has been guilty of any fraud.
- the bankrupt has failed to perform the duties imposed on him under the *Bankruptcy Act* or failed to comply with any other order of the court.

Receivership

Receivership is a concept which is often confused with bankruptcy but which is an entirely separate remedy. Generally, a business is said to be in receivership when a *secured* creditor takes action under a security (i.e., debenture, mortgage, etc.). The debtor is in default under the security and the creditor appoints a receiver who will seize the security (and often operate the business) with a view to ultimately selling the business or property. In Ontario, anyone can act as a receiver but usually a licenced trustee is appointed. The appointment of a receiver can be made by a court in response to a request from a secured creditor, or it can be made directly by a debenture holder if there are specific powers in the debenture to appoint a receiver. The powers of the receiver are

determined by the court order or by the terms of the debenture, and so may vary from case to case.

Liquidation

Liquidation involves the orderly winding-up of a solvent company. Ontario companies are wound up under the *Business Corporations Act* and there are similar Acts in other provinces. There are basically two types of liquidation.

Voluntary Liquidation

This occurs when the shareholders pass a resolution for the winding-up of the company. They usually also appoint a liquidator. In this case, the winding-up is under the supervision of the shareholders, although it may subsequently be brought under the supervision of the court if that is desirable. For example, while the shareholders may agree that the company ought to be wound up, they may not agree on the mechanics of liquidation. If such disagreements cannot be resolved, the Acts provide a procedure by which the shareholders may turn to the courts for direction. The liquidation may then take place under the supervision of the courts thus avoiding a stalemate situation which would have resulted from squabbling among the shareholders over details.

Involuntary Liquidation

This occurs when one or more of the shareholders or an interested party petitions the court for an order winding up the company and appointing a liquidator. In this case, the winding-up is carried out under the supervision of the court.

When a liquidator is appointed, the powers of the directors are suspended except insofar as sanctioned by the liquidator.

KEY TO YOU ARE THE JURY

IN RE ESTATE OF CHECKETS, IN BANKRUPTCY In making a voluntary assignment in bankruptcy Checkets, in effect, turned all of his affairs over to the Trustee in Bankruptcy who must now act as an agent for the creditors. The following decisions were made in the Checkets bankruptcy proceedings:

- Checkets had no legal right to give his friend an undertaking that he would see him paid in full after the bankruptcy. This amounted to a bankruptcy offence which entitled the judge at the discharge hearing from granting Checkets the discharge he sought.

- The bank argued that Checkets obtained the loan by fraud and that the *Bankruptcy Act* was not designed to discharge debts which were obtained by fraudulent misrepresentation. The bank declined to participate in the bankruptcy and sued Checkets in the ordinary courts for the full amount of its claim. The court agreed and gave judgment against Checkets personally. Over the course of several years, the bank diligently collected the entire amount of the judgment so obtained.
- The trustee has the power to review transactions and settlements made by the bankrupt before the assignment. Investigation revealed that the intent of Checkets was to see the relative paid in full and that the relative had sufficient knowledge of Checkets' affairs to know she was receiving a preference. The relative was required to pay back the amount received to the trustee for distribution among the creditors of the bankrupt estate.
- The trustee traced the $5 000 into the wife's bank account. The settlement on the spouse took place at a time when Checkets was insolvent to the knowledge of the spouse. The trustee attached (seized) the $5 000 from the account and made it available for distribution among the creditors.
- The trustee settled with Bedard. The transaction between Bedard and Checkets was reviewed. The trustee concluded that the payment of the debt was not made in the ordinary course of business and that Bedard had unjustly benefited by the difference between his debt and the value of the equipment. However, the trustee found that Bedard was probably far enough removed from the affairs of Checkets so that it would be difficult to establish that he knew he might be getting a preference over the general creditors. There were arguments available to both sides, so they decided to compromise. Bedard kept the equipment but paid $1 500 to the trustee for a release of the claim on behalf of the creditors.

Checklist: Creditors' rights

BANKRUPTCY

1. Obtain copies of *Bankruptcy Act* of Canada and *Fraudulent Transfer Act* of your province from government bookstore.

2. Review purposes of bankruptcy laws to effect equitable distribution of debtor's property; discharge debtors from their debts; give debtors opportunity to start fresh; regulate trade transactions.

3. Consider alternate remedies for collection including settlement, suit, attachment of property, garnishment, applications to set aside transactions by debtors under provincial fraudulent transfer Acts and foreclosure.

4. Possible proceedings include: voluntary bankruptcy, proposals and involuntary bankruptcy.

VOLUNTARY BANKRUPTCY

5. If debtor voluntarily files for bankruptcy by filing an Assignment for General Benefit of Creditors, follow these steps:

a) On receiving notice, make copies of all records, notes, invoices. Review debtor's file. Gather all known relevant information concerning debtor's assets and credit status. Be alert for any statement made to you by debtor which may prove fraudulent and allow you to avoid being "shutout" in the bankruptcy.

b) Obtain details of any security you hold against any asset of debtor which could give you a priority claim in the bankruptcy. Put present value on the security from your own records or have it appraised.

c) Request Proof of Claim form from Trustee in Bankruptcy. Complete form, state nature of debt owing to you and advise trustee of value of your security. Ask trustee to inform you of all proceedings.

d) If your claim is substantial, consult with lawyer. Consider retaining lawyer to look after your interests and advise on how to avoid debtor obtaining discharge of your account.

e) Receive Notice of First Meeting of Creditors. Prepare carefully by reviewing records and examining information contained on notice which might indicate fraud on part of debtor.

f) Attend meeting. Make certain trustee records your presence. Listen to the trustee who will advise of the debtor's Statement of Affairs. Examine the statement (if permitted by trustee) as it relates to your claim. Be prepared to question debtor on matters of your claim and any assets of which you are aware which appear to have "disappeared." Part of your questioning should aim at obtaining evidence of any debtor fraud in his obtaining credit from you.

g) Trustee may be required to appoint inspectors; if so, try to be appointed (but only if you do not intend to challenge the bankruptcy proceedings).

This ensures you some control over decisions.

h) Trustee will adjourn meeting and immediately re-convene a meeting of the inspectors. Be prepared to assume control. Remember trustee at this point works for inspectors as representatives of creditors. Trustee will outline duties of inspectors. Follow list.

i) In alternative to participating as inspector, consider your records, the evidence given at the hearing and the bankruptcy rules. Decide whether you qualify for court order that the bankruptcy will not discharge your debt on grounds of fraud. Retain lawyer. Instruct him to commence action to collect debt in full without participation in bankruptcy through regular court action. If successful you may obtain judgment in full and may be in collecting position while other creditors have debt discharged without payment or payment of percentage of original debt.

INVOLUNTARY BANKRUPTCY

6. If usual collection methods fail, consider putting debtor into bankruptcy through Petition, appointment of Receiver and Receiving Order. Follow these steps:

a) From your records and public information gather list of other creditors. Write or meet with larger creditors to discuss co-operative effort to petition debtor into bankruptcy. Object to having receiver appointed to take over business and assets of debtor forthwith to preserve assets, prevent shrinkage (i.e., disappearance of assets), correct mismanagement of business and in most cases to supervise orderly liquidation of business and assets for distribution among creditors.

b) By examining bankruptcy rules, decide whether debtor has committed any bankruptcy offence including any fraudulent conveyance, preference or debtor not meeting obligations generally as they arise.

c) Fraudulent conveyance is a transfer of property without adequate consideration *and* with intent to defraud or defeat creditors.

d) Preference is a payment or transfer of any property to any particular creditor (usually within last three months) which would give that creditor payment of a greater percentage than other creditors of the same class if such payment not made in ordinary course of contract between debtor and creditor (i.e., under contract, debtor required to pay instalments; now pays debt off in full).

e) Consult lawyer or Trustee in Bankruptcy regarding costs, procedures. Consult lawyer regarding need to appoint receiver immediately and con-

sider risks which may result from forceful interference with debtor's business or property.

f) Application for Petition in Bankruptcy to bankruptcy court. May appoint Receiver to immediately seize and take over debtor's property without notice or may require applicants to give eight days' notice of intention to appoint Receiver. In any event debtor given opportunity to have application dismissed or discharged.

g) If Receiving Order granted, Trustee in Bankruptcy legally entitled to take over debtor's business and assets, run business, hold liquidation sale, auction or do anything debtor might have done to preserve assets and pay creditors. Proceeds of business, auction or sale then divided among creditors.

TRUSTEES IN BANKRUPTCY

7. The *Bankruptcy Act* creates the Office of Trustee in Bankruptcy. The federal government appoints individuals or corporations to act as trustees on a year-to-year basis. In each voluntary bankruptcy, the creditors appoint one such trustee to be the trustee of a debtor at the first meeting of creditors. Trustees also handle Proposals and Petitions. Consider the following checklist of trustees' duties:

a) Must instruct and follow directions of inspectors.

b) Obtain legal title to the assets of an insolvent debtor; convert assets into money by sale or auction; distribute proceeds among creditors according to priorities set out in *Bankruptcy Act* and under direction of the court. Wind up affairs of the bankrupt.

c) Deposit all funds received in designated trust account.

d) Retain a solicitor to assist in investigation of debtor's affairs and legal transfers of title to assets.

e) Prepare a detailed Statement of Affairs listing debtor's assets, liabilities, names and addresses of creditors and securities held by secured creditors.

f) Keep records of accounts.

g) Examine the debtor, usually at the first meeting of creditors.

h) Provide each creditor with proof of claim form; receive and examine same; decide whether claim valid, unforceable or not. Reject invalid claims.

i) Provide interested parties with such information as may be requested.

j) Make final report to Superintendent in Bankruptcy. Submit account for services for approval.

k) Make final report to creditors.

l) Assist bankrupt in obtaining discharge and make final report to the bankruptcy court.

Review

1. List the steps you would take to collect a large sum of money from a debtor who is unwilling to make satisfactory arrangements for payment.

2. Define an "execution" and list the ways in which a creditor might use this device.

3. You have left goods with Ruban with instructions to repair them. You learn that Ruban is in financial difficulty and you have difficulty contacting her. She is evasive about the progress she has made with the repairs and you learn from others that creditors have begun to sue her. You ask her to return the goods but this is not done. What is the quickest and most appropriate remedy available?

4. You hold a second mortgage on commercial property which is in arrears and you must take steps to protect and liquidate your security. You are satisfied that your mortgage combined with the first and other debts (such as municipal taxes) exceeds the value of the property so that you will end up with a deficiency. Describe the most appropriate remedy and give reasons for your choice.

5. The Perfection Business Systems company owes your firm $11 000 which it has on one pretext or another refused to pay. You learn that the company is in default or behind in accounts with ten other companies. You are about to sue the company when you learn that the directors of Perfection have formed another company to which they have transferred all of the assets of the Perfection company. You attempt to get two other creditors to share in the responsibility of applying for a Petition in Bankruptcy, but they refuse. Assume that you will be able to show that the new company gave very little in consideration for the assets. What steps would you now take?

6. Krum has persuaded you as sales manager of your firm to sell him a quantity of machine equipment. In doing so Krum deposited with you a financial statement showing a net worth of $150 000 which also listed his creditors and amounts owing to them. In reality his debts exceeded his assets and Krum failed to disclose the existence of some of his largest obligations. The equipment was forwarded to him and two weeks later he made an assignment for the general benefit of creditors. You now wish to reclaim your goods but the other creditors object. You now either want your goods back through court ap-plication or you wish to pursue Krum for the money owed in full without having to "prove in the bankruptcy" by court action against Krum. What are your chances of success on either count? List the steps which might be taken on your behalf.

7. What is a Petition in Bankruptcy, a Receiver and a Receiving Order?

8. What are the main differences between an Assignment for the General Benefit of Creditors and a Receiving Order?

Solutions to Cases

CHAPTER 2

CASE 10 TINKERS, EVERS AND CHANCE v. CUMMINS

In this case Cummins will be liable for the damages to Tinkers but not for those of Evers and Chance. Tinkers, having been invited to the premises to do business, is an invitee and is entitled to a high degree of care. Cummins as a prudent owner is liable for injuries to an invitee caused by a hazard of which he had no actual knowledge, but of which he ought to have been aware under the circumstances. Evers can only claim the rights of a licensee and therefore can hold Cummins liable only for injuries caused by hazards of which Cummins was aware. Cummins is therefore not liable for Evers' injuries even though a reasonable owner under similar circumstances ought to have realized the danger existed. Chance is a trespasser to whom Cummins owes no duty whatsoever.

CHAPTER 3

CASE 1 BASSFORD v. WILLIS

Bassford loses. In this case the letter from Willis did not have the value of a definite contractual offer. It was no more than an extension of the bargaining process in which Willis undertook to make an offer based on agreed figures provided Bassford allowed the accountants to participate in the bargaining process through auditing the books of the business. There was at this stage no offer for Bassford to accept and no possibility of reaching a mutual agreement unless the bargaining process suggested by Willis resulted in an audit satisfactory to the accountants.

CASE 2 PIERCE v. CRAWFORD

In this case Pierce has not made a legal offer to sell. At best it is reasonable to suppose that he is in the bargaining process and is still trying to manoeuvre Crawford to the point where she will make an offer which he will then be free to accept or reject. The statement, "Will you give me $500?" is also ambiguous because it is capable of having two meanings. The first is obvious. It could be a suggested price for the car. The second is not so obvious. It may be a request for a gift or loan from Crawford. Vague statements such as this will not support a contract. Pierce also contended that because the statements were oral they should not be binding; but of course an oral statement will in fact support a contract for the sale of goods such as vehicles.

CASE 6 LINCOLN v. LAVINE

Lincoln loses. The display of merchandise in a store does not amount to an offer to sell by the owner to prospective customers. It is an invitation to customers to do business by making an offer to buy to the merchant. Lincoln made an offer to buy which Lavine was free to accept or reject. He chose to reject the offer. Therefore, there was no mutual agreement and no binding contract.

CASE 7 SKEFFINGTON v. SALLY SHOPPES

Skeffington loses. In this case the display of the coat along with other merchandise is an invitation to customers to make offers to buy. This is so even if prices are fixed and customers are not expected to compete with each other or haggle with the shopkeeper. In this case the owner has two competing offers to consider. She may accept one and reject the other or reject them both if she chooses. The "political" decision to sell to the older, more-valued customer was legal. The sale of the coat to that customer amounted to a rejection of Skeffington's offer and therefore she had no contract with the store.

CASE 13 SPOTISWOOD v. DORIAN

Spotiswood loses. In this case there was no contract. In order to legally accept Dorian's offer, Spotiswood had to accept unconditionally. Two conditions were actually attached to his so-called acceptance. First, it was subject to a satisfactory credit check; second, to unspecified terms in a formal agreement yet to be drawn-up and signed. In effect, there was no legal acceptance, no mutual agreement and therefore no contract. Spotiswood could have avoided this unfortunate result by running her credit check before preparing the Dorian agreement and by incorporating into the agreement a complete list of the terms which would be part of the eventual lease in that agreement.

CASE 14 DOWNES v. SMYTHE

In this case Downes could have had Smythe sign an agreement under seal undertaking to provide the right-of-way. The seal would have taken the place of consideration so that the lack of consideration would not have invalidated the arrangement. In the alternative, Downes could have agreed to give some form of legal consideration in return for the right-of-way. Examples of this from other cases include:

- $1 a year for the term of the lease.
- a turkey at Christmas each year.
- snowplowing services given in exchange.

Even if the consideration is nominal, it will provide a sufficient consideration to bind promises such as those given by Smythe.

CASE 17 LEHAY v. RUSS

In this case the main issue is whether or not the transaction can either be varied or set aside on the basis of lack of, failure of, or inadequacy of consideration. The general rule will apply: that the courts will not interfere with, vary or set aside contracts once made on the grounds that one party or the other did not get full value. Lehay can only argue that the consideration given by Russ was inadequate. My advice to Lehay (in the absence of evidence of fraud – and on the facts as given there is none) is that he has bought himself an apartment building. He should try to negotiate with Russ to get himself out of the deal on the terms if possible and chalk it up to experience. He is of course at the mercy of Russ who is free to voluntarily let Lehay "off the hook on terms." If Russ insists on the transaction closing as signed, he is entitled to that as well because we have here a valid binding contract.

CASE 20 JANEWAY v. GIGILO

Gigilo loses. Past consideration is no consideration. Gigilo was originally promised and received as part of the original transaction an all-expense trip and nothing more. As an afterthought, presumably to reward Gigilo for his past attentiveness, Aunt Mary gratuitously provided him with an unexpected windfall, the promissory note. The law states that if a person wishes to reward a person who has previously done an act or provided a service, the promise is not binding. The promise is gratuitous and, as we have seen, a gratuitous promise is not enforceable. The personal representatives of Aunt Mary were therefore entitled to reject Gigilo's claim.

CASE 23 DISNEY v. COHOL

Disney wins. Under the agreement Cohol had the right to return the set within one week. This period therefore becomes significant in that the parties have agreed that one week would be a sufficient time for the purchaser to change his mind. Cohol's only real defence to the contract is to raise his incapacity to contract through alcohol. However, to set up such a defence Cohol must demonstrate that either he or his legal representatives did some clear act repudiating the contract within a reasonable time – such as notification to Disney that Cohol would not be responsible on the contract, returning the goods or taking such other steps to put the parties back into the position they were in before the contract was signed. Watching the set and defacing it over a period of several weeks now negatives that defence. Cohol is legally liable on the contract and must pay.

CASE 25 PIONEER v. ADARO

Pioneer loses. To support the agreement between the father and himself Pioneer, as the person benefiting from the contract, must show that he gave consideration. The only consideration he could point to was his "refusal to give evidence at a criminal trial and co-operation in having charges dismissed against the former employee." This resulted in the dropping of a public prosecution by a private agreement between two citizens. The consideration given by Pioneer was accordingly illegal and the contract on which it was based was unenforceable through the civil courts. (In this case the fact that the criminal court permitted the dismissal of the charge is not relevant and has no bearing on the remedy sought by Pioneer. The author was involved as counsel in the civil case and was convinced that the criminal court was not fully aware of the underlying arrangement made by Pioneer.)

CASE 29 MITCHELL v. LEGROS

Yes, this is an example of a common mistake. Both parties were mistaken about the same fact, the destruction of the subject matter of the contract.

CASE 34   IN RE FLANNIGAN'S WILL

In this case the will was submitted to the court for directions as to its validity. The court found that Father Murphy's conduct was beyond reproach and it did not criticize his role in the drawing up of the will. However, the court said that in cases in which one party is considered to be the ''superior'' of another, whether it involves a contract or a will, the other party must always have the benefit of independent legal advice. Flanningan should have had the opportunity to sign the document before a lawyer of his choice, free of the influence of any other party. Had this been done, all other things being equal the will would have been valid and enforceable as it related to the gift to the church. As this was not done, the court declared the gift to the church invalid but allowed other gifts unrelated to the church.

CHAPTER 4

CASE 4   VENUS ELECTRIC LTD. v. BREVEL PRODUCTS LTD.

The court rejected Venus' claim since it did not advise Brevel of the change in the design of the dryers and therefore Brevel did not know of any special use to which the motors would be put over and above the trade norm. There was also no evidence that Venus had either expressly or by implication relied on the seller's judgment so as to bring Section 15 into play. In order to do this, Venus would have had to inform Brevel of the modifications in such a way that it would have been brought home to Brevel that its skill and judgment were required.

CASE 6   TALBUT v. SQUIRE

The seller may sue for the unpaid price but cannot require Squire to return the goods or otherwise seize them. In this case, the failure of the purchaser to pay for the goods amounts to a breach of warranty which gives rise to damages equivalent to the unpaid price but not recission.

CASE 11   LAFRENTZ v. HOGAN

In this case the issue is whether or not title to the goods had passed to Hogan. If the work had been done and Hogan had been notified that the work had been done, title would have passed under Rule 2 and Hogan would have been responsible for the loss. If the work had been done but

Hogan had not yet been notified at the time the theft occurred, the seller would still have had title and accordingly would bear the loss. If the theft had occurred before the work was done the seller would likewise have been responsible for the loss.

CHAPTER 5

CASE 9   MUNDY v. MUNDY

The court held that, having regard to all the circumstances, Kaye's breakdown and her disorientation at the time she agreed to sell the business, the transaction was unconscionable. The court did not set the transaction aside completely, but did substitute as a new price the amount proved to be the actual cash value of Kaye's interest at the time of the sale. Herman was ordered to pay the difference between what he paid and what he should have paid. In this way the court deprived Herman of an unjust profit.

CHAPTER 6

CASE 3   DEANE v. NATIONAL COLLEGE BOARD

The court based its decision on evidence presented to indicate what was generally expected of university professors in relation to teaching, testing and research. Deane's performance was compared against the standard this evidence established. Professors had the right to cancel some classes, but being a ''no-show'' was unprofessional. Successful research was described as published materials or procedures actually put into practice at the university or in the community. Those professors who failed to accomplish these ends were considered ineffective. Deane lost on these points and was judged sufficiently incompetent to have been legally discharged for cause. However, he did win a small victory regarding the testing procedures because evidence was adduced supporting his claim that he had not been told his method of testing did not conform to that of the university. The court held that an employee who did not perform a function satisfactorily had the right to be given an opportunity to respond and correct his actions before dismissal could be justified.

CASE 4   MYERS v. PETERS

The employer is correct. Illness which leads to the impossibily of performance and the likelihood of the situation continuing indefinitely justifies dismissal even though the employee is able to perform properly in intervals of good health. This should be true even though the employee has been with the firm an exceptionally long time.

CASE 8   BAXTER v. GEORGROPOLIS

The owner of the business was right. Employers are vicariously liable for acts done by employees in the ordinary course of employment. When the bartender became involved in a heated racial argument begun by the customer, he actually took himself out of his role as employee and was acting in his personal capacity. The boss was right. He had not hired the bartender to get involved in such arguments and could not be expected to be responsible for their consequences. While Baxter (the customer) had a good cause of action against the bartender, he could not claim damages against the employer. On the other hand, if the argument had been about the quality of the liquor served the result would have been different. While the employer does not hire the employee to argue with customers, he is entitled to the employee's loyalty and as defending the product served (to a point) is within the scope of employment, the employer must be responsible for damages caused by an overly zealous employee who takes company loyalty too far.

CHAPTER 7

CASE 3   IN RE BEST

Best could have avoided this substantial loss by placing his own insurance through the insurance agent of his choice. In this way coverage would have been in place immediately when he became owner. In this case he would have been insured at the time of the loss. Whenever buying property or a business, be sure to arrange insurance coverage as soon as the offer to purchase is signed because you then have an insurable interest without having to wait for the actual day of closing or transfer of official papers. The second thing Best could have done was to contact the insuring agent or company by telephone for an oral confirmation that the company accepted the transfer. This can be done by telephone. Most agents have authority to give a binder of such coverage over the phone, provided you undertake to forward the transfer papers forthwith.

CHAPTER 8

CASE 4   LAYCOCK v. FRASER

The court held that an agent is in a position of trust and thus owes the principal a duty to make full disclosure of all relevant facts. Fraser was in breach of a duty owed to his principal and accordingly judgment was entered against him in an amount equivalent to his unjust profit.

CASE 10   PHILPOTT v. COSTELLO AND VALENTINE

The *Partnership Act* of your province provides that every partner is liable for all debts of the firm while a partner thereof. The two issues raised are 1) whether Costello was a partner at the time of the Philpott contract 2) whether Valentine had real or apparent authority to bind the firm at the time.

The court gave Philpott judgment against Valentine but dismissed the case against Costello. In summary the judge said, "Costello was not a partner at the relevant time but this fact alone did not necessarily relieve her of obligation unless Philpott, who had dealt with the firm in the past knew or ought to have known that she was not a partner. The letter, advising of the dissolution of the partnership when read with the first order under the name of Valentine alone was a sufficient notice that the partnership had effectively been dissolved. Philpott should have been suspicious of the second order and will not be allowed to succeed on an argument based on apparent authority. Neither did Valentine have any real authority. Therefore the claim against Costello fails." Notice that the court fixed the Philpott company with responsibility for the knowledge held by one of its own agents.

CASE 11   ELIAS v. TYSON AND UNDERHILL

Elias was awarded judgment against both partners. "Underwood had no apparent difficulty accepting sales agreements which arose out of his partners backyard marketing," said the judge. "They extended the usual course of their business to include personal demonstrations during off-business hours in such a way as to recognize Tyson's real authority to bind the firm. Tyson's negligence was negligence on behalf of the firm for which Underwood must bear responsibility as well."

CASE 15 REDRUPP v. DELPAPPA AND MANTELLO

The court held that while DelPappa did not have any legal interest in the business and while he never directly referred to himself as a proprietor or partner, he was liable as though he were a partner because his conduct, in the absence of a specific disclaimer to the contrary, created the impression that he had a partnership interest in the business.

CHAPTER 9

CASE 1 IN RE MONTEITH

No, Monteith should not succeed. The knives must be something new created by Monteith as inventor not copied from some other source no matter how remote. Monteith's intended application will fail the "novelty test." Monteith would be ill-advised to attempt to obtain Letters Patent by deceit: it is an offence to make false statements in an application. Monteith may be prosecuted if he does. In addition, because competitors are entitled to ignore apparent patent rights based on fraud, protection obtained by such means is worthless.

CASE 2 IN RE DEAN

Dean should fully disclose the existence of the other device to a patent agent. It is unlikely that he will qualify for patent protection in Canada. He will be denied a Canadian patent if the American device has been patented in the United States or any other country. Even if the device has not been so patented but has been described in a publication anywhere more than two years before her intended Canadian application, that application will fail.

CASE 3 IN RE BOYER

It is now too late to patent her invention. If an inventor actually sells a device, puts it to public use or publishes details, the application for patent must be made within two years of such sale, use or publication or the right to monopoly is lost. After ten years of sales and publication, anyone is free to market a similar device.

CASE 7 ANDERSON v. BURGHARDT

As Anderson neither commissioned nor paid for the photograph the copyright therein belongs to Burghardt the photographer. The case raises the issue of the extent of the right to privacy in Canada which is more limited here than, say, in the United States. Anderson does not have a legal right to forbid the taking of her picture under these circumstances. Anderson would not be able to restrain Burghardt or any person to whom he sells the photographs from copying those in which she appears.

CASE 8 PETERSON v. PIONEER COLLEGE

As Peterson at the time was an employee who under normal working conditions was required to develop and produce materials which could be used to instruct students the right to copy belongs to the employee. This is a general rule of copyright law. In this case Peterson was a member of a faculty union and the terms of his employment were set out in a collective agreement which specifically stated that educational developments and materials created by employees would be the property of the employer. Peterson was not entitled to royalties and he could not restrain the college from the intended commercial use of the materials.

CHAPTER 10

CASE 4 IN THE MATTER OF THE ESTATE OF REGINALD WELLINGTON, IN BANKRUPTCY

The Trustee was correct. Mother Wellington was ordered by the court to discharge her mortgages and prove in the bankruptcy as an unsecured creditor. While the Wellingtons anticipated that the loans would be paid off, they were not to be paid until Wellington was solvent. The effect of the mortgages was to give the mother a settlement at a time when the debtor was insolvent. This amounted to an unlawful preference over the repayment of principal and interest with suspicion: "The parties at no time prior to April 1st ever considered that the loans would be secured in any way. The only purpose of the mortgages was to give the mother an unfair preference over other creditors."

Index

Absconding debtors, 13–16, 196
Actuaries, def. 126
Affidavit, def. 5
Argument, 4
Articles of incorporation, 170, def. 167
Auctions, 94–96
Authority, 6
    apparent, 148
    express, 147
    implied, 147, 148

Better Business Bureau, 103
British North America Act, 6, 9, 102
Bulk Sales, 93, 94
By-laws, 170, def. 167

Canada Business Corporations Act, 169 ff.
Canada Labour Code, 121, 122
Canadian Bill of Rights, 122
Canadian Consumer, 103
Canadian Standards Association, 103
Caveat emptor, 78, def. 71
Classes of shares, 171
Colour of right, 197, def. 195
Combines Investigation Act, 102–108
Conditions, 76, def. 71
Consensus ad idem, 36
Consideration, 43–47, 137, def. 43
    adequacy rule for, 45, 46
    past, 46
    rules of, 44
Consignee, def. 90
Consignment, 96, 97
Consignor, def. 90
Consumer Protection Act, 106
Consumers' Association of Canada, 103
Contracts
    acceptance, 41, 42
    breach of, 61–67, def. 61
    C.I.F., 92
    C.O.D., 93
    counter-offer, 39, def. 36
    essential elements of, 36
    F.O.B, 90
    offer, 37–41
    recision, 57, 65–67, def. 54
    revocation, 39–41, def. 36
    void, def. 48
    voidable, def. 48
Contract of carriage, def. 90
Convention
    Copyright, 182, 183
    International, for the protection of
    industrial property, 180, def. 176
Copyright Act, 182 ff.
    caution notices, 105

Damages, 63, *passim*, def. 21, 61
Deliverable state, def. 81
Delivery, 77, 78, 84, def. 71, 81
Directors, 171–173
Discharge, 62
Discrimination
    in employment, 120–122
    price, 103
Dismissal for cause, def. 111
Disparagement, 28, 29, def. 21
Dividends, 171
Duress, 57, 58, def. 54
Duty to deliver, 77, 78

Employee-inventor, 178
Estoppel, 148, def. 147
Examination for discovery, 10, 17
Exclusionary clauses, 87–89, 127, 130,
    def. 126
Execution, 14–16, 195, 196, def. 5, 195
    against goods, 14
    against land, 14, 15
    against the person, 16

Fair dealing, 186, def. 182
False advertising, 104
Firm name, 158, def. 154
Fitness of goods, 78, 79
Fixed term, 160
Forbearance, 46, 47, def. 43
Foreclosure, 197–199
Fraudulent conveyances, 196
Fringe benefits, 123

Garnishee, 16, 121, 201, def. 119
Goods
    future, 83, 84
    specific, 82, def. 81
Gratuitous promise, 44, def. 43

Illegal object, 51
Indemnity, def. 133, 147
Industrial design, 180, 181
Infants and minors, 48, 49
Injunction, 65, def. 61
Insolvent buyer, 87, def. 85, 200
Insurance
    adjuster, def. 126
    agent, def. 126
    application for, 128, 129
    assignment of, 131
    automobile, 135, 138
    business interruption, 134
    cancellation of, 130, 131
    claim, 132
    co-insurance, 134
    contract of, 129, 130

fire, 134, 138
    glass, 135
    guarantee, 136
    machinery, 135
    renewal of, 130
    term, 136, def. 133
    theft, 135
Invitation to buy, 38
Invention, def. 176

Judgment, 12, 13, def. 5

Lapse, def. 36
Law
    common, 7, 8
    def. 6
    equity, 8, 9
    essential elements of, 6, 7
    statute, 9
Legal capacity, 48–50
Legal problems
    how to solve, 3, 4
Letters patent, 169, 177, 191, def.
    167, 176
Libel, 24, 25, def. 21
Lien, 120, def. 85
Liquidation, 205
Litigation, def. 5
Luxuries, 48, 49

Master and servant, 119
Maternity leave, 122
Memorandum of association, 169, def.
    167
Mercantile agent, 90
Misrepresentation, 56, 57, def. 54
    of product quality, 106
Mistake, 54–56, def. 54
Mitigate, def. 85
Mitigation, def. 61

Necessities, 49
Negligence, 27, 28, 114, def. 21, 111
Non est factum, 57, def. 54
Notice, 112–114, def. 111
Nulla bona, 14

Onus, def. 187

Partnership
    Agreement, 158, def. 154

dissolution of, 160–162
  Limited, 158, 159
Partnership Registration Act, 158
Patent, 177–180, def. 176
Patent pending, 179, 180
Personal security, 21
Petition, 202, 203
Plagiarism, 186, def. 182
Pleadings, def. 5
Pledging credit of the firm, 157,
  def. 154
Power of sale, 198
Predatory pricing, 104
Premium, 129, def. 90, 126
Promissee, def. 43
Promissor, def. 43
Promotional contests, 105, 106
Promulgation, 6
Proposal, 203, 204
Public policy, 52, def. 51

Quantum meruit, 64, def. 61, 111
Quiet possession, 79, 80

Receivership, 205, def. 85
Replevin, 65, 197, def. 61, 195
Resolutions, 170
Restraint of trade, 52, def. 51
Retail sales management, 104
Rider, 130, def. 126
Rights and duties, 21
Right to sell, 76, 77
Risk of loss, 127

Sale of Goods Acts, 72 ff.
  conversion table, 75
Sale on approval, def. 81
Share capital, 171
Shareholders, 173
  Agreement, 170, 171
Shares, def. 167
Specific performance, 65, def. 61
Stare decisis, 7
Statute of Frauds, 37, 38
Statutory conditions, 127, 130, def. 126
Subrogation, def. 126

Title to goods, 81–84
Torts
  assault, 22, 23, def. 21
  business, 28
  def. 21, 51

defamation, 24, 25
false arrest, 23
intentional to property, 25–27
intentional to the person, 22–25
malicious prosecution, 24
meaning of, 22
nuisance, 25
Trade secrets, 180, 191
Trial, 9–18

Unconscionable transaction, 106

Vicarious liability, 117, 118, def. 111
Voluntary assignment, 200, 201

Warranty, 79, 80, def. 71
Wrong, 21, 22, def. 21
Wrongful dismissal, 116, 117, def. 111